# THE SOVIET UNION IN ASIA

# THE
# SOVIET UNION
# IN ASIA

GEOFFREY JUKES

UNIVERSITY OF CALIFORNIA PRESS

Berkeley and Los Angeles

UNIVERSITY OF CALIFORNIA PRESS
Berkeley and Los Angeles, California
First published in 1973

© The Australian Institute of International Affairs 1973

ISBN 0-520-02393-5

*This book has been sponsored by The Australian Institute
of International Affairs. Having as its object the scientific
study of international questions, the Institute, as such, does
not express opinions or advocate policies. The views
expressed in this book are therefore the author's own.*

Printed in Australia

# Contents

# Foreword

This book resulted from the discovery that while there are numerous specialised works on subjects such as the Sino-Soviet dispute, or Soviet trade and aid policies in the Third World, no general study has attempted to deal with Soviet interests in the Asian area on a broad basis, taking account of the fact that the Soviet Union is itself one of the most important Asian states and cannot 'pack up and go', as certain other great powers have done or intend to do. More specifically, the decision to include a description of the general characteristics of Soviet Asia arose from conversations during a journey through Siberia in 1969, and the realisation that some Soviet apprehensions about Asia are similarly grounded to those of Australia.

My thanks are due to: Academician Lavrentyev (Head of the Siberian Branch of the Academy of Sciences), whose skilful comparisons between Australian and Siberian conditions started a number of chains of thought; Mrs Robyn Ward, whose assiduity in collecting English-language material unearthed innumerable relevant facts and eased the task of assimilating material in other languages; Paul Dibb, whose comments not merely made valuable additions to the chapter on 'trade and aid', but also relieved it of a number of embarrassing solecisms; Miss Marsh, Mrs Gant and Mrs Mattocks of this Department whose skill in typing a much-amended text often approached clairvoyance. The residual errors are mine.

G. JUKES
Department of International Relations
Research School of Pacific Studies
Australian National University

20 February 1972

# I

# The Soviet Union in Asia: general propositions

The growth of Soviet interest in the Third World in general, and Asia in particular, since the death of Stalin, has sometimes been regarded as an alarming and unnatural phenomenon, with particularly sinister overtones of expansionism. Without denying the problems it could create for Western countries whose influence in Asia it challenges and could possibly come in due course partly or wholly to supplant, it is the aim of this study to indicate some other ways in which the Soviet presence can be viewed. In brief these may be summed up as follows:

1. Unlike other European powers which for long dominated Asia politically and economically, and still do to a considerable extent, the Soviet Union is inextricably part of Asia, being its largest state in territory, and one of its largest in population, even if the European population be excluded. It cannot therefore 'pack up and go' if events in Asia do not develop to its satisfaction.

2. In dealing with problems of underdevelopment, the Soviet government has had not merely to raise a European society which was backward compared with its neighbours, but to raise the standards within its state of non-European races which were economically and socially retarded compared with the dominant Europeans (Russians and Ukrainians). It has done so with very considerable success, and in so doing acquired expertise which the developing countries of Asia are finding welcome in their own situations.

3. In its possession of thinly inhabited terrain with immense natural resources, the Soviet Union resembles Australia. And

1

its proximity to a potentially hostile neighbour (China) gives both its apprehensions about Asia, and its desire to influence the course of events there. These are bases at least as realistic as those which have governed Australian (and American and British) policies towards Asian countries.

4. Given this situation, it is not Soviet interest in Asia which is 'unnatural' but the almost complete lack of interest in it during the years of Stalin's rule, and the Soviet role in Asia may be more usefully interpreted as arising from these conditions than as an intrusion from outside. In particular, the concentration of attention upon incumbent governments rather than upon local Communist-led movements can be better explained by reference to the realities of geography, politics and economics, than by allegedly revolutionary imperatives. This study therefore attempts to examine the general bases of the Soviet approach to Asia, the Asian USSR, the Soviet military role, its relations with the countries of the area, especially India, Indonesia and China, and its policies in the field of 'aid and trade'.

## THE GENERAL FRAMEWORK

Geographically Europe is no more than a peninsula of Asia, and the division between continents is purely arbitrary; the Ural Mountains constitute only a minor natural barrier, with no major differences between the terrain, flora and fauna on the Eastern and Western sides. And, while the watershed of the Caucasus range marks a more obvious natural break, there, too, the division is an arbitrary one. Politically, the distinction is even more meaningless, as the continental division along the Urals is not accompanied by any distinction of sovereignty or statehood: the territory both sides of it forms part of the Russian Soviet Federated Socialist Republic, largest of the fifteen republics which make up the Soviet Union; while in the Caucasus it serves only to mark off the Armenian and part of the Azerbaijani Soviet Socialist Republics from the rest of the USSR.

The history and culture of Russia have shown it to balance for centuries between Europe and Asia, but for lack of rigorous definitions of what may be regarded as 'European' or 'Asian', it is not proposed to argue to what extent the Soviet Union may be represented as a 'mixture'. The bulk of its population is of European stock; most of its industrial production takes place within the European USSR; and 71.1% of the Soviet population lives there.[1]

As with population, so with trade, 56.7% of which is with the

---

[1] 1970 census, preliminary data.

Soviet Union's Warsaw Pact partners, 21.9% with the countries of Western Europe, and only 12.7% with the Third World.[2] Essentially, therefore, the Soviet Union is a society in which the European element predominates, and whose links are mainly with Europe. There are 28 railroad and 36 road crossings along the European borders of the USSR; only 12 railroads and 34 roads (most of them unsurfaced tracks) cross from the Soviet Union into the Asian countries between the Black Sea and the Pacific.

But to prove that the Soviet Union is mainly Europe-oriented is not to dismiss its connections with Asia. Almost exactly 75% of the territory of the Soviet Union is in Asia. 70 millions (28.9%)[3] of Soviet citizens live in Asia, (Transcaucasus, Siberia, the Far East, and the Central Asian Republics), and the proportion is growing because the annual rate of increase in Soviet Asia, 1.7%, is almost twice as high as the 0.9% of the European Soviet republics.[4] Its population makes it the most populous Asian state except for China, India, Indonesia and Japan. Its territorial extent (16.8 million square kilometres) is far more than that of any purely Asian state—almost twice as large as China (9.6 million km[2]), and slightly more than twice the size of Australia (7.7 million km[2]). As for trade, it is the largest customer for Malaysian rubber, and third most important of India's trading partners, while the United Kingdom, for long its most important non-Communist trading partner, is now yielding this place to Japan.[5]

Strategically, Russian history has been one of expansion eastwards and southwards into Asian lands, uninhabited or sparsely populated by peoples whose lower level of technological advancement rendered them ripe for conquest. During the latter part of the nineteenth century this movement ceased as it came up against the British sphere of influence in South Asia, reached the Chinese heartland (though not before large tracts of peripheral Chinese territory had been seized), or collided with Japanese expansionism which for a time (in 1904-5 and again in 1917-25) caused it to recede. But always the major strategic emphases, and the troop deployments which gave them concrete expression, remained along

[2] *Vneshnyaya Torgovlya SSSR Za 1969 god.* (Foreign Trade of the USSR, 1969) Ministry of Foreign Trade, Moscow 1970, p. 16. Hereafter cited as *V.T.*

[3] *Narodnoye Khozyaysto SSSR v 1969 god.* (The National Economy of the USSR in 1969), Moscow, 1970, tables of population distribution by regions and republics (hereafter cited as N.E.) and 1970 census.

[4] *N.E.,* 1969, table 'National Increase, by Union Republics,' and *N.E.* 1967, table 'National Increase by Regions'.

[5] *V.T.* 1968 & 1969, Table IV 'Foreign Trade', (Moscow), 1970 pp. 56-57.

the vulnerable Western borders where the turbulent, expansionist and technologically better-endowed European states pressed constantly from the seventeenth century to 1945 and where, since then, their presence (as the Russians see it) has been made even more threatening by their formation of an alliance headed by America. Of the 150 or so known Soviet divisions (about half of them at or near full strength), about 100 still face westwards, and the remaining 50, with much longer borders to guard, include few of the full-strength ones. Yet even here, the importance of Asia to the Soviet Union's defence is far from negligible, because it is in Siberia that most of its strategic deterrent forces is located—the intercontinental ballistic missile force, mostly deployed in sites served by branch lines from the Trans-Siberian railway.

IDEOLOGY AND NATURAL INTEREST

Soviet domestic and foreign policies are avowedly ideological, in that actions and decisions are explained to the world in terms of the body of doctrine generally known as Marxism-Leninism, however tortuous the process involved. In practice Soviet leaders are no more prone to consulting Marxist-Leninist sacred texts before taking decisions, than are Christian leaders to seek guidance from their Bibles. But since Marxism-Leninism denies an after-life, and claims predictive abilities in respect of this one, it is necessary within the international Communist movement for the Soviet leaders to justify their actions not merely with reference to their short-term goals, and their role in furthering purely national interests, but also as aimed at promoting long-term objectives and in the interests of world Communism as a whole. This naturally lends to Soviet pronouncements a more revolutionary colouring than their actions would justify of themselves.

It is not proposed in this study to examine the vexed question of the relationship between the ideological and the pragmatic elements in Soviet policy making. The Soviet state can be viewed as one which attempts to maximise its position within an existing system of states, or as one which essays to overturn that system and replace it with a new one. Quotations may be adduced to support either interpretation, and neither posture excludes the other, since acquisition of influence within a system may increase the incentives to sustain it, but equally may provide the leverage with which to overturn it. Questions of this kind are not to be decided by reference to 'sacred texts', and to the extent that there is a contradiction at all, it is an artificial one. In Lenin's time, and still more in Stalin's, the survival of the Soviet state was laid down as the primary requisite for the prospects of world revolution, so that the Soviet national interest was closely identified with the ideological interests of world Communism. The same theme was highlighted again in 1961, with the publication of the draft 20 year plan for 'laying the foundations of Communism' in the USSR by the 1980s. Chinese anger at the self-centredness of this plan, and its lack of provision for assistance to the poorer Communist countries, was countered by claims that an affluent Soviet Union would serve as a magnet to the workers of the world, and that concentration on achieving affluence was therefore consistent with the interests of foreign Communist partners.

It is therefore necessary to look at the ideological concepts advanced by Soviet statesmen, publicists and Party theorists to explain their actions with respect to Asia, and to bear in mind that while in some cases these concepts are used to cover straightforward power politics, those who use them see no inherent contradiction between the Soviet national interests and those of the international Communist movement. The belief that the two are synonymous leads naturally to the assumption that Soviet pursuit of national interest, for example by dealing with those who actually hold power in Asia, however anti-Communist they may be in internal policy, strengthens the long-term attractiveness of a Communist movement which in any event is not working to a timetable.

The policy of Soviet governments towards the Asians within their own borders is dealt with in the next chapter. Here it is proposed to deal only with Soviet doctrines and policies towards the other Asian countries, in the hope of clarifying the general lines of their approach to Asia.

The most important ideological concept within which Soviet doctrine views relations with newly-independent countries and with the few remaining colonies is that of 'the national liberation struggle'. This is conceived as being a struggle for both political and economic freedom, in which the grant of political independence marks only an intermediate stage. The concept can be traced back to Lenin[6] but in fully developed form dates back only to the late 1950s and early 1960s, especially to the 20th Party Congress of 1956. In the Soviet definition, the 'national liberation struggle' has entered a new stage with the virtual disappearance of colonialism, but has not ended. Economic independence of the former colonies and semi-colonies requires, on the one hand, raising their national economies, developing productive forces, increasing labour productivity, and on the other, taking away the levers of imperialist

---

[6] Lenin, *Collected Works*, vol, 22 p. 187 'they leave out economic liberation. But in fact that is the main thing'.

control, putting an end to domination of the economy by the monopolies, and a struggle against international finance capital; in other words, it is a question of relieving the liberated countries of the yoke of world capitalism. In practice these 'are two indivisible tasks. Taken together they determine the main direction of the present-day national liberation movement—the road to full economic independence.'[7]

But taken by itself there is nothing especially remarkable or definitive about the concept of national liberation. It is in the matter of application and in historical context that it acquires meaning, especially when viewed in the perspective of Marxist ideas about the role of colonies in a capitalist world.

Less than a month after its seizure of power, the Bolshevik government issued an 'Appeal to all Moslem workers of Russia and the East', on 3 December 1917, which called on Moslems of Russian Central Asia, Persians, Turks, Arabs and, (oddly, in view of its title) Hindus for support. The effect of this appeal was negligible, addressed as it was, in the pre-broadcasting era, to a mainly illiterate audience, and not disseminated to any great degree. Its main interest is that it shows continuity between Lenin's optimistic vision of the East as a source of revolution, expressed in *Imperialism, the Highest Stage of Capitalism* in 1916, and his turning to it in 1920. The Bolsheviks' appeal was 'opportunistic'; they did not regard the East as ripe for 'socialist' revolutions, but, noting the rise of nationalist movements in some Eastern countries, expected them to result, if successful, in diminution of the colonies' role as captive markets and sources of raw materials to the 'imperialist' countries. Nationalist revolution in India, for example, would cause economic chaos in the United Kingdom, and the hardships thus caused to the British worker would spur him to overthrow capitalist rule. Therefore nationalist revolution in India would lead in short order to socialist revolution in England. That was the doctrinal position; more pragmatically, and more immediately relevant, risings in India would, it was hoped, divert British attention and forces away from anti-Bolshevik intervention in Russia.

At the Second Comintern Congress in July 1920, Lenin advocated Communist support for the non-Communist ('bourgeois-democratic') elements in bringing about the overthrow of the colonialist or colonialist-supported 'feudal-landlord' order.[8] Lenin

---

[7] Yegorov, Yu. (Ed.) *The National Liberation Movement* (in Russian), Moscow, Political Literature Publishing House, 1967, pp. 235-6.

[8] Carr, E. H. *The Bolshevik Revolution, 1917-23*, Macmillan 1953, pp. 251-9.

was concerned more to weaken anti-Soviet action by the 'imperialists' than to further the short-term fortunes of local—and very small—Communist Parties (in 1919 the Indian Communist Party had twenty members,[9] in 1923 the Chinese Communist Party had 432);[10] he therefore took a pragmatic view, told the Congress 'any national movement can only be a bourgeois-democratic one' —which was true of every Asian country at the time—and advocated a 'two-stage' revolution. In the first stage the Communists would assist the non-Communist nationalists to gain power, but would then begin to fight against them, eventually overthrowing them in the second stage.

This argument was opposed vehemently by the Indian Communist M. N. Roy. Roy pointed out that the objective of fighting foreign overlordship was not to 'underwrite the nationalist aspirations of the homegrown bourgeoisie, but to liberate the people from capitalism', whether foreign or indigenous. He therefore held that Communists should undertake no cooperation with movements they could not control, and should work for a 'one-stage' revolution which would bypass capitalism altogether.

The Congress adopted Lenin's view, but published Roy's arguments as a 'Supplement to the Theses on the National and Colonial Questions'. The question of 'one-stage' or 'two-stage' revolution later became an important factor in the Sino-Soviet dispute, when Soviet support for the 'two-stage' concept in the 1950s led them to extend massive aid to nationalist leaders (Nasser in Egypt, Kassem in Iraq, Nehru in India, Sukarno in Indonesia and Castro in Cuba), all of whom were at times strongly at odds with their indigenous Communist Parties, while terminating or curtailing their aid to China. The Chinese, who believed strongly in alliances in which the non-Communist elements were subordinate (their experience of following Soviet advice and co-operating with the Nationalists in 1926-27 having been disastrous), were to use Soviet practice as evidence that the Soviet leaders had betrayed the interests of the revolution. But in this, at any rate, the Soviet practice was thoroughly Leninist.

The Second Party Congress's 'Theses on National and Colonial Questions' led to the convening by the Comintern of the 'Congress of Peoples of the East' at Baku in September 1920. This included delegates from Russian Central Asia as well as from Countries between Turkey and China, and was addressed by a number of

---

[9] Kautsky, J. H. *Communism and the Politics of Development,* Wiley, New York, 1968, p. 85.
[10] Müller, K. *The Foreign Aid Programmes of the Soviet Bloc and Communist Asia: an Analysis,* Walker & Co., New York, 1967, p. 6.

leading Bolsheviks, whose speeches showed preoccupation with the British and with the Moslem world, where British influence was predominant at the time.[11] Attempts by the Comintern to form a national liberation movement foundered on Soviet *raison d'état,* because at the Congress a number of the delegates from Russian Central Asia complained so strongly of oppression and maladministration by some of the Soviet representatives in Turkestan that the Congress itself sent a delegation to Moscow to protest; and a few months later the Soviet Union invaded and absorbed the briefly independent republics of Transcaucasia which had supplied so many of the delegates. As to the resolutions passed by the Congress itself, they expressed an orthodox Leninist view that the national liberation movement of the oppressed peoples of Asia could triumph only under leadership by the industrial proletariat of the 'progressive' countries (ie., at that time, the Russian Republic). Thus the idea of close interconnection between the security of Russia and the prospects of success for world revolution, already firmly established in relations with other European Communist parties, was extended to cover those of Asia, and, in Stalin's hands, to lead to the simplistic doctrine that the prime duty of any Communist was to support the Soviet Union.

In the light of later developments in Sino-Soviet relations, it is interesting that the first Soviet 'satellites' were acquired from China's sphere of influence while Lenin was still at the head of affairs. Outer Mongolia, which had been a Chinese tributary until 1911 became in 1921 the scene of a prolonged campaign between the Red Army and the anti-Communist forces of Baron Ungern-Sternberg and Hetman Semenov, in the course of which its definitive independence was proclaimed. In the neighbouring area of Tannu-Tuva, Chinese until 1912 and a Russian 'protectorate' after that, an independent republic was proclaimed in August 1921. It was incorporated into the Soviet Union in 1944, as the 'Tuva Autonomous Region'.

The 'Theses on National and Colonial Questions', adopted by the Second Comintern Congress, committed all Communist parties to support revolutionary liberation movements in the colonies and backward countries, and fight feudalism, landlordism, the church and its missions, as well as Pan-Asian movements such as Panturanianism (which sought to unite all Turkic peoples, ie. the Turks, Azerbaijanis, Uzbeks, Turkmens and Kazakhs, into one state). The support of the peasants was to be sought, and an attempt made to impart a revolutionary character to their move-

---

[11] Eg., Zinoviev's call for a 'Holy War on the British and French Capitalists, and uprisings in the rear of the British'. Müller, *op. cit.,* p. 13.

ments by organising peasant Soviets wherever possible. Communists could ally themselves with 'bourgeois' revolutionary movements, but must not merge with them, and must identify the elements within them which could form the nucleus for future 'proletarian' parties. In an apparent concession to Roy, Lenin advised the Comintern to put forward the thesis that the backward countries 'could' avoid the stage of capitalism, and proceed directly to Communism once they had attained their 'true', that is, economic, independence.

Stalin's ascent to hegemony after the death of Lenin led to a sharp decline in Soviet interest in nationalist movements in Asia and Africa. In 1925 he stigmatised non-Communist nationalist leaders such as Nehru as 'more afraid of the revolution than of imperialism', and adopted a position towards them which appeared closer to Roy than to Lenin. But in fact, his attitude towards non-Communist nationalism amounted to refusal to believe it effective or even genuine. Under his influence the Sixth Comintern Congress declared not simply that the national liberation struggle could only be won under proletarian leadership, but that capitalism, because of its exploitative nature, would deliberately hinder industrialisation of its colonies. This resolution implied (a) that there could be no successful revolution without an industrial proletariat to lead it, and (b) that under capitalism, the development of industry, and therefore the creation of a proletariat in Asia was impossible. If there could be no liberation without a proletariat, and capitalism could not create one, revolution in the colonies could therefore come only as a by-product of the victory of revolution in Europe.

Stalin's writings, and the memoirs of those of his contemporaries who survived, do little to illuminate the reasons for an action which in effect cut the Soviet Union off from the anti-colonialist movement that it had done much to sponsor in its early days. Certainly, Stalin thought little of the effectiveness as revolutionaries of men such as Nehru and Gandhi, and he persisted in stating the belief that they were imperialist 'stooges'. Even after many of them had led their countries to independence, he professed to regard that independence as illusory, and refused to grant them any forms of aid. This attitude persisted until his death, and undoubtedly cost the Soviet Union opportunities to gain influence in what became known as the Third World. Its persistence suggests that Stalin found it impossible to believe in any form of revolution other than that carried out in the Soviet Union (a seizure of power by a small disciplined and centralised Party supported by a larger, but still relatively small, force of class-conscious workers, with the peasantry playing an almost passive role), and that he was unable to transcend the belief, derived by the Old Bolsheviks from the writings of Marx and Engels, that the key to world socialism was revolution in Europe.[12] Whatever the reasons, he abandoned the formula of 'two-stage' revolution, not in favour of the harder-line 'one-stage' revolution of M. N. Roy (and, later, of Mao Tse-tung), but in favour of a proposition which ruled out the idea of revolution altogether and with it, any idea of self-generated radical change in Asia and Africa. It is sometimes argued that he foresaw war with Germany, and had no wish to antgonise the 'imperialist' British and French, whose alliance he might need. But this is to credit him with an excess of foresight. In the late 1920s Soviet-German collaboration was at its height; German forces were evading the limitations imposed in the Treaty of Versailles by training secretly in Russia while Germany was in return assisting in Russian industrial development. This cooperation ceased only with the Nazi advent to power in 1933, and not until 1935 did Communist doctrine begin to make sharp distinctions between 'bourgeois democracy' on the one hand, and 'fascism' on the other, paving the way in foreign policy for a division of the capitalist states into 'aggressive' and 'non-aggressive'. Even as late as 1948, the Soviet Union showed evidence of its rigid adherence to the Soviet concept of revolution when in a letter of May 4 it charged Tito with according to the peasantry a leading role which could be held only by the industrial working class.

The conclusion therefore seems inescapable that Stalin's downgrading of Asia resulted from plain lack of imagination; only after his death did his successors reopen the doors which he had closed in the 1920s. In the meantime Chinese Communists had conducted a successful war, on the basis of a peasant army, over a period of more than 20 years, and Vietnamese Communists, basing their tactics and strategy on those of the Chinese, were on the verge of victory in their war with the French. Neither of these movements owed its success to Soviet support more than marginally, and neither had followed Soviet reasoning on the relative importance of the industrial worker and the peasant to revolution.

The newly independent non-aligned governments of Asia and Africa held no important place in Soviet thinking until Stalin's death; he refused to believe in the reality of decolonisation or to contribute with economic aid to the development of the former colonies. That Soviet interests were not felt to require stability in the area was shown by policies such as that enunciated by Zhdanov,

---

[12] See Kautsky, *op. cit.* pp. 82-83 and quotations therein from Benda, H. J., 'Communism in South East Asia', *Yale Review,* Spring 1956, pp. 417-429.

one of Stalin's chief henchmen. At the inaugural session of the Cominform (Communist Information Bureau, successor to the Comintern) in September 1947, he declared the world to be divided into 'two camps',[13] thus denying the possibility of genuine neutralism. This was followed by intensification in the scope and pace of insurrections, not merely in countries such as Malaya, for which no date for independence had then been fixed, but in those newly independent (such as India, Burma, Indonesia). At that time none of the countries concerned could pose a threat to Soviet national security, while most were still colonial in status and viewed, as they had been by Lenin, as part of the sinews of anti-Communism, both as providers of industrial raw materials and agricultural products to the advanced capitalist world, and as captive markets for its products. Their main function, as the Soviets saw it, was to enable capitalism to 'buy off' the proletariat of the colonial powers at the expense of the colonials; to that extent, the colonies and newly-independent countries (which were dismissed as neocolonialist because they were not economically independent) were of little or no intrinsic interest in themselves. Soviet preoccupations still took the form of strategic concern over the threat posed from Europe, and insofar as the colonial territories were worth attention, this related solely to their place in the colonialists' scheme of things. Unrest and disruption of colonial rule was still expected to lead to economic (and consequently socio-political) breakdown of the European 'imperialist' countries, and that was regarded as its main function.

This relative indifference to Afro-Asia did not long survive Stalin. On the one hand, reevaluation of his policies after his death showed that opportunities of enhancing Soviet influence were being missed through doctrinal rigidity; political analysts[14] 'detected' a will to 'independent' (and therefore from time to time pro-Soviet or at least anti-Western) action on the part of their governments. Furthermore, the rapid increase in the numbers of non-aligned states, as one colony after another gained political independence, brought an end to 'automatic' pro-Western majorities in the United Nations, and opened an era in which Soviet interests could be

---

[13] *For a Lasting Peace, For a People's Democracy,* 10 Nov. 1947, pp. 2-4.

[14] In recommendations for cooperation with non-Communist nationalists by Asian Communist parties, the 'discovery' came much earlier. The Cominform journal *For a Lasting Peace, For a People's Democracy,* urged it on the Indian Communist Party in January 1950, and in December 1950, R. Palme Dutt, a British Communist leader of Indian descent, in a letter to the CPI, referred to Nehru's neutralism as 'a very important development'. But changes in the *Soviet* attitude came only after Stalin's death.

furthered in that body without the defensiveness implicit in continual use of the veto. These considerations combined to give the new states of Asia and Africa an importance which Stalin and the Zhdanov 'two camp' theory had denied them. But, since Communism is an ideology which requires that major tactical shifts be justified as consistent with a framework of universally valid principles, it was necessary to establish a doctrinal basis for the change in attitude towards the 'Third World'. This doctrinal base was found in Lenin's works of 1916 *Imperialism, the Highest Stage of Capitalism,* and the less well-known *The Socialist Revolution and Nations' Rights to Self-Determination.* Neither of these works had been written on a basis of knowledge of the East, nor was either in fact primarily concerned with colonial countries. *Imperialism, the Highest Stage of Capitalism* was primarily concerned to explain why the proletariat in the advanced countries had become not universally poorer, as predicted by Marx, but on the whole richer, and to explain the force of nationalism which had resulted not merely in wholesale support by the peoples of the First World War belligerents for their countries' war aims, but in the collapse of the Second International in 1914, when the Socialist Parties themselves placed country before class. Lenin's tactical purpose was to show that this unity based on nationalism was temporary, and he therefore argued that a 'workers' aristocracy' had been created in the countries which held Empires, at the expense of the exploited peoples of the colonies. Thus a large section of the workers had been 'bought off' by capitalism, and the competition for markets among the capitalists had not immediately resulted in the ruthless driving down of workers' wages which Marx foresaw. However, the alleviation of conditions was only temporary, because with the world already divided up among imperialist powers, further recourse to this device would no longer be possible. The First World War was, in Lenin's view, an indication that imperialist expansionism had given place to an intensified struggle to divide the spoils. Whatever its outcome, it would be followed by resumption of the process of impoverishment and hence of revolutionary resistance by the workers, in which those of the colonies would join. In *The Socialist Revolution and the Nations' Rights to Self-Determination,* Lenin had exhorted Communists to further the expulsion of 'imperialist' (British, Russian, French and German) influence from the semi-colonial countries of China, Turkey and Iran, by supporting the 'bourgeois-democratic national liberation movements' in those countries. Since the Communist Parties in these countries were virtually nonexistent, Lenin was doing no more than making a virtue of a necessity—any resistance to imperialism would serve to weaken the belligerent powers, hence bringing forward both the revolution in Russia (a multinational state which would be particularly exposed to disintegrative pressures if the right to self-determination were invoked by its non-Russian peoples), and the general revolution in Europe without which a 'Soviet' Russia seemed then unlikely to survive for long.

Lenin's statements on the East were in a sense *obiter dicta,* prompted by the tactical considerations of European left-wing politics, but they implied that in dealings with what later became the Third World, *any* anti-Western movement was worthy of support, whether or not it was Communist. They therefore provided handy texts for the post-Stalin leadership, seeking to increase contacts with the Third World. But whereas in 1916 and 1920 Lenin's arguments could be justified on the pragmatic grounds that Communist Parties in Asia were nonexistent, or too weak to provide leadership for revolutions, in 1954 this was no longer the case. Communists were in power in China and North Korea, and were soon to assume it in North Vietnam; none of them had come to power by 'two-stage' revolution, and the Chinese chose to interpret their success as the outcome of simultaneous military resistance and social transformation, in which non-Communist nationalists had played their part, but with leadership firmly in Communist hands, as Roy had advocated in 1920. Thus the attempt to found the new policy in Leninism was to involve the Soviet Union in ideological and practical difficulties with the Chinese, who felt that they were more entitled to Soviet aid than the 'bourgeois' nationalists of Egypt, Iraq, India or Indonesia. Nor were their difficulties confined to relations with China, because large Communist parties now existed in many Asian countries, and these, too, resented the lavishness of Soviet support for regimes which often acted vigorously against them, as did for example, Nasser in 1958 and Nehru in 1959. Thus wherever the Soviet government sought to support nationalist movements in developing countries, a conflict between expediency and doctrinal purity arose. On the one hand, the local Communists expected Soviet support primarily for themselves; on the other, the Soviet Union as part of a system of states, was influenced to support the movement which either held power or appeared most likely to win it—and rarely was this Communist. The dilemma became more acute as the non-Communist independence movements one by one transformed themselves into governments, often turning against their local Communists, whom they saw as symbolising yet another form of 'direction from outside'. Yet only in Indonesia after 1965 did anti-Communism lead to a withdrawal of Soviet support—and even there it was compounded by Indonesia's inability to pay the massive debts incurred by Soekarno, reluctance to proceed with Soviet projects, and the greatest massacre of Communists since Stalin's purges in the 1930s. Thus, long after it had become clear that the Soviet Union's ability to survive was independent of the short-term prospects of world revolution, Communist parties continued to expect the Soviet Union to behave like an embattled citadel, supporting 'world revolution' however remote its local prospects. Soviet leaders, on the other hand, behaved like those of a state concerned to maximise its influence within an existing state system, making alliances with and lending support to those countries and movements deemed most likely to enhance Soviet influence and power, or to assist in reducing threats to its security. It is therefore hardly surprising that local Communist parties in Africa and Asia often found themselves at cross purposes with the 'Socialist motherland'. With their sense of identity with Soviet Communism weakening as the Soviet party invoked sacred Leninist texts for unintended purposes, many turned towards China, implicitly conceding Peking's claims to be the guardians of a pure revolutionary tradition which the 'bourgeoisified' Soviets had betrayed.

According to the accepted Leninist view up to the 1950s a 'national bourgeois' independence movement played a 'progressive' role as long as it was fighting a foreign ruler, but by strict definition could no longer do so once it had taken power itself. When the first wave of newly independent countries emerged after the Second World War, the reactions of both the superpowers were to doubt the feasibility of their professed neutralism, but the Soviet scepticism was more early and more rigorously expressed than the later American reaction, which did not so much deny it as label it immoral. By contrast, when Zhdanov stated the 'two camps' doctrine in 1947, he expressly denied the possibility of a 'middle way' between capitalism and communism and urged a revolutionary struggle to establish 'people's democracies' along the lines of the Eastern European states then recently brought into the Soviet sphere of influence, and cited China and Vietnam as models. While cultivation of neutral states in Asia, notably India and Indonesia, began soon after Stalin's death, the 'two camps' doctrine was clearly an obstacle to the growth of closer relations, both because it was unrealistic and, by branding all non-Communist states as still part of the capitalist world, it insulted the susceptibilities of the neutralist leaders. It was therefore essential to revise the doctrine, in respect to both the 'national bourgeoisie' and the states governed by it.

Revision of the attitude towards the national bourgeoisie in a post-independence situation took the form of conceding to it a dualistic nature, ie. allowing for it a 'progressive' role which '. . . may be judged by how consistently it carries out agrarian reforms and other forms of social reconstructions; by its sincerity, or lack of it, in developing economic and cultural contacts with the Socialist countries; by its stand on questions of war and peace, and so on . . .'[15]

After the initial refusal to recognise the new states as independent, the Soviet theorists had compromised with reality by tacitly continuing to recognise them as independence *movements*[16] rather than governments, but clearly this semantic device was of limited and short-term utility. In his 'Report of the Central Committee' to the Twentieth Congress of the Soviet Communist Party, held in February 1956, Khrushchev announced the demise of the 'two camps' doctrine, dividing the world instead into a 'zone of war' (the advanced capitalist countries and members of US-sponsored alliance systems) and a 'zone of peace' which comprised the Soviet Union, its allies, and countries which officially professed neutralism. Having thus brought the new states (and the doctrine was especially designed for them, because it was never said to have any application to Europe's longstanding neutrals, Sweden and Switzerland) into a closer doctrinal relationship, it was possible to broaden exchanges with them, but never totally to ignore the continued dissatisfaction of Communist Parties which existed within many of them. At about the same time, doctrinal guidelines were laid down for economic aid programmes to the Third World countries. These, too, utilised an existing concept—that of 'state capitalism'—and imparted a new gloss to it.

The concept of 'state capitalism' as applied to non-Communist societies had been evolved in examination of the question whether state ownership of industry in advanced capitalist states was consistent with a view of capitalist society as dedicated to the pursuit of private wealth and power.[17] The conclusion in that respect had been that it was 'reactionary', in that it constituted a coming

---

15 For a discussion of the Soviet adaptation to the facts of non-Communist nationalism, see Shinn, W. T. 'The National Democratic State: a Communist programme for less developed areas', *World Politics,* April 1963 pp. 377-389, and Löwenthal, R., 'On National Democracy', *Survey,* April 1963, pp. 119-133.

16 Eg., in the Party Programme adopted at 22nd Party Congress 1961.

17 The concept as applied to *Soviet* society is different. See Djilas, M. *The New Class,* 1966 edition pp. 48 ff., and Trotsky, L., *The Revolution Betrayed* pp. 248-255. Both argue that having taken power in a capitalist Russia which was not yet fully developed, the Communists were forced to develop capitalism, including its exploitative aspects, and coined the phrase 'state capitalism' to describe the resulting social order.

together of the coercive state and monopoly capitalist financial power, not a transfer of means of production to the people. Abandonment of Stalin's line, that the new states were not independent because of their continued economic dependence, did not mean that the Soviet leaders had reconciled themselves to that dependence. The fact was accepted, but so, too, were the desirability and feasibility of changing it. Most of the newly independent countries were industrially weak, and concerned to create industrial capacity, but lacked the capital, particularly private risk capital, to do so. These factors made it inevitable that industrialisation would be inadequate to fulfil the often unrealistic expectations of the newly independent countries and that such as there was would mostly be undertaken with state resources and under governmental control, even in countries where the government lacked any specific bias against private enterprise. Once the Soviets had determined on a more flexible outlook towards the non-Communist governments of the new states, it was a logical decision to channel aid into industrialisation, and into strengthening the public sector of industry, in part because this corresponded directly to their own experience of the 1920s and 30s, in part because it bypassed the ideological problems involved in aiding private 'capitalist' industry. At the same time, because control was in the hands of non-Communist leaders, it was ideologically repugnant to classify the resulting economic structure alongside that of a Communist state; to do so would imply that the means of production could pass into the control of 'the people' without the need to erect a Communist political superstructure. The term 'state capitalism' was therefore used from 1956 onwards to describe the nationalised industries rising in the new states, but in order to dissociate it from the pejorative overtones of the term as previously used, it was argued that it differed radically from the state capitalism of former times, which resulted from a fusion of monopoly capitalism with an aggressive state apparatus; that it resulted from the weakness of indigenous monopoly capitalism; was capable of developing further (sc. into genuine 'ownership by the people'); above all, that unlike the older state capitalism, its purpose was to reduce dependence on foreign monopolies and facilitate a 'non-capitalist road of development'; and that therefore it possessed 'progressive features' and should be supported.

The Soviet journals have also pointed out[18] that to strengthen state capitalism by expropriating foreign assets, thereby reducing

---

[18] Eg. Rubinshtein, M., 'A non-capitalist path for under-developed countries', *New Times,* Moscow, No. 28, July-August 1956, or Shamray, V. 'On the transition to socialism of economically weak countries', *Voprosy Ekonomiki* (Problems of Economics), 6/59.

the influence of foreign capital, constitutes an attack on imperialism, liquidates foreign monopolies over trade, and, by increasing the degree of governmental control over the economy, simplifies the task of directing it and mobilising national resources for socially desirable ends. No doubt they also have in mind that expropriation creates tension between the expropriating country and the expropriated concern (usually Western), therefore increasing their own opportunities for influence. But there is no evidence that the granting of economic aid to an Asian government has ever been made conditional upon its willingness to expropriate foreign assets—though they have stepped in to support one subsequently faced with Western counteraction (as in supplying oil to Cuba, after Castro's nationalisation of foreign-owned refineries and the consequent Western oil embargo) and pre-emptively assisted another—Ceylon—by stepping up supplies of oil and economic aid in 1963-4, when US aid was suspended after Ceylon had nationalised some of the assets of Western oil companies. They have persisted in aiding non-Communist governments in the face of repeated Chinese allegations that to do so merely strengthens the 'reactionary forces'.

In the later 1950s, a number of the new states intensified activity against their domestic Communist parties, especially in India, where tension between the central government and the Communist state government elected in 1957 in Kerala persisted throughout 1958, and culminated on 31 July 1959 in a central government decree, unseating the state government which had held power for 28 months.

At the Twenty-First Soviet Party Congress, Khrushchev and others referred critically to anti-Communist measures by Asian and African nationalist leaders, but refused to give any hint that their economic aid would be imperilled if they did not desist. (It later emerged that the Chinese had unfavourably compared Soviet aid given to them with that given to anti-Communist nationalists such as Nasser and Nehru, and it may have been Chinese advocacy of economic pressure which Khrushchev rejected.) This stand was perfectly comprehensible in terms of a balance of interest policy—however unpalatable the behaviour of Nasser and Nehru might be to their local Communist parties, or to Marxist theorists, each was an unchallenged national leader with an important voice in Third World councils. If either should be brought down by denial of Soviet economic aid neither would be succeeded by a pro-Soviet Communist and either or both might be followed by a pro-Western successor. In any event, the scope and volume of Soviet aid was not large enough for its withdrawal to be decisive, nor was it irreplaceable from other sources, notably the Western powers. But whatever the practical arguments for not using Soviet aid as a lever in the crude fashion suggested, the policy lacked doctrinal respectability. There were many in the affected Communist parties, as well as in the international Communist movement (not least within the Soviet party itself) who would readily accept Chinese charges (still at that time being made in private, but soon to become public) that to give aid to anti-Communist bourgeois nationalists was a betrayal of proletarian internationalism.

There were additional reasons for seeking a new and more comprehensive doctrinal formula. Fidel Castro had taken power in Cuba on New Year's Day 1959; although considered to be a typical bourgeois nationalist, by himself, by the Cuban Communist Party and the Soviet leadership,[19] he had found relations with the United States difficult, and by the end of 1959 was facing an imminent US-imposed cut in the sugar quota on which the Cuban economy depended. Given the poor state of Cuban financial reserves after a two-year civil war, the reluctance of US and other Western suppliers to grant credit, and the low level of world sugar prices in 1959, Castro's difficulties could be solved only by recourse to another supplier. As it happened, the Soviet Union was in the second year of its 1959-65 Seven Year Plan, an important element of which was improvement of living standards, and had already in October 1959 concluded a trade agreement with Brazil under which Brazilian coffee would be exchanged against Soviet machinery. Inherent in the plan for improved living standards was an increased consumption of sugar, which the Soviet sugar industry was unable to supply. Castro's problem therefore arose at a time when the Soviet Union was not merely able but willing to increase its imports of sugar, and, no doubt, not unmindful of the political opportunities offered by expanding Soviet trade in areas which had for many years been dominated by United States commercial and political influence. The outcome was the Cuban-Soviet trade agreement of February 1960. In view of Castro's previous vociferous anti-Communism, and his constant disputes with the Cuban Communist Party, the agreement with Cuba needed an ideological justification which that with Brazil did not—Castro's political survival could well depend on the trade agreement, which was not the case with the Brazilian government. The deal with Castro was therefore an additional reason to seek to provide doctrinal justifica-

---

[19] 'The political leadership of the armed struggle was in the hands of the petty bourgeoisie . . . ' Blas Roca in *World Marxist Review*, August 1959, p. 18.

tion for giving economic and political support to anti-Communist bourgeois-nationalist regimes.

Pending also was an international conference of Communist Parties, to be held in autumn 1960, and having as one of its objectives an attempt to compose the growing differences of outlook between the Soviets and Chinese. Since the question of attitudes to non-Communist nationalism was one of the important issues between them, it was clearly important to devise a formula to which not merely the Chinese and Soviets could subscribe, but also the Eastern European states (which on the whole supported the Soviet attitude, but saw some advantage to themselves, in the form of increased room to manoeuvre, arising from a situation in which Soviet doctrinal hegemony was subject to challenge), and the Communist Parties in non-Communist countries, for whom any new definition would serve as part of an action programme. But above all, it must take account both of the hitherto underrated forces of nationalism and 'non-scientific' (ie., non-Communist) socialism in the new states themselves.

The doctrinal formula to fit the situation in the new states of Asia and Africa was the concept of 'national democracy'. The first 'official' formulation of it was contained in the 'Statement of the Conference of 81 Communist and Workers' Parties' published on 6 December 1960. The Statement described the 'breakdown of colonial slavery under the impact of the national liberation movement' as 'a development which in historical significance ranks second only to the formation of the world socialist system', and went on to define the characteristics of a new type of state, the 'independent national democracy'. It was a state which:

1. 'Upholds continually its political and economic independence, fights imperialism, imperialist military blocs, and military bases on its territory' (ie. pursues a policy of non-alignment with an anti-Western slant);
2. 'fights the new forms of colonialism and penetration by imperialist capitalism' (ie., carefully controls or rejects outright all forms of Western economic penetration, whether trade or aid);
3. 'rejects dictatorial and despotic forms of government' (ie. abjures the anti-Communist measures then being pursued in, among other recipients of Soviet aid, Egypt, Iraq and India).

The Statement justified the concept doctrinally by describing the 'national bourgeoisie' as 'progressive' in that it was 'anti-imperialist *and* anti-feudal' (ie., hostile to both the colonial regime and its native supporters), but argued that after independence had been gained it became 'more and more inclined to compromise with domestic reaction and with imperialism'. By this gloss it both justified support for the 'national bourgeoisie' by Communists in ejecting colonialism, and kept alive the possibility of revolt against them by Communists after independence. In this respect, the doctrinal formula adhered to the concept of 'two-stage revolution' of classical Leninism. By its references to elements of 'feudalism' persisting in former colonies it equated them with pre-capitalist societies, where a bourgeois revolution would have to take place simply to create the conditions for the later socialist revolution in which the Communists would displace their erstwhile allies. This was in no sense innovatory, though the active participation of Communists in furthering the bourgeois revolution was a reversion to the 'Popular Front' strategy of the middle 1930s. The 'national democracy' was clearly presented as a transitional state,[20] though naturally no attempt was made to set time limits for its supersession by 'socialism' (even if considered desirable this would hardly have been possible, since in many of the states later to be defined as actual or potential 'national democracies' there was in fact no Communist Party in 1960). In the theoretical progression of social advancement, 'national democracy' appeared destined to precede 'people's democracy', a term coined by Stalin to describe the states of Eastern Europe, in which 'socialism' was being built under Communist direction, but which had not yet liquidated all vestiges of the capitalist order and earned the right to join the Soviet Union in being described as 'socialist'.

The Statement gave no indication which states were appropriately to be described as 'national democracies', but the first to be so described was Cuba, in a speech by Ulbricht made on 20 December 1960. Subsequently, however, Castro (on 15 April 1961) for the first time described his revolution as 'socialist', and after some hesitation[21] the Soviets indicated in their 1962 May Day slogans that Cuba had passed from the 'national democratic' to 'people's democratic' stage. To this day, however, they have declined to confer the same accolade on any other of the developing countries which claims its ideology to be 'socialist', and Cuba remains an isolated exception to the rule that countries in which leadership is exercised by non-Communists cannot be classified higher on their scale of historical progression than 'national democracy'.

---

[20] Eg. by Kim, G. in *Aziya i Afrika segodnya* (Asia & Africa Today) 10/1962.

[21] Eg. Ponomarev, B., in *Kommunist* No. 8, described Cuba as a national democracy in May 1961, several weeks after Castro had made his claim.

Although the concept of 'national democracy' served to cover pragmatic diplomacy with a doctrinal mantle, it by no means eliminated the problem of reconciling nationalism with Communist orthodoxy. In part, this arose from the manifestly transitional nature which the 'national democratic' state bore in the minds of its devisers; although delegates from some non-Communist parties which might take part in 'national democratic fronts' were invited to attend the Soviet Twenty-Second Party Congress in 1961, the attractions of the Communist concept remained more apparent to its creators than to non-Communists in the countries likely to be affected by its application.

By subscribing to the Conference Statement, China appeared to endorse the concept of 'national democracy', but in fact it took no action to explain or justify it either to Party members or the public at large, and subsequent statements indicated that its criticisms of the Soviet practice of aiding anti-Communist regimes had not been abandoned. With fewer possibilities for enhancing their influence by means of aid and trade, the Chinese consistently adopted a more 'pure' doctrinal approach which saw danger for Communist parties in assisting the national bourgeoisie to take power, and accepted the idea of united fronts only where the local Communists were in a controlling position. They also argued against the Soviet policy of granting aid to develop the publicly-owned sector of industry in 'national-democratic' states. This may partly have been 'sour grapes' (they were later to disclose publicly their displeasure at the amount of aid granted by the Soviet Union to non-, or even anti-Communist leaders, instead of to China, from which Soviet aid was almost wholly withdrawn in 1958), but they based their argument not on this but on the belief that to enlarge the publicly-owned sector merely strengthens the hand of nationalist leaders against their own local Communists, rejecting (where they did not totally ignore) the Soviet contention that enlargement of industry improves the long-term prospects for a Communist takeover by creating a class-conscious industrial proletariat.

Although Soviet charges that the Chinese denied the possibility of peaceful takeover were as exaggerated as Chinese counter-charges of Soviet betrayal of revolutionary ideals, it was neverthe-less the case that the Soviet approach aimed at securing short-term influence over nationalists actually in power, while the Chinese attitude was more calculated to appeal to the local Communist parties whom both saw, in doctrinal terms, as eventually destined to supplant the nationalists. Since a number of the most important states of Asia fall into the category of potential 'national democracies', the difference in approach to the doctrinal issue has tended to be expressed in the way they have since handled their dealings with the non-Communist unaligned states of the Indo-Pacific area. Although the real world has, as is normal, diverged from the theoretical model in a number of instances, it has remained true as a general proposition throughout the 1960s that Soviet wooing of established governments in Asia, whatever their political colour and attitude to Communists, has been more assiduous than that of the Chinese.

The concept of the 'national democratic state' was developed in order to preserve a fiction: that Leninist postulates on the inevitable breakdown of capitalism, and unavoidable conflict between the exploiters and exploited, were still valid. Neither Marx nor Lenin foresaw the importance of 'bourgeois' nationalism or non-Communist socialism in the development of former colonies after independence, nor did they or their successors foresee that in many cases the newly independent states of Asia and Africa would consider their national interests furthered by continued association with their former colonial masters. The pursuit of diplomacy has therefore been hampered during the 1960s by the discovery that the formula of 'national democracy' itself fails to fit reality at a number of points. Most of the countries described as in this category (Ghana, before the overthrow of Nkrumah, Guinea, and Mali, for example) are in sub-Saharan Africa. Here the Soviets argue that conditions for 'transition to the non-capitalist road' are especially favourable, because the proletariat and bourgeoisie are coming into existence simultaneously, and the bourgeoisie is therefore unable to entrench itself before the proletariat becomes class-conscious and militant. They also see the lack of a private industrial sector as favouring the buildup of a state sector free of private competition. Among non-Arab Asian countries, only Burma is described in the same terms.[22]

Developments in Indonesia after the abortive *coup* of 1965 have shown that the process of establishing a 'national democracy' is subject to rapid reversal, and while the Soviet propaganda apparatus, after considerable hesitation, now draws hostile attention to increased Western economic and political activity there,[23]

---

[22] Eg. in Brezhnev's speech 'Report of the Central Committee of the CPSU' to the 24th Party Congress, 30 March 1971. Novosti Press Agency Publishing House, Moscow, 1971, pp. 23-24.

[23] Eg. TASS 18 Dec. 1970, 'The colonialists that were expelled by the Indonesian people a quarter of a century ago are now returning to the country through another door'. BBC Summary of World Broadcasts SU/3565/A3/1.

Soviet scholarly comment inclines to a less simplistic view.[24] As in most Soviet studies of developing countries the trend is towards explaining events more in terms of specific local circumstances than by rote references to 'universal' laws. As the decade progressed, comment in Party journals laid less emphasis on the supposedly transitional nature of the national democratic state, and more on the desirability of supporting it in the search for a non-capitalist road of development, while policies towards South-East Asian states have aimed more at enhancement of area stability than at fostering of either a 'one-stage' or 'two-stage' revolution.

Thus military aid programmes in general have been calculated to create balances rather than to disturb them; Afghanistan received arms to balance those provided by the United States to Pakistan as a member of CENTO and SEATO; aid to India was calculated to some extent to counter Pakistan's new aircraft and tanks, but in the main was more oriented to improving the balance against China; Indonesia received quantities of naval and air force equipment beyond its capacities to man, operate or maintain, though the army received very little, despite the fact that successful pursuit of confrontation in Borneo depended more on the army than on the other services. North Vietnam's imports from the Soviet Union exceeded her exports to it by up to 150 million roubles per annum from 1961 onwards, suggesting that economic aid has been important in determining its ability to support the war and withstand American bombing; but military aid became important only after 1965, and neither has played as significant a role for either the North Vietnamese Army or the National Liberation Front as has US military and economic support for South Vietnam. Significant, also, has been the total abstinence from clandestine arms supply to insurrectionists; the most striking example of the Soviet approach occurred during the 'Che Guevarist' revolt in Ceylon in early 1971. North Korea was accused of supporting it; the Soviet Union was one of several countries (including the UK and India) which supplied weapons to assist in suppressing it.

The doctrines of 'two-stage revolution' and 'national democracy', and the revised version of the concept of 'state capitalism' have remained the bases of the Soviet approach to the non-Communist neutrals of Asia, despite attacks on them by the Chinese and local Communists. From the Soviet point of view, these doctrines have provided flexibility in building relationships with the new states;

---

[24] Eg. Yu. Arkhipov, 'Indonesia' in Dinkevich, A.I. (Ed.), *Credit and Credit Systems of the Asian Countries*, USSR Academy of Sciences, 1968, pp. 111-151.

on the one hand, they provide a 'theological' justification for support of non- or anti-Communist leaders; on the other, they place such support within a framework of 'eventual' socialist revolution, and may therefore be defended as consistent with Communist aims, against Chinese charges of 'revolution betrayed'. They do not constitute a strategy for subversion, though they do provide one for erosion of the influence of other powers, whether Western or China. Their main weakness from the revolutionary's point of view is their lack of appeal to 'the masses' and from the Soviet angle their chief drawback has been that their heavy emphasis on trade and aid can be backed up in practice only to a limited extent compared with the similar but much larger Western-sponsored programmes.[25] Steady development of the Soviet economy has permitted aid and trade programmes to expand by impressive percentages, but their overall volume is less impressive when compared with those of their ideological antagonists. However, the decision to proceed on a largely economic basis derived from Khrushchev's doctrine of 'peaceful economic competition' presented in 1956; even then, when prospects of 'overtaking' America economically were assessed with considerably more optimism than proved justifiable, it was clear that major results were not to be expected in the short term.

A new departure in Soviet foreign policy in 1969 was Brezhnev's brief reference to the desirability of a collective security system in Asia, made at the conference of Communist Parties in Moscow on 7 June. Soviet writings and commentaries on the proposal were vague, but indicated that if such a system were set up, containment of China would be one of its objectives,[26] though one commentator mentioned the possibility that China could participate, provided it ceased to be interested only in 'raising tension and chauvinist great-power plots against other countries'.[27]

Although the reactions from Asian countries to Brezhnev's suggestion was unenthusiastic, Soviet media from time to time refer to the proposition in terms which suggest that, though not of high priority, they retain an interest in it. But an unusual reference was made in a Moscow Radio broadcast in Chinese on 21 December 1970, which said 'The Soviet Union maintains that the form of collective security system in which the Soviet Union, China,

---

[25] This issue is discussed in more detail in the chapter on Economic Relations.
[26] For a detailed discussion of the Brezhnev proposal as reflected in the Soviet media, see Howard, P., 'A System of Collective Security' in *Mizan*, July/August 1969, pp. 199-204.
[27] Matveyev, V., in *Izvestia* 3 Aug. 1969.

Pakistan, India and other countries which are concerned with the task of turning the densely populated Asian continent into a region of permanent peace should participate, would constitute a major obstacle to the expansionist designs of imperialism. Regrettably, the Chinese leaders have treated this proposal with prejudice and have made false reports about it to the Chinese people, purporting that this is the product of anti-Chinese collusion.'[28]

It is difficult to estimate what this statement means. The suggestion that both the Soviet Union and China should form part of the collective security system in Asia is contrary to previous indications (a) that the Soviet Union did not intend itself to claim membership of any collective security body in Asia, and (b) that containment of China was one of the Soviet purposes in floating the proposal in the first place. The selection of countries named is peculiar in another respect, namely that the four countries mentioned by name seem rather improbable partners for any collective security arrangement envisaged for the near future. Pairing of India with Pakistan, of China with India, or of the Soviet Union with China, seems likely only after a number of major border issues and ideological disputes have been settled. But this reference was an isolated occurrence, not referred to in Soviet home service or other foreign language broadcasts, nor in the press; its contact with reality seems slim, and in any event the Chinese are said in the broadcast to have wilfully misrepresented the proposal—though not to have rejected it.

At the highest level, there seems to be no compulsion to urge an Asian collective security arrangement; Brezhnev introduced it in one brief sentence in 1969, and in presenting the Central Committee Report to the Twenty-Fourth Party Congress in March 1971 referred to it not at all. But at lower levels, commentators continued to make low-key references to it on subsequent occasions. An article in *International Affairs* for March referred vaguely to 'growing support for the idea of collective security in Asia',[29] and another in April commended Singapore for being 'not against collective security in Asia'.[30]

From the Soviet foreign policy angle, non-alignment is a virtue only to the extent that the non-aligned can be presented as making common cause with the Soviet Union and its allies against 'imperialism' in all its manifestations. This naturally imposes limits

[28] *BBC Summary of World Broadcasts*, Pt.I, SU/3567/A3/1.
[29] Nikhamin, V., 'Diplomacy of Developing States', *International Affairs* (Moscow), March 1971.
[30] Shatalov, I., 'At the Junction of Eras and Continents', *International Affairs* (Moscow) April, 1971.

on their approval of it, since, to the extent that the non-aligned see themselves as a differentiated group, they are likely to view their interests as divergent from not only the 'imperialist' but also the 'socialist' countries, and, perhaps, to view sympathetically Chinese attempts to organise small and medium power opinion against 'joint world domination' by the superpowers. Since many leaders of non-aligned countries have tended to express their neutralism by refusing to adopt viewpoints which would unconditionally support one superpower against another (eg., the Indian reluctance to condemn outright Soviet actions in Eastern Europe, or to support Soviet demands for immediate withdrawal of American forces from Vietnam), they often take a middle position which Soviet ideologists regard as unsatisfactory. Thus Soviet writers have objected both to 'equation' of the Warsaw Pact and NATO,[31] and to acceptance of a formula which divides the world into 'poor' and 'rich' halves (eg., the 'rich North—poor South' concept), instead of drawing a formal distinction between countries on a 'class' basis (which in their view, would isolate the West from the bulk of the world).[32]

The Soviet view of non-alignment seeks to ally it to socialism, whether implicitly (as in Khrushchev's 'zone of peace') or explicitly as when Soviet writers argue that it is the very existence of the 'socialist system opposing imperialism' which makes non-alignment possible. But whatever dissatisfaction has existed on the ideological side, government support has been given throughout to non-Communist nationalists, even when facile expectations voiced in the mid-50s (presenting the bourgeois nationalist stage as temporary) proved incapable of fulfilment, and the alternative 'national democracies' failed to increase in number. A book published in Moscow in 1970 contained a convenient summary of a widely held Soviet view of non-alignment, showing it to be regarded with a relative detachment, and accepted as a force in its own right—though one whose very existence depend on the 'socialist system's' ability to deter Western action against it.

> ... the new states occupy an intermediate position between the two opposing social systems. They can take advantage of the existence of the powerful socialist system to pursue a relatively independent foreign policy course, the so-called policy of non-

---

[31] Sidenko, V., 'Perspectives of the Policy of Non-Alignment', *New Times* 31/1969, p. 19.

[32] In Lavrishchev, A.A. (Ed.) *The Developing Countries in World Politics* (in Russian), Moscow, 1968, quoted by Morison, D. in 'USSR and the Third World: Questions of Foreign Policies', *Mizan*, November 1970, p. 76.

alignment and neutralism. In the practical activity of the United Nations, the policy of non-alignment shows itself, on the one hand, in a desire to rise above the fundamental opposition of the modern age, that between the two social and economic systems, and to smooth it over and reconcile it, or seek compromise solutions satisfying both sides. This finds expression in the new states' support for declarations and resolutions on the problems of maintaining peace, disarmament, human rights, etc., usually of a broad and general character. On the other hand, the policy of non-alignment constitutes a balancing between the two groups of countries, and an attempt to turn their present opposition to use and profit.[33]

From time to time Soviet publications attempt to categorise countries of the Third World in terms of their progress towards the goal of 'non-capitalist development'. One such list was given in an article by Yu. Alexandrov in early 1966,[34] on the peasant movements in Asia and North Africa. None qualified for description as a 'national democracy', but in 'ascending order of merit', the countries were grouped as follows:

1. 'Ruled by reactionary imperialists': Thailand, South Vietnam, South Korea.
2. Feudal structure preserved, feudal landowners and top stratum of bourgeoisie dominant: Libya, Saudi Arabia, Jordan.
3. Feudal landowners deprived of power, replaced by 'landlord-capitalism': Turkey, Philippines.
4. Top stratum of feudal landlord class 'liquidated', future of large and middle landowners in question: India, Pakistan, Iraq, Indonesia.
5. Agrarian order transformed beyond 'usual bourgeois-democratic reforms': Algeria, UAR, Syria, Burma.

Over recent years it has become apparent that Soviet expectations of social change in the Third World are modest. This may be seen from an article on the 'non-capitalist path' of development which appeared at the beginning of 1971. The author was at pains to point out that the 'non-capitalist path' is not socialism, 'because it presupposes an *extremely prolonged* coexistence of contradictory tendencies', some of which are not merely not socialist, but 'contradict the principles of socialism'.[35] Similarly, an article published in 1970 named only seven countries (UAR, Algerian, Syria,

---

[33] *Ibid.* p. 77.
[34] Alexandrov, Yu. G., 'On the Character of the Peasant movement in the developing countries of Asia and North Africa'; *Narody Azii i Afriki:* (Peoples of Asia & Africa) (in Russian) No. 2/1966, pp. 3, 14.
[35] Ulyanovsky, R. A., *New Times,* 1 Jan. 1971.

Burma, Guinea, Congo (Brazzaville) and Tanzania) as actually 'proceeding' on the non-capitalist path, named two others (Sudan and Libya) as 'having achieved the conditions for transition' to it, and South Yemen 'and others' as 'having declared their resolve' to proceed along it.[36] Comparison with Alexandrov's list of 1966 is possible, though neither the areas nor the categorisations match directly. Four countries (UAR, Algeria, Syria and Burma) are in the 'top category' of both lists (the other three in Ulyanovskiy's list are in sub-Saharan Africa, which the 1966 article did not cover), and none had been added in the four years which separate the two articles. Perhaps more significantly, none of the key countries in Soviet policies towards Asia rate a mention: in the whole of Asia outside the Arab world, only Burma is rated as having actually taken the 'non-capitalist road'; no other is considered even to have 'declared its resolve' with sufficient firmness to be named.

At the highest policy level, Brezhnev provided an informal ranking of a number of states of the Third World in his Central Committee report of March 1971. Its correspondence with the 1970 list given above was close, and it also indicated the criteria by which a state is judged to be taking the 'non-capitalist road', when compared with the 1970 list. Brezhnev's list of countries 'oriented towards socialism' ran as follows:

1. Foreign property nationalised wholly or substantially: UAR, Burma, Algeria, Guinea, Sudan, Tanzania, Somalia.
2. All land and minerals nationalised: Congo (Brazzaville).
3. Substantial agrarian reforms: UAR, Syria, Sudan, Somalia, Algeria.

Apart from his omission of Libya and the addition of Somalia, Brezhnev's list of countries 'oriented towards socialism' corresponds exactly to those described in the 1970 article as either 'proceeding' on the non-capitalist road or 'having achieved the conditions for transition'. The fact that all except Burma are countries of the Arab world, or in Africa, or both, suggests that those, at least for the near future, appear to the Soviets more hopeful than non-Arab Asia as areas where the trend of events favour their political philosophy of non-capitalist development based on a state-owned industrial sector. Assuming Brezhnev's 'list' to be the more authoritative of the two, as well as the more recent, five countries in sub-Saharan Africa, two in Arab Africa and one in Arab Asia achieve commendation, for expropriation of foreign

---

[36] Popov, V., *Aziya i Afrika Segodnya* (Asia & Africa Today), 11/70, pp. 2-4.

assets, agrarian reform, or both; Congo (Brazzaville) received approval for nationalisation of all land and minerals, which, could, of course, in the absence of an industrial sector, be seen as extending state control to all future industrial activity, as well as forming a prerequisite to a far-reaching agrarian reform.

A complication not foreseen by the constructors of the ideological framework in the mid-1950's was the outbreak of a doctrinal dispute with China. In practice this made little difference to the policies followed; China was in any event ill-equipped to woo wielders of power in non-aligned countries because its doctrinal position was hostile to them, and its ability to acquire influence through aid programmes was very limited compared with the Soviet Union. China's appeal was mainly directed to the insurrectionists whom the Soviet Union declined to support, and as these were not successful in winning power, Soviet influence on the non-aligned governments was not materially harmed by the lack of unanimity in the Communist movement. To a large extent, in fact, Soviet espousal of the 'moderate' side in the dispute increased the readiness of those governments to accept its advice, assistance, and offers to expand trade relations. Therefore Soviet post-1954 policies towards Asian countries have shown themselves sufficiently flexible to adapt to reverses, and to the failure of events to develop as quickly as expected in directions favourable to the Soviet Union.

In the short run, they have, on the whole, been moderately successful, in that few Asian countries now maintain an attitude of out-and-out antagonism to Soviet interests, while the specifically anti-Communist alliance systems—the Baghdad Pact (later CENTO) and SEATO—have shown marked disintegrative tendencies. Policies covered and explained by the doctrines of 'national liberation struggle', 'national democracy' and 'the non-capitalist road' are therefore likely to continue to figure largely in Soviet dealings with Asia during the seventies.

# 2

# Soviet Asia

Soviet territory in Asia comprises Transcaucasia (the Republics of Georgia, Armenia and Azerbaijan), Central Asia (the Uzbek, Turkmen, Kirghiz and Tadzhik Republics, plus the very large Republic of Kazakhstan, which Soviet usage normally classifies separately but which is here regarded as part of Central Asia), and Russia east of the Urals (West Siberia, East Siberia and the Far East). Taken together these contain three-quarters of Soviet territory and just under 30% of its population, distributed as follows:

Population (000's), Soviet Asian Territories
*Transcaucasia* (1970 census)[1]
    *Total*: 12,295

|  | of which | Georgia | 4686 |
|---|---|---|---|
|  |  | Armenia | 2492 |
|  |  | Azerbaijan | 5117 |

*Central Asia* (1970 census)
    *Total*: 32,801

|  | of which | Kazakhstan | 12849 |
|---|---|---|---|
|  |  | Uzbekistan | 11960 |
|  |  | Kirghizia | 2933 |
|  |  | Tadzhikistan | 2900 |
|  |  | Turkmenia | 2159 |

*East of Urals* (1968 official estimate)
    *Total*: 25,231

|  | of which | West Siberia | 12201 |
|---|---|---|---|
|  |  | East Siberia | 7321 |
|  |  | Far East | 5709 |

*Grand Total, Soviet Asia,* 70,327,000

[1] Memorandum compiled by V. D. Ogareff, Australian National University, from preliminary data on the Soviet census of 1970.

CENTRAL ASIA AND TRANSCAUCASUS

In their excellent short study[2] of this area, Alec Nove and J. A. Newth entitle it 'The Soviet Middle East'. While the description is a pithy one, it must be used with caution. It is apposite in respect of some of the products of the area (cotton, citrus fruits, tobacco and oil), of the racial affinities of some of the inhabitants, and of the Moslem religion, which is widespread in parts of Transcaucasia and throughout Central Asia. But it must not be pushed too far; ethnically the Moslem inhabitants are linked not with the Arab world but with Turkey, Iran and Afghanistan; the living standards of the Soviet southern republics more closely approximate the Slav republics of the Union rather than their co-religionists and ethnic cousins to the south; and the area as a whole, but especially Kazakhstan, contains a far larger European population (mostly Russians and Ukrainians) than do the Middle Eastern states.

Russian hegemony over Transcaucasia began with the conquest of the hitherto independent Kingdom of Georgia in 1801, and the areas south of it were acquired from Turkey and Persia between 1813 and 1829. Numerous and fierce revolts occurred during the 19th Century, and anti-Russian feeling remained so strong that when Tsarism collapsed in February-March 1917, Georgia, Armenia and Azerbaijan attempted to seize their independence. Reestablishment of Russian authority had to await the end of the Civil War, but Soviet governments were set up in Azerbaijan and Armenia in 1920, and in Georgia in 1921, following invasions by the Red Army. The three republics are ethnically very mixed— both Georgia and Azerbaijan contain almost half a million Armenians, and about as many Russians,[3] but their links with the nations to the south of them are more tenuous than in the case of Central Asia; few Georgians or Armenians live in Turkey. Insofar as religious tradition still plays a part in the area, it too divides the Georgians (mostly Christian, except for those around Batumi, who are Moslem) and Armenians (Christian) from the Moslems of Turkey. The Azerbaijanis, however, are both Moslem and Turkic, and their antipathy, especially towards Armenians, is marked, having been frequently expressed in the past in bloody pogroms, such as marked the revolution of 1905 in the Baku oil-fields.[4] Azerbaijan, however, is relatively primitive and under-developed, and its usefulness as a magnet to Turks is limited.

---

[2] Nove, A., and Newth, J. A., *The Soviet Middle East; A Communist Model for Development* Allen & Unwin, London, 1967.
[3] Soviet 1959 census data.
[4] Described in Broido, E., *Memoirs of a Revolutionary*, pp. 101-115.

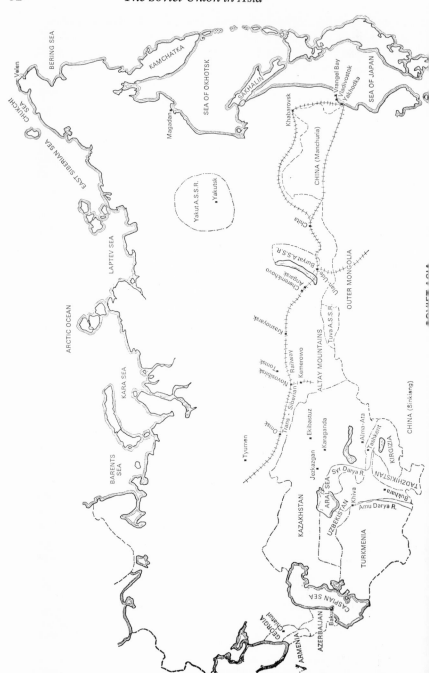

Economically, the prime importance of Transcaucasia to the Soviet Union lies in the Baku oilfields and the manganese deposits of Chiaturi.[5] The Baku field was the first Russian one to be worked, and appears to be approaching exhaustion, though production is maintained by the drilling of new wells further and further out in the Caspian Sea.[6] Although industry in the area is being diversified, exhaustion of the Baku oilfield is likely to create local employment problems and to lend greater urgency to Soviet negotiations for Iranian or Middle Eastern oil, for which there are economically sound arguments—in view of the distances and extraction difficulties involved, it has been estimated that oil from distant Soviet Asian fields would cost from 25 to 200% more delivered in European Russia than would Arab or Iranian oil.[7]

In pre-revolutionary Russia, virtually no other industries existed in Transcaucasia. Soviet policy has been to channel investment so as to ensure a higher growth rate for previously unindustrialised republics, and Transcaucasia has benefitted from this—even allowing for the fact that the original base for calculation was very low. Industrial output in Armenia increased about one hundredfold between 1928 and 1965, and in Georgia slightly over forty times. Azerbaijan did not do so well; but even there the increase was about seventeenfold, compared with that for the USSR as a whole of about fifty times over the same 37 year period. However, even the striking increase in Armenia left it less industrialised than the average for the USSR, and with per capita incomes which, at between $500 and $600 per annum, were in 1963 slightly less than three-quarters of the Russian average, though three to four times as large as those of neighbouring non-Communist countries.[8]

Central Asia presents a more varied picture. To begin with, it is very much larger than Transcaucasia: whereas the three Transcaucasus Republics have an area little larger than the State of Victoria or the United Kingdom between them, the Kazakh Republic alone is almost half as large as Australia; it is the second largest of the fifteen Republics of the Soviet Union (the Russian Soviet Federated Socialist Republic is larger, but Kazakhstan has more territory than the remaining thirteen put together).[9] The

---

[5] *Narodnoye Khozyaystvo SSSR v 1969 g.* (National Economy of the USSR in 1969), (hereafter cited as *N.E.*) pp. 197 & 207.

[6] *N.E.* 1969 p. 197, shows that post-war production from this field has never reattained the 1940 level, and has been falling since 1965.

[7] Berreby, J. J., 'Oil in the Orient', in *The New Middle East*, December, 1969, p. 44.

[8] Nove and Newth, *op. cit.*, pp. 42-43.

[9] *N.E.*, 1969, pp. 13-18.

Kazakh Republic also resembles Australia in being very largely arid or semi-arid. Northern Kazakhstan has been the scene of the 'Virgin Lands' experiment, a grandiose venture embarked on by Khrushchev after Stalin's death, in an attempt to expand grain production by increasing the area under cultivation. After a few good years, yields fell off drastically and soil erosion proved a major problem.[10] However, the experiment was not abandoned, though less dramatic methods of husbandry are now in vogue, and the hundreds of thousands of workers brought in from the European USSR added to those brought in during the nineteenth century, make the Kazakhs a minority in their homeland. (At the 1959 census Kazakhs formed only 30% of the population, while immigrants of European stock amounted to over 60%; the proportions had changed slightly in favour of the Kazakhs by 1970 because of their higher birth-rate.) The majority of the indigenous Kazakhs were to be found in the semi-arid zone of Central Kazakhstan, where they were mostly engaged in nomadic rearing of livestock.

Agriculture, however, is less important to Kazakhstan's and the Soviet Union's economy than minerals, particularly coal (at Karaganda and Ekibastuz), copper (Jezkazgan), iron ore and bauxite (Central Kazakhstan) manganese, chromium, lead, zinc and silver (the Altai Mountains).[11]

The southern zone comprises Soviet Central Asia proper (the southern border areas of Kazakhstan and the four Central Asian Republics). This area is relatively mountainous and, unlike the two climatic belts to its north, comparatively well-watered by the two river systems of the Amu-Darya and Syr-Darya, which empty into the Aral Sea and provide the basis for a settled agriculture based on oases and irrigation, on which a stable civilisation of great antiquity exists. Because of the mountainous nature of the terrain between the river valleys, and the concentration of populations around the oases, the states which existed prior to Russian penetration of Central Asia in the nineteenth century were small. Much of their revenue was derived from taxing or robbing the caravans of traders passing between the Mediterranean and China, and they decayed as these routes were supplanted by sea routes. As the states were small and backward, they proved no obstacle to the extension of Russian influence south towards the borders of India.

A major impetus to Russian penetration of Central Asia was given by the American Civil War. The interruption of cotton supplies which resulted, led to a renewed Russian advance into

[10] Nove and Newth, *op. cit.,* p. 61.
[11] Nove and Newth, *op. cit.,* pp. 25-26.

cotton-growing areas. As the reasons for their presence were mainly economic and strategic, the Russians in most cases ruled indirectly through native emirs and did not disturb the existing society; and where they did establish settlements, these usually took the form of new suburbs alongside the existing cities but separate from them. The races were very varied, the Tajiks being closely akin to the Persians, and found in large numbers in both Persia and Afghanistan, Kazakhs of Turkic-Mongol stock (and forming a large minority in the Chinese province of Sinkiang), and the Uzbeks also spreading across the then virtually nonexistent borders into Afghanistan. The Turkmen and Kirghiz were also Turkic, and all were backward. A sense of nationalism was slow to develop in these circumstances, and the entire region was administered as the province of Turkestan, together with the nominally independent vassal Emirates of Khiva and Bukhara. Apart from the extension of cotton-growing in the irrigated areas, and Russian peasant settlement in the northern steppes, little change was apparent to the average Central Asian peasant until 1916. In that year, as a consequence of the Russian Army's appalling manpower losses in the campaigns against Germany, Austro-Hungary and Turkey, the Russian government proposed to conscript Central Asians, who had hitherto been exempt, for non-combatant service. The outcome was a revolt, which was suppressed, but not before it had given the Kazakhs and Kirgiz a national focus, even if a negative one. In addition, the religious and racial affinities of most of the area with the Turkish Sultan, the titular Caliph of Islam, who had proclaimed a Jehad (Holy War) against the Entente Powers, provided a focus for Islamic sentiment, even though the response to the Sultan's call was nowhere strong. When the Tsar abdicated in the spring of 1917, enough nationalist feeling had been generated for both modernisers and the more traditionally-minded to raise the question of autonomy. Despite Lenin's pre-revolutionary espousal of self-determination for the subject nationalities of the Empire, and toleration of the proclamation of a Turkestan Republic, there was in fact no national movement for independence in Turkestan—the traditionalist nationalists tended to support the Whites and the modernisers the Bolsheviks, but the majority in both groups saw Turkestan's future as lying in continued association with Russia. Furthermore, Lenin's views on self-determination in the Russian Empire had been in part tactically motivated; he put them forward in the belief that they would contribute to the Empire's disintegration, but hoped that nationalities which did secede would return to the fold voluntarily once the monarchy had been overthrown.[12] After the Bolshevik seizure of power he insisted throughout that Communist Parties in the Empire's non-Russian border areas were to be regarded as regional branches of the Russian Communist Party, subject to direction by its Central Committee, and in no sense autonomous or equal.[13] This meant that irrespective of nationalist sentiment or theoretical rights to self-determination, areas in which Bolshevik rule was established were forthwith subject to direction from Moscow, and as Bolshevik officials effectively ran the Turkestan Republic and later the People's Republics of Bokhara and Khiva, their independence would have been notional even if racial diversity had not precluded an all-embracing Turkestan nationalism.

Soviet nationalities policy was more responsible for creating national feeling among the Central Asians than any deeds of their own. The brutalities and acts of injustice of Bolshevik officials were the subject of a protest by the 'Congress of Peoples of the East' held at Baku in 1922, and the hardships resulting from the First World War, the 1916 revolt, the disorganisation caused by the Russian Civil War, and the misdeeds of local Bolshevik officials, caused discontent among the peasantry which lent ready support to the 'Basmachi', traditionalist bands who were anti-Russian in character and tended to engage in banditry. The Emirs of Bukhara and Khiva were expelled in 1920, but fighting against the Basmachi forces continued for several more years. However, Bolshevik control was strong enough by 1924 to allow the Turkestan Republic to be dissolved, and replaced by administrative units based on the various races. Two new Republics—the Turkmen and Uzbek were established in that year; Tajikistan became an autonomous unit within the Uzbek Republic; Kirgizia in 1926 receiving similar status, but inside the Russian Republic; while Tadzhikistan became a full Union Republic in 1929.[14]

Kazakhstan was not regarded as part of the Turkestan Republic, and had already become an autonomous unit within Russia in 1920. In December 1936, along with Kirgizia it became a full Union Republic. In shaping the boundaries of the new Republics and autonomous units, a definite attempt was made to form them on a basis of nationality.

In part, this was doubtlessly a 'divide and rule' policy dictated

---

[12] Schapiro, L., *The Communist Party of the Soviet Union*, Methuen, 1963, p. 149.

[13] Lenin, *Collected Works*, Vol. xvi, p. 512.

[14] Rakowska-Harmstone, T., *Russia and Nationalism in Central Asia*, John Hopkins Press, 1970, p. 31.

by the fear of Pan-Islamic or Panturanian sentiments arising in an undivided Turkestan. But the Party's commitment to self-determination (short of secession) for the non-Russians of the Empire was of long standing, and, in any event, the grant of Republic status to Tadzhikistan came three years after the crushing of the Basmachi and could therefore hardly have been motivated by fear of Islamic traditionalism. In the states other than Kazakhstan the majority nationality after whom the Republic was named formed from 41 to 65[15] per cent of the total population, though in every one there were large minorities both of other Central Asian nationalities and of immigrants of European stock. Only in Kazakhstan is the titular nationality outnumbered by the Europeans; elsewhere Europeans form between one-seventh and one-third of the total. In this important sense, therefore, Central Asian nationalism is a creation of the Soviets, both through dissemination of ideas on self-determination before the Revolution, and the formation of states on a basis of nationality after it. However, a number of checks and balances operate within the Soviet system to keep nationalism within bounds, notably the strongly centralised Communist Party organisation.

Each of the Republics has its own Communist Party, which is a component part of the Communist Party of the Soviet Union (CPSU) and hence bound by its decisions. Since the CPSU's supreme body, the Politburo, is effectively the government of the Soviet Union on all issues beyond day-to-day administration, and since the Councils of Ministers, both of the Union and the Republics, consists of Party members, CPSU control of the Republics is near absolute. The Union government is able also to control the Republics by its financial powers, both in determining Republic revenues (eg., by varying the amount of turnover tax it permits each Republic to retain), and in deciding what projects in each Republic shall be financed out of central government funds. In the final resort, it also has the secret police—the State Security Committee (KGB), which is a central government organ directly responsible to the Council of Ministers of the Union, and is, as far as can be judged, largely staffed by Russians.[16]

Education also helps to keep nationalism within bounds. On the one hand, Soviet authorities have promoted literature and other aspects of native culture in Central Asia: but on the other, the imposition in 1939 of a Cyrillic script (in place of the Arabic script employed before the Revolution and the latinised alphabets with

[15] 1959 census data.
[16] Rakowska-Harmstone, *op. cit.*, pp. 113, 118-123.

which it was replaced in the late 1920s) has helped to separate the Soviet Central Asian from his fellows beyond the Soviet borders. An Uzbek may speak a language closely allied to Turkish, but he could not read a Turkish newspaper, even if such were available to him. Furthermore, given the processes of linguistic borrowing, the fact that the Turk borrows his loanwords predominantly from the languages of Western Europe, while the Central Asian takes most of his from Russian, tends to drive the languages further apart. Russian is a compulsory second language in all Soviet Central Asian schools, and, not unnaturally, progress for the ambitious depends on ability to understand Russian. The armed forces are another powerful institution for reinforcing the Central Asians' identification with the Soviet Union as a whole, since although reserve divisions are constituted on a territorial basis, the peacetime army is not; there are no Uzbek, Kazakh, Turkmen, Kirgiz, etc., units as such, and conscripts of these nationalities will serve in predominantly European units, where all commands and instruction are given in Russian. The sense of 'belonging' in a multi-racial society is hence reinforced, and, of course, the opportunities for developing 'armed nationalism' in peacetime, or defecting in war, are minimised.

It is sometimes alleged that the non-Russian areas of the Soviet Union constitute the colonies of an empire. There are a number of ways in which to determine whether a country has colonial status, but they are not mutually agreed. One criterion is the presence of control over internal or external affairs, especially the latter. Nominally, all Republics have the right to conduct their own external dealings, and a few of them have their own foreign ministries. But these are shadowy organisations with no real substance,[17] and in the sense that ultimately their external, and many of their internal relations, are run from Moscow by a government of alien race in which they are only minority participants, the Transcaucasian and Central Asian Republics possess elements of colonial status. However, it is doubtful whether this could be said to have been forced on Central Asia as a whole. There was, and no doubt still is, considerable resentment of Russians as aliens, but local tensions (such as the mutual dislike of Uzbeks and Tadzhiks) are probably at least as strong, and there was never at any time an independence movement with wide popular support, such as existed in Transcaucasus or the Baltic States during the Russian

---

[17] The Ukraine and Belorussia are separately represented at the UN, but this reflects a wartime arrangement between the 'Big Three' rather than the independent conduct of external affairs.

Civil War. To that extent at least, Central Asia is not 'colonial'. In the social structure, with Russians occupying large numbers of skilled jobs in urban centres, and locals performing unskilled or rural work, they resemble colonies; but it is argued further that this is a consequence of their relative underdevelopment, not of colonial status.

The Leninist view[18] of colonies is that their function is primarily an economic one, namely to provide markets for the products of advanced capitalist countries, to serve as sources of raw materials and food, and to provide profits, some of which will be used to buy off the workers in the mother country, thus sapping their revolutionary zeal. To examine the cardinal features of the Transcaucasian and Central Asian economies is therefore to examine the Soviets' own attitude towards them; to attempt in fact to see whether the predominantly Russian government has treated them as colonies by its own definition.

The first criterion to be examined is that of industrial development. Industry, apart from the Baku oilfields, was virtually nonexistent in Transcaucasus and Turkestan in 1913, and a study of the growth of industrial production during the Soviet period should indicate whether any attempt has been made to industrialise the formerly backward areas. The following is the official Soviet assessment for 1969.

Table 1: Growth of Industrial Production 1913-1969[19]

|  | 1913 | 1950 | 1960 | 1969 |
|---|---|---|---|---|
| USSR | 1 | 13 | 40 | 84 |
| Georgia | 1 | 16 | 40 | 78 |
| Armenia | 1 | 22 | 68 | 162 |
| Azerbaijan | 1 | 8.3 | 17 | 30 |
| Kazakhstan | 1 | 18 | 57 | 132 |
| Uzbekistan | 1 | 8.7 | 20 | 37 |
| Kirghizia | 1 | 21 | 61 | 164 |
| Tajikistan | 1 | 13 | 38 | 79 |
| Turkmenia | 1 | 4.3 | 15 | 40 |

On this basis Armenia, Kirghizia and Kazakhstan compare well with the Soviet average, and Georgia and Tajikistan not badly, while industrialisation in Azerbaijan, Uzbekistan and Turkmenia has lagged considerably behind. Industrialisation is not merely an

18 Lenin, *Imperialism, the Highest Stage of Capitalism*, 1916.
19 *N.E.*, 1969, p. 148.

act of social policy; for it may make little *economic* sense to establish industry in a border area, remote from central markets, perhaps vulnerable to invasion, possibly poorly endowed with raw materials, or with a labour force which is difficult to train because of backwardness, language difficulties, or the lack of an industrial tradition. Soviet data on industrial productivity indicate that labour problems have been more acute in Transcaucasus and Central Asia than elsewhere, and that one of the reasons for low industrial growth in the non-Russian republics of Soviet Asia is the mundane one of low productivity, which would be one of the factors in a decision, based on purely economic grounds, as to where new plants should be sited.

Table 2: Growth of Industrial Productivity (1940 = 100)[20]

|  | *1960* | *1969* |
|---|---|---|
| USSR | 296 | 460 |
| RSFSR | 318 | 500 |
| Georgia | 197 | 289 |
| Armenia | 273 | 375 |
| Azerbaijan | 214 | 284 |
| Kazakhstan | 256 | 375 |
| Uzbekistan | 231 | 291 |
| Kirghizia | 222 | 341 |
| Tajikistan | 193 | 241 |
| Turkmenia | 222 | 308 |

That economic considerations count may also be seen from Soviet 1969 figures for production costs (in roubles per ton) of various agricultural products.[21] These were:

Table 3

|  | *Grain* | *Cotton* | *Cattle* | *Wool* |
|---|---|---|---|---|
| **RSFR** | 60 | — | 1260 | 4078 |
| Ukraine | 35 | — | 1130 | 3432 |
| Baltic | 85 | — | 1130 | 7154 |
| Caucasus | 99 | 433 | 1884 | 5575 |
| Central Asia | 97 | 404 | 1496 | 2879 |
| Kazakhstan | 61 | 344 | 1359 | 4108 |

[20] *Ibid.* pp. 171-2.
[21] *Ibid.* pp. 414-5, by derivation.

From these figures it emerges that Central Asia and the Caucasus are uneconomic producers of wheat, that the Caucasus is also a very uneconomic producer of cattle and wool, and that of the three cotton-producers, it is the most expensive. It is hardly surprising that this should be so, in view of the hilly terrain; the Caucasus therefore concentrates on tea and grapes, while Central Asia is the main cotton-growing area (extension of cotton-growing in Kazakhstan is limited until more irrigation has been provided), that both Central Asia and Kazakhstan concentrate on wool and Kazakhstan in addition specialises in cattle.

The following table indicates the contributions made in total by Transcaucasia, Central Asia and Kazakhstan to various Soviet fields of economic activity in 1967.[22]

Table 4

| Commodity | Production | % of Soviet total |
|---|---|---|
| Oil | 41,200,000 tons | 13 |
| Natural Gas | 35.1 million m³ | 20 |
| Steel | 4,000,000 tons | 4 |
| Fertilisers | 5,600,000 tons | 14 |
| Cement | 13,200,000 tons | 15.1/2 |
| Cotton Textiles | 686 million metres | 9 |
| Cotton Fibre | 2,033,000 tons | 100 |
| Raw Cotton | 5,970,000 tons | 100 |
| Meat | 640,500 tons | 10 |
| Tea | 230,800 tons | 98 |
| Wool | 188,700 tons | 46 |

From the table (which is far from a complete list of products of the area), it will be noted that raw materials and agricultural products play a more significant role than industrial goods—in particular, though the area produces all the Soviet Union's cotton fibre, 91% of it is sent elsewhere for textile manufacture. It seems therefore that in this respect, despite the high degree of industrial progress in most of the republics, non-Russian Soviet Asia still to some extent meets the Marxist definition of colonial status.

However, there are yet other comparisons which must be made, especially in the field of social services, employment, and incomes.

The frontiers in Central Asia do not seal off the various nationalities: Tadzhiks have links with Persia; Turkmens, Uzbeks, Kirgiz, Kazakhs and Azerbaijanis speak languages very closely allied to Turkish; all have ties to the Moslem countries of Turkey,

[22] *N.E.*, 1967, by extraction and combination from tables in sections 'Industry', 'Agriculture' & 'Fuel'.

Iran and Afghanistan, and therefore comparisons with those
countries also have some point; and since the Sino-Soviet dispute
erupted, comparisons between the Kazakhs of the Soviet Union and
of Chinese Sinkiang would be relevant, were Chinese data available
(many thousands of Sinkiang Kazakhs fled into the Soviet Union
in the early 1960s, perhaps an eloquent comment on their view of
the position).[23]

The statistics of the neighbouring states are of varying reliability,
but those on the Soviet side are detailed, comprehensive and
generally regarded as reliable by those who have to use them, provided allowance is made for differences in definition between Soviet
and Western practices. In 1967 there were in Iran one hospital bed
per 960 population, and one doctor per 3820. In Turkey the position was slightly better, with one bed for 560 population and one
doctor for 2760, but Afghanistan was considerably worse off, with
5,810 population for each hospital bed and 21,360 to one doctor.[24]
In 1959 the average for the five Soviet Central Asian Republics was
one doctor for every 742 persons. By 1967 the Soviet average had
improved to one doctor for every 430, and of hospital beds to one
per hundred.[25] Soviet Central Asia lagged slightly behind the
national average in 1959,[26] and may have continued to do so, but
clearly the diffusion of Soviet health services was on an entirely
different plane from that of the southern neighbours, and this was
reflected in death rates per thousand population of 12.9 in Turkey
(towns only; rural mortality was probably much higher, since the
villages are less well supplied with medical facilities than the
towns),[27] compared with rates between 5.7 and 6.3 in Soviet
Central Asia[28] (birth rates in Turkey, Iran and Soviet Central Asia
were all in the range 30-40 per thousand, and women of child-
bearing age formed between 20.37 and 22.2% of the total populations, indicating that the difference in death rates is unlikely to be
due to significant differences in the population structure).[29]

In tertiary education also the comparison favours the Soviet
Central Asian. In 1967 approximately 1 Afghan in 3,200, 1 Turk
in 224, and 1 Iranian in 383 was a full-time university student[30]

23 Nove and Newth, *op. cit.*, p. 132.
24 *UN Yearbook of Statistics,* 1969, Table 198, pp. 675.
25 *Ibid.* p. 676.
26 Nove and Newth, *op. cit.*, pp. 108-9.
27 *Ibid.* p. 109.
28 *Ibid.* p. 106, and Soviet 1959 census data.
29 *N.E.* 1969 pp. 34-35. By 1969 the Soviet Central Asian birth rates had
   dropped to between 32.7 per 1000 (Uzbekistan) and 34.7 per 1000
   (Tadzhikstan), not sufficiently to affect the argument.
30 *UN Yearbook of Statistics,* 1969, Tables 16, pp. 57-71 and 201.

(the figure for Australia was 1 in 61)[31] while the average for the five Central Asian Republics (1962) was 1 in 127.[32] This was slightly worse than the USSR national average for that year (1 in 125)[33] but the three Transcaucasian Republics bettered it (1 in 108), and even the worst Soviet case (Tadzhikistan), 1 in 173,[34] was considerably better than in the neighbouring states.

Since much of the Soviet effort in Central Asia can be looked upon as modernisation of a traditional Islamic society of a kind similar to that essayed by Ataturk in Turkey and Nasser in Egypt, a possible additional comparison relates to the status of women.

Moslem institutions such as polygamy, child betrothal, bride-price and purdah have long been abolished by Soviet law, though there have been indications that some of them survive in remote rural areas. However, a fairly reliable indicator of the status of women in any society is their access to higher education compared with that of their male coevals. The following table compares the ratio of males to females undergoing tertiary education in the USSR as a whole, the Ukraine, the Central Asian Republics, the adjacent Moslem countries, Egypt (as a Moslem society with a 'modernising' and socialistic philosophy), and some advanced non-Communist countries, during the 1960s.[35]

Table 5

| (1) | (2) | (3) | (4) | (5) |
| --- | --- | --- | --- | --- |
| | | | | Ratio, males to |
| Country | Year | Males | Females | females |
| USSR | 1968 | 2,369,600 | 2,100,100 | 1.1 to 1 |
| Ukraine | 1968 | 432,322 | 358,860 | 1.2 to 1 |
| Turkey | 1967 | 101,032 | 24,515 | 4.1 to 1 |
| Iran | 1967 | 44,769 | 13,975 | 3.2 to 1 |
| Afghanistan | 1967 | 3,573 | 747 | 4.8 to 1 |
| Egypt | 1966 | 140,071 | 39,029 | 3.6 to 1 |
| Central Asia | 1959 | 160,200 | 68,700 | 2.3 to 1 |
| USA | 1967 | 4,132,800 | 2,778,948 | 1.5 to 1 |
| England & Wales | 1966 | 195,737 | 114,969 | 1.7 to 1 |
| Australia | 1967 | 108,000 | 45,000 | 2.4 to 1 |
| New Zealand | 1966 | 18,819 | 10,734 | 1.8 to 1 |

[31] *Ibid.* p. 716.
[32] Data from *Statistical Yearbooks* of the individual Central Asian Republics, 1962, 'Education' tables.
[33] *UN Yearbook of Statistics*, 1965, Tables 16 and 201.
[34] *N.E.* 1962, 'The Soviet Middle East', p. 110.
[35] Figures derived from *UN Yearbook of Statistics*, 1969, table 201, and Soviet 1959 census data.

From column (5) it can be seen that in Central Asia the proportion of women among students in tertiary education was considerably lower than in the USSR as a whole, or in the Ukraine, USA, or UK, but was considerably higher than any of the Moslem countries in the table, and not greatly different from that of Australia. In terms of their access to higher education, and hence of the professions to which it gives entry, women in Central Asia enjoy a status which is intermediate between their Moslem neighbours and the European USSR, but much nearer to the Soviet standard than to that of their neighbours.

Although nurturing of national culture has been accompanied by a repression of the religious element which formerly provided the region with its strongest unifying force, there are some signs that Islam retains a hold, especially in rural areas, and that Communism is accepted with more reservations than in the European-settled parts of the Soviet Union. One such indicator is Communist Party membership, which in all the Central Asian Republics is significantly lower as a proportion of the population than in the USSR as a whole, as the following table shows. The figures relate to the year 1968.[36]

Table 6

| Area | Population (millions) | Party membership (thousands) | Proportion in Party |
|---|---|---|---|
| Whole of USSR | 238.9 | 13,180 | 1 person in 18 |
| Kazakh | 12.9 | 486 | 1 person in 26 |
| Kirghiz SSR | 2.9 | 91 | 1 person in 32 |
| Turkmen SSR | 2.1 | 61 | 1 person in 33 |
| Uzbek SSR | 11.7 | 336 | 1 person in 33 |
| Takzhik SSR | 2.8 | 72 | 1 person in 38 |

Too much should not be made of the discrepancy. Although admission to the Party is easier than it was in Stalin's time, and it has more than doubled in size since 1952, joining is more like seeking admission to a club than joining a political party in a Western country. It is subject to a probationary stage of candidate membership and to checking of credentials, and because of the worker-oriented philosophy of Communism, membership is proportionally higher in industrial areas than rural ones.[37] Party member-

---

[36] *The Far East and Australasia 1969,* Europa Publications, 1969, pp. 887–891.

[37] For a breakdown of the membership of the CPSU by nationalities, see Avtorkhanov, A., *The Communist Party Apparatus,* Regnery, Chicago, 1966, p. 171.

ship also tends to be higher among white-collar workers than manual workers. Since the Central Asian Republics are 'under-developed' compared with the European USSR, Georgia and Armenia, with proportionally fewer industrial or white-collar posts, it is only to be expected that they would contain a lower proportion of persons (a) deemed by the Party sufficiently 'class-conscious' (in the Marxist sense) and therefore sought as recruits, or (b) sufficiently 'class-conscious' (in a status-seeking sense) to wish to advance their careers by joining. The importance of these factors in determining the level of Party membership cannot be quantified with sufficient precision to determine their relative importance, compared with putative policies of racial discrimination on the one hand or reluctance to join an 'alien' (Russian-sponsored) party on the other. But evidence from other non-Russian areas of the USSR (eg., Georgia and Armenia) on the proportion of higher Party posts held by 'natives' suggests that there is a correlation between socio-political 'advancement' (expressed by the proportion of the population in non-agricultural employment or undergoing higher education) and Russian control, in that the proportion of Russians in the higher Party and state apparatus declines as a Republic becomes more 'advanced', that is, that the criteria are social and economic rather than racial.[38] Furthermore within the Central Asian Republics themselves, those with the higher percentages of Europeans among their populations also have the higher propor-tions of Party membership, as shown in the table.[39]

Table 7

| (1)<br>Republic | (2)<br>% Europeans | (3)<br>% Party members | (4)<br>% Industrial Workers (1959) |
|---|---|---|---|
| Whole of USSR | — | 5.55 | 38.2 |
| Kazakh SSR | 50.9 | 3.85 | 35.1 |
| Kirghiz SSR | 36.8 | 3.21 | 25.6 |
| Turkmen SSR | 17.3 | 3.01 | 27.1 |
| Uzbek SSR | 13.5 | 2.92 | 21.5 |
| Tadzhik SSR | 13.3 | 2.63 | 19.2 |

[38] The process of localisation is not necessarily continuous. From 1945 to 1953, the proportion of Russians in the Tadzhik Communist Party increased from 23 to 30%, and in the Party Secretariat from 50 to 67%. Localisation then resumed, and the proportion of Russians in both bodies began to fall. See Rakowska-Harmstone, *op. cit.*, pp. 99-122.

[39] Derived from data in *The Far East and Australasia 1969*, pp. 887-891, Nove and Newth, *op. cit.*, pp. 30-31, and 1959 census.

The fourth column, based on the 1959 census, illustrates the tendency for low percentage levels of industrial employment and of Party membership to go together. In all cases, the percentage of Europeans, of industrial workers, and of Party members is below the national average; in every case except Turkmenia and Uzbekistan the Republics come out in the same rank order under all three headings and all come out in the same order under two of the headings. The inference is that as in the case of Russianisation at the top of local parties, the criteria are those of socio-economic advancement rather than race. It could, of course, be argued that the low industrialisation and low party membership result from policy decisions taken in Moscow to 'keep the natives down', but in view of the Soviet investment in industrialising Central Asia, in raising educational standards, and ensuring availability of social services on as wide a scale as possible, the argument would seem hard to justify.

That having been said, however, the figures do raise some questions, in that while they correlate in rank order, they do not do so perfectly, and in particular indicate that the proportion of Central Asians in the Party is disproportionately low. In 1959, 38.2% of the Soviet work force as a whole was engaged in industry, and one Soviet citizen in 18 was a Party member. With 35.1% of its labour force industrial, Kazakhstan was not far below the national average, yet its Party membership, at one person in 26, was substantially lower (3.85% versus 5.55) and in all the other Republics the Party membership is lower than might be expected if the degree of industrialisation was the sole criterion. The most recent official membership figures for the Central Asian Communist Parties do not divide them by nationalities within parties, but if it is assumed that Russians or Ukrainians living in Central Asia are as likely to seek Party membership as they would if living in Russia or the Ukraine (and the tendency for Party membership to be higher in the Republics with large European populations would indicate that such is the case), then Central Asian nationalities are even less abundant in the Party ranks than the tables indicate. If one European in 18 among the population of Central Asia belongs to his Republic's Communist Party, the 1,046,000 Central Asian Communists include among their number only some 504,000 members of the 'local' nationalities, Europeans being in the majority in the Kazakh and Kirgiz Parties, (about three quarters and two-thirds respectively), slightly more than a third of the Turkmen party, and just over a quarter in those of the Tadzhik and Uzbek republics.[40] To the extent that the Central Asians think along nationalist lines (and bearing in mind that their nationalism is of recent origin and largely Soviet-created), they would seem to regard Communist Party membership as something more appropriate to Europeans. While this attitude may not reflect a feeling that the Party in non-Russian areas follows any definite policy of excluding indigenes (Armenians, for example, not only form the overwhelming majority of the Armenian Communist Party, but are prominent in those of other Republics), the fact remains that the ruling party in the Central Asian Republics contains large numbers of Russians, Ukrainians or Belorussians who are likely on issues involving nationality to identify themselves with Moscow rather than Tashkent or Alma Ata, and that this is apparent at least to the politically active or ambitious Central Asian.

There has been no policy of 'Russification' as such; although the Central Asians are continually reminded of Russian cultural superiority by the daily facts of life, and are constantly pressed to regard the Russians as their 'Big Brothers' (and cultural superiors), much has been done to foster the native cultures, not least by education, which has raised the level of literacy from less than 2% at the turn of the century to virtually 100% now. The one outstanding exception to this general rule has been in the case of religion.

Prior to 1917, Soviet Central Asia was overwhelmingly Moslem. As part of the general Communist policy towards religion, and with the aid of indigenous 'modernising' elements, who regarded Islam as a positive obstacle to progress (as did Kemal Ataturk in Turkey), the Soviet government embarked in the late 1920s on a thoroughgoing attack on Islam. Large numbers of mosques were closed, religious leaders deported or imprisoned, and a number of customs made illegal (among them the 'Haj', pilgrimage to Mecca; the 'Waqf', or pious donation of a tithe on income; and marriage customs such as polygamy). Resistance from the Basmachi bands was at least in part motivated by the anti-religious campaigns of the Soviet government, but the attack on Islam did not arouse nation-wide opposition in Central Asia or among the Moslems of Transcaucasia, and today the influence of Islam, while difficult to gauge, does not appear great. Certainly, the Moslem populations of areas occupied by the Germans in the Second World War, notably the Tatars of the Crimea, collaborated with the Germans

40 In respect of the Tadzhik party the assumption is confirmed by official figures cited in Rakowska-Harmstone, *op. cit.*, pp. 100-101, which showed Russians to constitute between 25 and 30% of membership in all years 1947-62.

to a much greater extent than Christians in the same areas, and the Germans were able to recruit a number of units to fight against the Red Army from Soviet Central Asian Muslim prisoners of war. But even this is not conclusive proof of a causal connection between Islam and anti-Communism. Defection and collaboration were also higher among non-Russian Europeans than among Russians, and were met in the same way—by mass deportations—while anti-Stalinism and the high mortality rate in German prison camps[41] led large numbers of European Soviet citizens also to volunteer for German units, and most Red Army soldiers of Central Asian or Transcaucasian origin proved reliable in combat. There are undoubtedly racial and regional stresses in the Soviet Union, as in any other multiracial society, and Soviet reluctance to admit their continued existence is ideologically motivated by the desire to present that society as superior to any other. But their lack of frankness should not be taken as evidence that they have more to hide about their treatment of non-Europeans than about past Soviet Government behaviour towards Russians, Ukrainians or Balts.

In summary, it could be said that through association with Russia the nationalities of Soviet Central Asia had achieved living standards, insofar as these may be expressed by wages, health and educational opportunity, somewhat lower than those of the European USSR, but a great deal higher than those of their independent neighbours. In those respects, at least, they had gained from their association within the larger society and markets of Soviet Union, and their economic success was an important factor in enhancing the image of Communism in adjacent countries. In Turkey and Iran at least, that success is not sufficient to overcome the traditional distrust of Russia (shared by governments and the majority nationalities in those countries) as a predatory power which annexed or laid claim to territories formerly under their sway; but it could be sufficient to influence minorities (such as the Turkmens, Tadzhiks and Azerbaijanis of Iran) in pro-Soviet directions, especially in the event of central government action against them. Whether the Soviet Central Asians regard the undoubted economic advantages of living under Soviet rule as adequate recompense for disruption of a traditional way of life, for the acceptance of large numbers of European immigrants, and for the restrictions imposed

---

[41] 3,461,338 prisoners had been taken by the Germans by March 1942, and the total for the whole war was in the vicinity of five million. Of these, 1,981,000 died in prisoner of war camps and 'Exterminations', not accounted for; deaths and disappearances in transit totalled another 1,308,000. *Kriegstagebuch des Oberkommandos der Wehrmacht*, vol. I p. 489, and Clark, A., *Barbarossa*, Hutchinson, 1965 p. 183.

on freedom of political choice by Communism, or by membership of a European-dominated federation, is less easy to assess. There have, however, been few signs of widespread dissatisfaction, though the high turnover at the top levels of some of the Central Asian Parties and Governments, and the uneven results in fulfilment of economic plans, indicate the existence of problems not always illuminated in official pronouncements. However the fostering of a sense of nationhood, and the long-sustained effort to raise levels of industrialisation, personal income, educational standards and availability of social services towards those prevailing in the European USSR go considerably beyond those made by the other colonial powers in their former major possessions, and suggest strongly that the Soviet leaders have consistently striven to avoid treating the Transcaucasian and Central Asian nationalities in ways which could be defined by a Marxist as 'colonial'.

For propaganda to Asia, the Soviet Central Asian states offer a number of undoubted showpieces; they may not appeal to the traditionalist Islamic leader, but these are declining in numbers, in favour of modernisers who themselves regard some of the traditional practices of Islam as a bar to modernisation. Such leaders may well wince at the sight of a desecrated mosque, but are no more likely to allow it to determine their foreign policy than is the leader of a Christian country on seeing a desecrated church. In any event, both can be placated to some extent (and often are) by being taken to a church or mosque that is still 'operating', as the Russians put it. The atheistic nature of the Soviet state, and its persecution of religion should not therefore be expected to nullify the appeal of its Moslem parts to Moslem leaders. While the economic advancement of Central Asia and Transcaucasia is an obvious success for the Soviet regime, it has in large part resulted from inputs of capital and expertise from the European USSR and the real problem of transferring the Soviet example to an Asian state which the Soviets wish to urge on to the 'non-capitalist road', is likely to be more one of finding the necessary capital than of overcoming revulsion at repression of religious feeling, or the imposition of a one-party system.

SIBERIA

With the transition from Central Asia to the adjacent sector of Soviet Asia—Siberia—the ethnic picture changes almost completely, and so does the historical background. Here the majority of the population is of European stock, Russian settlement began earlier than in Central Asia and the chief problems were not those of conquering and holding down recalcitrant native populations, but of overcoming vast distances and severities of climate. Russians reached the East Coast in 1638, established control over Kamchatka by the end of the century and crossed the Bering Strait to Alaska, which remained Russian until sold to the United States in 1867.

Collision with Chinese power in the Amur Valley caused Russian activity to be directed further north and east, so that part of Kazakhstan and much of Southern Siberia passed under Russian control only in the nineteenth century, their sovereignty over the Maritime Province being recognised by the Peking Treaty of 1860. As the rivers run mostly south to north, and both terrain and climate are difficult, lack of communications inhibited Siberia's development. This situation was radically altered at the beginning of the twentieth century, with completion of the Trans-Siberian Railway in 1905, linking European Russia with the Pacific Coast and providing a means for access to its raw materials.

Siberia resembles Australia in a number of ways though climate is not one of them. Convict settlement was important in the development of it, though use of convict labour remained significant in Siberia until much later than in Australia. No precise data have been made public, but the prison and concentration camp population of the USSR was at its peak during the late 1930s and 40s, and has been estimated at ten million,[42] most of them in Siberia and the Far East. As the free population of Siberia and the Far East in 1939 was 17.3 million,[43] the proportion of prisoners to free citizens must have been over one to two. Convict labour (consisting mostly of 'purged' members of the Party, intelligentsia, armed forces and the political parties abolished by the Bolsheviks, deportees from Eastern Poland and the Baltic States, and prisoners of war) was employed mostly in forestry and mining, under a regimen so harsh that life expectation in the camps was of the order of three years. The main concentration was in the Kolyma Valley Goldfields in the far North-East, run by an MVD organisation with the innocuous name of Dalstroy (an abbreviation for 'Far Eastern Construction'). Former prisoners have estimated that the normal convict population of the Kolyma Valley was about half a million, with an annual mortality rate of 30%.[44] After the death of Stalin, a series of amnesties resulted in the release of most of the prisoners. The camps still exist, but their population is a very small fraction

[42] Conquest, R., *The Great Terror,* Macmillan, 1968 pp. 530-535.
[43] By totalling, from *N.E.,* 1969, p. 12.
[44] Lipper, E., *Eleven Years in Soviet Prison Camps,* Landon, 1951, p. 108.

of what it once was, and their contribution to Siberia's economy very much reduced.

Siberia also resembles Australia in the possession of large natural resources, especially timber and minerals. Like Australia, it is not abundantly endowed with the two most important minerals—soil and water—and most of its territory is virtually unusable for agriculture, being covered by snow for most of the year, and having a permanently frozen subsoil, which, as the melted snow cannot percolate downwards, turns the surface of the ground into swamp during the short summer. Low population density and proximity to the dreaded 'teeming masses' of Asia are other features which it shares with Australia.[45]

Outside the Soviet Union it is common to refer to all Russia east of the Urals as 'Siberia', but in Soviet usage the area is divided into three—West Siberia, East Siberia, and the Far East, all entirely east of the Urals—and parts of a fourth—the Urals region—which straddles the mountain chain. In this study the Urals region is not treated as belonging to Soviet Asia.

West Siberia consists of the Altay region, and the provinces (oblasts) of Omsk, Novosibirsk, Tomsk, Tyumen and Kemerovo. Its area (about 950,000 square miles) is about one-third that of Australia, or 10.8% of the Soviet Union, and its population (12,110,000 in 1969) was just over 5% of the Soviet total. Over 90% of the population is of European stock, and none of the native Siberian national groups numbered more than 250,000.[46] The largest city, Novosibirsk, had a population of 1,161,000 in 1969, while populations of the other centres ranged from 821,000 (Omsk) to 339,000 (Tomsk).[47] It is the most heavily industrialised part of Russia East of Urals, as well as the most developed agriculturally. The growth of its importance in the Soviet economy can be briefly illustrated by the volume of goods dispatched by its transport system during 1966.[48] At 220.25 million tons it ranked fifth among the nineteen economic regions into which the USSR was then divided, and in excess of outgoing goods over incoming (37.48 million tons), a measure of its importance as a supplier to other parts of the country, it was outranked only by the Volga and Donets-Dniepr regions. As an importer from other regions it ranked sixth. Capital investment in the zone in 1967 (3575 million roubles) was seventh highest, and not much less than in Central

---

[45] For Soviet expressions of fear of Asian pressure, see eg. Harrison Salisbury, *The Coming War Between Russia and China*, pp. 30-38, 208.

[46] Soviet 1970 census.

[47] *N.E.*, 1969, pp. 23-28, incorporating 1970 census figures.

[48] *N.E.* 1967, table 'Transport balance of all goods, by economic regions'.

Asian economic region (3859 million) or Kazakhstan (3879 million).[49] These indicators give sufficient idea of its relative importance to the Soviet economy, which will not be laboured further.

East Siberia consists of Krasnoyarsk region, Irkutsk and Chita provinces, and the mainly Mongolian-inhabited Buryat and Tuva autonomous republics. Its area (1,610,000 square miles) is slightly more than half that of Australia, but its population (7,464,000 in 1970) is considerably less than Australia's or Western Siberia's. The largest towns are Krasnoyarsk (648,000) Irkutsk (451,000), Chita (242,000) and Angarsk (204,000).[50] It is industrially much less diversified than West Siberia, but is a large-scale producer of timber and minerals. Its economic ranking can be gauged from the level of capital investment in 1967; at (2,376 million roubles) it was tenth among the nineteen economic regions.[51] Level of economic activity, as indicated by the loads carried on its transport system was as follows:[52]

Table 8

|  | Volume (million tons) | Ranking among 19 economic regions |
|---|---|---|
| Loaded | 126.87 | 9 |
| Unloaded | 100.30 | 10 |
| Movement within region | 81.89 | 7 |
| Exports to other regions | 44.98 | 9 |
| Imports from other regions | 18.41 | 18 |
| Excess of exports over imports | 26.57 | 4 |

THE SOVIET FAR EAST

This region lies to the east of Eastern Siberia, and comprises two 'Regions' (Khabarovsk and Maritime), four 'Provinces' (Amur, Kamchatka and Magadan on the mainland, plus the island of Sakhalin and others administered from it), and the Yakutian Autonomous Republic. In area it constitutes 14% of the land surface of the USSR, but it contains only 2% of its population. From Vladivostock in the south to Uelen in the north is 2,673

49 *N.E.* 1967, table 'Capital Investment of State and Cooperative enterprises and organisations, collective farms and the population, by economic regions'.
50 *N.E.* 1969, pp. 23-28.
51 As for (49) above.
52 As for (48) above.

miles, and from Vladivostock to the nearest developed industrial area within the Soviet Union (the Irkutsk-Cheremkhovo region of Eastern Siberia) is more than 2,500 miles. By comparison with the areas to the west of it, it is thinly populated and poorly developed, partly because of its remoteness. However, its population has grown rapidly from 370,000 in 1897 to 5,780,000 in 1970—though even so the population density is less than four persons per square mile.

The Far East is very mountainous (only one fifth of the land area is level); over 50% of it is in the permafrost zone; on Kamchatka, Sakhalin and the Kurile Islands are a number of active volcanoes; and earthquakes are frequent in this area. The low temperatures of winter (in the warmest part of the mainland the average day temperature of the coldest month is —12.1°C, or 10°F, in the coldest part —47.1°C, or —53°F) and the short growing season render agriculture difficult; only 1% of the total agricultural land of the Soviet Union lies in the Far East, most of it along the Amur and Ussuri Rivers in the south. Although there are extensive mineral deposits, distance and difficulty of extraction have lent their utilisation low priority compared with those further west, and the area's main contribution to the Soviet economy is in timber (16% of the Soviet total) and fishing industries (34% of the Soviet fish catch is made by trawlers based in the Far East).[53] Despite this, the area is not economically self-supporting; in 1967 it imported (by tonnage) about 2½ times as much from other areas of the Soviet Union as it exported to them.[54]

Almost all its trade with the rest of the Soviet Union is carried by rail, practically none by sea,[55] and very little of its traffic is with the European USSR—the bulk of it is with Siberia and some with Central Asia.[56] It would be wrong, therefore, to attribute undue importance to it either as an area for settlement of land-hungry Chinese (it offers little attraction for settlement, and China is, in any event, not suffering from overpopulation), or to link Soviet naval policy in the Indo-Pacific region to a need to maintain sea communication between its European and Asian parts. But to caution against exaggerating its importance either to China or to the Soviet Union is not to dismiss its political or strategic signifi-

---

53 *Dal'niy Vostok* (The Far East), USSR Academy of Sciences, Moscow, 1966 pp. 9, 21, 40.

54 *N.E.*, 1967, table 'Transport balance of all goods by economic regions'.

55 *Ibid*. Total volume of seaborne traffic to and from other regions of USSR in 1967 was 200,000 tons, versus 24.4 million tons by rail.

56 In 1963, only 18% of the Far East's imports from the rest of the Soviet Union came from the European USSR, and 22% of exports were to it. *Dal'niy Vostok*, Table 13 p. 225.

cance in the eyes of both. Politically it is a potential source of conflict, since most of it was 'ceded' to Russia by 'unequal treaty' in the nineteenth century, and strategically it is a back door to Russia, through which both American and Japanese troops penetrated to Siberia during the Russian Civil War in 1918 and after. It is, furthermore, possession of a coastline which makes the Soviet Union a Pacific Power, and with the growth of Russo-Japanese trade, for which the raw materials of Siberia offer great potential (Japan already rivals the UK as the Soviet Union's most important non-Communist trading partner) the importance of Far Eastern trade will increase. The most significant elements of this trade at present are timber, coal and fish, but the discovery of large oil, natural gas and coal reserves in Yakutia raises possibilities of further expansion.

The following table does not attempt to give a detailed picture of the contribution made by the Asian USSR (Central Asia, Siberia and the Far East) to the Soviet Economy, though it does give some idea of its range. It has been compiled mainly to show the growth in its percentage contribution to Soviet production in most categories of goods, and to give some idea of the absolute levels of production in 1967.

Table 9: Percentage contribution of Asian USSR to Soviet output, 1940 and 1967[57]

| Product | 1940 (%) | 1967 (%) | Actual output 1967 |
|---|---|---|---|
| Electric power production | 9.2 | 24.9 | 146,400 million kw-hrs |
| Oil | 6.3 | 9.8 | 28.1 million tons |
| Natural gas | 0.5 | 22.5 | 35,400 million cubic metres |
| Coal | 28.7 | 41.1 | 244.7 million tons |
| Iron | 10.3 | 9.9 | 7.4 million tons |
| Steel | 10.6 | 8.3 | 8.5 million tons |
| Tractors | 0 | 11.6 | 47,100 tractors |
| Combine harvesters | 0 | 18.4 | 18,600 |
| Iron Ore | 1.7 | 16.8 | 28.3 million tons |
| Mineral fertilisers | 6.9 | 16.2 | 6.5 million tons |
| Artificial fibres | 0 | 16.2 | 82,500 tons |
| Timber | 23.4 | 32.3 | 92.6 million cubic metres |
| Cellulose | 0 | 15.2 | 612,000 tons |
| Cotton textiles | 3.8 | 9.3 | 690 million metres |
| Meat | 23.0 | 20.5 | 1,327,000 tons |
| Vegetable oils | 29.4 | 20.0 | 212,000 tons |

[57] N.E. 1967, derived from table 'Development of industry of the eastern regions of the USSR'.

The large increases in percentage of USSR production of electricity, natural gas, iron ore fertilisers and agricultural machinery are obvious, but even where the increases have been less spectacular, as in the case of coal, the large absolute production figure should be borne in mind. The combined output of the Kazakhstan and Siberian coalfields in 1967 exceeded that of any other country except the United States.[58] Where production has gone down as a percentage, as in the case of iron, steel, meat and vegetable oils, this reflects larger increases in other parts of the USSR, not absolute reductions in Soviet Asia—for the absolute increases in these products have been large:[59]

Table 10

|  | 1940 | 1967 |
|---|---|---|
| Iron (million tons) | 1.5 | 7.4 |
| Steel (million tons) | 1.9 | 8.5 |
| Meat (thousand tons) | 345 | 1327 |
| Vegetable oils (thousand tons) | 67 | 212 |

THE FUTURE OF SOVIET ASIA

The preliminary results of the 1970 census have shown that the high rate of population increase characteristic of Central Asia and Transcaucasia from 1917 has been maintained. Whereas in 1959

Table 11: Comparative increases, Central Asians, Transcaucasians, Ukrainians and Russians[60]

|  | 1959 (thousands) | 1970 | % increase 1959-70 | % of population 1970 |
|---|---|---|---|---|
| USSR total | 208827 | 241720 | 15.8 | 100 |
| Russians | 114164 | 129015 | 13.1 | 53.4 |
| Ukrainians | 37253 | 40753 | 9.4 | 16.9 |
| Uzbeks | 6015 | 9195 | 52.9 | 3.80 |
| Kazakhs | 3622 | 5299 | 46.3 | 2.19 |
| Tajiks | 1397 | 2136 | 52.9 | 0.88 |
| Turkmens | 1002 | 1525 | 52.2 | 0.63 |
| Kirghiz | 969 | 1452 | 49.5 | 0.60 |
| Azerbaijanis | 2940 | 4380 | 49.0 | 1.81 |
| Armenians | 2787 | 3559 | 27.7 | 1.47 |
| Georgians | 2692 | 3245 | 20.5 | 1.34 |

[58] *Ibid.* and *UN Yearbook of Statistics* 1969, Table 51 pp. 164-5.
[59] As for (57) above.
[60] Memorandum on 1970 preliminary census data, V. D. Ogareff, ANU.

the eight republics in question, with a total population of 33 million, contained 15% of Soviet citizens, by the end of the decade, with a 45 million total, 18.6% of the Soviet population was to be found within their borders.

Examination of 1970 census figures of population divided according to first language rather than place of residence confirmed that since 1959 the Transcaucasus and Central Asian nationalities had increased by far more than the two major European Soviet nationalities, as indicated in the table.

These nationalities had increased from 10.5% of the Soviet population in 1959 to 12.97% in 1970.

But there are so many more Europeans to begin with that even a much higher non-European growth rate can significantly affect the balance only if continued for a very long time—as an example, the number of Russians increased by 14.9 million, that of all Central Asians and Transcaucasians combined by 9.5 million, despite the fact that the Russian increase was only 13.1%, while the other ranged from 20.15 to 52.9%. Hence, even if the present trends should continue, a drastic change in the balance between races will not occur. Should the present differential rates of increase continue for the rest of the century, the Soviet population would rise to about 320 million, of which Central Asians would constitute about 63 million, while there would be about 170 million Russians. It is therefore unlikely that the Soviet leaders have yet begun to have nightmares over the prospect of being swamped by their internal segment of the 'teeming masses' of Asia. Very likely the Central Asian rate of increase will begin to slow down before the year 2000 as the present high rate of population growth is typical of a developing area, in which the endemic diseases have been brought under control and infant mortality drastically reduced, while the birth rate continues high. It is likely to be reinforced to some extent by the fact that the post-war European settlers constitute a young population, and that the birth rate among Russians in Central Asia is probably higher than in the European USSR. With further economic advance, the rate of increase will probably slow down drastically, as it has already done in the European USSR, and is beginning to do in Transcaucasia.

The problems posed by population growth are hence not so much those of nationalism; rather, since Soviet achievement in Central Asia has been so solidly based on economic betterment, the continued rapid rate of population growth presents some very definite difficulties of a socio-economic nature, in the demands which it makes and will continue to make upon Soviet society as a whole. One of the Soviet Union's proudest claims is that it has 'abolished' unemployment, and while the most casual visitor can see that often this claim has been made good only by inefficient use of labour, it is nevertheless an important feature of Communist doctrine that everyone who can must work, and must therefore have his right to do so guaranteed by the provision of employment opportunities. The rapid rate of population growth in Central Asia therefore presents difficulties which increase with every year that it continues: with the demands it makes on the building industry in providing housing, schools, hospitals, and factories; on the economic planners, in channelling resources adequate to ensure that economic growth keeps pace with the population increase; on agriculture, to feed the annual increase in hungry mouths; on education and the social services, to keep pace with the annual increase in demand. Examination of the Soviet Budget Laws shows that the Central Asian republics have usually been permitted to retain a much larger proportion of turnover and income taxes raised within their boundaries than the European republics, and have in addition received a direct subsidy, while much of the industrial investment within them has been financed out of central government funds. While their development was unquestionably in the interests of the Soviet Union as a whole, it has largely been financed at the expense of the other republics of the Union. This situation is likely to continue, and may even be intensified by the allocation of extra projects under the new Five Year Plan. But with the absolute increase in the number of new citizens born every year, the burden will increase until the growth rate begins to level off, as it has begun to do in Transcaucasia and Kazakhstan.

The population of Western Siberia grew during the 1960s from 11,251,000 to 12,201,000, partly through immigration from other parts of the USSR, but its natural increase was lower than the national average (though higher than the Moscow region and RSFSR as a whole) while that for Eastern Siberia and the Far East was higher. The table below compares the natural increase of the three East-of-Urals areas in 1967 with those of some other parts of the USSR, and indicates what the population may be by 1980 if the present trends continue.[61]

---

[61] *N.E.* 1969, pp. 34-35, indicate that in all areas the rate of increase has declined further compared with 1967. But as post-1967 editions do not break the RSFSR data down by regions, no post-1967 figures are available for Moscow, Siberia and the Far East, and the 1967 data have therefore been used as the basis for projection to 1980; actual increases appear likely to be somewhat less than those given here, but the proportions substantially the same.

Table 12

| Region | Natural annual increase per 1000 population, 1967 | Expected population, 1980 | % of Soviet total 1970 | 1980 |
|---|---|---|---|---|
| All USSR | 9.8 | 265    million | 100 | 100 |
| RSFSR | 6.5 | 139    million | 53.7 | 52.4 |
| Moscow | 3.1 | 13.2 million | 5.3 | 5.0 |
| West Siberia | 7.6 | 13.1 million | 5.0 | 4.9 |
| East Siberia | 10.1 | 8.2 million | 3.0 | 3.1 |
| Far East | 10.3 | 6.3 million | 2.4 | 2.4 |
| Transcaucasus | 19.2 | 14.6 million | 5.1 | 5.5 |
| Central Asia | 26.8 | 25.3 million ⎱ | 13.6 | 15.2 |
| Kazakhstan | 18.3 | 15.1 million ⎰ | | |

Thus the percentage of the Soviet population living in Soviet Asia will probably increase from 70.5 million in 1970 to about 82.6 million by 1980; as a proportion of the total Soviet population it will probably increase from the present 29.1% to about 31%, almost entirely as a result of the higher natural increase in the non-Russian Republics of Transcaucasus and Central Asia, while the population increase in Siberia will probably be about the same as that in European Russia.

Another indication of the preservation of culturally-based differences between 'Russians' and 'others' is evident in the frequency of divorce. Whereas divorce rates are rising in all parts of the USSR, they remain far lower in Transcaucasus, Central Asia and Kazakhstan than elsewhere. Figures for Russia East-of-Urals are close to those of the RSFSR as a whole, and Kazakhstan occupied an intermediate position, probably because just over half its population is European.

Table 13: Divorce rates, USSR, 1960 and 1967, per thousand population.[62]

| | 1960 | 1967 |
|---|---|---|
| USSR | 1.3 | 2.7 |
| RSFSR | 1.5 | 3.2 |
| Moscow Region | 2.0 | 4.0 |
| West Siberia | 1.1 | 2.8 |
| East Siberia | 0.8 | 2.5 |
| Far East | 1.6 | 4.4 |
| Transcaucasus | 0.4 | 1.0 |
| Central Asia | 0.4 | 1.1 |
| Kazakhstan | 0.4 | 1.6 |

[62] *N.E.* 1967. From table 'Marriages and divorces per 1000 population'.

The differences in the divorce rates between the Russian and non-Russian areas are striking. Unfortunately, Soviet statistics do not divide divorce rates by nationalities, but it could be that the rise in divorce rates in Transcaucasus, Central Asia, and Kazakhstan is mainly due to a rise in frequency of divorces among their European populations—quadrupling of the divorce rate in Kazakhstan between 1960 and 1967 could be associated with the arrival of large numbers of young Russians to work in the new state farms of the 'Virgin Lands' scheme. This cannot be proved, but it is known that the primitive conditions provided in the early stages of the scheme resulted in mass departures back to the European USSR, and conditions such as this favour family break-downs, especially when the spouses are young and childless. Certainly the remoteness and poor living conditions have caused similar defections of immigrants attracted to the Soviet Far East by the high wages offered there, and the divorce rate (4.4 per 1000) is the second highest in the USSR. Without fuller information it is not possible to explain the difference in divorce rates either between the Russian and non-Russian areas, or between Siberia and the Far East except in general and rather hypothetical ways. Persistence of an older and less 'love-oriented' tradition of arranged marriage in the non-Russian areas is an attractive hypothesis, but could only be validated statistically if it could be demonstrated that Russian residents of these areas conform to the pattern of the RSFSR. Islamic tradition could be invoked, but would not explain why divorce rates in Christian Georgia and Armenia (1 per 1000) are lower than in Moslem Azerbaijan (1.4) or the Central Asian republics (1.1 to 1.3). Remoteness does not explain why the divorce rate in the Far East (4.4) is almost double that of the almost equally remote Eastern Siberia (2.5), or why it is less than in Kaliningrad region (part of the former East Prussia) which is closer to the main centres of the USSR, enjoys a less severe climate than Siberia and more urban amenities of its own, yet has the highest divorce rate in the Soviet Union (4.9 per thousand).

A clue may be found in the statistics of marriages, since the areas with high divorce rates also have high marriage rates, suggesting that marriage is there more readily undertaken and terminated, though not explaining why this should be so. For the purposes of this study it is sufficient to note:
1. That the natural increase of the population of Soviet Siberia and the Far East is typical of regions of the European USSR rather than of Central Asia or of other Asian countries.
2. That West Siberia's population is increasing more slowly than

that of the regions to its east, but faster than most parts of the European USSR (Moscow 3.1, Ukraine 7.1, Baltic States 6.7, per thousand for example). Hence, if the trend continues (as the censuses of 1926, 1939, 1959 and 1970 have shown it to do, despite fluctuations in its actual magnitude), the proportion of the Soviet population living in Russia East of the Urals will rise slightly from the 10.6% of 1967 to perhaps 11% by 2000, but its numbers will increase to about 28 million by 1980 and 33 million by 2000. Elucidation by the Soviets of the causes for the steep decline in the birth rate of Europeans (from 26.9 per 1000 inhabitants of the RSFSR in 1950, it fell to 23.2 in 1960 and 14.2 by 1969)[63] could enable them to take steps to change the situation, if they wish to do so, but if present trends continue the population of Siberia will in both 1980 and 2000 be noted more for its relative affluence than its numbers, as economic growth, at about 5% per annum, is well ahead of population increase.

At present, the Soviet part in Asian or Pacific trade is not large, and a relatively small part of it passes through the Asian USSR— the outlets for it to reach the Pacific direct comprise only the eastern end of the Trans-Siberian railway and the single port of Nakhodka. However, the rapid increase in trade with Japan (mostly timber, fish, coal and mineral ores from the Soviet side, and machinery from the Japanese, but with some consumer goods) is already outrunning Nakhodka's capacity, and agreement has been reached with the Japanese to build an additional port nearby, at Vrangel Bay,[64] as well as to extend and improve the facilities at Nakhodka itself. Apart from this, the Soviet Union has for some time been negotiating with Japanese firms for joint exploitation of the reserves of coking coal and oil in Southern Yakutia, some 1500 miles from the coast, while import of natural gas from Yakutia and Sakhalin is also under consideration.[65] Although the idea that the 'empty spaces' of Siberia are being eyed by China is a some-what superficial one (most of the empty space is less habitable than the Nullarbor, while any minerals in it are difficult to extract because of the permanently frozen subsoil beneath which they lie, and the difficulty of building roads and railways for bringing them out in permafrost areas), building up the economies of the peripheral areas is for the Soviet government a desirable end in itself, especially as the assets which can be reached and exploited—

[63] *N.E.*, 1969, pp. 34-5.
[64] Moscow Radio, 28 Dec. 1970. BBC Summary of World Broadcasts SU/3571/A3/1.
[65] *Ibid.*

timber, minerals, oil and natural gas—are potentially rich sources of convertible currency.

Increased development of trade between Eastern Siberia, the Far East and Japan offers a number of other attractions. The Yakutian oil and gas fields are almost twice as far from Western Siberia as from the coast of the Sea of Japan, and would probably be most economically exploited by sending oil eastwards, even at the expense of buying Middle Eastern oil to replace it. At present Japan obtains nearly all its oil from the Middle East, and might find it cheaper to replace a proportion of it with Yakutian oil. For its part, the Soviet Union has a dying oilfield on the Caspian Sea at Baku. The Caspian offers easy access both to refineries at Baku and, via the Volga, to those at Astrakhan and Saratov-Engels. There may well be scope for a triangular arrangement, under which the Soviet Union supplies Yakutian oil to Japan, and buys oil from Iran, hitherto Japan's major supplier and also possessed of a Caspian coastline. Negotiations took place in 1969-70 between the Soviet Union and Iran, over the possible construction of a pipeline from the Persian oilfields to the Caspian coast, and though they did not lead to an agreement, there is no reason why they should not be resumed when the Japanese-Soviet negotiations over Yakutia reach a more definite stage. Iran is already supplying natural gas to the Soviet Union, as is Afghanistan, and under the Soviet-Iraqi agreement for development of the Rumaila oilfield in Southern Iraq, payment for Soviet equipment and services is to be made in oil.[66]

Moreover, profitability of the Trans-Siberian line would be higher if the problem of unbalanced traffic flows could be eliminated. Because of the concentration of industry in West Siberia, the Urals, and the European USSR, the predominant traffic flows west of Irkutsk are in a westerly direction, comprising raw materials (chiefly coal, oil and timber) as well as industrial products, and this results in large eastward return flows of empty wagons. East of Irkutsk, the predominant loaded flow is eastward, as the Far East is not self-supporting either in industrial or agricultural products —it imports from elsewhere in the USSR 60% of its oil products and wheat—and there are therefore large empty train flows westwards, amounting in 1966 to 10.39 million tons,[67] or approximately 20 empty trains a day. At the standard movement cost of 2.295 kopeks per 10 ton-kilometres,[68] and average lengths of interregional

[66] Moscow Radio, 5 Mar. 1971, quoted in *USSR and Third World,* vol. I No. 3 p. 122.
[67] *N.E.* 1967, table 'Transport balance of all goods by economic regions'.
[68] *N.E.* 1969, p. 443.

haul to or from the Far West of 6-7000 kilometres, it is not difficult to appreciate that the movement costs associated with these empty flows are high—at a standard empty train weight of 1100 tons, return of empty wagons would have cost about 15,000 roubles per train, or about 110 million roubles per annum. If the movement costs of products brought in by rail are also taken into account (to rail diesel oil from Omsk trebles its cost, to bring wheat from Kazakhstan adds 50-60% to its price),[69] it can be seen that the case for some reorientation of Far Eastern trade is a strong one. To purchase some commodities in Japan would be likely to reduce substantially the cost of transport to the Far East, and would improve the balance of traffic flows over the Trans-Siberian east of Irkutsk, while by reducing the eastward flow over the Omsk-Novosibirsk section (one of the most heavily worked anywhere in the world), it would ease the pressure on the western section of the line as well. Viewed in this light, the use of Japanese capital and expertise to develop the Soviet Far East appears a natural and sensible step on economic grounds, quite apart from any fears the Russians might have of a 'populate or perish' variety.

The pursuit of economic autarky was a cardinal feature of Soviet policy during Stalin's lifetime, and this was mainly responsible for the inwards-turning of the Soviet Far Eastern trade. Before the First World War the Soviet Far East's population was not large enough to generate significant foreign trade, but during the war the Trans-Siberian line became a main supply route for Russia, and Stalin's later aversion to development of trade through the Pacific coast ports arose mainly from the realisation that the chief potential trading partner — Japan — was also the most likely potential antagonist in the area. The pattern of traffic flow, by which Eastern Siberia and the Far East exchange goods mostly with Western Siberia and Central Asia, rather than with suppliers and customers closer at hand, was built up in the 1920s and 30s, and Soviet eagerness to enlist Japanese capital in the development of these areas indicates that they are well aware of its economic short-comings. In view of the prospects for continued growth in Japanese demand for raw materials, and its compatibility with Soviet plans for development of Russia East of Urals, the 1970s are likely to see an increase in the importance of the Soviet Far East, and of Soviet foreign trade through its Pacific ports.

This brief review of Soviet Asia has suggested that its record of economic and social development has been uneven but impressive. There remains the unresolved question of the political price which

---

[69] *Dal'niy Vostok, op. cit.,* p. 223.

has been paid, more particularly in the thwarting of nationalism among the non-Slav minorities. As has been pointed out, nationalist feeling barely existed among the Central Asian peoples, and the same was true of the Azeris of Transcaucasia and the Siberian minorities. However, a strongly developed sense of nationhood existed among the Georgians and Armenians, and both set up short-lived independent republics in 1918. The Azeris had virtually no part in the contemporaneous Republic of Azerbaijan in which Russians (Red and White) and Armenians played the leading roles, under sponsorship of outside powers, so nothing further will be said of it. But in the Georgian and Armenian cases, there was no doubt that both were homogeneous enough to be considered as potential nation-states, and the question to be answered is whether incorporation into the Soviet Union deprived them of a prospect of independent political existence.

In both cases the answer must probably be in the negative. The independent Georgian Republic was set up by German action in 1918, contrary to the provisions of the Treaty of Brest Litovsk. Its existence was prolonged by the historical accident that the Georgian left was dominated by the Mensheviks, a faction of the former Russian Social Democratic Party hostile to Lenin's Bolsheviks and justifiably afraid of what the Bolsheviks would do to them if Soviet rule was established in Georgia. Georgian nationalism, resurgent since the late nineteenth century, aimed at autonomy rather than independence, because of the value attached to Russian protection against Turkey, and one effect of the Republic's Sovietisation in February 1921 was the removal of Turkish forces which had occupied its southernmost part.

The same consideration applied even more strongly to Armenia. Turkish massacres of Armenians in 1896 and 1915 had left little doubt of their likely attitude to the former Russian Armenia. Return of the Armenian Republic to its former allegiance in May 1920 secured the withdrawal of the Turkish forces which had invaded it and were about to seize its capital. In respect of both Georgia and Armenia the conclusion must therefore be that the alternatives open to them were to be under Soviet or Turkish rule, and that the third option, prolonged independence, did not exist. The prominence of individuals of both nationalities in politics, the arts and the armed forces suggests that at least one cause of resentment among minorities—exclusion from access to high office—is not of great force in the Soviet Union. Lack of a significant 'Free Armenia' movement among the large Armenian diaspora in Western countries also tends to suggest acceptance of the protection afforded Armenia by its membership of the Soviet Union. While anti-Slav resentments undoubtedly exist in Georgia and Armenia, as among minorities in other multinational states, the federal structure of the Soviet Union provides some scope for assertion of national individuality, and while the political structure makes it necessary for aspiring leaders to be Communists, it does not require them to be Russians.

In their dealings with the 'Third World', the Soviets make judicious use of 'their' Asians. Visiting Asian or African leaders are usually taken to Transcaucasian, Central Asian or Siberian minority areas where they may view conditions for themselves. Soviet delegations to Asian or African countries normally include at least one Central Asian, and a proportion of Soviet technical specialists on aid projects will be drawn from the Soviet Asian nationalities. Beyond this, it is worth remembering that among the European nationalities of the Soviet Union, only about 20 per cent were literate in 1918. The Soviet Union in the past fifty years has conducted social experiments both in converting a predominantly peasant society into a developed industrial one, and in raising the standards of its Asian minorities well above those of the neighbours from whom they were virtually indistinguishable in 1917. That the 'experiments' in places involved great suffering, are incomplete, or may be doubtfully transferrable to other contexts, is in Soviet eyes of less importance than the fact that they were recent. To newly independent countries, aspiring to similar economic betterment, the Soviet experience is relevant, even though some of its political aspects are repugnant to them. The gist of the Soviet 'message' is that a developing country can convert itself reasonably rapidly into a developed industrial one precisely as the Soviet Union has done —with minimal dependence on Western capital, little or no abatement of political hostility to the West, without the introduction of a fully-fledged capitalist system, and with concomitant advancement of education and the social services. There is a certain amount of disingenuousness in the argument, as pre-revolutionary Russia possessed an incipient heavy industrial base to which only India has an analogue among the non-aligned countries of Asia and Africa, but it is true in the sense that the Soviet Union has achieved what most Asian and African countries aspire to without becoming reliant on a private business sector, i.e. under 'socialism'. As most non-aligned countries profess to be 'socialist' in one way or another, the entire Soviet Union is a showcase, and however shoddy some of the goods displayed, there is no denying that the institution functions. Within the Soviet Union, the Asian parts are presented as being of special relevance to the developing countries, being an illustration of what can be achieved with the right kind of assistance. These points are too self-evident to be laboured further, eg., by citing numbers of apparently Uzbek engineers found on Soviet aid project sites, but should be borne in mind constantly when considering Soviet political and economic dealings with Asian states and the ideological constructs used to justify them.

# 3

# Soviet Military Power and Asia

In terms of total deployed forces and weapons, the Soviet Union is Asia's only superpower. Because of uncertainties about pricing policies, defence-associated items not formally included in the defence budget, and the artificiality of the exchange rates for the rouble, estimates of actual defence spending range between $US19.7 and 53 billion, and their wide range indicates their low reliability.[1] All that can be said with confidence is that the Soviet defence budget exceeds that of all the states of Asia combined, and is second only to that of the United States.[2] With deployed forces totalling about 3.3 million men, it is on paper far stronger than any Asian state or combination of them.[3] Nor is the exercise of military power in Asia by the Russians any novelty. Apart from some very thinly populated areas of Siberia, all Russian or Soviet territory from Georgia to the Kurile Islands was acquired by military conquest, occupation, or 'unequal treaty', and much of it was acquired at the expense of Asian imperial powers, in particular Turkey, China and Japan, beginning in the 18th Century and continuing until 1945. Alone among the powers of Asia it has a fully-operational force of intercontinental ballistic missiles with thermonuclear warheads, deployed mostly in Siberia, and its Pacific Fleet, based upon Vladivostok, Sovetskaya Gavan and Petropav-

---

[1] For a discussion of problems in assessing the Soviet defence budget, see *The Military Balance 1970-71*, Institute for Strategic studies, London, pp. 10-11.
[2] *Ibid.*, pp. 110-111.
[3] *Ibid.*, pp. 60-71.

lovsk-Kamchatski, has more combat ships than the navies of any six Asian powers combined.[4]

In theory, therefore, the Soviet Union has large capabilities for military adventures against Asian countries, and in the not too distant past has displayed willingness to use them. But capabilities and possible intentions are not in themselves enough in assessing what Soviet military power means in relation to Asia or Asia to the Soviet Union. To do that with any hope of success necessitates a much closer evaluation of military deployment patterns, the putative threats which they are designed to create, or to which they respond, and the objectives, in so far as they are known or may be inferred, to which military deployments add force.

The Soviet Ground Forces comprise some 150 divisions, about half of them at or near full strength of around 10,000 men.[5] About two-thirds of these divisions (rather more of the full-strength divisions) are, however, deployed to face NATO, along Soviet bloc frontiers from Northern Norway to the Caucasus.[6] In theory, large numbers of these could be redeployed eastwards if necessary, but in practice the Soviet Union would be reluctant to do so because of the almost equally large NATO forces which face them. Of the 70-75 full strength divisions, 30 are located in Eastern and Central Europe (20 in East Germany, 2 in Poland, 4 in Czechoslovakia and 4 in Hungary),[7] where they not merely serve as earnest of the Soviet intention to support its Warsaw Pact allies, but by their presence help to keep the governments of some of those allies in power. Major withdrawals of these forces could result only from a radical change in the situation in Europe, so to all intents and purposes they are not available for use elsewhere in the foreseeable future. The same is true of the back-up divisions in the Western USSR, especially of those maintained in the Carpathian military district. This borders on Poland, Czechoslovakia, Hungary and Roumania, and its importance to the stability of the Soviet sphere of influence in Eastern Europe is manifest by the fact that from it invasions of two of those countries were mounted, in 1956 and 1968. While the ten divisions or so in the Caucasus could be used to exercise military pressure upon Turkey or Iran, their presence there is primarily dictated by Turkey's membership of NATO and

[4] *Ibid.,* pp. 60-71: see also 'The Indian Ocean in Soviet Naval Policy', Adelphi Paper No. 87, International Institute for Strategic Studies, London, 1972, by the present author, and *Jane's Fighting Ships 1969-70,* pp. 578-9.

[5] *The Military Balance 1970-71,* pp. 6-9.

[6] *Ibid.,* pp. 6-9, 13-19, 91, 99-101.

[7] *Ibid.,* pp. 90-98.

CENTO, to which the 400,000-strong Turkish Army is an important contribution, and their employment outside a general NATO or CENTO-Warsaw Pact confrontation is improbable. Turkish-Soviet relations have improved considerably since the 1950s, but antagonism between them is of very long standing; Turkish reservations about NATO became apparent during and after the Cyprus crisis of 1963, but are far from the point at which Turkey would be prepared to jettison an alliance which secures it against Soviet pressure over the Eastern frontier or control of the Straits. In any event, the sheer size of the Turkish Army (the largest in NATO except for the American) renders confrontation with it unlikely, except in a context of general war, or a total breakdown of alliance systems accompanied by a local crisis of major dimensions for which there is no apparent rationale.

From Transcaucasia, pressure could also be brought to bear on Iran. This happened in 1941 when the British and Russians jointly occupied the country, and in 1945-6 when pro-independence agitation in Persian Azerbaijan was given impetus by Soviet reluctance to withdraw their occupying force, apparently in the hope that an autonomous Persian Azerbaijan would in due course join the Soviet Republic of Azerbaijan. With armed forces of only 221,000 Iran hardly seems a formidable antagonist, but American involvement in the future of Iran is evinced both by the large Western oil interests there, and Iran's membership of CENTO. Soviet diplomacy has for some years been improving ties with Iran in ways to which military pressure, short of invasion, would be counter-productive, while invasion itself would risk confrontation with the United States, Turkey and, through Turkey, not merely the moribund CENTO but the far from moribund NATO.

Afghanistan was the scene of British and Russian struggles for influence during the nineteenth century, but both finally agreed to regard it as a buffer zone. Because of its dispute with Pakistan over the North-West Frontier Province, it proved receptive to Soviet influence after Pakistan received American aid through joining CENTO. The Afghan Army is small and almost entirely Soviet-equipped. It offers no threat to the security of Soviet Central Asia and neither Afghan-Pakistani nor Soviet-Pakistani relations indicate a Soviet belief that any incidental threat to their borders is likely to emanate from the sub-continent.

East of Afghanistan begins the border with China. This extends almost to the Pacific coast, and is in two sections, divided only by the border with Outer Mongolia—which in view of its weakness, its very close ties with the Soviet Union and relatively poor relations with China, forms an addition to the perimeter which Soviet troops must guard, greater than any contribution Mongolian forces can make to its defence.

The Western sector of the Sino-Soviet border adjoins Sinkiang, which Russia (and the Soviet Union, as recently as 1946) has in the past attempted to detach from China. Sinkiang contains a large Kazakh minority, indistinguishable from the Soviet Kazakhs, which in the early 1960s reacted to Sinification of the province by unrest and large-scale defection into Soviet Kazakhstan. The terrain, though mountainous, has not proved a barrier to movement of armies in the past, and location of the Chinese nuclear weapons production and test facilities in Sinkiang and the industries of Alma Ata and the Fergana Valley, as well as the Soviet anti-ballistic missile test centre on Lake Balkhash, make it a sensitive area for both countries. This is reflected in both Chinese and Soviet arrangements for military command.

Until recently China maintained about four army divisions and two or three divisions of border troops in the area, and may have increased these in response to Soviet changes in command arrangements. Close political control over events in the border areas is maintained by subordination of the military command for the area direct to the Chinese government instead of through the High Command of the Chinese armed forces.[8]

The Soviet Turkestan Military District is believed to contain twelve to sixteen army divisions, plus about 50,000 border guards.[9] The Turkestan Military District was responsible not merely for the Sino-Soviet border but, further west, for that with Iran east of the Caspian. Increasing tension with China persuaded the Soviet High Command to end this undesirable division of responsibility, and in 1969 or early 1970 it set up a Central Asian Military District command, responsible solely for the Sino-Soviet border area.[10] It is also said to have moved at least one additional division into the area.[11]

The Sino-Soviet border is in many places not officially accepted by the Chinese, but in the Far East it mostly follows the line of the Argun, Amur and Ussuri Rivers, whereas in Central Asia no such convenient lines of demarcation exist. According to recent

---

8 *The Military Balance 1969-70*, p. 39.
9 *The Military Balance, 1970-71*, p. 99. Derived by subtraction from totals given in Col. I of the Table.
10 First mentioned in *Krasnaya Zvezda* (Red Star), Moscow, 6 February, 1970.
11 By comparison, *The Military Balance, 1969-70 and 1970-71*, Soviet Union sections.

Chinese atlases, about 440 miles of it north-eastwards from the junction with Afghanistan, are in dispute, and many violations have been alleged by both sides, though none have been on the scale of the Ussuri River incidents in the Far East in March 1969.

Outer Mongolia (The Mongolian People's Republic) has very small armed forces (an army of about 24,000 and an air force of about 700),[12] but has a defence agreement with the Soviet Union. Under this agreement about three divisions of Soviet troops are stationed there.[13] The viability of this small force against strong opposition is doubtful, as it is at the end of a tenuous supply line: a single-track railway which branches off the Trans-Siberian at Ulan Ude and runs across Mongolia into China, and a low-capacity road which runs parallel to it. However, the symbolic value of the three Soviet divisions far outweighs their military worth. In 1945, along these same tenuous supply lines, the Red Army in less than four months concentrated four armies in Mongolia for the final stage of the war against Japan. A mixed cavalry and tank group crossed the Gobi Desert into the narrow waist of China, heading for Peking, which is only some 400 miles from Dzamin Ude on the Sino-Mongolian border, and reached it in twelve days. The bulk of the force concentrated in Mongolia headed eastwards to meet other Soviet armies from the Maritime Province. Between them these forces conquered Manchuria (China's main industrial region then as now) in less than two weeks, against a Japanese army whose firepower, though inferior to that of the Red Army, was relatively no poorer than that of the present Chinese Army.[14]

Naturally it would not be wise to push the comparison with 1945 too far, as a Soviet military victory would be harder to achieve against a hostile population and an army trained to regard military defeat as the prelude not to capitulation but to a prolonged guerrilla-type war. Nevertheless, the strategic importance of Mongolia as base for a mobile campaign against China's industrial heartland is significant, if only for its value in ensuring that border incidents to do not grow into anything bigger. The Soviet Union would be reluctant to undertake a prolonged conventional campaign in the Far East and could not attempt to repeat the 1945 campaign without large-scale mobilisation, but has already shown itself capable of a highly mobile and effective short campaign there. The Chinese leaders mostly have personal cause to remember the

[12] *The Military Balance 1970-71*, pp. 66-67.
[13] *Ibid.*, p. 7.
[14] *Istoriya Velikoy Otechestvennoy Voyny Sovetskogo Soyuza 1941-45* (History of the Great Patriotic War of the Soviet Union, 1941-45), Vol. V, pp. 546-583.

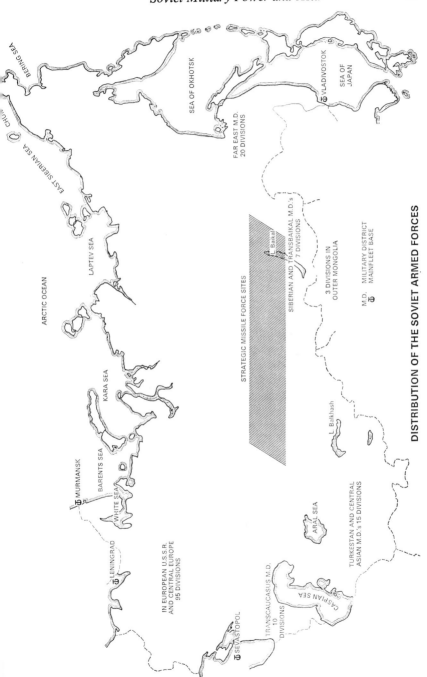

**DISTRIBUTION OF THE SOVIET ARMED FORCES**

FAR EAST M.D.
20 DIVISIONS

SEA OF OKHOTSK

VLADIVOSTOK

SEA OF JAPAN

BERING SEA

CHU...

EAST SIBERIAN SEA

ARCTIC OCEAN

LAPTEV SEA

KARA SEA

STRATEGIC MISSILE FORCE SITES

L. Baikal

SIBERIAN AND TRANSBAIKAL M.D.'s
7 DIVISIONS

3 DIVISIONS IN
OUTER MONGOLIA

M.D.    MILITARY DISTRICT
        MAINFLEET BASE

MURMANSK

BARENTS SEA

WHITE SEA

LENINGRAD

IN EUROPEAN U.S.S.R.
AND CENTRAL EUROPE
95 DIVISIONS

L. Balkhash

ARAL SEA

TURKESTAN AND CENTRAL
ASIAN M.D.'s 15 DIVISIONS

CASPIAN SEA

TRANSCAUCASUS M.D.
10
DIVISIONS

SEVASTOPOL

speed with which Soviet superiority in modern equipment enabled them to swamp in a few days a Japanese army which they themselves had fought with only limited success for over seven years. While Soviet manpower resources do not match those of China (the Soviet population at 242 million, is only about one third that of China), the Chinese forces' mobility and firepower are greatly inferior.[15]

The twenty or so divisions of the Soviet Far East Military District were maintained there in the 1920s and 30s to guard against Japanese attack from Korea and Manchuria. After 1945 their main task was to guard the Maritime Province and the naval bases of Vladivostok and Sovetskaya Gavan against attack from the sea by US/Japanese forces, but from 1962 they have exercised defence against attack from China,[16] and in March 1969 elements of them were involved in the largest of the many Sino-Soviet border incidents—that on Damansky Island in the Ussuri River in which they claim 31 Russians and about 100 Chinese were killed. The air force units based in Siberia include some long range bombers, most of which have been converted for naval reconnaissance and strike tasks against US carrier forces.[17] At the western end of the Soviet Asian perimeter, the Caspian oilfields are heavily guarded by surface-to-air missiles and interceptors of the Baku Air Defence District, against attack by NATO aircraft based in Turkey or operating from US aircraft carriers in the Eastern Mediterranean. Otherwise most of the Soviet air forces east of the Urals are deployed for army support and protection of the Trans-Siberian railway (which in places is less than 20 miles from the Chinese border), as well as the industrial areas and administrative centres situated along and south of it. As most of the area is remote from risk of Western air attack, and the Chinese air force, though dangerously close, has few bombers (and most of those obsolete) Soviet air forces there are small compared with those deployed in the European NATO area.

More important to Soviet war-making capability is the Intercontinental Ballistic Missile force, which provides the largest single element of deterrence against Western attack and the main striking force against America in the event of general war. As the shortest route from the Soviet Union to America is via the Arctic, there is no operational need to deploy ICBMs in the European USSR, and

[15] *The Military Balance 1970-71*, pp. 99-101. See also *Current Affairs Bulletin*, 6 April 1970, pp. 146 ff.
[16] Victor Zorza in *The Guardian*, 9 November 1963.
[17] *Janes' Fighting Ships 1969-70*, Naval Aircraft section, p. 21.

a number of reasons why they should not be deployed there. Most important is the security of the force, which requires both immunity from espionage and maximum warning of enemy attack. When the Soviet Union began to install ICBMs in the late 1950s, the only means of photographing or attacking sites was aircraft. Maximum security against this possibility (as well as against the residual danger of espionage by agents or subverted citizens) could be attained by locating the ICBM force in Siberia. However, there are very few roads outside the major centres in Siberia, and transport of the very bulky early missiles, plus the ancillary equipment for the sites, could be carried out only by rail, which necessitated locating the force within a relatively narrow band along, though out of sight of, the Trans-Siberian railway. The later advent of the reconnaissance satellite and the US ICBM reduced the advantages of Siberia, and some of the later complexes were located in thinly populated areas of the European USSR, and, later still, the availability of smaller missiles (which could be carried to site in a large aircraft such as the AN-22) reduced reliance on the railway to some extent. But to counterbalance that, the realisation of the need to protect missiles by 'hardening' (emplacement in underground reinforced-concrete silos) tended to restrict deployment to areas where the subsoil was not permanently frozen, thus leading to a perpetuation of the South Siberian deployment where, in any case, there had been heavy investment already in site facilities, command posts, communications and living quarters. The strip along the Trans-Siberian railway has therefore remained important to the Soviet Strategic Missile Forces, and is an extra factor in determining Siberia's significance to Soviet military power as a whole. However, since its application is mainly against US targets, and only secondarily against those in the Indo-Pacific region, it is not proposed here to do more than note its existence.

Undoubtedly the force which played the least role in development of Soviet Asia, and in the exertion of Russian influence upon Asian states, was the Navy. Russian expansion took a different form from that of the Western European states. To its west was the heavily populated, politically and technologically dynamic heartland of Europe, in comparison with which Russia was backward and weak. To the east and south, opportunities were greater. All the way to the Pacific Coast and the Hindu Kush were weak and disunited neighbours, most of them technologically backward compared with Russia, few of them capable of prolonged or successful resistance. Russian imperialism, therefore, unlike that of Spain, Portugal, Holland, Britain and France, took the form of annexing

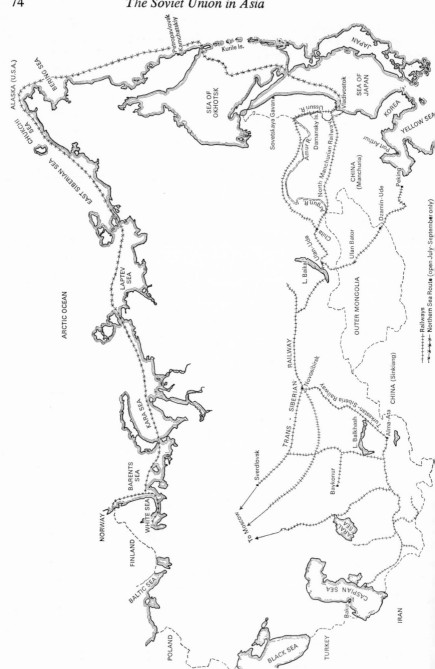

geographically contiguous areas, so that in the expansion which eventually made it the largest state of Asia, navies and shipping played a relatively unimportant part. Rivers, land routes and, ultimately, railways, were all of much greater significance, and even where sea routes were available they tended to be of secondary importance because of the detours which they involved. Their prime significance was in local transits between, for example, the ports of the Soviet Far East, where land routes are bad and in many cases longer.[18]

This fundamental difference in the means by which the Empire was established naturally affected the status of the Navy. In the case of the other Empires of European states, communication between heartland and provinces required not merely a merchant navy, but a combatant fleet, strong enough both to counter the fleets of the other imperial powers in time of war and, in war or peace, to deter interference by pirates, or by small states which might control bottlenecks upon the sea routes and attempt to exploit the fact politically or economically. Establishment of empires dependent upon maritime links therefore had international repercussions far beyond those incurred by Russia in the mere acquisition of remote areas little known to the outside world and little desired by it. Only with attempts to accelerate the decay of the Ottoman Empire in Eastern Europe (in the expectation of becoming patron of the mostly Orthodox Christian successor states), did Russia come into serious conflict with the British, and then more because of the balance of power in Europe than through imperial rivalries. Russian penetration of Central Asia towards Afghanistan and the Indian border was designed at least in part to moderate British attitudes to Russian ambition in Eastern Europe, by creating trouble for Britain elsewhere.[19] Limits were set to Anglo-Russian competition in Central Asia by the approach of the First World War, and the desire to settle differences in order to face the threat from Germany. This settlement left Afghanistan as a buffer between the two Empires. Despite apprehensions about the Russian Navy (such as those which led to the building of forts in Sydney Harbour and elsewhere), it did not acquire the forces

---

[18] See Table on 'Movement between economic regions by mode of Transport' in *Narodnoye Khozyaystvo SSSR za 1967 god* (The National Economy of the USSR for 1967), Moscow, Central Statistical Directorate, 1968, and *Dal'niy Vostok* (The Far East). An economical-geographical survey Academy of Sciences, Moscow, 1966, pp. 222-251.

[19] Eg. General Skobelev's argument of January 1885, that a force of 15,000 Russians sent into India could provoke a general uprising against British rule.

or bases necessary for any real confrontation of British interests in Asia.

Only towards the end of the Nineteenth Century did naval forces become important in the Russian Far East. In 1896 Russia seized Korea from China, and, in so doing, pre-empted Japanese territorial ambitions in the same area. In Japanese plans for wresting Korea from the Russians, destruction of Russia's Pacific Fleet naturally rated high, because the ferrying of an army to the Korean mainland, and its maintenance there throughout a campaign, depended on naval supremacy in the Sea of Japan. In 1904, therefore, Japan opened the war with a surprise attack on the Russian Navy in Port Arthur, and wiped most of it out at its moorings. The Russian response was to send its Baltic Fleet, which the Japanese likewise destroyed in the Battle of Tsushima. More important, however, than the outcome of the battle was that the Baltic Fleet's voyage illustrated graphically a problem which faced all Russian admirals in the Indo-Pacific area, and still plagues their Soviet successors—that of communications. The Russian Baltic Fleet's journey took $7\frac{1}{2}$ months, and it was subjected to considerable harassment on the way, ranging from ostentatious surveillance by the Royal Navy to denial of port and coaling facilities.[20]

The Soviet Navy is divided into four Fleet areas—Northern, Baltic, Black Sea and Pacific, which are virtually incapable of reinforcing each other except by long journeys through waters not under Soviet control. Furthermore, in any kind of war situation, two of the fleets (those of the Baltic and Black Sea) are easily bottled up or at most confined to flank support of land campaigns. Only via the Northern Sea Route, between the Northern and Pacific Fleets, is there a seaway which avoids foreign-controlled waters; but at its eastern end this route passes close to Alaska and Japan and in any event can be used for only three months or so each year. Each Fleet, therefore, and in particular that in the Pacific, must be self-contained. In this respect the Soviet Union is at a considerable strategic disadvantage compared with the United States, where a worldwide network of bases facilitates the transfer of major units from one fleet area to another relatively quickly, and where most transits are made wholly or mainly through waters controlled by the United States or its allies.

When it comes to the actual exercise of land or naval power in Asia, the theoretical capabilities have to be greatly modified by the practical requirements of the likely situations. It is therefore neces-

[20] *The Fleet That Had to Die,* by Richard Hough, Hamish Hamilton, 1958, describes the voyage and the difficulties encountered.

sary, before considering in what ways and circumstances Soviet armed force might be used in Asia, to examine more closely the scale of deployment and circumstances in which Soviet (or Russian) armed force has been used in the past, and what tasks it is designed for in the present.

For most of the present century, the main threat envisaged to the Soviet Far East was Japan, which defeated Russia in the war of 1904-5, and occupied large parts of the Maritime Region and Eastern Siberia during the post-revolutionary Civil War. In 1938 and 1939, Japanese forces of considerable size encroached into the Maritime Region and into Outer Mongolia (which invoked its defence pact with the Soviet Union).[21] In both cases they were defeated after heavy fighting, but thereafter a Soviet force of twenty-five divisions was maintained in the Far Eastern Military District and Transbaikalia; although most of it was withdrawn to fight in the Battle of Moscow in 1941,[22] this was only after it had been ascertained from a reliable spy that Japan intended to attack the Western colonial dependencies in Asia, not the Soviet Far East. Apart from relatively minor incidents during the Boxer Rising of 1900 and attacks on the Soviet-managed North Manchurian Railway during 1929, China itself provided no problems for the Russian or Soviet armed forces in the Far East.

After 1945, Japan was still seen as a possible threat to Soviet territorial integrity: annexation of South Sakhalin and the Kurile Islands, while improving the defences of the Soviet coastline in the Japan and Okhotsk Seas (where 13% of all Soviet shipping movements take place),[23] had created a potential issue of irredentism in Japan. More importantly, the possibility that American forces would assault Soviet territory from Japanese bases could not be excluded from Soviet contingency planning, especially when the Americans ignored the European precedent and rejected Soviet requests for an occupation zone. The post-war force therefore comprised about twenty divisions to defend the coast. Along the rest of the frontier defence was left to the light-armed Border Guards, and all army divisions in Siberia were of low readiness.[24]

Even during the Korean War, which led to a doubling of the Soviet armed forces (from 2.9 to 5.7 million, according to Khrushchev's 14 January 1960 speech), deployments in the East

---

21 *Vospominaniya i Razmyshleniya* (Recollections and Reflections), by Marshal G. K. Zhukov, Moscow 1969, pp. 157-181.

22 *History of the Great Patriotic War of the Soviet Union 1941-45* (in Russian), Vol. 2, pp. 257, 274.

23 *Dal'niy Vostok* (The Far East), p. 242.

24 See 'Soviet Union' sections of *The Military Balance* from 1960 onwards.

were not substantially increased. The bulk of the newly-raised forces remained in the European USSR or Transcaucasus, facing the NATO area, and neither during the war nor in the 18 years since have there been any indications that Soviet defence of its Far Eastern areas involves collaboration with or by North Korea.

Soviet Far East military doctrines changed radically with the outbreak of the Sino-Soviet dispute at the end of the 1950s and by 1962 the Far East Military District had begun to exercise defence of its Western border against invasion from China. Nevertheless, no large transfers of Soviet forces from the West took place until after the major incident at Damanski Island in March 1969. Even after it, no major diminution of Soviet forces elsewhere has been reported, nor have there been any indications of a major increase in the total armed forces, so it seems that reinforcement of the frontier with China has not been on a scale sufficient to alter radically either the balance between Soviet forces deployed in West and East or that between Soviet and Chinese forces along the border.[25]

As a general proposition, use of Soviet land power in Asia against any of the Asian states with which the Soviet Union has borders, carries the risk of escalation to all-out war, either with US-sponsored alliance systems, or with China, under circumstances likely to be difficult for Soviet military planning, even if the Soviet military were notably bellicose—which on the whole they have not proved to be, except in regard to maintaining the status quo in Eastern Europe.

Against a threat from China, deterrence by threat to use nuclear weapons is of limited effectiveness. While the Soviets have found Mao Tse-Tung's professed willingness to incur 300 million casualties a godsend for propaganda purposes, they are well aware that most of China's violence has been verbal only. In any event, a number of Soviet Siberian and Central Asian cities lie very close to the Chinese border, well within range of nuclear weapons carried by unsophisticated short or medium range delivery vehicles. While ability to destroy Moscow may not be within China's reach for some years, a number of important Soviet provincial centres are already within range of Chinese nuclear weapons, and only a threat to the very existence of the Soviet state, which China is not in a position to pose, would be considered sufficient to justify sacrificing areas such as the Kuznets Basin, Khabarovsk, the Pacific Fleet's main base at Vladivostok, Novosibirsk or the Fergana Valley.

[25] Cf. *The Military Balance,* Warsaw Pact section for years 1963-64 to 1970-71.

Naval power presents more opportunities for a number of reasons. Certainly, in a warlike context, the Pacific Fleet's opportunities are somewhat limited; as the Soviet Navy possesses no aircraft carriers, surface units could not operate with safety beyond the range of land-based air cover, and in view of the land-locked nature of the Sea of Japan (whose widest outlet, the Straits between Japan and Korea, is split by Japanese owned islands into two channels, each less than fifty miles wide), prospects of their ranging far afield would not be high. In any event, their probable role in a war situation would be to defend the approaches to the coast against carrier strike forces or amphibious assaults. For a general war, the main strength of the Pacific Fleet resides in its force of about 120 submarines.[26] Of these the missile-firers would in part be used to supplement the coastal defence by surface ships and air forces, using a ship-to-ship cruise missile (code-named 'Shaddock' by NATO), in part to attack targets in Japan and South Korea, mainly cities and bases. The conventional attack submarines would be used, along with some of the missile firers, to seek out and destroy the US Seventh Fleet and the Japanese naval self-defence force, as well as in general anti-shipping activity.[27]

But the 'general war' task, while it is the 'worst case' for which the Soviet Navy, along with most others, is designed, is not the most likely case for naval involvement. Warships play an important part in manifesting a presence in peacetime, and can do so in circumstances where use of other armed services is not possible. Unlike the other armed forces, units of navies regularly visit the territory of other countries and spend much of their time in international waters. The concept of 'showing the flag', well understood by the older maritime powers, has been enthusiastically espoused in the post-war years by the Soviet Navy, which has consequently appeared in areas where it had hitherto been seen rarely or not at all. For the Soviet Union, visits by naval units have the advantage of bringing its presence to the awareness of countries with which it has no land frontiers, and for whom its puissance as a land power is of little account.

From the Battle of Tsushima (1905) to the early 1930s, Russia had virtually no Pacific Fleet; the loss of two of her three fleets (Tsarist Russia had no Northern Fleet) placed Russia in serious need of a naval construction programme, in which the Baltic Fleet naturally received priority, because of the dangers presented to

---

26 *The Military Balance 1970-71*, p. 9.
27 Marshal V. D. Sokolovsky (ed.) *Military Strategy*, 3rd edition, 1968, Moscow, Ministry of Defence Publishing House, pp. 335, 362-368.

Russia's Baltic provinces, and the then capital (St. Petersburg, now Leningrad), by Germany's naval expansion. Much of the reconstituted Baltic Fleet was destroyed during the First World War and by British naval action in the ensuing Russian Civil War, while most of the major units of the Black Sea Fleet were scuttled to avoid capture by the Germans in 1918, and the remainder removed by the Whites when they evacuated the Ukraine and Caucasus. The Soviet government was therefore forced to re-establish the Navy almost from scratch, and the Pacific Fleet was accorded low priority, again reflecting the greater importance attached to the threat from Europe. When re-established in 1932, it consisted of only a few destroyers and submarines,[28] and its major expansion had to await the large naval shipbuilding programme which began in 1950 and continued for approximately 11 years. As part of this programme, some small shipbuilding facilities were established in the Far East,[29] but large surface units for the Pacific Fleet are built in European yards, and Soviet warships en route to Vladivostok have been passing through the Indian and Pacific Oceans for a good many years. However, it was not until the 1960s that Soviet Pacific Fleet units began to pay 'good-will' visits in the Pacific, and it was April 1968 when the first such visit to Indian Ocean countries took place.[30]

Since 1968 there has been a steady flow of Soviet naval units from the Pacific into the Indian Ocean, but its volume has remained low; in 1970 a total of seven surface warships, four submarines and nine auxiliary vessels visited states on the Indian Ocean littoral at various times[31]—the typical pattern of activity was for a force of two warships and two auxiliaries (one a tanker, the other a dry goods ship, thus making the force self-contained for supplies), sometimes accompanied by a submarine, to enter the Indian Ocean via the Malacca Straits, visit several ports between Singapore and Mauritius and return to Vladivostok after a stay of two to three months in the Indian Ocean. Western press sources have at various times carried reports suggesting that base facilities are being negotiated or have been granted, by countries as diverse as Indonesia, Singapore, India, South Yemen, Tanzania and Mauritius. None of these reports has stood up to investigation, and all the governments concerned except Singapore have strongly

[28] Herrick, R. W. *Soviet Naval Strategy,* U.S. Naval Institute, Annapolis, 1968, pp. 13, 43.

[29] *Dal'niy Vostok,* p. 164.

[30] *Current Affairs Bulletin,* 6 April 1970.

[31] Speech by British Prime Minister, Edward Heath, at Commonwealth Heads of Government Conference, Singapore, January 1971.

denied any intention of granting bases.[32] Singapore has indicated willingness to provide facilities to Soviet ships on normal commercial terms, but a 'facility' unaccompanied by a certain degree of extraterritoriality is of little use. If the Soviet Union did wish to use Singapore, it would require much more than the right to have ships serviced and supplied by the Singapore Government or local contractors; it would require secure areas under its own control, ammunition storage, and facilities for repairing secret equipment, such as on-board electronics, without surveillance. Rights less than these—namely repair and supply—which are normally available in any neutral port at the government's discretion, do not require elaborate negotiation and may be withdrawn at any time, making them far too tenuous a foundation for the basing of a fleet with military or political tasks to perform.

When considering evaluations of Soviet naval intentions in the Indo-Pacific area, it is well to bear in mind that some extremely circumstantial reports made in the past have proved to lack any basis in fact. Late in 1970 a British newspaper reported that a Soviet 'Alligator' class landing craft, laden with marines and stores, was on its way to the island of Socotra, near the entrance to the Red Sea. Subsequent reports in newspapers from as far afield as Japan and the United States, spoke confidently of construction of a 'command facility' with radio masts, and of Soviet naval construction troops at work, while speculation as to the purpose of the exercise included control of an Indian Ocean Fleet and stockpiling of small arms for African guerrilla movements. Eventually the owners of Socotra, the People's Democratic Republic of South Yemen, flew a correspondent from the London *Times* to the island in January 1971. He returned to report[33] that five months after the alleged arrival of the Soviet marines, there was nothing on Socotra —no port facilities (except for small dhows), no aerials, no roads of any kind, that the waters around the island were very shallow, and its future could be seen only in terms of animal husbandry and tourism, the latter of which is of low compatibility with a 'secret base' on an island of only some 1400 square miles.

In July 1970, Mauritius concluded an agreement covering landing rights for Soviet shipping and the Soviet state airline 'Aeroflot'. Despite speculation that this agreement might serve to provide the Soviet Navy with base facilities, examination of the text indicates otherwise. Soviet trawlers are allowed to berth, up to a

[32] See eg., statement by Indian Deputy Foreign Minister, 19 November 1969.
[33] *The Times,* London, reprinted in *Canberra Times* 12 December 1970.

maximum of one ship a month, for rest and recreation and exchange of crews, while Aeroflot is permitted to land at Mauritius up to a maximum of twelve times in a year, for the purpose of bringing in new crewmen and taking away those due for home leave. Soviet fishing fleets, with headquarters at Sevastopol in the Black Sea and at Vladivostok have fished the Indian Ocean for a number of years; the fleets consist of large trawlers, and include factory ships capable of processing and preserving the catch, as well as depot ships equipped to carry out heavy repairs. Fish forms an important part of the Soviet diet (only Peru and Japan catch a larger annual tonnage),[34] and in view of the large capital investment which the fishing fleets represent, it is economically sensible to keep them at sea as much as possible. The very limited rights granted by Mauritius make sense in this context, and there is up

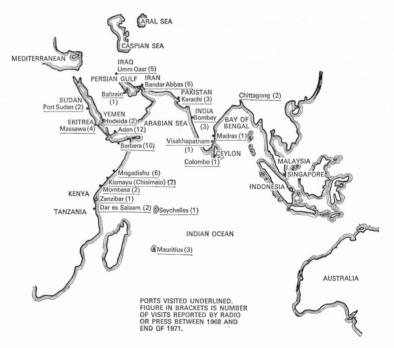

**INDIAN OCEAN: VISITS BY SOVIET WARSHIPS 1968-71**

to the present no evidence or reason to interpret the agreement in any more apocalyptic sense. No doubt electronic intelligence (ELINT) trawlers operate in the Indian Ocean as elsewhere, but

[34] *UN Yearbook of Statistics,* 1969; Table 47, pp. 137-8.

they are not spy vessels disguised as fishing boats; they are special purpose vessels which use the standard trawler hull and machinery, but carry a considerable amount of extra gear, much of which is visible and none of which is of any conceivable use for fishing. In the 1950s, when large Soviet fishing fleets began to fish the Western Atlantic, the Soviet Navy was much concerned over the danger posed to Soviet territory by Western aircraft carrier strike forces. To station early warning radar ships on the routes taken by such forces was deemed prudent; to use the standard trawler as the basis for these ships meant that spare parts fuel and lubricants of appropriate grades could readily be obtained from the fishing fleet tankers and depot ships, thus allowing maximum time on station for the early warning ELINT ships. The policy has been followed in the Indo-Pacific region, where ELINT trawlers regularly appear off US bases such as Pearl Harbour and Guam, presumably to monitor the arrivals and departures of US naval units, such as the seven missile submarines stationed in the Pacific.[35]

A further Soviet naval presence in the Indian and Pacific has been that of naval auxiliary vessels associated with oceanography and the space programme. Among the work carried out by the hydrographic ships is surveying of the ocean bottom, work which is obviously of use to the Navy, especially the submarine fleet, but the ships are also employed in marine biology, particularly in study of fish movements. The Soviet Union's fleet of 55 survey ships is more than twice as large as that of the United States;[36] in part this is due to the low importance of fish in the American diet, in part to the fact that with much longer coastlines than the USA, more ships are required for hydrographic work off the coasts. Nevertheless, the increase in Soviet naval presence on the high seas has been matched by increases in the survey fleet, and while this does not prove a causal connection, it indicates a strong possibility of one.

Space-associated ships are also classified as naval auxiliaries, and in the Indo-Pacific region appear in two distinct contexts. Usually four or so missile observation ships are stationed in the expected descent areas of Soviet missiles launched from Baykonur test range in Central Asia, to splash-down in the Pacific. They also tend to appear when American missiles or French nuclear weapons are being tested, obviously in order to record telemetry or operators' radio conversations for processing in the Soviet Union. In that sense they perform a spying function similar to that of ELINT trawlers,

---

[35] *The Military Balance 1970-71,* p. 2.
[36] *Jane's Fighting Ships, 1969-70,* pp. 578-9.

but practised as a matter of course by all powers whose resources permit it. Soviet space-programme ships in the Indian Ocean frequently perform a different function. Both the United States and the Soviet Union make extensive use of reconnaissance satellites to safeguard themselves against surprise attack. These are normally launched into polar (north-south) orbits, so that rotation of the earth beneath them enables a different strip of the adversary's territory to be scanned on each orbit. Film or tape for subsequent analysis is normally ejected in recoverable capsules, which it is desirable to recover over water—partly because there is less risk of impact damage, and partly because a malfunction over dry land could result in a capsule's landing on neutral or adversary territory, with a risk of international complications far worse than the inconvenience attendant upon occasional loss of a capsule sunk at sea. US-launched satellite capsules are usually recovered in or over the Pacific or Western Atlantic, Soviet ones in the Indian Ocean.

An aspect of Soviet Indian Ocean activity so far unexplained has been the laying of mooring buoys in international waters off the East coast of Africa.[37] These could serve as rendezvous points for merchant, fishing or warships. Whatever their purpose, they are not 'bases', but information as to the types of ships which use them, or the frequency with which they are used, has not been released by any of the governments which monitor them (for example the South African or British, whose forces can, and presumably do, maintain surveillance by ships or aircraft from Simonstown).

The Soviet presence in the Indian Ocean, modest though it is, has given rise to some speculation[38] on possible intentions to interfere with Western oil traffic from the Persian Gulf to Europe, and the British Government used this argument in an attempt to justify its decision to resume arms sales to South Africa.[39] From a purely naval point of view, the argument makes little sense. If such interference is contemplated, it is most expediently conducted in places where the targets (tankers) must funnel into relatively narrow channels, for example at the exit from the Gulf itself, the English Channel, or the Western Mediterranean. There is no bottleneck at the Cape of Good Hope; tankers are not compelled to 'hug the corner' and can in fact utilise a lane several hundred miles wide between the Cape and the northern limits of the Antarctic ice. Also, as a logistic proposition, the Cape is the furthest possible point from

---

[37] *The Times*, 18 December 1969.
[38] Eg., in *The Gulf: Implications of British Withdrawal*, Georgetown University Centre for Strategic and International Studies, Washington, 1969.
[39] Edward Heath, speech at Singapore Conference, January 1971.

Soviet bases, whether in the Pacific or in Europe, thus prolonging the transits of the vessels destined to do the 'interfering'. It is also about as far removed as any point on the earth could be from Soviet air support while it is very close to an active Western base (Simonstown). Any Soviet intention to 'interfere' with Western oil traffic could be far better realised in the Northern part of the Indian Ocean, near the points where all tankers must pass through a relatively restricted exit, nearer to Soviet fleet bases and to Soviet airfields in Southern USSR, or in Egypt, and, equally important, also several days' steaming from Simonstown. The importance of the Cape route to Australia should not be allowed to obscure the fact that very little of the shipping which passes the Cape is Australian. Most of it sails under the Liberian flag (but is usually US-owned), or those of Britain, Norway, Italy, Greece, France and West Germany—and to interfere with it is to interfere with NATO, which controls the narrow exits of the Baltic and Black Sea, used by most Soviet shipping engaged in foreign trade. Approximately a quarter of the shipping passing the Cape is Soviet-owned (though this includes trawlers which pass the Cape more than once a year in transit between East and West African fishing grounds),[40] and this constitutes a 'hostage' for good behaviour, a fact which Soviet admirals are probably as aware of as anyone.

Although viable combat missions for the Soviet 'flag-showing' forces are not easy to find, some possibilities suggest themselves. Of the 41 American missile-firing submarines (all nuclear propelled, and therefore of practically unlimited radius of action), 7, with 112 missiles, are deployed in the Pacific. All are armed with the Polaris A-3, a missile of 2500 nautical mile range, and are in course of conversion to the Poseidon missile, of similar range, greater payload, and capable of taking a larger number of warheads than the A-3.[41] Although what little is known of these submarines' movements indicates that they remain in the Pacific (and are intended to attack targets in the Soviet Far East, East Siberia and perhaps China in the event of nuclear war), a far wider range of targets would be open to them from the North-West Indian Ocean, including all the European USSR as far north as Moscow, the whole of Transcaucasus and Central Asia, and much of Western Siberia. The status of anti-submarine warfare is not promising—since the Second World War improvements in detection capabilities have not been sufficient to offset the increases in range of sub-

---

[40] See *South African Digest* 5 March 1971, pp. 8-10, for some data on Soviet shipping movements around the Cape.
[41] *Jane's Fighting Ships 1969-70*, p. 387.

marines and of their missiles, which have vastly enlarged the areas to be searched. But anti-submarine warfare continues to develop, presumably in the hope of a technological breakthrough in detection, currently its major area of weakness. It is possible therefore that both the naval expeditions to the Indian Ocean and the basing of bombers in Egypt represent a Soviet attempt at 'area familiarisation', in the expectation that the US Navy will eventually utilise the Indian Ocean as a deployment area for Fleet Ballistic Missile Submarines. In this connection they may well, rightly or wrongly, have linked the building of a US Navy communications station at North West Cape in Western Australia (agreed 1963, completed 1967), the Polaris A-3 (operational since 1964), the Poseidon (operational 1970) and the plan for a joint US-UK naval facility on Diego Garcia, as indicating an operational plan for missile submarine deployment in the Indian Ocean, and decided to preempt Western action to the limited extent possible. If the Soviet Navy has a mission in the Indian Ocean beyond that of 'showing the flag', an anti-submarine mission is consistent with its post-war role, and responds, however inadequately, to a tangible threat to the Soviet Union. Putative missions to 'interfere' with Cape route shipping are, in any event, more easily carried out by submarines than by small surface forces with no organic air support, and are therefore less convincing as tasks for the Soviet surface ships so far seen in the Indian Ocean.

A possible explanation for the small Soviet presence in the Indian Ocean suggests itself if the requirements not merely of naval but also of arms control policy are taken into account. The potential attractiveness of the North-West Indian Ocean would have become apparent in 1963-4, with progress of the Polaris A-3 test programme (realisation of its potential required no more than routine map-work such as had already been applied to the Mediterranean in 1962-3), and probably led to representations from the naval staff to the government. During the period in question, Khrushchev was engaged in pursuit of detente, and is likely to have reacted adversely to the idea that the Soviet Navy should begin to expand its activities into yet another ocean, while the squadron in the Mediterranean was just being built up (from May 1963 onwards). His preferred solution would have been to seek a mutual self-denying ordinance with the United States; this line of reasoning is consistent with the Soviet proposal of 7 December 1964, that the Indian Ocean should be 'denuclearised', that is, that the Powers should agree to maintain no forces with nuclear capability (submarines or strike carriers) in it. The West rejected the proposal; this should perhaps have led to an early appearance of 'area familiarisation' forces, but none appeared for over three years. There are a number of possible explanations for this, all conjectural but none apparently unreasonable. The newly-elected British Labour government was undecided about the future of its East of Suez policy, and if the Soviets considered British withdrawal from the Indian Ocean to be in their interests, it would have been unwise to weaken the arguments for withdrawal by moving into the area until the British had committed themselves to moving out. From the naval point of view, the force most conveniently located to supply an Indian Ocean squadron (i.e. the Black Sea Fleet, until closure of the Suez Canal in June 1967), was heavily engaged in building up the Mediterranean Fleet, while the much more distant Pacific Fleet was building up its experience of long-range cruising with visits to such countries as Indonesia.

The government and the Navy were very probably pursuing conflicting objectives. The government (and the strategic planners) would have no reason to disagree with the Navy about the potential attractiveness of the Indian Ocean as a deployment area for missile submarines and strike carriers (the US Navy acquired two types of long-range aircraft, capable of carrying nuclear weapons to distances not much less than those of a submarine missile), but would also note that the area offered no such attractive targets for the Soviet Navy. Their objective would remain that of persuading the US to stay out of the Indian Ocean, and having failed to secure this by means of the December 1964 proposals, they would have to seek other means. The most obvious would be to enlist the local powers of the Indian Ocean littoral in opposition to a great power arms race in that area. To raise such a spectre would require action on the Soviet part, as the United States was at the time making clear its unwillingness to take up any commitments shed by the British. To send in a small force of ships, for short visits, could arouse the spectre of an arms race without the reality of one, and give time for opposition to ripen, without forcing the Americans to react at once. At the same time, it would enable the Navy to proceed with area familiarisation, thus lessening the importunities of the admirals, and insuring against the possibility that no agreement would be reached.

So in April 1968, when the British decision to withdraw had been taken, a small force was sent in. Too small to constitute a credible threat, its mere appearance nevertheless aroused concern about the future, especially in Australia. Rumours of a Soviet search for bases were retailed, and neutral countries helped to create a state of alarm, because although indignantly denying intention to provide bases themselves, they were prepared to believe that hostile neighbours might. In the United States, the prospect of indefinite extension of Soviet naval power led to agitation for a riposte, including a massive programme of reconstruction and renewal of naval tonnage. In due course the US Administration, faced with the possibility of enlarged naval responsibilities and costs on the one hand, and a perceived need to counter the Soviet presence on the other, was to announce that it intended to detach units of its Seventh Fleet in the Pacific for occasional cruises in the Indian Ocean, and, more importantly for the Soviet leaders, that it was prepared to discuss the neutralisation proposal which it had rejected in 1964.

This line of reasoning is, of course, largely conjectural but is consistent with:

1. The postponement of visits until the British had announced their decision to withdraw.
2. The smallness of the presence, which has averaged no more than four warships at a time in the first half of each year, and two in the second.
3. The inclusion in most of the forces of SAM and SAM/SSM ships as well as anti-submarine ships, designed to provide protection against a carrier's aircraft long enough to sink the carrier, and to provide anti-submarine capability as well.
4. The periodic inclusion of submarines, to provide additional capacity against a carrier, at least to keep it at a distance, at most to provide an additional means of sinking the carrier.
5. Failure of the 'presence' to escalate appreciably since 1968. In 1969, nine surface units spent some part of the year cruising the Indian Ocean, in 1970, 11, and in 1971, 10. This suggests that the military requirement is less important than the political one of appearing in just enough strength to arouse and sustain debate. In the Mediterranean, the presence escalated very fast to about 40 ships between the first 'cruise' in May 1963 and the Suez Canal crisis of 1967. There, because of the presence of the US Sixth Fleet and other NATO navies, a definite combat task existed.
6. Soviet tardiness in commenting on even the more ludicrous suggestions concerning bases (eg. in Mauritius, which has a defence agreement with the UK, and offered it a base there as an alternative to Simonstown, which it would hardly have done if the landing rights agreement of July 1970 was to serve as a basis for a semi-clandestine Soviet facility). If one of the

objectives of the exercise is to 'create an atmosphere', there is nothing to be gained by denying even the most absurd rumours. They can, after all, be checked by US or British intelligence organisations with little difficulty, so there is no danger that the *governments* concerned will be misled by them, and if gullible publicists are, so much the better.

7. The dispatch of two naval units past Singapore, while the British arguments for resuming arms sales to South Africa (hinging, as they did, on a purported Soviet naval threat) were being hotly debated.

8. The US 'leak' (Melbourne *Age,* 27 April 1971), of an alleged proposal to discuss neutralisation of the Indian Ocean, said to emanate from a committee of the National Security Council, and subsequent official admission in February 1972 that discussions had been initiated.

9. The US decision, made public a few days before the 'leak' to send a squadron to cruise the Indian Ocean, and later announcement that occasional but regular visits would be undertaken. This squadron was larger than any the Soviets had sent in (one anti-submarine carrier, four destroyers and a nuclear submarine), suggesting that the US sees itself as in a 'stick and carrot' situation, the 'carrot' being the leaked proposal to talk about neutralisation, the 'stick' the threat to send in larger forces. That the US itself wishes to observe a very graduated escalation was perhaps shown by the composition of the force, the carrier being twice as large as any Soviet warship, but not a strike carrier, the submarine nuclear-powered but not a missile-firer; the force, in short, avoiding fulfilling the Soviet naval staff's 'prophecies'.

10. Brezhnev's disclosure (*Canberra Times* 14 June 1971), that among the subjects which the Soviet Union wishes to discuss with the United States is that of 'limiting the cruises of navies in distant waters'.

The hypothesis that the Soviet objectives are twofold—primarily, to achieve a limitation on nuclear strike forces in the Indian Ocean, by restricting naval appearances there to low-level 'flag showing', or perhaps eliminating them altogether, and secondarily, to achieve area familiarisation in case the primary objective proves unattainable—appears to fit the observed facts better than other hypotheses of unrestrained naval ambition, intent to interfere with commercial traffic, or preoccupation solely with the potential danger from nuclear submarines or strike carriers. However, detailed information is insufficient to permit firm conclusions.

The arguments against the likelihood of peacetime Soviet interference with shipping in the Indian Ocean also apply to the Pacific but with even greater force because of the strong US and growing Japanese naval forces deployed there. In theory a blockade of the Malacca Straits could cut off most of Japan's oil supply. In practice, advanced industrial countries, warned by the problems which arose from blockage of the Suez Canal in 1956, no longer live from hand to mouth where oil is concerned; most have stockpiles adequate to cover interruption of the supply for some weeks, during which time Japan and its allies (notably the United States) would be expected to bring pressure to bear for removal of the blockade as well as to arrange supply from sources immune to it (eg. by re-routing of tankers from Indonesian, US or South American oilfields). In general war, of course, all belligerents could be expected to interfere with enemy shipping, but neither superpower expects this to be a major contribution to winning a nuclear war,[42] and neither allocates a large proportion of its naval budget to the anti-shipping role, since neither apparently expects a nuclear war to last long enough for attrition of seaborne supplies to have decisive effects. Most submarines are designed to attack other warships (carriers or guided missile ships), to fire missiles at civilian targets, or to attack other submarines in defence of their own side's surface fleets or missile submarines. With the shift in power from European states to superpowers whose survival does not depend on seaborne food and raw materials (as did Britain's in all circumstances, and Germany's if Russia was not allied or conquered), the emphasis on naval blockade in general war has diminished; the main exception to this—the North Atlantic route between America and its European allies—has become less important with increases in airlift capability, prepositioning of heavy equipment, and abandonment by NATO of the concept of a long conventional campaign in Europe.[43]

In the Pacific itself, as opposed to the boundary areas between the Indian and Pacific Oceans, Soviet ambition to exercise naval power is inhibited by the lack of aircraft carriers (without which its surface units can operate only within reach of land-based air cover), by its landlocked situation in the Sea of Japan, and by the countervailing power of United States naval forces and the far from

---

[42] The Soviet view is plainly expressed in Sokolovsky (ed.) *Military Strategy,* Ministry of Defence Publishing House, Moscow, 1968, pp. 362-3 'Combat operations in naval theatres in a future world war would be of wide scope, but these operations can scarcely have a decisive effect on the outcome of the war'.

[43] British Defence White Paper, 1968.

negligible Japanese Maritime Self Defence Force. Nevertheless, the ability to 'show the flag', which has little connection with actual combat capability, is open to it here as elsewhere, and will be increasingly exercised in the future, both to counter Western influence and to bolster the resolve of countries deemed liable to succumb to Chinese influence or pressure.[44]

In common with other aspects of Soviet conduct of policy, strategy is formulated within a doctrinal framework, which it is now appropriate to examine. The doctrinal framework is laid down at a political level (eg. in Khrushchev's speeches of 14 January 1960 or 6 January 1961), and elaborated for the military in their specialist press (the newspaper *Red Star,* and a number of periodicals). Occasionally a comprehensive treatment of problems of war and strategy is given in book form. The standard work of this kind for the professional enlightenment of the Soviet officer is the book *Military Strategy,* first published in 1962 and extensively revised before republication in 1963 and 1968. Its authors (a team of 15 officers of the rank of colonel or above, headed by a former Chief of the General Staff, Marshal of the Soviet Union, V. D. Sokolovski) include no airmen or sailors,[45] despite the fact that the book is intended for all-service use, and in that is typical of the army-centred Soviet defence structure. However, a number of complaints by naval officers about the sketchy treatment of naval matters in the first edition[46] have resulted in some expansion of the sections devoted to naval operations, but shed no light on the role of the Indian Ocean in future war. In discussing the role of the missile-firing submarine in American war planning, for example, the authors said 'At the start of a war [US] missile firing submarines may be deployed at launching points up to a distance of 1800 kilometres from the [Soviet] coast, above all in the Arctic Ocean and the northern seas, the North-Eastern Atlantic, the Mediterranean and the Western Pacific',[47] but made no mention of the Indian Ocean. The authors' position on nuclear and local war was unambiguous; nuclear war was so potentially destructive of world civilisation that it must be avoided (not so much by 'capitulationism', as the Chinese alleged the Soviets to interpret it, but by

---

[44] See the author's 'The Soviet Military and Asia', *World Review,* June 1970, and 'Soviet Naval Policy, East of Suez', *World Review,* July 1971.

[45] Sokolovsky (ed.), *op. cit.,* Ministry of Defence Publishing House, Moscow, 1962, 1963, 1968, title page (all editions), prefaces to 2nd and 3rd editions.

[46] Of which that by Admiral V. A. Alafuzov 'On the Appearance of the work "Military Strategy"', *Morskoy Sbornik* (Naval Anthology), January 1963, pp. 88-96 was the most comprehensive and authoritative.

[47] Sokolovsky (ed.) *op. cit.,* 3rd edition, p. 365.

deterrence); local war was also to be avoided or deterred, because of its potential for escalation into world nuclear war.[48] 'National liberation wars', however, posed a more difficult problem of definition. Khrushchev's own formulation of January 1961, which is still 'official' doctrine, stressed the need to support them—without any attempt to define 'support'—but described them as 'not wars between states'. While this definition covered the case of internal insurrection, it could not doctrinally be stretched to cover a government which, faced with such an insurrection, calls for assistance from allies, unless it was assumed additionally that the statement 'these are not wars between states' implied 'they must not *be allowed to become* wars between states'. The practical interpretation of the actual and implied statements was that in such cases a Soviet intervention *in support of insurgency* would convert the war from one of national liberation (to be supported) into a local war (to be avoided); that therefore Soviet troops would not be used to support wars of national liberation; but that intervention *at the request of a government* would not constitute a 'war between states'. In the United States it was assumed that Khrushchev's speech might herald an era of more aggressive Soviet support for left-wing insurrections; in practice, this did not prove to be the case. Soviet aid, economic and military, continued to flow predominantly to non-Communist governments, and such actual involvement of Soviet military personnel in combat as occurred was all at governmental invitation—manning of SAM sites in North Vietnam in 1966 (while North Vietnamese were being trained to take them over), manning of SAMs and some interceptor aircraft in Egypt in 1970 and in assisting a neutralist government of Ceylon in 1971 to mount counter-insurgency operations against the ultra-Left 'Che Guevarist' guerilla movement. While the Soviet definition of support has ranged from the purely verbal to heavy supply of arms and support of the economy, as in the case of North Vietnam, offers to supply combat forces to insurrectionary movements have not formed part of the doctrine. The only apparent exception to this was a public declaration of willingness to send 'volunteers' to North Vietnam if requested; but to send them to *North* Vietnam would not violate the doctrine, provided they were not then dispatched to *South* Vietnam; and as North Vietnam did not need manpower, it was probable that the offer would not be taken up. Besides, in view of North Vietnam's dependence on Soviet economic aid, it would have been easy to ensure by a behind-the-scenes warning, that North Vietnam would, as it did, disclaim any need for volunteers.

[48] *Ibid.*, 2nd ed. pp. 7-8, 80-96, 3rd ed. pp. 9-10, 71-89.

The Chinese attacked the Soviets for alleged lack of support for the national liberation movement on a number of occasions,[49] and after one especially violent onslaught, in November 1963, Soviet defence of its record became more assertive, Khrushchev in December making the first public claim of Soviet assistance to the Algerian rebels—though without stating that the war in Algeria had been in progress for several years before Soviet arms aid was given. But even when attempting to defend their past record, Soviet leaders were careful to give no hostages to the future, either by indicating where they considered the maximum and minimum limits of support to lie, or the areas where they expected to provide it. Even when a North Vietnamese writer (in *Hoc Tap,* Hanoi, April 1964) berated them for over-preoccupation with nuclear weapons and the dangers of escalation, and for abandoning Leninism by taking the view that in the nuclear age war had become too dangerous to be an instrument of politics, no notice was taken at the political level.

In professional military circles, however, senior Soviet officers were showing considerable interest in problems of limited and local war. This interest was prompted by a number of factors, not all of which were explicit. Under the impact of the 'MacNamara Doctrine', unveiled publicly by the then US Secretary of Defense in a speech made at Ann Arbor, Michigan, in July 1962, but heralded in a number of President Kennedy's statements on defence during 1961,[50] the United States was engaged in increasing its conventional capabilities by raising new combat divisions, developing new non-nuclear weapons, and increasing the versatility for non-nuclear missions of existing weapons, especially strike aircraft. It was also urging its NATO allies (on the whole unsuccessfully) to do the same. Since Khrushchev's argument against involvement in local wars was based on the risk of escalation by use of nuclear weapons, moves by NATO to reduce its dependence on tactical nuclear weapons struck at its philosophical basis, and necessitated re-examination of the Soviet assumption that its conventional theatre forces were sufficiently strong to deter a NATO-initiated local war. There was also the example of American efforts to increase strategic mobility by introduction of larger transport aircraft, and of the successful use of strategic mobility by the Americans and British in a number of situations since 1945 to influence local situations with forces which by Soviet standards were minuscule. In December 1963 the Commander-in-Chief of

---

[49] Discussed in the Chapter on Sino-Soviet relations, q.v.
[50] Eg., those of 25th March, and 25th May 1961.

Ground Forces, Marshal Chuykov, drew attention to NATO increases in conventional capabilities, without denigrating them, and thereby implied to his professional readers that the Soviet Army should follow suit.[51] About this time—though its existence was not disclosed until July 1964—a Marine force was set up for the first time.[52] It was not clear whether the Soviet interest related solely to peripheral local wars around the frontier of the bloc; because though Chuykov drew specific attention to the NATO area, the Marines could indicate an interest in distant limited wars, for example in Asia or Africa. This might have indicated a possible intention to compete in militancy with the Chinese and provide highly mobile forces, which the Chinese could not, to aid anti-Western governments or even insurgent movements.

In the event, it turned out to mean none of these things. The outcome of Marshal Chuykov's statements was his retirement and the temporary abolition of his post, while the Marines remained a small force, with limited afloat support, suggesting that their primary role was amphibious assaults on coastlines or islands auxiliary to ground force operations in large-scale war, rather than independent operations at great distances. Speculation by Soviet officers in professional journals continued until well into 1966,[53] but Khrushchev's successors eventually reiterated that the primary objective of the Soviet armed forces was deterrence of wars, rather than the fighting of them.[54] This did not imply neglect of the conventional forces; on the contrary, they continued to receive new equipment and in 1967 several new models of ground attack aircraft were displayed.[55] But their equipment, training, and doctrines for their employment remained oriented towards a highly mechanised mobile war in the European theatre, while the major increases after 1965 came in the strategic nuclear forces, indicating that, as the Brezhnev-Kosygin regime had emphasised, deterrence remained the chief preoccupation and NATO the main enemy. When redeployment did take place—in 1969—it took the form of movement of a few divisions towards the borders with China, in the

---

[51] *Red Star,* 10 December 1963.

[52] It was widely taken in the West as a 'reconstitution' of a force—the 'Naval Infantry' which existed in W.W. II. But the 'naval infantry' were in fact formed *ad hoc* from the crews of sunken, immobilised or redundant ships, and fought as conventional infantry, far from the sea.

[53] Eg. Colonel E. Rybkin in *Kommunist Voouzhennykh Sil* No. 17, (Armed Forces Communist) September 1965, pp. 50-6, Colonel Bondarenko, in the same journal in September 1966.

[54] *Red Star,* 24 January 1967.

[55] Discussed in *Strategic Survey 1967,* Institute for Strategic Studies, London 1968, pp. 13-21.

wake of the Ussuri River incident of 31 March. Throughout the 60s, therefore, Soviet military policy showed no tangible interest in the development of capabilities for giving direct support to wars in Asia, except around the Soviet periphery, and there only in connection with the Sino-Soviet border. In that sense it remained profoundly conservative. In military, as in political and economic terms, despite the obvious importance attached to some of its component countries (India throughout, Indonesia until 1965, and Vietnam from 1964 onwards), Asia as a whole figured well below Europe in Soviet thinking.

# 4

# Political Relationships—Indian Ocean Asia

It is impossible in a short space to deal with every feature of Soviet relationships with all countries in Asia. Because of the Soviet Union's position within an international movement, its foreign relations with most countries comprise two main strands—on the one hand its dealings with the elements which actually wield power within each country, and, on the other, its relationship with the indigenous Communist Party, or, where that Party is banned, with the left-wing party which most closely approximates it, subsumes it, or, in some cases, conceals it.

## TURKEY

Of the countries which geographically form part of Asia, not all regard their interests as lying in giving importance to an Asian role. Turkey has for many years given priority to its associations with countries west and north of it, in part through Atatürk's determination to divorce it from its Ottoman associations with the Moslem world, which he regarded as a bar to essential modernisation,[1] and also, more recently, through the belief that protection against the only neighbouring country strong enough to pose a threat to Turkey —the Soviet Union—was to be sought through association with the technologically advanced countries of the West and by membership of American-sponsored alliance systems, first NATO and later CENTO as well.

The Turks were given a powerful push into alliance with the

[1] Luke, Sir H., *The Old Turkey and the New*, Bles, London, 1955, pp. 174-229.

West through Soviet attempts in 1946 to secure totally unfettered exit from and entry to the Black Sea. Stalin sought revision of the Montreux Convention of 1888, and a Soviet base on the Straits, as well as hinting at the possible revival of Soviet territorial claims in respect of the Kars and Ardahan areas of Eastern Turkey.[2] These tactics assisted to propel Turkey both into NATO and into the Balkan Pact, in which it allied itself with long-standing enemies, Greece and Yugoslavia. Turco-Soviet relations remained almost non-existent well into the 1960s, but in the second half of the decade improved considerably, particularly after the progress of the Cyprus crisis showed that Turkish membership of NATO was of no assistance in gaining a settlement on terms favourable to Turkey. Soviet support for the Greek Cypriots, which extended at first to provision of arms, was moderated somewhat after the Turkish government hinted in 1964 at its willingness to invoke its right of search against Soviet merchant shipping passing through the Bosporus, and during the latter part of the decade Turco-Soviet relations have improved somewhat, especially in trade. However, Turkey's international position has not altered radically, as however good relations may be with the Soviet Union, it remains the only power in the area against which Turkey might require protection. Short of a complete political bouleversement within Turkey, this situation remains a fact of international life. Turkey is atypical of Asia in its orientation towards Europe and its comparative indifference to the Moslem world, most of which it once ruled. Insofar as Soviet relations with it are not determined by its NATO membership, they focus on the fact that most Soviet Central Asians are Turkic by race, language or both. Turkey's economic performance has been unimpressive alongside that of Soviet Central Asia (though less so compared with Azerbaijan), and Central Asian nationalism, being very largely Soviet-created, does not look upon union with Turkey as an alternative to membership of the Soviet Union. Turkey's 'drawing power' for Soviet Central Asians is therefore small, and, in the reverse direction, the economic attractions of Soviet Central Asia are not sufficient to outweigh for most Turks who think about them (very few do) either their suspicion of Russia or their hostility to Communism.

IRAN AND IRAQ

The same arguments apply, though with considerable qualifications, to Iran and Iraq. In the case of Iran, trade has been an important indicator of political detente; Soviet interest in Iranian

---

[2] For an account of the Soviet claims see *Keesing's Contemporary Archives* 1946, pp. 7737-8 and 8076.

oil and natural gas, which could conveniently be piped to the refining and loading facilities on the 'dying' Soviet oilfield centred around Baku, has been described elsewhere in this book, and this interest will probably grow during the 1970s. But a further indication of Soviet interest in '*détente* via trade' has been shown in the 1971 Soviet-Iranian trade agreement,[3] which is similar to trade agreements with India in providing for large increases in Soviet imports of Iranian manufactured goods. In the military field, Iran, which formerly purchased all its weapons systems in the West, has in recent years purchased some of its artillery equipment from the Soviet Union,[4] but remains a member of the Central Treaty Organisation, partly no doubt as reinsurance against a repetition of the Soviet attempts in 1946 to sponsor an independent state in its wartime occupation zone in Persian Azerbaijan.

Unlike Turkey and Iran, Iraq belongs to the Arab world proper, and as such Soviet policy towards it has formed part of its nexus of obligations and undertakings in the Middle East. Changes in political alignment have been frequent. At first a member of the Baghdad Pact, its secession after General Kassem's *coup d'état* of 1958 forced that body to change its name to Central Treaty Organisation. Arms were purchased in the Soviet Union, Iraqi officers sent there to train and the influence of the Iraqi Communist Party in the trade unions, student movement and armed forces increased greatly. When Kassem refused to take Communists into the government in mid-1959, he was accused of 'treason to the revolution' by Communist press and leaders, and it began to appear that a Communist *coup* against him was imminent. Instead the Soviet leadership intervened; it charged the Iraqi Central Committee with 'incorrectness' in allowing large numbers of ultra-left extremists to join it in the National Front, in playing into the hands of counter-revolutionaries by encouraging mob violence, accusing Kassem of treason, and seeking places in the government. It 'advised' the Iraqi party to acknowledge its errors publicly, demote the leaders responsible for the mistaken policies, expel the ultra-leftists, dissociate itself from violence, and acknowledge Kassem as leader. The Iraqi Communist Party did as 'advised'.[5]

Soviet motives were probably connected with Khrushchev's

---

[3] The same is true of recent trade agreements with India, Pakistan, UAR, Brazil, Iraq and Turkey. See *USSR and Third World*, Vol. I No. 3, February-March 1971, p. 95.

[4] *The Military Balance, 1970-71*, Institute for Strategic Studies, London 1970, p. 39.

[5] Deutscher, I., *Russia, China and the West*, Oxford University Press, 1970, pp. 186-8.

impending visit to the United States; a Communist rising in the Middle East would certainly have been taken by the US government as Soviet-inspired. Besides, with the American and British interventions of 1958 in Lebanon and Jordan not far behind, Khrushchev, who appears to have feared that Western invasion of Iraq was imminent in 1958, would not have wished to see a pretext given for it in 1959. When Kassem was overthrown in 1963, and many Iraqi Communists killed, the Soviet Government protested at the arrests and executions, but was one of the first to recognise the new Government, on 11th February, 1963, three days after the *coup*. Chinese verbal militancy contrasted with Soviet conciliatoriness in this situation, as in those of 1958 and 1959.

THE INDIAN SUB-CONTINENT

The main centre of Soviet foreign-policy activity in 'Indian Ocean Asia' has undoubtedly been the Indian sub-continent. There are a number of reasons for this, some going far back into European history, others more closely linked to the emergence of Communism in Russia.

Trade links between Russia and the Mogul Empire began in the 17th century, and in 1801 the 'mad Tsar', Paul I, reached an accord with Napoleon to expel the British from India.[6] Napoleon's failure in Egypt, and preoccupation in Europe, rendered it impossible for French troops to be provided, and Paul despatched a small army on his own initiative, but the expedition was abandoned after he was assassinated. The project was revived by his successor, Alexander I, but collapsed with the breakdown of the Franco-Russian alliance. However, British knowledge of its existence, and the subsequent advance of Russian forces towards Central Asia, caused lively concern to the British in India, which expressed itself in attempts to ensure that Afghanistan remained subject to British control. However, no evidence has yet been found to suggest that Russia ever seriously contemplated annexation of India[7] rather than the mere exploitation of the India issue in order to influence British behaviour in Europe, and the St. Petersburg convention of 1907 regulated the situation to the north of British India, in order to enable both Powers to concentrate their efforts against the emergent threat from Germany.

For the early Marxists,[8] India's main importance was its role in

---

[6] Naik, J. A., *Soviet Policy Towards India*. Vikas, Delhi, 1970, pp. 3-4.
[7] Fischer, L., *The Soviets in World Affairs*, Princeton, 1951, Vol. I, p. 420.
[8] Eg. Marx, 'British Rule in India' and 'The Future Results of British Rule in India', *Collected Works* (Russian edition), Vol. II, p. 9.

'propping' British capitalism as a source of raw materials and a captive market for industrial goods. After the seizure of power in 1917, Soviet concern was mainly with Europe, both as a military threat and as a possible source of support through proletarian revolutions. The deserts and mountain barriers between Russia and the Indian sub-continent, and the unlikelihood of any threat to Russian security arising from that quarter, combined to make the Soviet southern frontiers their calmest during the interwar period. But the importance which Marx had attached to India was reflected in Lenin's writings, and the Indian Communist Party actually came into existence in Tashkent during 1919-20 with seven members, led by M. N. Roy.[9] However, firm action by the British in India put an end to the short-term prospects of a mass Communist movement, and Comintern interest then turned to the more hopeful prospects offered by cooperation with the Kuomintang in China. Lenin himself was preoccupied both with the practical problem of restoring the Russian economy (which required improved relations with the British among others), and the inevitability that independence movements in the colonial countries would at that time be led by 'bourgeois' nationalists. The one dictated a reduction in revolutionary activity in Britain's largest overseas possession, the other suggested that Communists should support the 'bourgeois' nationalists, rather than fight them. M. N. Roy disagreed, but did not prevail, and for a time the Indian Communist Party followed the Leninist line of collaboration with the Indian National Congress, even though it opposed the policy of non-violent resistance espoused by Gandhi. In 1928, the Comintern virtually dismissed the possibility of proletarian revolutions in the colonies, denounced Gandhism, Nehru and the Congress, and sanctioned non-cooperation with the nationalists by the Indian Communist Party (though undoubtedly, with no reason to believe that it mattered very much what the Indian Communists did, in view of their very small numbers, their lack of mass appeal compared with Congress, and the stiffness of British measures against them).

At this time, the Comintern decided to entrust the overseeing of Indian Communist affairs to the British Communist Party,[10] which dispatched two of its members to India for the purpose. This decision probably reflected lack of Soviet interest in India on the one hand, and, on the other, a belief that the need for tutelage could be far more easily met by British Communists than by any

---

[9] *Narody Azii i Afriki,* (Peoples of Asia and Africa), 1/1969, p. 69.
[10] Degras, J., *Comintern Documents, 1919-43,* Oxford University Press, 1956, Vol. II, p. 526.

other, because of their relative ease of access to India.[11] However, M. N. Roy protested that the move 'smacked of imperialism' and later stated that his opposition to the Comintern's decision was a key factor in his expulsion from the Comintern in 1929.[12]

The rapid changes in Soviet policy during the late 1930s caused difficulties for the Indian party, as for most others, and not until the German attack on the Soviet Union in 1941 did clear foreign policy lines emerge. Soviet ignorance of India during the 30's was almost total; the British refused entry to Soviet nationals, and in any event, the Soviet government's attention was almost wholly taken up with its west and east border problems. The Indian Communist Party during this period vacillated from hostility to the Indian National Congress, to cooperation with it and even, at the end of the 1930s, to absorption within it. The attitudes of Congress leaders varied considerably, but in view of his prominence then and later, the views of Jawaharlal Nehru are worth noting. In 1936 he referred to the Soviet Union in the following terms:

> ... Much has happened there which has pained me greatly, and with which I disagree, but I look upon that great and fascinating unfolding of a new order and new civilisation as the most promising feature of our dismal age ... It is interesting to note in that monumental and impressive record, the Webbs' new book on Russia, how the whole Soviet structure is based on a wide and living democratic foundation ... There has been no such practical application of the democratic process in history ...[13]

The passage is more interesting for its indication of the source of his views than for its accuracy as description of Stalin's USSR. Nehru had not then visited the Soviet Union, and the quotation shows that his ideas on it were derived from those of British Fabian Socialism, in particular the thoroughly misleading *Soviet Communism: A new Civilisation* by Sidney and Beatrice Webb. Given that this was his view, he was not at that time hostile to the Communist Party of India, and did not object to its joining the Congress.

In 1940, the defeatism of the British Communist Party (then obliged to support the Soviet-German alliance) led to a ban on its newspaper, and serious consideration to a ban on the Party itself.[14] This did not eventuate in Britain, but was put into effect in many parts of the Empire, including India. When Russia entered the

---

11 Naik, *op.cit.,* p. 19.
12 Roy, M. N., *Our Differences,* Saraswati, Calcutta, 1938, p. ii.
13 Speech at the Lucknow meeting of the Indian National Congress, 1936.
14 Brome, V., *Aneurin Bevan,* Longmans, 1953, pp 130-1.

war the CPI, like the British Communist Party, ceased to oppose the British war effort, and in 1942 the ban was lifted. However, the circumstances attending on legalisation were to prove politically harmful to it in the post-war situation, because CPI support for the British from 1942 onwards put it in opposition to the Congress. The British defeats in Asia at the end of 1941 had been welcomed by some of the Congress leaders as foreshadowing Indian independence. Gandhi had some reservations, and Nehru welcomed Japanese success not at all, since his internationalist background had made him profoundly anti-Fascist. Nevertheless Gandhi launched the 'Quit India' campaign in 1942, and the Congress was therefore declared illegal and its leaders interned, rendering Congress politically impotent until their release in 1944. During the two years hiatus, the newly-legalised Communists, hitherto a very small band of intellectuals, began building a base of mass support, with no opposition from the British. The resentment which this action aroused in the Congress leaders was manifested in 1945, when the CPI was expelled from the Congress, and on a number of occasions after independence. Mass demonstrations against the British broke out in mid-1945, but the CPI refrained from supporting them until the beginning of 1946, and did so only after the Soviet Union's relations with Britain had begun to deteriorate into the Cold War.

As antagonism between Congress and the Muslim League mounted, and the British began to plan against the wishes of Congress for a divided sub-continent, the Soviet Union denounced the device as a means to perpetuate their control over India, by creating two hostile states and acting as arbiter between them.[15] In April 1947 the Soviet and Provisional Indian governments announced their intention of exchanging ambassadors, but indications were soon forthcoming that Stalin's attitude was hostile. These indications were confirmed, when the Cominform (Communist Information Bureau, successor to the Communist International, which had been disbanded in 1943) held its inaugural meeting in September 1947. At this meeting Andrey Zhdanov, a leading associate of Stalin, advanced the thesis that the world was divided into two camps, the anti-imperialist (the Soviet Union and its allies) and the imperialist (the rest of the world, including the states which professed themselves non-aligned).[16]

The effect of the 'two camps' thesis was to strengthen pressures for a 'left strategy' of non-cooperation with, extending even to

[15] For an account of Soviet comments on partition see Druhe, D. N., *Soviet Russia and Indian Communism 1917-47*, Bookman Associates, New York, 1959, pp. 269-283.

[16] *For a Lasting Peace, For a People's Democracy*, 10 November 1947.

violent opposition to, non-Communist nationalism, and India was one of the countries in which Communist militancy erupted into violence in 1947-8, along with Burma, Indonesia and Malaya. It does not appear that this violence was directly orchestrated by Moscow, but had Moscow not approved, the Cominform machinery would certainly have been invoked to stop it then, as it in fact was to be in 1950.

In India implementation of the 'left strategy' was immediate. A 'South-East Asian Youth Conference' held in Calcutta in February 1948 endorsed the 'two camps' thesis, and the Second Party Congress of the CPI, held simultaneously and also in Calcutta, did the same.[17] The General Secretary, P. C. Joshi, was replaced by the militant B. T. Ranadive. Although Party membership had increased considerably, it was still minute on the Indian scale, at 89,000 members,[18] mostly middle-class intellectuals, and in refusing to become a mass party like the Congress, followed closely Lenin's concept of the pre-revolutionary party as a small, tightly disciplined and highly organised force. However, unlike the Russian party, the CPI was plagued by dissent between its central organisation and the regions both over the desirability of violence at all, and, between those who did accept violence, over the desirability or otherwise of enlisting as allies the 'richer' peasants and the bourgeois nationalists, or between violence in the cities and peasant uprisings in the countryside. At first the national leadership prevailed, and uprisings took place in Andhra Pradesh, West Bengal, and Travancore-Cochin. The peasant revolt in Telengana was especially fierce, but the Andhra Provincial Committee of the CPI, which was directing it, had doubts about the wisdom of confining revolutionary efforts to the poorer peasants, and in June 1948 submitted a document to the Indian Politburo suggesting they enrol the richer peasants and left-wing 'bourgeois' nationalists as allies, as the Chinese Communists had done. Ranadive refused, attacked Mao Tse-Tung by name (he classed him with Tito, who had just been expelled from the Cominform as a major heretic), described his strategy as 'counter-revolutionary', and ordered violence to continue, especially in the cities. It went on throughout 1949, but firm action by the Indian government and state authorities (including the banning of the Communist Party in the areas then in revolt, and detention of about 2,500 Party members) was

17 Rothermund, Indira, *Die Spaltung der Kommunistischen Partei Indiens*, Harrassowitz, Wiesbaden, 1969, p. 5.
18 Smirnova, A. A. (Ed.), *Strany Yuzhnoy Azii (Politiko-ekonomicheskiy Spravochnik)* (The Countries of Southern Asia, a Political-economic Handbook), Moscow, 1968, p. 83.

successful in suppressing or containing the insurgencies. Pursuit of the violent and unsuccessful policies alienated many supporters, and Party membership fell from 89,000 in 1948, to about 25,000 in 1950.[19]

At this point the Cominform intervened. On 27th January 1950 its journal *For a Lasting Peace, for a People's Democracy* condemned the CPI's tactics, declaring armed uprisings 'inappropriate' to the situation and recommending that the CPI form a united front with 'all classes, parties, groups and organisations' which were prepared to defend India's independence and freedom.

The CPI agreed to implement the Cominform directive, but regionalism and factionalism made this a slow process. Ranadive was replaced only in June, his place being taken by Rajeshwar Rao, leader of the Andhra Provincial Committee, and the violence in Telengana continued throughout the year, despite the Cominform's condemnation of it.

In April 1951 the Indian Politburo rejected the Chinese guerilla warfare model, dismissed Rao (replacing him by Ajoy Ghosh), and ordered an end to the Telengana insurrection (which in fact continued for some months thereafter).[20] The episode showed the limitations of the CPI as an instrument of Cominform (i.e. Soviet) policy, in that the Telengana revolt could not be stopped by Cominform fiat, but continued almost to the end of 1951, nearly two years after the Cominform denunciation of armed risings, and six or seven months after the CPI itself ordered it to stop. This reflected in part its scattered nature (it was strong only in a few areas, such as Hyderabad in Andhra Pradesh, West Bengal and Travancore-Cochin, while in many others no Party organisation existed at all).

Nevertheless, the switch to a more moderate policy, and the concentration of strength in a few areas, bore fruit in the political arena. The ban on the Party in Madras and West Bengal was lifted in mid-1950, leaders were released, and in the first Indian general election (end of 1951—beginning of 1952) the CPI contested 70 of the 489 seats, winning 16 of them, and thus embarking on a course of Parliamentary participation which it has followed with varying fortunes ever since.

Signs of direct Soviet interest in India were lacking until after the death of Stalin; the Cominform directive of 27 January 1950 marked more the abandonment of an unsuccessful policy than initiation of a new one aimed at short-term results. The small size of

[19] *Ibid.*, p. 84.
[20] Rothermund, Indira, *op. cit.*, pp. 6-8.

the Party, the appeal of the Congress to the masses, and Stalin's own scepticism about both the genuineness of India's independence and the prospects for proletarian revolution in it combined to perpetuate the low level of Soviet interest characteristic of the pre-war years. A leading Soviet Indologist summed up the accepted Soviet view of Congress government in 1951 with the words 'India . . . is a country in which the dictatorship of bourgeoisie and landowners appears in its most nakedly terroristic form',[21] while the *Greater Soviet Encyclopedia's* hostile evaluation of Gandhi in 1953 ('Gandhi's role in the evolution of the national liberation movement reflects the treacherous outlook of India's upper classes and liberal landowners. These made common cause with the imperialists against the people, and regarded their own people as their main enemy')[22] was no more than typical of Soviet disdain for a country still at that time hovering only on the periphery of Soviet interest.

One of India's first important acts as an independent non-aligned country was its role in helping to end the Korean War. Although Stalin took no public note of it, the Indian mediation both helped to extract the Soviet Union from an unsuccessful and burdensome foreign policy adventure, and illustrated its willingness to play an autonomous part in international affairs, which cannot have gone unnoticed in Moscow. Shortly before Stalin's death he indicated in *Economic Problems of Socialism in the USSR*[23] a waning of the belief in inevitability of war inherent in the 'two camps' doctrine, suggested that conflicts between capitalist countries were more likely, and mentioned a need for greater flexibility in Soviet policy. Although he died before any signs of policy change had become apparent, his death occurred at a time when change was necessary. In January 1953, two months before Stalin's death, the Eisenhower administration took office in the United States with a foreign policy based, at least verbally, on the concept of 'rollback' of Communist power rather than the 'containment' which had satisfied President Truman. On the one hand, its determination to end the Korean War on conditions short of total victory promised some relaxation of an important source of US-Soviet tension, but on the other, its attempts to extend and tighten the ring of 'containment' presaged new dangers for the Soviet Union. American efforts were directed primarily at the formation of blocs analogous to NATO along the southern and

---

[21] Dyakov, A. M., in *India and Pakistan,* Moscow, 1951.
[22] *Bolshaya Sovetskaya Entsiklopediya,* Vol. XVIII (1953), p. 68.
[23] Published by Foreign Languages Publishing House, Moscow, 1953.

eastern periphery of the Soviet Union, and India at once became important for several reasons: it was large; it was not only non-aligned but a main centre for the development of the non-alignment philosophy, which made it a potential medium for influencing other Afro-Asian countries; its success in helping to arrange the Korean Armistice (approved in July 1953) had given it an international 'status'; it was attracted by the idea of 'peaceful coexistence'; and it was resistant to United States efforts at drawing it into a formal alliance. Its dispute with Pakistan over Kashmir was an additional reason for seeking close relations with it, as Pakistan, separated from the Soviet borders only by a thin strip of Afghanistan (which was also in dispute with Pakistan), appeared willing to join the US-sponsored alliance system. It was not likely that India would ally itself to the Soviet Union, because of the importance played by non-alignment in Nehru's world outlook, but this was not necessary. A non-aligned India, friendly to the Soviet Union, would serve as an entry-point for Soviet relationships with the unaligned countries in general, would help to keep Pakistan preoccupied within the sub-continent and prevent the American-sponsored alliances (CENTO and SEATO) from becoming geographically continuous and mutually reinforcing.

The then Soviet Prime Minister, Malenkov, was identified with internal policies giving priority to consumer well-being, as part of the reaction from the austerities of Stalinism, and these required some reduction in the costs both of the armed forces and of the heavy industries which supplied their hardware. Diplomatic action to limit the success of the new American forward policy, liquidation of the Korean War, and attempts to lower tension in Europe, all offered prospects of reducing defence costs and freeing military manpower for the civilian labour force, and these were the policies which the post-Stalin collective leadership pursued. India had played an important role in the second of them, was crucial to success of the first, and, as a Commonwealth country with strong British ties, may have been expected to play some indirect part in furthering the third.

The first high-level indication of a change of attitude towards India came in a speech by Malenkov to the Supreme Soviet in August 1953,[24] where he paid tribute to India's role in bringing the Korean War to an end, described Soviet-Indian relations as 'strong and growing', and expressed the hope that they would increase and develop 'in a spirit of friendly cooperation'.

One problem faced by Soviet policy was the reluctance of the

[24] *For a lasting Peace, For a People's Democracy,* 14 August 1953, p. 3.

CPI to abandon its longstanding preoccupation with British 'imperialism' to the exclusion of all others. In an interesting survival of the practice which had so annoyed M. N. Roy in 1928, the task of reorienting the CPI was again entrusted to the British Communist Party. Its Secretary-General, Harry Pollitt was the chief foreign guest at the III Party Congress (December 1953) and his main effort was devoted to stressing the importance of realising that not British but American imperialism was the Party's most dangerous enemy. From the Soviet point of view this made sense in two ways. Firstly, it corresponded to the reality of the Cold War in general and the situation in South Asia in particular, where not the British but the Americans were committed to building an anti-Soviet alliance system. Secondly, it was likely to make Soviet relations with the real rulers of India easier. Most of them had been strongly influenced by the British non-Communist left in their pre-war struggle; many had been educated in Britain and associated with the Labour Party; some, including Nehru, had favoured the popular front tactics which had brought about a temporary association of Congress with the CPI in the late 1930s. If the CPI could be persuaded to concentrate its attacks upon American 'imperialism', this would both fit reality better than a continued hammering of the British, and would reduce social embarrassment in dealings with the Congress leaders. To cultivate relations with the Indian Government would be less difficult if the CPI (which most Congress leaders regarded as a Muscovite mouthpiece) could be persuaded to tone down its attacks upon the British and to concentrate instead upon the Americans, with whom few Congress leaders had personal ties, and whom most of them regarded with suspicion.

But Pollitt was only partly successful in his mission. The leading group around Ghosh accepted his arguments, but the left-wing refused to abandon the view that the Indian non-Communist nationalists were tools of the British, and the Andhra Communists in particular took the 'national communist' line, that the Soviet Union's main enemy was not necessarily the CPI's as well. In the end the Party compromised, by declaring the United States to be the main obstacle to world peace and Britain that to national liberation, but refraining from defining which of the two was the more dangerous.[25]

Similar uncertainty resulted from attempts to urge the Cominform and Soviet line of peaceful cooperation with the non-Communist left. The Party Congress agreed only to end its

[25] Rothermund, Indira, *op. cit.,* pp. 6-8.

self-imposed isolation; the more difficult question of whether to link up in a genuine united front or to ally itself only with those it could dominate, was remitted to the Central Committee for further consideration. The III Party Congress therefore ended with the Party's attitude both to the Nehru government and to the rest of the Left unresolved.[26] In practice, however, the Party found itself unable to avoid endorsing the Soviet position that peaceful transition to socialism was possible, since violence had failed, had cost the Party most of its members and many of its votes, and since under Nehru's influence Congress had declared its objective to be the construction of a socialist type of society. To oppose Congress was possible only on a basis of argument and continued participation in elections, on the basis that Congress was incapable of developing 'real' socialism.

Western efforts to extend the barriers of containment eastwards, through the formation of the Baghdad Pact (later CENTO) and SEATO, during 1954, soon involved Pakistan, which accepted American military aid early in 1954 thus improving Soviet prospects of a fruitful counterbalancing relationship with India. More directly connected to Soviet security was the future of Afghanistan once Pakistan was drawn into the American-promoted alliance system. Having about 1200 miles of border with Soviet Central Asia, Afghanistan's viability as a buffer state between a Western-aligned Pakistan was important to the Soviets, who saw it as endangered by the Afghan-Pakistani dispute over the Pushtunistan issue. The Afghans had long contended that the Pathans of Pakistan's North-West Frontier province wished for, and were entitled to, self-determination, and demanded a plebiscite on the issue of an independent state of Pushtunistan. The dispute eventually led in 1955 to closure of the Kabul-Karachi road on which most of Afghanistan's trade with the outside world depended, thus prompting a reorientation of Afghanistan's trade towards Soviet Central Asia (a process already set in train by the modest Soviet-Afghan technical aid agreement of April 1953, but given new impetus by the dispute), and prompting the first Soviet-Afghan military aid agreement—but only after Afghan overtures for American military assistance had been rejected because Afghanistan was unwilling to ally itself to CENTO or SEATO. Thus the first deliveries of Soviet military aid to Southern Asia, which began early in 1956, resulted directly from a perceived threat to the Soviet southern borders, which coincided with Afghanistan's own fears of the danger to itself from a United States-armed Pakistan, reinforced

[26] *Ibid.,* p. 8.

by United States rejection of Afghanistan's request for arms with which to protect itself. Soviet willingness to supply arms without requiring an alliance was noted in India, but there were no immediate consequences.

The importance which the Soviets had begun to attach to India was reflected in the position it occupied in the annual slogans issued to mark May Day and the anniversary of the 1917 seizure of power. Beginning with 1st May 1954, India has been mentioned first among the greetings to non-Communist countries. 1954 was unquestionably the year of a 'great leap forward' in Soviet-Indian relations, with Soviet efforts to seat India in various international forums (on Indo-China, Korea and Arms Control) all being successfully opposed by the West and serving to increase Indian goodwill towards the Soviet Union. At the Geneva Conference on Indo-China America alone of the great powers opposed India's inclusion, and although this opposition was successful, a strong Indian delegation attended as 'observers', whose views were treated with deference by the Russians. India was nominated as the neutral member of the three-nation International Control Commission, and mutual exchanges both of compliments and of delegations increased. India's conduct of the chairmanship of the Neutral Nations' Repatriation Commission, which handled the return of prisoners of war in Korea, had aroused the opposition of the South Korean government, in whose support the United States rallied a bloc of Latin American countries against India's inclusion in the Korean peace conference. Because of this, India failed to secure the necessary number of votes to be seated, but expressed gratitude to the Soviet Union for its support.

On the arms control issue, 1953-4 saw the first Soviet intercontinental bombers enter service,[27] and the first Soviet thermonuclear weapon tests. These gave the Soviet Union the ability to attack United States territory, and thus put an end to the strategic imbalance of the post-war years during which America had been able to threaten nuclear attack on the Soviet Union, but Russia, for lack of overseas bases, had been unable to pose a counter-threat except to United States allies on her borders. To that extent the Soviet position either in an arms race or in negotiation to reduce arms was strengthened, but the stockpile of weapons and number of bombers was small compared with that of the United States, and the real Soviet advantage lay in the large conventional forces which it could put into the field at short notice. Soviet proposals for disarmament therefore tended to stress the abolition of

[27] They were first displayed at the Moscow air show in July 1953.

nuclear weapons and percentage reductions of conventional forces (which, if carried far enough, would take the smaller Western forces below the minimum effective level while leaving the Soviet Union above it).[28] India was an enthusiastic advocate of a total ban on nuclear weapons, and the Soviets proposed that India be added to the membership of the Disarmament Subcommission of the United Nations, along with the Chinese People's Republic and Czechoslovakia. The Western countries, which until then had enjoyed a 4-1 majority on the Subcommittee, opposed the addition of the new members and India did not in fact become one until the subcommittee was expanded to include 18 nations in 1962. But on this issue, also, the significant fact for India was that it received Soviet support and American opposition. Improvement of the Soviet Union's image in Indian eyes was therefore assured, despite the lack of tangible results from the Soviet initiatives.

The opportunities for Soviet acquisition of influence in Pakistan were more limited. Although the Soviets had frequently described partition as a British device to ensure a continued position as 'arbitrator' between the two new states, no attempt was made to contest the permanence of the division. Lenin had acknowledged the right to self-determination of the non-Russians in the old Russian Empire and tolerated temporary secessions from it, but he had always envisaged reunion, and organisational measures to facilitate it and included a firm continued subordination of the Communist Party in the seceded areas to Party headquarters in Moscow.[29] After the partition of India, however, the CPI Politburo made no attempt to assert authority over the Communists in Pakistan, nor did the Cominform journals assert that they should. Partition was accepted as a fact, and no suggestion that reunification was desirable or feasible was made. Pakistan consistently showed a more pro-Western orientation than India, made no virtue of non-alignment, and showed itself receptive to American overtures, joining both the Baghdad Pact (later Central Treaty Organisation) and South-East Asia Treaty Organisation (SEATO). The inflow of American arms to Pakistan placed extra strains on Indo-Pakistan relations, and provided further opportunities for enhancing Soviet influence in India.

If 1954 had been a year of major growth in Soviet-Indian ties,

---

28 Eg. Draft Resolution on ' . . . prohibition of the atomic weapon and one-third reduction of Great Power Forces', introduced in First Committee of United Nations General Assembly, 23 October 1950.

29 For Lenin's views see *Theses on the National Question* (1913 and 1917), *Imperialism, the Highest Stage of Capitalism* (1916) and *The State and Revolution* (1917).

it was also the year in which Indian amity with China reached
unprecedented heights. In April the Tibet Agreement was signed,
including the formal enunciation of the 'Panch Shila' (the Five
Principles of Peaceful Coexistence), in June Chou En-Lai visited
India, and in October Nehru visited China. But whereas the level
of amity shown in Sino-Indian affairs was never subsequently
reattained, the progress in Soviet-Indian relations during 1954
served only as a springboard for further advances. In January 1955
*Pravda* endorsed India's foreign and internal policies, despite the
fact that by so doing it undermined the CPI's chances of overturning
Congress in the state elections in Andhra Pradesh.[30] In February
the agreement to build a major steelworks at Bhilai was signed,
in June Nehru visited the Soviet Union, and in November
Khrushchev and Bulganin visited India. They praised what they
saw there, and made no contact with the leaders of the CPI.

Nehru's visit to the Soviet Union in June was unusual in that
he was permitted to make public speeches in a number of cities,
including Moscow, Leningrad and Kiev and several in Soviet
Central Asia, the first time in the entire history of the Soviet state
that a non-Communist leader had been permitted to expound his
views in public at government invitation. In his speeches he praised
Soviet initiatives towards peaceful coexistence, but reiterated his
opposition to some of the Cominform's activities as interference in
other countries' internal affairs. At the Bandung Conference in the
previous month he had denounced the Cominform as 'not com-
patible with non-interference',[31] and his continued references to it
in the Soviet Union and during his subsequent tour of Europe,
as an instrument of overt Soviet interference in the affairs of other
countries may well have influenced its dissolution on 18th April
1956. It is not possible to prove cause and effect, but in view of
the determined Soviet wooing of Nehru during 1954-55, and his
constantly repeated references to the Cominform as an obstacle to
normal relations with the Soviet Union, it is difficult to avoid the
conclusion that his views played an important role in the decision
to dissolve it.

During Nehru's visit he and his entourage described themselves
as impressed by Soviet tact in avoiding attempts to present India
as a Soviet ally; for example, the then Indian Ambassador to
Moscow, K. P. S. Menon, later pointed out that the drafting of

---

[30] Windmiller, E., 'The Andhra Election' in *Far Eastern Survey*, 4/1955,
pp. 57-46.
[31] *The Hindu*, 1 June 1955.

the joint communique was left to the Indians.[32] But when Khrushchev and Bulganin came to India in November-December 1955, they behaved with less restraint. Their rejection of Pakistan's request that they not visit Kashmir was very acceptable to India, as was Khrushchev's strongly pro-Indian statement in Srinagar, while the Soviet support for India's case on the Portuguese enclaves of Goa, Daman and Diu made a particularly favourable impression, as John Foster Dulles, then United States Secretary of State, was at the time engaged in talks with his Portuguese opposite number and had made statements which could readily be taken as suggesting that Goa was covered by the NATO agreement (Dulles denied this a few days later, but the damage had been done). However the crudeness of some of Khrushchev's anti-British remarks and his identification of the Indians after his return to Moscow as 'our allies in the struggle for peace' caused some offence, leading the *Times of India* to suggest that he had 'failed to grasp the spirit of non-alignment.'[33] Nehru was sufficiently concerned by this and by Western suggestions that India's non-alignment was taking on a pro-Soviet tinge to argue that 'the area of friendship should not be confined by a wall of hostility to others'.[34]

The bases for Soviet-Indian relations were enunciated by Khrushchev and Bulganin in speeches made before, during and after their visit, and were summarised by Sisir Gupta as follows: 'the promise of aid; endorsement of India's unity; the acceptance of Indian national leadership as a progressive and desirable phenomenon; the promotion of India's status in the world; the acceptance of the desirability of India's friendship with the United States and of American aid to India; and finally, the use of Soviet influence to prevent the irresponsible functioning of its followers in India.'[35]

Of these, the promise of aid was fulfilled by the construction of the Bhilai steelworks and later (in 1964) by agreement to build a second (Bokaro) after negotiations with the United States broke down; the endorsement of India's unity was exhibited by support for India over the Kashmir issue (most immediately by the vetoing in the Security Council in February 1957 of a proposal for a plebiscite in Kashmir which India opposed); the acceptance of Indian non-Communist leadership as desirable and progressive was

---

[32] Menon, K. P. S., *The Flying Troika,* Oxford University Press, 1963, pp. 118-9.

[33] *Times of India,* 23 November 1955.

[34] *The Hindu,* 27 December 1955.

[35] Gupta, S., 'India and the Soviet Union', in *Current History,* 3/1963, pp. 144-5.

pursued despite Nehru's continued anti-Communism and notably his deposition of the Communist State government of Kerala in July 1959; the promotion of India's status was shown particularly in relation to China for Soviet refusal to back China in the border dispute of 1959 was the first occasion where Soviet verbal support was not forthcoming to a Communist state in dispute with a non-Communist one; Soviet aid to India was greater than that to China, and continued long after the programme of aid to China had been terminated, while after 1960 military aid was granted in the full knowledge that India was now more preoccupied with achieving a military balance with China than concerned about the US-supplied and-aligned Pakistan. That India should continue to maintain friendship with the United States and receive United States aid was beyond Soviet ability to influence, especially as the Soviet Union would have been unable to replace it if withdrawn, but that the Soviets saw aid-giving as a competitive activity was indicative of the importance they attached to India.

Use of their influence to moderate the behaviour of CPI was perhaps the most difficult undertaking to fulfil, especially since Nehru pursued no self-denying ordinance in respect to anti-CPI activity. Less than a month after the Soviet leaders' visit, he was taunting it for its alleged desire to copy the Russian revolution in preference to taking account of Indian conditions.[36] The CPI's factionalism, while rendering it less effective than it might other-wise have been as an opponent to Nehru, also made it less amen-able to suggestions from Moscow. The then Secretary-General, Ajoy Ghosh, visited Moscow during the Khrushchev-Bulganin visit, but even at that stage, while the Soviet leaders were lauding Nehru's foreign and internal policies, published a statement which made a sharp distinction between them, praising the 'peaceful aspects' of his foreign policy and denouncing 'reactionary elements' of his domestic policies.[37] Only in mid-1956 did CPI criticism of Nehru's foreign policy abate—almost two and a half years after the Soviets had ceased to denounce it—and criticism of his domestic policies remained at a far higher level than the occasional mild rebuke which appeared in Soviet periodicals during 1956-58. The disparity reflected not merely the factionalism of the CPI, but a conflict of interests. An indigenous Communist Party which ceased to criticise had no intellectual basis for continued existence, and it had no ground for political support unless it could differen-

---

[36] Stein, A., *India and the Soviet Union,* Chicago University Press, 1969, p. 77.

[37] Ghosh, A., 'Communist Answers to Pandit Nehru', *New Age,* Delhi, 5 December 1955.

tiate itself from the Congress in the minds of the electorate. To the Soviet Union, the fate of the Indian Communist Party was less important than its own relations with the actual government of India, and it lacked the concern with Nehru's domestic policies which was vital to the CPI.

By mid-1956 trade relations had progressed far, while aid offers had been made by several other East European countries, apparently at Soviet encouragement. India was particularly anxious to reduce its foreign exchange expenditures on oil, and both the Soviet Union and Roumania in November 1955 offered to assist in oil prospecting and refining. In March 1956 Soviet Deputy Prime Minister, Anastas Mikoyan (who had made the first anti-Stalin speech at the Soviet 20th Party Congress in February, and was widely believed to favour both greater consumer welfare and the reduction in cold war tensions which would make it possible) arrived to sign a new trade agreement. He emphasised the USSR's desire to avoid straining India's balance of payments and the new agreement, as had the old, stipulated that the value of Indian exports to the USSR should equal that of imports. In fact the provision was as much in the Soviet as the Indian interest for the Soviet balance of payments was also in no position to stand a great drain on it, in view of the shortage of convertible currencies and the demands likely to be made on them by the programme for improved consumer welfare.

Nehru greeted de-Stalinisation as 'taking the USSR more and more towards one kind of normalcy which is to be welcomed . . .'[38] as 'based on a more realistic appreciation of the present world situation', and representing 'a significant process of adaptation and adjustment'.[39] He naturally welcomed the abolition of the Cominform in April, and at the Commonwealth Prime Ministers' Conference spoke out strongly in favour of increased contacts with the Soviet Union.

The first major strains upon Indo-Soviet relations came with the crises of late 1956. On the iniquity of the British-French action at Suez there was no disagreement; India had made several efforts during the summer months to reconcile the rights of canal users with those of Egypt, and had received Soviet support but had been rejected by the Western powers. The budding crises in Poland and Hungary were far from the forefront of Indian attention (its ambassador to Moscow was accredited also to Budapest, but visited it only occasionally) and emotionally made far less impact on

[38] Stein, *op. cit.,* p. 81.
[39] Speech in Lok Sabha, 20 March 1956.

Indian opinion than the 'colonialist' action against Egypt. Nehru was clearly disquieted at the Soviet invasion of Hungary, but only once during November 1956 (at a UNESCO meeting on 5th November) did he equate it with the Anglo-French invasion observing that 'we see today, in Egypt as well as Hungary, both human dignity and freedom outraged . . .'.[40] At the emergency session of the UN General Assembly India abstained on one resolution which included a condemnation of the Soviet action and a call for the withdrawal of Soviet troops, and voted against another which called for elections to be held in Hungary under United Nations supervision. The government's tepidity on Hungary, compared with its vehemence on Suez not only roused displeasure in the West, but exposed Nehru's foreign policy to more widespread and prolonged criticism within India than it had ever before received.

Nehru's own explanations of his actions indicate that he feared the Hungarian crisis to have a potential for escalation into world war, which was not inherent in the Suez affair, as both superpowers were opposed to the Anglo-French action. After the Hungarian rising had been crushed he joined the Burmese and Indonesian Prime Ministers on 15th November in the call for Soviet withdrawal which India had opposed ten days earlier in the UN debate. On the same day he explained that to vote for an election in Hungary under UN auspices might create a bad precedent.[41] Undoubtedly he had in mind Kashmir, and the belief that India might in due course need Soviet assistance in repelling UN attempts at a plebiscite among the mainly Moslem population. Events were soon to justify his refusal to embarrass the Soviet Union; on 14th February 1957 the British, United States, Australian and Cuban delegations jointly introduced a draft resolution in the Security Council, calling for demilitarisation of Kashmir 'preparatory to the holding of a free and impartial plebiscite'.[42] The Soviet Union opposed the resolution and eventually vetoed it. When the subject was raised again in November 1957, the Soviets again opposed attempts to impose a solution unacceptable to India, and with clear evidence of Soviet willingness to resort again to the veto on India's behalf, the Western powers did not press the matter to a vote.

The Soviet ICBM successes of 1957, culminating with the launch of the first artificial earth satellite, Sputnik-1, on 4th October,

---

[40] Stein, *op. cit.*, p. 89.
[41] Speech in Lok Sabha, 15 November 1956.
[42] United Nations Security Council, 12th Session, 768th meeting.

prompted an Indian 'peace offensive', in which a revered former Congress leader and ex-Governor-General C. Rajagopalachari, wrote to Khrushchev suggesting that in the light of its technological advances the Soviet Union could unilaterally abjure the use of nuclear weapons, as the West could no longer interpret such a decision as prompted by weakness and would be morally compelled to follow suit. Shortly thereafter, on 28th November 1957, Nehru proposed to Khrushchev and President Eisenhower that they end the arms race. Khrushchev replied with a polite rejection of Rajagopalachari's suggestion, but in response to Nehru's appeal offered to end nuclear testing if the Americans and British would do the same.[43] As the Americans refused, the Soviet undertaking did not come into effect, and they conducted a series of tests beginning in October 1958, which the Indians denounced. Having completed the series, they announced a unilateral moratorium on nuclear tests, which remained in force for three years, so that the nuclear issues played no further part in Indo-Soviet relations until late in 1961. By then Soviet arms control policy had been modified; in the search for economy in defence, the numbers of the Soviet armed forces had been heavily reduced and Khrushchev had proclaimed that reliance would be placed on the deterrent capability expressed by missiles with nuclear warheads. India's advocacy of a total ban on nuclear weapons therefore did not correspond to Soviet realities, and by the mid-60s when Soviet and American interest shifted to the prevention of proliferation, China had conducted its first nuclear weapon test and indicated its unwillingness to accede to any US-Soviet sponsored Non-Proliferation Treaty. Since India, while not exercising the option to manufacture its own nuclear weapons, was reluctant to sign it away without a corresponding Chinese signature, or, at the least, a specific nuclear guarantee from both superpowers, Indian arms control policy moved into conflict with Soviet wishes after 1964. To obtain an Indian signature to the Non-Proliferation Treaty then became a Soviet objective, pursued with varying degrees of enthusiasm, but without success up to the time of writing.

Nehru's equivocal behaviour during the Hungarian crisis had showed that his major concern was to avoid a Soviet-Western confrontation, and this manifested itself again in India's support for the Rapacki plan for disengagement in Europe, put forward by the

---

[43] The letters were later published in Khrushchev, N.S. *For Victory in Peaceful Competition with Capitalism,* Hutchinson, London, 1960, pp. 9-21.

Polish Foreign Minister late in 1957[44] and discussed at intervals thereafter until the mid-60s. In the Lebanon-Jordan crises which followed General Kassem's seizure of power in Iraq in July 1958, Nehru proposed withdrawal of American and British troops, fearing possible Soviet involvement and escalation to world war. However Khrushchev's reluctance to confront was manifest (especially when compared with Chinese statements on the crises), and Indian concern at the danger was unjustified, indicating that a grasp of Soviet strategic difficulties was lacking.

In some other respects, 1958-59 saw the development of strains on the relationship. Nehru's concern for good relationships with Communists did not extend to the CPI; domestically he remained fiercely anti-Communist, and continued to stress (even to exaggerate, in view of its factionalism) the CPI's subservience to outside forces of doubtful relevance to Indian conditions. In an article 'The Basic Approach'.[45] he castigated both capitalism and Communism as based on violence, contempt for spiritual and moral values, and intolerance of opposition. In reply, the Soviet ambassador to China, P. Yudin, wrote in the *World Marxist Review* in December 1958 a fierce criticism of Nehru's domestic policies, charging him with espousing an unrealistic concept of socialism, failing even to consider how poverty and exploitation were to be ended, and comparing India's continued economic dependence on 'the imperialists', as well as its slow economic progress, most unfavourably with the Chinese record. However, like the CPI, he praised Nehru's foreign policy, and he pledged continued Soviet support for Indian industrialisation.

The expression of Soviet reservations about India was more outspoken in Yudin's article than on any occasion before or since, and his removal from his post in 1959 appears to have been the result of excessive zeal in espousing the Chinese point of view, but it is most unlikely that his article would have been published if it had not reflected views which the leadership held but could not openly express. The purpose was to warn Nehru not to go too far in criticism of the Soviet Union's behaviour within the Communist bloc (he had been particularly outspoken over Soviet pressure on Yugoslavia and the execution of the former Hungarian Prime Minister, Imre Nagy), rather than to indicate intention to

---

44 Address by Polish Foreign Minister to General Assembly of the United Nations, 2 October 1957. U.S. Department of State, *Documents on Disarmament 1945-59,* Vol. II, pp. 889-892.

45 Nehru, J., 'India: A Basic Approach: Inaugural address at Commonwealth Press Union Conference,' New Delhi, 2 November 1961.

force change in domestic policy. His rough treatment of the CPI was not commented on, and Yudin assured his readers of continued Soviet assistance in industrialising India, as well as disclaiming any suggestion of intent to meddle in its internal politics.

The year 1959 saw a deterioration in China's relations with both the Soviet Union and India. The role played by Chinese discontent at India's favoured treatment by the Soviets is discussed in the chapter on the Sino-Soviet dispute and may be summarised here as irritation with the generous scope and terms of aid to India compared with the niggardliness of assistance to China, as well as at the Soviet persistence in propping up a bourgeois-nationalist regime to the detriment of the truly revolutionary forces which, in the Chinese view, that regime was oppressing.

The proximate cause of the crisis was the revolt in Tibet in February.[46] The Chinese alleged that the rebels were using Kalimpong in West Bengal as a base; despite Nehru's denials some early Soviet radio commentaries repeated the Chinese charge, but after mid-April Soviet media deleted all allegations of Indian complicity when relaying Chinese reports on the situation in Tibet. From mid-1959 occasional clashes occurred between Indian and Chinese patrols in border areas which were under dispute, and after one such clash in late August a Soviet official news agency statement described the incident as 'deplorable'. It ostensibly took a neutral line, but in describing cooperation between the USSR and India as 'successfully developing in accordance with the idea of peaceful coexistence' and describing the 'inspirers' of the dispute (unidentified) as 'trying to discredit the idea of peaceful coexistence' it appeared to point at the Chinese as the instigators.[47] That interpretation was too esoteric for most observers, but the unprecedented Soviet step of declaring neutrality in a dispute between a Communist and a non-Communist state was not lost on either the Chinese or the Indian governments.[48] As if to underline their support of India, the Soviets chose September 1959 to confirm credits for $357 million towards India's Third Five Year Plan, under the agreement signed in May, despite the intensification in the interim of the Sino-Indian border dispute and Nehru's dismissal (in July) of the Communist state government of Kerala. In October Khrushchev urged a solution by 'friendly negotiation'.[49]

The deterioration of Sino-Soviet relations after this resulted in an

[46] Doak Barnett (ed.), *Communist Strategies in Asia*, Praeger, New York, 1963, p. 111.
[47] TASS, 12 September 1959.
[48] *The Hindu*, 21 September 1959.
[49] Speech to the Supreme Soviet, 30 October 1959.

upsurge of Soviet official visits to India during the early months of 1960, including in January a 74-member delegation headed by President Voroshilov, and in February Khrushchev himself. Although his journey was partly prompted by a desire to counter the very successful visit paid by President Eisenhower two months earlier, his very appearance could be interpreted as an overt indication to the Chinese that India was assured of Soviet support; for though he undoubtedly urged Nehru to negotiate with the Chinese, he brought with him Mikoyan and a group of experts, who finalised the project aid to be given towards the Third Five Year Plan and concluded the definitive Credit Agreement to cover it. Nehru told the Rajya Sabha on 12th February, after talks with Khrushchev, that he saw at present 'no bridge between the Chinese position and ours'. Although Chou En-Lai came to India in April to discuss the border issue, the ambience surrounding the visits by the Soviet leaders had made it clear to both sides that they had put no pressure on the Indians to compromise, whatever the inconvenience to the Soviet Union of an open dispute between the two countries. During 1960 supplementary credits for new Five Year Plan projects were granted to India, while Soviet technicians were beginning to be withdrawn from China. Aid to India became a symbol of Sino-Soviet differences, and increased as they did, while trade with India expanded as that with China fell off.[50] In November 1960 the scope of aid was enlarged to include military assistance, beginning with an agreement to deliver aircraft and helicopters and gradually broadening to include weapons for all three armed services.

India's own policies appear to have been little affected, and on a number of issues it pursued lines contrary to those of the Soviet Union, or embarrassing to it. Opposition politicians in both houses cautioned against the danger of over-involvement with the Soviet Union,[51] whether politically or economically, or suggested privately that India's 'trust' might be betrayed by the Soviets as it had been by the Chinese. On the Congo issue, the Soviets supported the government of Patrice Lumumba and contended that all UN forces should be withdrawn. India, on the other hand, insisted that the UN remain, and after several African countries withdrew their forces, speedily provided Indian replacements for them. And when the Soviet objections to UN intervention focussed on the Secretary-General (Dag Hammarskjöld) personally, so that in autumn 1960 they called for his replacement by a 'Troika' (one

[50] *Mizan*, 11/12 1968, p. 225.
[51] Eg. Sudhir Ghosh, quoted in Stein, *op. cit.*, p. 129.

Westerner, one Soviet bloc representative, and one neutral), India opposed that also.

Judging from Nehru's own statements and actions, he regarded Soviet friendship as a counterweight to India's heavy dependence on Western (especially American) aid, and, increasingly from 1959 onwards, as a guarantee against China whose intransigence he frequently contrasted with Soviet willingness to reach an accommodation with the West.[52] In both senses, therefore, relations with the Soviet Union were seen as defence of non-alignment, and an essential part of it.

The Soviet resumption of nuclear testing at the beginning of 1961 occurred on the eve of a major conference of non-aligned countries in Belgrade. Nehru did not condemn the Soviets for their unilateral breach of the moratorium, but expressed the view that the 'crisis' was the most dangerous since the end of the Second World War, urged East-West discussions, and emphasised India's opposition to all forms of nuclear tests.[53] There is no reason to believe that the Soviets expected Indian support for their action, or were surprised that Nehru treated their resumption of testing with more concern than did Tito, Nasser and Soekarno. Equally, there is no ground for believing that Nehru's reaction to it was inhibited by fear of incurring Soviet displeasure. He regarded India's role as essentially central between the superpowers, taking no sides as between one and the other, and acting where possible to bring them together—hence in this situation his urging of East-West negotiations, as in autumn 1960 he had urged an Eisenhower-Khrushchev meeting as a way out of the crisis in Soviet views of the UN structure. A certain tendency for rebukes to the West to be more sharp in tone than those addressed to the Soviet Union was manifest, and was occasionally the subject of adverse comment from other Indian public figures. Nehru's reasons for this were complex. Although he himself frequently said that he could afford to be franker with Westerners because of a shared background, it is also clear from his writings as far back as 1927 that the Soviet Union in his eyes 'carried no stain of original sin' for Western colonialism in Asia.[54]

As often happened in Soviet-Indian relations, Indian opposition to Soviet wishes carried no penalty when India itself needed Soviet support. At the 22nd Party Congress (October 1961), Khrushchev

[52] Stein, *op. cit.*, p. 127.
[53] Speech at the Belgrade Conference of non-aligned nations, reported in *Times of India*, 19 August 1961.
[54] Moraes, F. R., *India Today*, Macmillan, New York, 1960, pp. 141-2 and 198-9.

called for the elimination of Portuguese colonialism from India, thus giving a public indication that if Nehru wished to annex the Portuguese enclaves Soviet support in international forums could be expected. In December 1961 Indian forces occupied the Portuguese enclaves of Goa, Daman and Diu. At the time Brezhnev, then President of the Soviet Union, was visiting India, and well aware that invasion was imminent (Portugal had protested against the Indian preparations on 7th December). On 17th December, he made a speech, a few hours before the invasion, in which he gave a public assurance of Soviet 'understanding and sympathy', and on the next day repeated the assurance of support.[55] It was forthcoming that same day in the shape of a veto in the Security Council against a Western-sponsored motion hostile to the Indian action.[56] Indian appreciation of Soviet support was greatly enhanced by the hostility of much Western government and press comment. India was unaccustomed to incurring international odium for its actions, and felt that the West's pro-Portuguese stance ignored the unacceptability to Indian opinion of Portugal's continued refusal to do what the British and French had done fourteen years earlier. It was felt, too, that the West was taking insufficient account of the pressure of public opinion on the Indian government for over ten years and that Portugal's record as a colonial power was not such as to make the West's verbal rush to her defence easily explainable, except on grounds of NATO solidarity (it was not lost on the Indians that the sponsors of the resolution vetoed by the Soviet Union were all members of NATO—USA, UK, France and Turkey). In the circumstances Soviet support, uninhibited by India's opposition to Soviet wishes over the Congo, the UN Secretariat, or the nuclear tests issue, was doubly welcome. As the *Times of India* pointed out, 'Not every aspect of Soviet policy . . . is acceptable to New Delhi, but Moscow's recognition of the fact that complete identity of views is unnecessary is most encouraging.'[57]

From the Indian point of view, the Sino-Soviet dispute was not an unmixed blessing. On the one hand, it increased India's importance to the Soviet Union as a counterweight to China, but on the other it reduced the extent to which the Soviets could influence Chinese behaviour towards India. As Sino-Indian relations declined during 1961-62 and border incidents became more frequent, India's defence problems became more acute, as most of its armed

[55] *Times of India*, 18, 19 December 1961.
[56] Security Council proceedings, 18 December 1961.
[57] *Times of India*, 20 December 1961.

forces were tied down on the borders with West Pakistan, in the Punjab and Kashmir. Soviet military aid deliveries to India had begun in 1961, but were not sufficient to make up for the lag in equipment and training for mountain warfare of the Indian troops in the North-East Frontier Agency and in Ladakh. Responsibility for the outbreak of hostilities is beyond the scope of this discussion; judging from statements made by Nehru and the Indian Defence Minister, Krishna Menon, in October 1962, Indian action was imminent, and the Chinese may merely have anticipated it, but the success of their campaign showed that they were themselves more prepared for offensive action that was India. Fighting began on 20th October 1962, and continued for exactly one month, during which time the Chinese expelled the Indians from the parts of Ladakh to which China laid claim, drove them out of most of the North-East Frontier Agency, and took several thousand prisoners.

From the Soviet point of view, the war occurred at a most inconvenient time, when they themselves were heavily embroiled in the Cuba crisis. At first they temporised, giving no circulation to China's allegations that India had attacked first, but urging the Indians to accept the Chinese proposals (made on 24th October) that both sides should halt at the 'line of actual control', withdraw their forces 20 kilometres (12½ miles) from it, and open negotiations. The Soviets first advocated acceptance of these proposals on 25th October,[58] and despite Nehru's rejection of them on the 27th (when he insisted that no negotiation was possible until the Chinese returned to the *status quo ante bellum*), urged them again at the United Nations on the 30th and in a letter from Khrushchev to Nehru on 3rd November.[59] But with the defusing of the Cuba crisis, the Soviet position began to firm up more in India's favour. A *Pravda* editorial on 5th November again urged a negotiated settlement, but dropped the previous endorsement of the Chinese proposals as a basis for discussion. Aid to India continued to arrive as scheduled,[60] and no adverse comment was made on the haste with which India had resorted to the West for military aid. But clear signs of concern were evident that Chinese action might drive India away from non-alignment into the arms of the 'imperialists', especially as in India the speed of the American and British response to requests for arms was being unfavourably contrasted with the Soviet Unions' temporising. So,

[58] *Pravda*, 25 October 1962.
[59] *The Times* (London) 5 November 1962.
[60] Morarji Desai in Lok Sabha, 8 December 1962.

too, were unfavourable comparisons being drawn of the Soviet Union's swift intervention on behalf of Egypt in 1956, and willingness to embroil itself with the United States on Cuba's behalf, with its slowness to throw its support behind India in confrontation with China. The Chinese announced on 20th November that they would cease fire at once and begin withdrawal to the pre-war positions. On 1st December Khrushchev addressed the Supreme Soviet,[61] and made several points against the Chinese. In particular, while welcoming their action in withdrawing, he said it would have been better not to have moved from their positions in the first place. As for India, he pointed out that while non-alignment had given India 'great moral and political weight', in the current situation 'militarists and reactionaries' were coming to the fore, and 'progressive elements' were being weakened; in other words, Chinese action was endangering non-alignment.

Under the pressure of the crisis, the Indian Government moved against the CPI, and a number of its members were arrested under emergency legislation during November. These came mostly from the pro-Peking faction, but included many who were not so identified, as well as seventeen left-wing members of the Central Committee including E. M. S. Namboodiripad, the former Premier of Kerala, and ten members of Parliament. Soviet protests against these arrests were muted and delayed; no reference was made to them at all in the Soviet press until late in December, and the most detailed statement was merely a reprinting in *Pravda* of 2nd February 1963 of an article from the CPI's own journal *New Age* of the previous week. Release of the pro-Soviet detainees took place only during the spring and summer, but Soviet media did not refer to the matter again after early February, and Soviet displeasure was vented only indirectly, through articles by non-Russians in the *World Marxist Review* and other Communist journals.

Apart from the disruption caused within the CPI by the arrests, and the dissatisfaction within its ranks at the Soviets' apparent indifference, the war itself intensified the differences between pro-Moscow and pro-Peking factions, and when the public exchanges of polemics between the Soviets and Chinese in 1963 revealed the full extent of their differences, events in the CPI moved steadily towards a split.[62] Soviet indifference towards the CPI's fortunes remained marked during the intra-Party debate of 1963-64. The Chinese media, on the other hand, made their interest known through shrill attacks on the right-wing Communists who formed a

---

[61] N. S. Khrushchev, speech of 12 December 1962.
[62] Rothermund, Indira, *op. cit.*, pp. 22-3.

majority of the central Committee,[63] 'Opposition' Party journals began to appear from June 1963 in Bengal, Andhra Pradesh, Madras and Kerala, and in October the Politbureau was forced to suspend the regional leadership in West Bengal and introduce 'Commissar's Rule' there. Finally, on 11th April 1964, 32 members of the Central Committee walked out, and in due course both 'left' and 'right' Communist Parties issued their own programmes after each had conducted its own 'Seventh Party Congress' in October and November 1964 respectively.[64] The fortunes of the Party were considerably harmed by the split, especially those of the 'left'. From the start, its support for China isolated it politically, and this isolation was deepened when the Chinese gave verbal support to Pakistan during the 1965 war over Kashmir. Communists, whether of right or left, regarded Pakistan as a tool of 'imperialism' with even more than the normal Indian mistrust, and the unexpected emergence of the Soviet Union as mediator in the conflict made it necessary for them to seek renewed contacts with the despised 'revisionists'. The 'right' Communists were less hampered in view of their continued identification with the Soviet Union. But as Soviet policy remained firmly wedded to dealing with the actual governing party, neither CPI bulked large in Soviet thinking. The fundamental issue between 'right' and 'left' Communists was that which had separated M. N. Roy from Lenin in 1920: whether to cooperate with other parties to hasten the 'bourgeois-democratic' revolution as the necessary prelude to the socialist one, or to collaborate only with those movements it could control, so as to bypass the bourgeois-democratic stage altogether. And on this issue the Soviet mind had long been made up, to the detriment of the CPI.

The year 1964 was notable for two events more important to Indo-Soviet relations than the fracture of the CPI. Since Stalin's death, their conduct at the highest level had depended on continuity of contact between two leaders—Nehru and Khrushchev. In May 1964 one died, and in October the other was deposed. Nehru had succeeded in attracting to India an international status far greater than its military or economic strength alone would have given it; however closely his successor adhered to Nehru's policies, it was not likely that he would be able to perpetuate the standing which Nehru's personal qualities had achieved for India in the international field. President Radhakrishnan paid an official visit to the Soviet Union in September 1964, and while there was at pains to emphasise that the continuity in Indo-Soviet amity did not depend

[63] Eg. in 'A mirror for revisionists', *People's Daily,* 9 March 1963.
[64] Rothermund, Indira, *op. cit.,* pp. 23-26.

on one person.[65] Scarcely had he returned to India when Khrushchev was displaced.

The reasons for Khrushchev's dismissal were probably more to do with failures in the domestic field (especially in agriculture) than with any specific foreign policy issue, but no single reason by itself is likely to have been crucial in bringing about his deposition by the men who had been his closest colleagues and were thus closely identified with the policies which they now denounced. Dissatisfaction with the extent to which relations with China had deteriorated may have been one of the factors; certainly two actions by the new collective leadership indicated that it had played some role in their decision to remove him. Firstly, they separated the functions of Head of Party and Head of Government, thus bringing an end to the ludicrous situation in which Khrushchev, as First Secretary of the Party, participated in polemical exchanges directed against the leaders of a state with which he, as Chairman of the Council of Ministers, maintained normal if distant relations on matters of routine diplomacy. This was not the only reason for the division of powers, nor even the most important—the Soviet leaders had had unfortunate experiences of the consequences of vesting total power in the State in one person, and prudence would have dictated that they abstain from conferring such power upon one of their number. But whatever the reasons, their action had the effect of creating a divorce, however spurious, between inter-Party and inter-State disputes, and their second action—the almost total suspension of anti-Chinese polemic for several months—indicated more unambiguously their desire to explore the possibility of lowering Sino-Soviet tension.

Yet even at this period of exploration, the Soviets set clear limits both on their willingness to make concessions of substance to China, and on the extent to which they were prepared to sacrifice their relationship with India. Naturally the possibility of Sino-Soviet rapprochement was not unduly welcome to an Indian government, which feared it might be made at the price of a loss of Soviet support, both against China and against China's quasi-ally, Pakistan. But one of the first acts of the new Brezhnev-Kosygin leadership was to assure India that all agreements, including those for arms deliveries, would continue to be met.[66] The new Indian Prime Minister, Lal Bahadur Shastri, visited Moscow in May 1965

---

[65] *Times of India*, 20 September 1964.
[66] Rothermund, Dietmar, 'India and the Soviet Union', in *Annals of the American Academy of Political and Social Science*, November 1969, p. 82.

to cement relations with the new Soviet leaders, and receive assurance of their continued support over the Kashmir issue, without, in turn, satisfying their hopes for an Indian demarche over the American bombing of North Vietnam—for although the Indian Government eventually denounced the bombing, it never echoed Soviet calls for unconditional United States withdrawal from the South.

The period following the downfall of Khrushchev was an anxious one for India's leaders for three other reasons. One was the attainment by China of a nuclear capability, as shown by the first Chinese nuclear test in October 1964, the second was the increase in signs that the Third World lacked the perceived community of interests necessary to function as any kind of political 'bloc'. A second 'Bandung Conference' was to be held in Algiers in 1965, and the Soviet Union, which had been excluded from the first Bandung Conference in 1965, was anxious to be present, firstly in order to refute Chinese charges that it was a chauvinistic great power colluding with the United States; secondly to strengthen its claim to be an Asian country; thirdly to bolster the concept of the Third World by its presence, and the recognition which presence implied. The third cause for Indian anxiety was the prevalence of change in the 'First' and 'Second' worlds—the industrialised West and the industrialising East. In the West, the post-Cuba period had seen a degree of relaxation in tension between America and Russia. From the Indian point of view this was not entirely unwelcome (Nehru was on record as believing the North-South differences to have more potential for trouble than 'the other, artificial, division of the world between capitalism, communism and all that'[67]), but to the extent that *detente* diminished the competitive search of the superpowers for allies and influence, it threatened to reduce India's importance to them. At the same time, tensions between them and their allies (European unwillingness to take an increased share of NATO burdens, and French opposition to American leadership on the one hand, Roumanian hostility to Soviet plans for economic integration of Eastern Europe, and the beginnings of the Czechoslovak debate on the economy which eventually burgeoned into the 1968 crisis on the other) were seen in India as likely to turn the attention of the superpowers away from Asia and back to Europe.[68] That Indian fears of diminished superpower interest

[67] Karanjia, R. K., *The Philosophy of Mr. Nehru,* Allen & Unwin, London, 1966, p. 67.
[68] Gupta, S., 'The Third World and the Great Powers', in *Annals of the American Academy of Political and Social Science,* November 1969, pp. 54-63.

proved unfounded (despite the complete failure of the Bandung movement after the 1965 *coup d'état* in Algiers made it impossible to hold its conference there, and the removal of Soekarno from power after the 30 September *coup* in Indonesia deprived the concept of the Third World of one of its most vociferous advocates), was largely due to Soviet acts of will. These were the assurances of continued economic and military aid; the progress with the Bokaro steel plant; assistance in finding or supplying and refining oil; maintenance of trade at a high and increasing level; and the seeking of a mediatory position between India and Pakistan. This marked for India something of a recessional from a position of unconditional Soviet support; but by serving notice of acute Soviet interest in the sub-continent's stability, it warned China to limit its support for Pakistan during the war over Kashmir in late 1965 and subsequently.

Pakistan had been growing more and more disillusioned with its pro-Western alignment. From 1960 onwards, the strategic importance to the United States of 'containment' in the purely physical sense had diminished as intercontinental ballistic missiles and the seaborne 'Polaris' missile came into service. Although political importance was still attached to preventing an increase in the number of Communist states, peripheral bases became less important for the purpose of major war against the Soviet Union, and the Kennedy Administration's attention had turned to non-aligned countries, such as India, to the inevitable disillusionment of Pakistan. This created an opportunity for a Soviet rapprochement with Pakistan, and at the same time, required of Soviet diplomacy a more subtle approach than had previously been necessary in relations with India, as moves towards a more neutral position on Kashmir were certain to incur hostile questioning in New Delhi. The then President of Pakistan, Ayub Khan, concluded that membership of the Baghdad Pact, by causing the Soviet Union to throw its support behind India on matters such as Kashmir 'more than nullified whatever economic and military advantages we gained from the Pact',[69] and visited the Soviet Union in April 1965, with the aim of establishing contact and seeking to present Pakistan's case in its dispute with India.

The first concrete sign of a change in Soviet policy came shortly after his visit and that of Shastri in the following month. In June fighting between Indian and Pakistani forces occurred in the Rann of Kutch; the Soviet Union maintained a neutral stance, confining

---

[69] Khan, Ayub, *Friends, not Masters,* Oxford University Press, 1967, p. 156.

itself to urging a peaceful settlement.[70] But the major test of the new Soviet relationship with Pakistan came later that year, in the Kashmir crisis which began in August 1965, escalated into war in September, and concluded with the Tashkent Conference of January 1966.

With its much smaller army and limited resources, Pakistan's hopes of success resided in rapid action, before India could redeploy forces from the frontier with China, and hopefully, in Chinese gestures designed to inhibit India's transfer of troops. In practice neither hope was fulfilled; China's militance was verbal only, and had little effect on events, as India was able to contain the Kashmir situation without major transfers from other theatres, and the war ended with Indian forces in Pakistani territory. Soviet mediation proved acceptable to both sides.

The Tashkent agreement probably marked the high point of Soviet influence in the sub-continent; Kosygin succeeded in securing a rapid withdrawal of Indian forces from Pakistani territory, in exchange for a Pakistani undertaking not to resort to force again in seeking a settlement of the Kashmir issue. For the Soviets it was marred only by Shastri's death of a heart attack in Tashkent, which was to introduce new complications into the Soviet-Indian relationship. He was succeeded by Nehru's daughter, Mrs. Indira Gandhi, and there were indications that the Russians for some time believed her to be a figurehead behind which reactionary elements were planning to turn India away from her father's avowed aim of achieving a socialist (albeit non-Marxist) society.[71]

An authoritative view of India's prospects and shortcomings in Soviet eyes during the early post-Nehru period was given in the journal *Peoples of Asia and Africa* in early 1966.[72] It drew attention to the low growth rate of the Indian economy since 1950, and blamed part of this on colonialism, for (a) removing part of India's national income; (b) leading to a predominance of small-scale trade, which hindered the transition to capitalism because of the slowness with which reserves accumulate; and (c) causing uneven distribution of income. But at the same time it laid some of the blame for India's slow development on the Indian government, on the grounds that the socio-economic structure and government policy had not only failed to prevent 'non-productive accumulation'

[70] TASS, 8 May 1965.
[71] Eg. in *Pravda* of 19 May 1966, 31 January 1967, 17 March 1967, 13 June 1967 and in *Mezhdunarodnaya Zhizn* (International Affairs) articles by O. Mayev (1/67) and N. Savelyev (4/67).
[72] Yegorov, I. L., and Rastyannikov, V. G., in *Narody Azii i Afriki* (Peoples of Asia and Africa) 2/1966.

(conversion of potential investment capital into gold, jewels, houses, land or foreign currencies) by the rich, but had in some cases positively encouraged it. While the authors claimed that the logic of the situation required a socialist policy of encouraging growth in the publicly-owned sector of industry, they pointed to inadequacy of investment in the private sector, arising from the 'non-productive accumulation' already mentioned, plus inflation and tax increases resulting from the increased post-1962 defence expenditures, as reasons for the poor performance of industry during the 3rd Five Year Plan. While the remedy (continued sponsorship of growth in the public sector) was orthodox, the diagnosis came close to suggesting that rich private investors should be given greater incentives to transfer their resources from gold or property into industrial investment. But when this step was in fact taken, some Soviet commentators greeted it with suspicion, using it as evidence of Right-wing resurgence.[73]

During 1966 bad harvests and increased taxes (largely resulting from increased defence expenditures) caused a serious worsening in India's economic situation. In an attempt to stimulate industrial production, especially for export, the Indian Government took steps to induce private investment and to attract foreign capital. The economic effects of these measures were beneficial, but deepened Soviet suspicions that right-wing elements were gaining the ascendancy. Despite Indira Gandhi's relative success at the elections of February 1967, Congress lost its majority in eight of the seventeen states, and found it necessary to enter into coalitions with various opposition parties, some of which (Hariana, West Bengal and Uttar Pradesh) had to be replaced by presidential rule within a year of the elections. The growing loss of unity and popularity of the Congress benefitted the Communists to some extent, but the CPI benefited less than the (originally) pro-Peking CPI(M).[74] However, this party found it necessary after Tashkent to be more Muscovite than the Muscovites, in view of the Soviet role in achieving a cease-fire, and the weird alliance of China with Pakistan, and it endorsed the Tashkent agreement even more vehemently than did the CPI itself.[75] At the 1967 elections the CPI(M) and CPI opposed each other directly only in Andhra Pradesh, and the split between them did not therefore result in a loss of strength compared with the previous elections in 1962—

---

[73] Eg. Savelyev, N., *loc. cit.* (note 71).

[74] On the difficulties for the CPI in opposing Congress policies, see Overstreet, G., and Windmiller, M., *Communism in India,* University of California Press, 1959, pp. 318 ff.

[75] Rothermund, Dietmar, *loc. cit.,* p. 87.

total votes remained about the same, but because of geographical dispersion almost twice as many seats were won. But the CPI(M) polled best in the traditional CPI areas (West Bengal, Kerala and Andhra), whereas the CPI's votes were garnered mainly in 'non-traditional' areas, thus in a sense the CPI(M) became the 'Communist establishment'. This had an unforeseen result: the two Communist parties were strong enough in West Bengal to form a coalition state government if they could sink their differences. They did so, and the CPI(M), by virtue of its larger number of seats, became the senior partner. The transition from revolutionary to governing party led to dissension within the CPI(M), some of whom reverted to the 1948 line and staged a peasant uprising in the Naxalbari area—from which they became known as 'Naxalites'. Measures to restore order led to denunciation of the CPI(M) by China, and the formation of a third Indian Communist Party, committed to a Maoist line which the CPI(M) was held to have abandoned.[76]

The decline in the Soviet belief that the Third World could be considered a cohesive political force with strong pro-Soviet, or at the least, anti-Western potential has been particularly marked since the mid-1960s, with the departure through death or deposition of leaders such as Nehru, Soekarno, Nkrumah or Nasser. This, plus the supersession in Moscow of the unpredictable visionary, Khrushchev, by the more inward-looking but more businesslike Brezhnev-Kosygin regime, reinforced the post-1960 decline in importance of peripheral bases to reduce both the strategic concern of superpowers about the Third World and their tendency to look at it in universalist terms. In the case of India and Pakistan, particular emphasis was placed on the continued development of trading relations as the basis for a true community of interest, while in the international political field, the Soviet Union ceased to sponsor India as a candidate for important international meetings. Whereas Khrushchev had proposed the inclusion of India in the Summit Conference on the Middle East which he requested in 1958, the Soviet proposal for such a conference in December 1968 did not mention India, and the annual May Day slogans, which since 1954 had greeted India first after the other Communist countries relegated it in 1966 to eighth position, behind three Arab, three sub-Saharan African and one Asian countries and just ahead of Pakistan.[77] From 1966 also, Soviet media while continuing to praise Indian foreign policy, have carried far more critical comment

[76] Rothermund, Indira, *op. cit.,* pp. 83-90.
[77] May Day slogans, *Pravda,* various dates around 17 April, 1954-67.

about the internal situation than was the case in the Nehru-Khrushchev years.[78] Indian support of the Arabs after the Six-Day War of 1967 attracted favourable but sparse comment in the Soviet press, while the refusal by Indira Gandhi to condemn out-right the Soviet invasion of Czechoslovakia (on the grounds that to do so would not help the Czechs) received far less attention in the Soviet press and radio than had her father's similar action in respect of Hungary in 1956. This was despite the fact that the refusal was the subject of considerably more hostile comment, both inside and outside India, than had been the case in 1956,[79] (in 1968 there was, of course, no Suez crisis to divert Indian attention). When a Soviet delegation arrived in India in September, elements of the press accused it of conducting itself 'in the manner of an imperial power', and of refusing to satisfy Indian concern on matters such as its arms deals with Pakistan, its position on Kashmir, or the activities of 'Radio Peace and Progress' (a Soviet-controlled radio in Tashkent, which broadcasts particularly uninhibited propaganda attacks, especially against Indian right-wing leaders, but for which the Soviets deny responsibility on the grounds that it is not 'official'—as Kosygin explained when pro-tests were made to him during his visit in January 1968).[80]

Charges of Soviet 'imperialism' were echoed by the Chinese. A Chinese view of Soviet-Indian relations, published in July 1969, and entitled 'India—a Vivid Specimen of how Soviet Revisionists push Social-Imperialism'[81] charged that the Soviets had seized control of India's heavy industrial sector, 'placed a stranglehold' on its foreign trade, and joined in collusion with United States imperialism and 'the big landlords and bourgeoisie in India' against China, including using it as a base for espionage and subversion against the Chinese People's Republic, and 'reduced India to a colony, both of Soviet revisionism and of US imperialism'. The direct effect of such diatribes within India is small, but illustrates the difficulties of the Indian government, in that charges of 'selling the country to the Russians' are made with equal force from right

---

[78] See note 71 and, eg. Smirnova (ed.) *op. cit.*, 1968, pp. 99-106, Skosyrev, V. in *Izvestiya*, 26 January 1969; Kodachenko, A. in *Ekonomicheskaya Gazeta* (Economic Gazette) No. 10 (March 1969); Vladimirsky, I. A. in *Peoples of Asia and Africa* 1/1970; Alexandrov, R. in *New Times*, 26 February 1971.

[79] *Times of India*, 28 September 1968.

[80] Naik, *op. cit.*, p. 140. See also Stein, A., 'India and the USSR: the post-Nehru period', in *Asian Survey*, March 1967, pp. 165-175.

[81] *Peking Review* No. 30, 25 July 1969.

or left.[82] The Soviet image was not helped by the collapse of a building under construction in Trivandrum in December 1969, which enquiries disclosed to be a Soviet 'cultural centre' being built without any permission sought from the Central Government.[83]

India continues to present Soviet political leaders with dilemmas of understanding, and publicists with problems of presentation. Its social structure, and the magnitude of its economic difficulties (which Marxists see as closely interconnected), make it impossible to present it as a model for other Asian countries, except in respect of its non-alignment which has been carefully defined as 'not neutralism, but a form of anti-imperialism'.[84] Its adherence to the forms of 'bourgeois' democracy, and its strong links with Western countries, economic, political and cultural, make it difficult to fit it into any Soviet schema of the future, while the complications of its social structure have proved difficult to fit into standard Marxist analyses based on presumed nationwide class interests. At the same time, Soviet support of India tends to show that its role as an 'alternative model' to China has not been lost sight of, and its possibilities as an adjutor in containing China are felt to be real. But its ability to fulfil this role is hampered by its long-standing dispute with Pakistan, and while Indo-Pakistan disagreement suited Soviet objectives as long as Pakistan was firmly wedded to US-sponsored alliance systems, it ceased to do so when Pakistan turned towards China. In fact, Pakistan and China have little in common save frontier disputes with India, and in the Soviet assessment it became possible to maintain good relations with both states of the Indian sub-continent, provided Pakistan's disillusionment with Western alliances, which had proved incapable of furthering her claims to Kashmir, was not accompanied by exaggerated ideas of what China might be able to do on her behalf. A complicated nexus of interests therefore came into existence, and deprived Soviet policy of its clear-cut pro-Indian character. Tashkent placed the Soviet Union in a position of mediator between India and Pakistan, but India's willingness to accept Soviet mediation was based on a belief confirmed by years of Soviet action on India's behalf in the UN and elsewhere, that it would favour India's case. From the Soviet angle, however, mediation, to remain acceptable to Pakistan, was not consonant with overtly pro-Indian behaviour, as Pakistani disillusionment with the Soviets could lead either to a return to pro-Western alignments, or to a deepening

[82] Eg. in *Hindustan Times,* 4 December 1969.
[83] *Times of India,* 18 December 1969.
[84] Nasenko, Yu. P., 'India: Evolution of the Policy of Non-alignment' in *Peoples of Asia and Africa,* 6/1968, pp. 15-24.

relationship with China which would be both anti-Indian and anti-Soviet in character. Furthermore, while there could be no return to the Sino-Soviet intimacy of the early 1950s, common prudence and ideological pressures for Communist unity dictated a moderation of the Sino-Soviet dispute to the extent possible. However, India's fortunate position as a non-aligned protege of the superpowers depended largely on the continuance of Sino-Soviet tensions, while a permanent solution of the Kashmir problem would considerably strengthen India's position vis-a-vis China by freeing most of the Indian Army for deployment along the Sino-Indian border. But the easing of Indo-Pakistani tension implied by this, would have deprived the Soviet Union of its mediatory function, and might also, by increasing Chinese willingness to settle the border issues on terms acceptable to India, have reduced Soviet importance in Indian foreign policy. Conversely, an easing of the Sino-Soviet dispute could cause a re-emergence of Indian fears (already expressed after the sale of weapons to Pakistan after 1968)[85] that Communist friendship is unreliable, and non-alignment no substitute for 'great and powerful friends'.

While the increase in Soviet-Pakistan trade created no special problems with India, military aid has naturally abounded in difficulties. Detachment of Pakistan from both pro-Western and pro-Chinese alignments was possible on a basis of arms supply, which offered considerable and immediate political dividends because of the armed forces' role in the government of Pakistan, but subject to the readiness of India to accept it as reasonable, during a period in which, as the Soviet media noted, with the split in the Congress, the growth of the right-wing Swatantra and Jan Sangh parties, the easing of restrictions on private and foreign capital investment, and tentative Indian steps to reopen discussion with China (announced by Mrs. Indira Gandhi on 1 January 1969), India's non-alignment was under pressure from a number of directions. Nevertheless, the Soviets persevered. Their economic aid to Pakistan between 1965 and 1970 was estimated at US$120 million, and it was expected that aid provided during Pakistan's Fourth Five Year Plan (1970-75) would be at least double this. Projects underway in 1970 included exploration for oil and natural gas (under an agreement signed in March 1961), industrial plants, radio transmitters, improvements to ports and airfields (agreed in April 1965 and September 1966), a heavy electrical equipment plant, a steel mill, a nuclear power station, and a television set

---

[85] Eg. in *Madras Mail,* 23 April 1969 and *Times of India,* 16 September 1969.

factory (announced during the visit of President Yahya Khan to Moscow in 1970).[86]

By the end of 1970, it was possible for a Soviet journal to describe Pakistan's position in reasonably 'optimistic' terms. Its author claimed that since 1960 Pakistan's policy had changed from a one-sided pro-Western orientation towards independence, activity on the international scene, and contacts with as many countries as possible. Its membership of SEATO and CENTO had become more and more a 'formality'; its advocacy of effective steps against Rhodesian and South African racism, support for the Arab cause, for a settlement of the Vietnam question on a basis of the 1954 Geneva agreements, for general disarmament, for a ban on nuclear weapons, for peaceful coexistence and for 'liquidating the remnants of colonialism' had conferred added international importance and prestige on it. Although the evidence submitted in support of this assertion was thin—election to Chairmanship of a UN General Assembly session, choice as a non-permanent member of the Security Council in 1968, and as a member of the expanded Disarmament Committee in 1969—none at all would have been possible without withdrawal of Soviet bloc opposition.[87]

However, the Soviet expectation that the neutral role could continue to be maintained fell by the wayside as the crisis in East Pakistan developed in 1971. Soviet relationships with Pakistan had shown no special awareness of the East Pakistan conviction that their half of the country was subjected to discrimination; aid given to Pakistan was on a 'no strings' basis, and the largest projects (eg. the steel mill) were located in West Pakistan. During the 1971 election campaign, the Soviet media singled out for approval not Sheikh Mujibur Rahman's Awami League, but the West Pakistan-based Pakistan People's Party led by R. A. Bhutto, suggesting a failure to appreciate either the multinational nature of Pakistan or the fragility of consensus between its two wings. The Soviet-Indian agreement[88] ratified on 18th August 1971 commits the two signatories to 'consult' in the event of attack upon either. It is not strictly a defence agreement, but the decision to enter upon it at a time of great tension between India and Pakistan signified partial

---

[86] *Christian Science Monitor*, 21 July 1970. See also Chaudri, M.A., 'Pak-USSR Relations', *Asian Survey*, September 1966, pp. 492-500 and Seth, S. P., 'Russia's role in Indo-Pak politics', *Asian Survey*, August 1969, pp. 614-624.

[87] Moskalenko, V., in *Aziya i Afrika Segodnya* (Asia and Africa Today) 9/1970, p. 30.

[88] *Soviet News Bulletin*, USSR Embassy, Canberra, No. 19/243, 23 August 1971.

abandonment of the mediatory position gained in 1965. That the hope of returning to a mediatory position had not been totally abandoned was, however, indicated in the relative coolness with which events in East Pakistan were described.

However, the East Pakistan crisis developed beyond the point at which the Soviets (or anyone else) could exercise mediation, and the Soviet-Indian agreement of August 1971 probably marked recognition by the Soviet leaders of the possibility that stability and the *status quo* could no longer be reconciled, and that the problems of the refugees from East Bengal could not be solved within India. The agreement served notice that Chinese intervention in support of Pakistan could result in Soviet involvement, and freed India's hands for a military solution. Soviet recognition of the new state of Bangla Desh indicated an intention to stay on good terms with at least two of the three major countries into which the Indian sub-continent was now divided, while cautiously welcoming comments on the new, civilian, government of Pakistan, suggested a Soviet expectation that any damage to Soviet-Pakistan relations could be repaired.

The post-1966 modesty in expectations of India continues in Soviet pronouncements. The most recent high-level statement, delivered by Brezhnev to the 24th Congress of the CPSU[89] was brief and delicately phrased, but showed the distinctions which the Soviets now make between Indian foreign and internal policies. Bank nationalisation, and Mrs. Gandhi's election victory, were cited as 'evidence that the masses of people in that country resolutely oppose the reactionary pro-imperialist forces, and stand for the implementation of a land reform and other socio-economic transformations, and for a policy of peace and friendship in international affairs', thus pointing out that reactionary forces are still strong, that land reform has not yet occurred, and that some elements in India oppose peace and friendship with the Soviet Union. Later in the speech, unreserved approval was given to Indian *foreign* policy, by a statement that 'The Indian Government's pursuit of a peaceable, independent line in international affairs, and the traditional feelings of friendship linking the peoples of the two countries, have all helped to deepen Soviet-Indian co-operation', but there was no hint that Indian policy was expected to affect other countries. Even compared with a year previously, this marked a downgrading of India as an example to others; a

[89] *Report of the Central Committee,* 30 March 1971, Novosti Press Agency, pp. 24 and 33-4.

Moscow Radio broadcast of 1 April 70[90] had said ' . . . all Asian countries will have to do much to maintain peace on the continent. However, . . . India's attitude to the basic problems of Asia *greatly assists this task*' and continued ' . . . India's efforts to check the extremists' imperialist plans in the Indian Ocean are significant in the struggle for peace in Asia . . . the Indian Government considers neither South-East Asia nor the Indian Ocean a vacuum that must be filled by outside forces. This point in the report (by the Indian Ministry of External Affairs) is a shattering blow to the American 'vacuum theory', which ignores the existence of scores (*sic*) of independent states on the shores of the Indian Ocean. The American extremists needed this absurd theory to set up their nuclear rocket bases in the Indian Ocean and to establish new military blocs . . .' thus claiming exemplary value for Indian foreign policy. However it remains true that whether measured by levels and planned rates of growth of trade, by amounts of aid, or by column-inches in the speeches of Soviet leaders, the Indian subcontinent remains the cornerstone of Soviet foreign policy in Asia, and India the most important Asian state in Soviet eyes. The limitations to Soviet aid and trade have been outlined in another chapter, but it remains to point to the advantages India sees accruing to it from Soviet interest. During the period of India's emergence as an independent state, the readiness of Stalin's successors to acknowledge non-alignment while serving their interests in impeding American attempts to create new blocs, also corresponded with Indian interests. That Soviet strategic interest in non-alignment has waned with the decline in importance of peripheral bases, and that the concept of a politically cohesive Third World bloc has proved illusory, has not greatly affected Indian gratitude for past Soviet sponsorship in international bodies. Some disillusionment has been apparent with the realisation that Soviet and Indian interests over Pakistan or over nuclear weapons policy are not identical, but this is partly offset by the belief that India is more important to the Soviet Union than Pakistan—whether as a partner in trade, in containment of China, or in developing an alternative to the Chinese socio-political model for other Asian countries to follow. There is also no doubt that in the Indian view Soviet provision of aid, however modest, has rendered Western aid cheaper, by its effect on interest rates,[91] as well as perhaps more readily forthcoming, and that Soviet willingness to increase imports of

---

[90] *BBC Summary of World Broadcasts*, SU/3341/A3/3.

[91] Roy, A., *Planning in India—Achievements and Problems,* Calcutta, 1965, pp. 329-30.

manufactured goods (a recent Soviet study[92] spoke of intention to increase imports of manufactures and semi-manufactures to total 25% of imports) will assist in freeing India from its traditional role as a supplier of primary products and raw materials.

For the Indian Communists, the Soviet role has been less beneficial. In the elections of March 1971 Mrs. Gandhi was able to divest herself of any need for CPI support. She rejected at the outset of the election campaign any alliance with the CPI on which she had previously relied for her Parliamentary majority, and in the event her supporters increased their seats from 228 to 350, gaining a clear majority. The CPI(M) won 25 seats, and the CPI 23, a slight improvement on the 1967 position, but totally nullified by the gains made by Mrs. Gandhi's Congress 'R'. The CPI sought an electoral alliance with Congress 'R', but now regards it as committed to preserving capitalism, and can find little comfort for itself in the continued Soviet approval of it, however qualified that approval may be by references to unrealised internal reforms.[93]

The other countries west of the Malacca Strait—Burma, Ceylon, Thailand, Malaysia and Singapore—have reflected altogether lower levels of Soviet activity, but nevertheless the pattern of activity is interestingly differentiated.

## BURMA

Burma has presented a consistent picture of unrest ever since it attained independence in 1948, and the split within its Communist movement dates back to 1945. Burmese Marxism owed little to Chinese or Soviet tutelage, and was of a particularly intransigent kind. Two factions had come into being, and differences arose between them as the British reoccupied the country. The larger of the two factions, the 'White Flag' Communists, proposed to follow a 'Popular Front' line, by working within the ranks of the Anti-Fascist People's Freedom League, a 'bourgeois nationalist' movement by Communist definition but clearly destined to be the ruling party when independence was attained. The smaller 'Red Flag' faction, on the other hand, refused to cooperate with non-Communists, and instead proposed to fight the British for independence.[94] The tactics of both factions proved fairly pointless

---

[92] Klochkovskiy, L. L., study prepared for United Nations Conference on Trade and Development (UNCTAD), summarised in *USSR and Third World,* Vol. I No. 3, February-March 1971, p. 95.

[93] *Indian Express,* 1 May 1971.

[94] Britwell, R., 'Burmese Political Development: Impact of a National Heritage', in Leifer, M. (Ed.), *Nationalism, Revolution and Evolution in S.E. Asia,* University of Hull Monographs on South East Asia No. 2, 1970, pp. 130-134.

(though in the case of the 'Red Flag' faction indicative of the uncompromising nature of Burmese Marxism), as the Anti-Fascist Freedom League was engaged in achieving independence by negotiation, while its basis of popular support was strong enough for it to have no need of the 'White Flag' movement which it expelled from the League in 1946. The 'White Flags', under Thakin Than Tun, denounced the treaty of independence negotiated by U Nu in January 1948 and, under the influence of the 'two camps' theory called for his overthrow as a 'tool of the British imperialists'.[95] In consequence, Burma, despite its independence, found itself faced in March 1948 by an armed Communist revolt which has continued until 1971 and is not yet concluded, though Thakin Than Tun himself was killed in 1968. Burma's economic and political problems were already serious before the Communist insurrection began; war-damage, especially to transport facilities, had been heavy, and the need to unite the minorities behind the new nation demanded a federal structure to guarantee the constitutional pledge of 'unity in diversity', as well as a minimum of discord within the governing party.[96]

In practice none of these requirements was achieved. Discontent among the ethnic minorities led to a number of revolts, while a split in the People's Volunteer Organisation (the combatant wing of the Anti-Fascist People's Freedom League) resulted in a majority of its members joining one or other Communist faction. The upshot of such disunity has been politically and economically damaging. No Burmese government since independence has been in firm control of more than two-thirds of the country. Reconstruction was severely hampered and the standard of living has never reattained its 1939 level (after 1963 even declining for several years). Vacillation has been apparent both in the economic structure (between strict state control of all economic activity and limited private entrepreneurship) and in politics where democracy eventually gave way to military rule, under which an attempt was made to evolve a 'Burmese way to Socialism', but without significantly winning the allegiance of the ethnic minorities. Burmese leaders moved to take trade out of the hands of long-resident Indian and Chinese minorities, but were unable to replace them adequately, while fear of giving offence to China was an important inhibitant to taking up offers of American or Soviet aid. Total

[95] Girling, J. L. S., *People's War,* Allen & Unwin, London, 1969, pp. 19 & 47.
[96] Silverstein, S., in *The Far East and Australasia 1969,* Europa, 1969, p. 355.

foreign aid has therefore been low, at between 1 and 2 per cent of gross national product, and only about one-sixteenth of it is of Soviet origin.[97]

But despite Burma's gloomy political and economic record since independence, it is the only country in Asia proper which the Soviet leaders describe as 'on the non-capitalist road of development'.[98] While the creed professed by the Burmese leaders is certainly socialist (though not Marxist) in content, Burma's record in development is among the worst in the Third World, while its internal unrest has been of such scale, diversity of causes, and duration, as to make it a most unlikely model for developing countries to follow. The sparsity of articles on Burma in Soviet learned journals indicates a genuine lack of expertise on it in the Soviet Union, and, in view of the very restricted access which the country allows to foreigners, it could be that Brezhnev's praise of Burma is based on ignorance. Equally likely, however, is that the Soviet view is ideological in origin, and based solely on the Burmese social order which, whatever its practical shortcomings, is certainly not capitalist. That the Soviet classification is purely a social one, taking little account of economic success, is suggested by the fact that some of the other countries said to be taking the non-capitalist road, such as Syria and Congo (Brazzaville)[99] are hardly likely to serve as models to their neighbours.

CEYLON

Pre-war Soviet influence in Ceylon was negligible, and the Communist Party of Ceylon came into existence only in July 1943. Prior to that, Marxist influence had been expressed only through minority membership in the Socialist Party (Lanka Sama Samaja), which was founded in December 1935 and split in 1940 over attitudes to the British war effort. After the split, Marxist influence was exercised within the Ceylon Trade Union Federation, set up in December 1940.

Despite active support of mass strikes, political acceptance eluded the Ceylon Communist Party. The newly-founded (1946) United National Party won power in the 1947 elections, and became the first government of independent Ceylon on 4th February 1948. Rifts within this party led to formation of the Sri Lanka Freedom Party in 1951. It joined with other left-wing parties to

[97] Pfanner, M. R. H., in *The Far East & Australasia 1969*, pp. 361 and 365.
[98] Brezhnev, L. I., 'Report of the Central Committee' to 24th Congress of the CPSU, 30 March 1971.
[99] *Ibid.*, and Popov, V., in *Aziya i Afrika Segodnya* (Asia and Africa Today) 11/1970, pp. 2-4.

contest the elections of 1956 on a strongly neutralist platform, which included the proclamation of a republic, abolition of British bases, establishment of diplomatic relations with Communist-ruled countries, and gradual nationalisation of foreign-owned companies. The coalition (known as the United People's Front) won a majority and proceeded to put its programme into effect. Some nationalisation was undertaken, tariff protection was given to local industries, a measure of land reform was begun, British withdrawal was negotiated and diplomatic relations were established with the Soviet Union and several other East European countries. In February 1958 a Soviet loan of $US30 million was made[1] to cover a number of projects ranging from mineral prospecting to irrigation and industrial plants.

Political instability continued, however, and in May 1959 the United People's Front began to disintegrate. In September, the Prime Minister, S. Bandaranaike, was assassinated. His successor, W. Dahanayake, announced his intention to end further national-isation and agrarian reforms. He was expelled from the Sri Lanka Freedom Party, and formed his own party. Elections held in March 1960 conferred no majority on any party, attempts to form a coalition failed, and new general elections were held in July. These were won by the Sri Lanka Freedom Party, now headed by Bandaranaike's widow, on a policy of non-alignment in foreign policy and extension of the 1956 programme in internal affairs.[2] Among the proposals for further nationalisation was one for a national corporation to distribute oil products, involving a takeover of the assets of Western oil companies operating in Ceylon. The Ceylon government professed disconent at the profit margins of the Western oil companies, and, no doubt, anticipated action to cut off oil supplies in the event of failure to agree on terms for their future operation. A preliminary agreement was therefore signed with the Soviet Union in March 1961, providing for Soviet supply of 40,000 tons of petroleum products, in exchange for tea, rubber, coconuts and other traditional Ceylonese exports. Similar agree-ments for smaller quantities were signed with the United Arab Republic and Iraq. Later, agreements for much larger quantities were signed: on 26 December 1961 with the Soviet Union for a minimum of 1.25 million tons of petroleum products over five years; on 7 February 1962 with Roumania for about 30 thousand

1 Müller, K., *The Foreign Aid Programmes of the Soviet Bloc & Communist China: an analysis*, Walker & Cox, New York, 1967, p. 222.
2 *Keesing's Contemporary Archives* 1959-60, p. 17356.

tons; and with the UAR on 20th March for about 40 thousand tons.[3]

Having assured itself of alternative sources of supply, the government took over a number of installations belonging to Western oil companies during 1962. Both the British and the American governments protested at the compensation terms offered, and eventually, on 8 January 1963, the United States government announced that economic and technical aid would be suspended until Ceylon took adequate steps to compensate the Esso and Caltex companies, while British aid, though not suspended, was severely scaled down. From 1963 until mid-1965, when American aid resumed after a compensation agreement had been signed, the Soviet Union was the largest single provider of economic aid to Ceylon (excluding the International Bank for Reconstruction and Development, which lent more in 1962), but its aid dwindled rapidly in 1966, as the table shows.

Table 14: Principal providers of long-term loans to Ceylon, 1962-66 (million rupees)[4]

|  | 1962 | 1963 | 1964 | 1965 | 1966 |
|---|---|---|---|---|---|
| Chinese People's Repub. | 0 | 14 | 14 | 10 | 9 |
| German Federal Repub. | 1 | 11 | 7 | 10 | 53 |
| UK | 9 | 8 | 6 | 2 | 33 |
| USA | 4 | 3 | 1 | 0 | 25 |
| USSR | 5 | 17 | 33 | 23 | 9 |
| IBRD | 27 | 23 | 15 | 11 | 7 |

In October 1963 Mrs. Bandaranaike visited the UAR, Czechoslovakia, Poland and the USSR, obtaining an agreement from the UAR for increased exports of petroleum products in return for tea; and communiques issued during her various visits lined Ceylon up in support of the Soviet bloc on disarmament, colonialism and the Palestine problem. Shortly after her return an air agreement was signed in February 1964 with the Soviet Union, giving Aeroflot and Air Ceylon reciprocal landing rights.

Ceylon's problems, however, remained economic rather than political. With its limited range of exports, most of which were affected by adverse movements in the terms of trade during the 60s, and heavy dependence on industrial imports, growth of national income barely kept pace with the population increase, and improved at less than 1% per annum.[5] Ceylon was therefore preoccupied

---

[3] *Ibid.*, 1961-62, pp. 18241 and 19115.
[4] *The Far East & Australasia 1969*, p. 156.
[5] Gunasekera, H., in *The Far East & Australasia 1969*, p. 152.

with internal problems, and heavily dependent on loans and grants on a scale which the Soviet Union was unable to advance on its own, given its already heavy commitments to Egypt, India and Indonesia. Nor was Ceylon able to cast a large shadow in international affairs; its political instability led to frequent changes of government, and deprived its party leaders of the permanence without which they could not become 'fixtures' on the international scene. Even had they done so, Ceylon was hardly likely to take a strongly pro-Soviet line in the Sino-Soviet dispute; its Communist Party did so, but this mattered little in view of its weakness in the political field. The Government, on the other hand, whatever its political complexion, was constrained in its attitude to China by the importance of the Chinese People's Republic as both a trading partner and a supplier of aid, while its close connections with the United Kingdom and United States also inhibited it in supporting the Soviet Union against the West. The United Kingdom remained by far its largest trading partner, with China second (mainly by virtue of the 'Rice and Rubber' agreement, concluded originally in 1952 and renegotiated at intervals since). Of the 182 million rupees' worth of aid drawn in 1966, 121 million came from NATO members (Canada, West Germany, UK and USA) and only 9 million from the Soviet Union.[6]

This resulted in part from change of government. In March 1965 the United National Party was able to form a government in coalition with five minor parties on a programme of neutralism in foreign policy combined with retention of private property rights and a determined effort to attract foreign capital. One of its first acts (in May 1965) was to conclude a compensation agreement with the oil companies, thus assuring resumption of loan aid by the United Kingdom and International Monetary Fund (in June), and by the USA (in July). However, the country's economic difficulties continued, the rice ration had to be reduced, and public satisfaction with the UNP government proved no greater than with its predecessors. Basically its problem was that of excessive dependence on three products—tea, rubber and coconuts, which accounted for about one-third of the national income[7]—and neither the left-wing governments' resort to Soviet assistance in building up a state-owned industrial sector (expressed particularly in provision of a steel mill and a tyre factory), nor the right wing's attempts to build up a private sector with Western aid, could alter this situation

6 *Ibid.,* p. 156.
7 *Ibid.,* p. 150.

quickly. In the circumstances, alternation of electoral favour between the two parties was to be expected.

So in May 1970 the left wing Sri Lanka Freedom Party again returned to power, in coalition with the LSS and pro-Moscow Communists, and in June took a number of steps favourably viewed by the Soviets, nationalising the banks, putting foreign trade under a state corporation, establishing diplomatic relations with North Vietnam and North Korea, and recognising the National Liberation Front's 'provisional revolutionary government of South Vietnam'. This policy suffered a severe setback in April 1971 when it became necessary to expel the entire staff of the North Korean Embassy, a mere ten months after recognition. The North Koreans were alleged to have given both 'ideological direction' and finance to the 'Che Guevarist' insurgency which began on 5th April. At the same time work on a Chinese aid project in the centre of Colombo was halted by government decree, though the government did not openly implicate China in the 'Guevarist' rebellion. However, the Chinese indicated support for the North Koreans by seeing them off at the airport. The Soviet Union, on the other hand, supplied by airlift a consignment of small arms, several Mig-17s, and some helicopters, for use in suppressing the uprising.[8] Among other suppliers of arms for this purpose were India and the United Kingdom, and the present diversity of Communism could hardly have been more dramatically illustrated than in this situation, where a left-wing government, including Communists, sought and received aid from the leading Communist power, an influential neutralist, and the former colonial power, in order to suppress a rebellion by a movement drawn largely from the youth movement of the pro-Moscow party, claiming to be inspired by the ideals of two South American and three Asian Communists (Guevara, Castro, Ho Chi-Minh, Mao and Kim Il-Sung) and alleged to be supported by two Asian Communist countries.[9]

It has been suggested[10] that the Soviet aid may form the cover for an Indian Ocean base, but it may be questioned whether the Ceylon Government, having shown its non-alignment by the catholicity with which it sought aid to suppress the rebellion, would wish to prejudice its foreign trade and aid (both of which are overwhelmingly with and from the West), by offering the Soviets such a base. Nor does the prospect seem likely to attract the Soviets; if they are actively searching for an Indian Ocean base (and there

[8] *Daily Telegraph,* Sydney, 17 April 1971.
[9] *Ceylon Tribune,* 16 August 1970.
[10] Eg. by C. L. Sulzberger in *New York Times,* 5 May 1971.

is as yet no reliable evidence that they are), Ceylon lacks the political stability which they would consider desirable for it, namely a guarantee that policy will not be reversed at the next election. Both parties profess neutralism in foreign policy, but the United National Party tends to be pro-Western in internal policy; and it has held power for thirteen of the twenty-four years of Ceylon's independence. Should the Sri Lanka Freedom Party depart from neutralism to the extent of granting the Soviets a base, it is not unreasonable to expect the United National Party to return Ceylon to neutralism by expelling them when it next gains power.

### THAILAND

The Communist Party of Thailand was founded in 1929, from the Siam Special Committee of the South Seas Communist Party, an organisation directed by the Far Eastern Bureau of the Comintern in China, and especially active among overseas Chinese communities. Ho Chi Minh (then known as Nguyen Ai Quoc) was at the time the Comintern agent for South-East Asia, based in Thailand. Because of these circumstances, and the inability of the CPT to invoke anti-colonialism among the Thais, it attracted few of them as members, and from the start was closely connected both with China and Vietnam, while its connections with the Soviet Union were indirect, through the Far Eastern Bureau.[11] In the Sino-Soviet dispute it consistently supported the Chinese line. Its pronouncements are normally conveyed to the outside world by the Chinese media, and its own radio station 'Voice of the People of Thailand' is apparently located in South China (certainly it is not in Thailand). On 31st August 1967 the Thai government announced that 33 CPT members had been arrested, and that it had been established that a skeletal CPT organisation had been set up within Thailand. While the senior member captured was of Vietnamese descent and a number of those arrested had been trained in China, there was no indication that any had had connections with the Soviet Union.[12] It would seem therefore that Soviet indifference to the CPT is as complete as in the case of most other Asian Communist Parties, and Soviet comments tend to confirm this view. For example, on 21 March 1970 the 'non-official' 'Radio Peace and Progress' described the leaders of the Communist Parties of Burma, Thailand and Malaysia as having isolated themselves

[11] As a Soviet source delicately puts it the first Thai 'Communist organisations' were established in the early 1920s, but the Thai Communist *Party* was founded only in 1942. *Malaya Sovetskaya Entsiklopediya* (The Little Soviet Encyclopedia), 3rd ed., Vol. IX, Moscow 1960, p. 62.
[12] *Asian Almanac,* Vol. V, p. 2345 and interviews in Bangkok 1969.

from the working class by the adoption of 'adventurist' Chinese ways. The 'official' Moscow Radio broadcasts in Thai concentrate on criticism of the United States presence and of the Thai government's support for South Vietnam, but comment on the activities of the Thai Communist insurgents is very rare. The nearness of China (less than 100 miles from the Thai border), the close Chinese connections of many of the CPT leaders, the regularity with which CPT documents pay tribute to Mao (compared to the extreme infrequency of references of any kind to Soviet experience), and the reported remark of the Soviet Ambassador to Singapore in late 1970 that 'he doubted whether the Communists in Indonesia, Malaysia or Thailand followed real scientific Marxism',[13] all suggested that the Soviet Union saw no hope of achieving substantial influence with the CPT, and preferred to improve its relations with the actual government of Thailand.

Relations with Thailand have been very limited. Trade has been small, consisting mostly of exports of Soviet light machinery in exchange for Thai rice and rubber. Even the normal air agreement (signed on 6 May 1971) took four years to negotiate. It provides for Thai offices in Tashkent and Moscow, and Soviet offices in Bangkok.[14] The probable Soviet assessment is that Thailand is more likely to regularise its relations with China in the event of American withdrawal than to expose itself by joining in a Soviet-sponsored containment; that Thailand's relative stability, derived largely from the absence of land-hunger and the lack of a colonial past, renders it an unfruitful prospect for socialist doctrines and that Soviet influence can be adequately expressed through participation in the work of the Economic Commission for Asia and the Far East (ECAFE), centred in Bangkok. On such an assessment the Soviet Union would see no scope for more than a modest diplomatic and economic effort there.

MALAYSIA

The long-drawn out Communist insurrection in Malaya owed its inception to Soviet influence, but very little else. It began, as did the Communist risings in Burma, India and the Philippines, early in 1948, after Zhdanov's speech to the Cominform, and the Youth Conference in Calcutta. But the Malayan Communist Party (like that of Thailand) was an offshoot of the former South Seas Communist Party with its membership almost wholly Chinese, its methods and inspiration Maoist, and its weapons in origin entirely

---

13 *The Hindu,* Delhi, 22 November 1970.
14 *Bangkok Post,* 9 May 1971.

British (supplied to the Communist resistance movement during the Second World War) or Japanese (acquired when the Japanese surrendered in 1945).[15] It received no outside supplies throughout the Emergency, and attracted very little support from Malays.[16] Its susceptibility to Soviet influence was, and remains, negligible, and in Malaysia, as elsewhere in Asia, Soviet relations have been established with the incumbent government on a mainly economic basis.

While the Soviet Union gave verbal support to the Malayan Communists, it became a heavy purchaser of Malayan rubber at the end of the 1950s. Again though it denounced Malaysia (founded in July 1963) as a British device to perpetuate colonial rule,[17] it had already in that year displaced the United States as the largest purchaser of natural rubber (in January-July 1963 it purchased 134,000 tons, compared with 96,000 by the United States).[18] However, most of its purchases were made through the London rubber market, thereby avoiding friction with Indonesia such as would have been generated by on-the-spot purchasing activity.[19] The level of purchases has tended to fluctuate from year to year but they have shown a general, modest rising trend,[20] although the position of 'largest buyer' has not been maintained in every subsequent year. The verbal support given to Indonesia against Malaysia was not matched by hardware supply, as it had been in the earlier campaign against the Dutch in West Irian, and during the latter part of 1964, while confrontation was still in progress, anti-Malaysia propaganda tapered off. The one major exception to the rule that hardware support for Indonesia in confrontation was at a lower level than during the West Irian crisis was the supply of six missile-firing fast patrol boats to the Indonesian Navy during 1964-5.[21] The purpose of these boats was

---

15 Author's interviews with former senior British police and military officers who served in Malaya between 1948 and 1957.

16 Osborne, M., *Region of Revolt: Focus on Southeast Asia,* Pergamon Press Australia, 1970, pp. 72-74.

17 Eg. in speech by Anastas Mikoyan in Djakarta, 25 June 1964, reported in *Indonesian Herald,* 26 June 1964.

18 *Far Eastern Economic Review,* 1964 Yearbook, Malaysia section.

19 Derived by comparison of Malaysian figures of rubber exports to USSR 1963-64, *(Far Eastern Economic Yearbook)* and the much larger Soviet figures of imports of Malaysian rubber (Soviet foreign trade yearbooks for those years). Soviet practice is to record imports under their country of origin, not place of purchase, and the difference in the Malaysian and Soviet figures represents purchases made on the London Rubber Market.

20 *Vneshnyaya Torgovlya SSSR,* (Foreign Trade of the USSR), volumes '1918-66', and annual volumes for later years, Malaysia import tables.

21 *Jane's Fighting Ships,* Indonesian Navy sections, 1966 onwards.

most likely to deter British use of their Singapore-based aircraft carriers against land targets in Indonesia, but they may have been procured under an earlier agreement not specifically connected with confrontation, as another six of these boats had been delivered between 1961 and 1963.[22]

The ending of confrontation in 1966 was welcomed by the Soviets; by reducing tension between Indonesia and its neighbours it afforded them greater freedom to cultivate political relationships with Malaysia, Singapore and the Philippines. While Malaysia offered no great opportunities as long as Tunku Abdul Rahman remained Prime Minister, there was some scope for the exercise of influence and attainment of goodwill by increasing the amount of rubber purchased locally, rather than in London, and a trade mission was established in Kuala Lumpur in November 1967. Establishment of diplomatic relations followed in 1968.

Current Soviet views of Malaysia are that the call by the Prime Minister (Tun Abdul Razak) for the neutralisation of South-East Asia was 'an important factor for peace and stability in the area'; that its development planning is good, and that prospects exist for closer economic ties with the Soviet Union. A factor making for potential instability is the Chinese population which is seen as susceptible to the driving of wedges between it and the Malays by 'pro-Peking elements'.[23] Soviet media have for several years played down the fact of Malaysia's involvement in ASEAN and SEATO, as well as its interest in the Five-power defence arrangements with Singapore, UK, Australia and New Zealand, and further development of relations may be expected. In the first instance, Soviet efforts are being directed to increasing their exports to Malaysia, whose negligible proportions during the 1960s meant that rubber imports had to be paid for in convertible currency, thereby imposing strains on Soviet resources. At the time of writing it appears their main efforts are directed to persuading Malaysia to buy mining machinery, and setting up 'joint ventures' (unspecified) with the Malaysians.[24]

SINGAPORE

Although politically the Soviet Union has been wary of involvement with Singapore (as a Chinese enclave in a Malay world where Indonesia once appeared a likely ally, and where Malaysia is the prime source of rubber, a commodity for which Soviet

---

[22] *Ibid.,* 1964.
[23] Kuala Lumpur Radio, 4th, 5th, 12th March 1971, quoted in *USSR & Third World* Vol. I No. 3, March 1971, p. 106.
[24] Kuala Lumpur Radio 19 March 1971.

demand is growing), it has shown considerable interest in its economic possibilities, especially in its facilities for ship repair. In view of the growth in Soviet merchant shipping traffic, and the importance of Singapore's entrepot trade (much of the Soviet-purchased Malaysian and Indonesian rubber is shipped from there), calls by Soviet ships at Singapore have been increasing steadily, and totalled 521 in 1970.[25] Some of this traffic consists of ships on their way to or from North Vietnam and hence is unlikely to grow indefinitely, since most of the shipments are aid, not trade. However with the large Soviet fishing fleet in the Indian Ocean, and the flows of Soviet shipping between Far East ports and India, for example, the number of Soviet ships passing through the Malacca Straits is like to continue to grow, especially if the Suez Canal reopens. Facilities for ship repair in the Soviet Far East are very limited: in 1965 they were capable of handling only slighty more than half the requirements of the Soviet ships based there,[26] and since they could not build large ships, it is probable they could not repair them either for lack of adequate dry docks. Singapore has available for commercial repair the former British naval dockyard, and a new yard at Jurong, Japanese-financed and capable of dry-docking ships far larger than any at present in Soviet service. A party of Soviet shipping experts visited Singapore in early 1971 to examine the possibilities of having large Soviet merchant ships repaired there—presumably as an alternative to heavy capital investment in the Soviet Far East shipyards. They were reported as pronouncing favourably on the facilities,[27] but Soviet negotiating procedures tend towards the ponderous, and a number of financial factors will have to be weighed in Moscow before it is known whether any firm proposal will eventuate. It has been suggested that they were possibly searching for a base for an Indian Ocean naval squadron. But it is hardly likely that they would seek a base in a state already providing hospitality to Western warships under a defence agreement or that would wish to install themselves in an area where security would be difficult to maintain, (a base requires far more than refuelling or provisioning facilities, which are readily available to any ship against payment). Nor is it likely that they would expect the Singapore government, whose entire development strategy is based on attracting capital from the Soviets' naval 'rivals' to jeopardise the chances of a continued flow of American, Japanese, British, German or other Western capital. For

[25] *Izvestiya,* 13 March 1971.
[26] *Dal'niy Vostok* (The Far East) USSR Academy of Sciences, Moscow, 1966, p. 164.
[27] *Financial Times,* London, 19 March 1971.

merchant ship repairs, on the other hand, the Soviet Union has a distinct requirement, which is likely to grow, and which can be met only by (a) expensive investment in their Far East shipyards; (b) return of ships to yards in the European USSR, themselves congested and overloaded (much Soviet ship repair is already contracted out to Eastern and Western European countries); or (c) use of facilities in Japan or Singapore.

To the extent that the Soviet media express doubts about Singapore's future, these are connected with its dependence on foreign capital. Typical of their view of it was an article which appeared in April 1971.[28] Its author said, 'In Jurong [the government-sponsored industrial complex] one feels the full impact of the contradictions in the government's economic policy; on the one hand, persistent efforts to overcome economic backwardness and latch on to the achievements of the scientific and technological revolution, and on the other hand, almost unlimited freedom for the activity of private capital, mainly foreign. What will personify the Singapore of the future; the Jurong complex, rousing the pride of the people, or the run-of-the-mill factories, producing electronic equipments parts and assemblies, founded on American and Japanese capital? This is a question that cannot yet be answered.' He pointed further to 'a unique geographical position, the pragmatism of its leaders, a hard-working population, emphasis on broad ties and a policy of non-alignment' as favourable factors for progress, but went on to say 'the definite inconsistency, as far as following a neutral course is concerned, in agreeing to be part of the Britain-sponsored military bloc, along with Australia, New Zealand and Malaysia, may prove to be detrimental to Singapore'. Whether this was a hint that Soviet purchases from Singapore may depend on its rejecting military alignments remains to be seen.

THE FUTURE

The dominant feature of Soviet relations with the Asian countries of the Indian Ocean littoral since the death of Stalin has been the establishment and maintenance of a firm relationship with India. This began in a period when the Soviet Union was obliged to react to American attempts to build a ring of alliances along the Soviet southern borders, and developed further when the two countries found themselves united in opposition to China from 1960 onwards. It has survived the decline in strategic importance to America of peripheral bases, and consequent decline of the

---

28 Shatalov, I., 'At Junction of Eras and Continents', *International Affairs*, (Moscow), April 1971, pp. 89-94.

CENTO and SEATO alliance systems, the departure of its principal architects, Nehru and Khrushchev, the Soviet attempt to play
a mediatory role in the sub-continent after the Tashkent Agreement
of 1966, and the Indo-Pakistan war of 1971.

The implications of the Bangla Desh crisis for Indo-Soviet
relations have yet to be seen. The indication of Soviet support
implied in the Indo-Soviet treaty of August 1971 was valuable for
India in the short term, since it reduced the likelihood of Chinese
intervention on Pakistan's behalf. However, the outcome of the war
has been to change the local strategic balance significantly in
India's favour, and thereby to reduce its future need for Soviet
military assistance. On the other hand, the possibility of U.S.
rapprochement with China is not particularly welcome to either
India or the Soviet Union and will tend to perpetuate the 'special
relationship' between them.

The most significant current development arising from Soviet
relationships with Indian Ocean countries concerns the 'Asian
collective security' proposal first advanced by Brezhnev in 1969.
Although Soviet ideas on the concept have still not been spelt out
in detail, there have been indications that 'collective security' is
viewed as linking economic betterment, and hence increased
internal stability as well as defensive capacity, with a network of
non-aggression treaties, concluded on a regional or bilateral basis.
Treaties concluded by the Soviet Union with Egypt, India and Iraq
have been cited as possible models for an Asian collective security
system.[29]

It therefore seems possible that the current Soviet relationship
with India, in both its political and economic aspects, is to some
extent a 'test-bed' for a wider collective security system in Asia.
Use of the Indo-Soviet relationship as a pilot project for both
economic co-operation and regional security arrangements would
be consistent with the high importance which Soviet leaders have
attached to the relationship since 1953. If this interpretation is
correct, Soviet offers of aid to Pakistan and Bangla Desh are likely
to be accompanied by diplomatic pressures on all three countries
of the sub-continent to engage in economic co-operation and to
sign non-aggression pacts with each other. At the time of writing
it is not clear whether such pressure is yet being applied, but in
view of the importance of the Indian subcontinent to Soviet policy-
makers, and the Soviet Union's past efforts to mediate in its affairs,
this objective may well figure higher than any other in their
approach to Indian Ocean Asia.

[29] E.g. Mayevsky, V., 'Pravda', 22 June 1972.

# 5

# Political Relationships—Pacific Ocean Asia

Whereas west of the Malacca Straits, Soviet relationships have been mainly centred on (a) the Arab world (mostly defined as outside the scope of this volume) and (b) India, east of the Straits the focal points have varied with the political and economic climate from year to year. Thus North Vietnam's importance to Soviet policy was low until the early 1950s, and restraint placed on the Viet Minh in 1954 was, in part at least, a function of Soviet policy towards France. Since 1961, however, it has grown, and with increasing American involvement in the Vietnam War, support of North Vietnam by all means short of direct confrontation gave it an importance out of all proportion to its size, resources, or attractiveness as a model (for development, as opposed to the conduct of armed insurrection). The moves towards involvement in Indonesia, originally most likely conceived as a counter-offensive against American treaty-mongering on the Soviet southern borders, developed into a struggle for influence over the Indonesian Communist Party (PKI), which, on the whole, was won by Peking, and then into a retreat from influence after the *coup* of 30 September 1965. Relations with Japan have been different in nature from those with most of Asia, as a general ideological framework devised for dealings with newly-independent and economically underdeveloped countries did not fit Japan on either count. But dealings with the Japanese Communist Party followed a similar course to that elsewhere, namely a struggle to prevent its adhering entirely to a pro-Peking line.

The area differs from Indian Ocean Asia also in that it contains the Asian Communist countries—Outer Mongolia, North Korea, North Vietnam, and the Chinese People's Republic. This classification is slightly artificial, since Outer Mongolia can hardly be said to have links with either ocean, while China's geographical extent brings it into close contact with countries of Indian Ocean Asia, and North Vietnam is close to Thailand (whose coastline is on the east side of the Malacca Straits, even though Bangkok's latitude is west of them). Soviet relations with the Asian Communist countries have been discussed in a separate chapter, but for the purposes of this one it should not be forgotten that their centres lie in Pacific Ocean Asia, and that each is technically a 'divided country'. In the Mongolian case, the 'other half' (Inner Mongolia) lies within the borders of China, and in any event the issue of Inner Mongolian autonomy, independence, or union with Outer Mongolia has not, as far as can be known, been a very lively one, nor one with much effect upon relations between them. But the division of the other three has resulted from war (in the case of China), or both resulted from war and caused war (in Korea and Vietnam), and therefore lent to Communist-capitalist, or inter-Communist, dissension, a sharpness and violence less apparent in the countries West of the Malacca Straits. A further factor which distinguishes Pacific from Indian Ocean Asia is the universality of connections with China within its Communist movements. All the major Communist Parties in the Pacific Ocean area except Indonesia had strong links with China from early revolutionary days, either through participation by some or all of their founders in the Chinese Communist risings of the 1920s, or through their being offshoots of the South Seas Communist Party, whose special appeal was to overseas Chinese. Throughout the Pacific zone, except for Outer Mongolia and North Korea, the connections between the local Communists and Moscow have always been more tenuous than on the Indian Ocean littoral.

### THE DIVIDED COUNTRIES—KOREA, VIETNAM, CHINA (TAIWAN)

In the case of at least two of the divided countries, (Korea and Vietnam), Soviet policy has been presented with neither the problems nor the opportunities inherent in a political relationship. In both cases division resulted from Soviet-American agreement to divide, envisaged originally as a temporary arrangement (until the surrender of Japanese forces in Korea in the one case, until Vietnam-wide elections in the other), but becoming quasi-permanent because of the commitment of a superpower to support of each half. In each case, by a curious coincidence, the Communist 'half' was the more industrialised; more to the point, in each case the Communist 'half' was adjacent to a Communist country (to both USSR and China in the case of North Korea). Commitment to support of the Communist part of each country virtually precluded relations with its non-Communist counterpart, while neither the South Korean nor the South Vietnamese government has sought a relationship with the Soviet Union for its own sake or for the purpose of ending the state of war.

The third Asian country divided between Communists and non-Communists, China, shows almost but not quite the same exclusiveness. For many years, the Soviet Union showed no interest whatever in cultivating Taiwan, which was frequently denounced as yet another American puppet state.[1] Were Soviet foreign policy run entirely on a basis of Realpolitik, it might have been expected that with the growth of the Sino-Soviet dispute, Soviet leaders would have seen some benefit in reactivating old contacts with the Kuomintang, and there have indeed been rumours that some such contacts (involving Chiang Kai-Shek's son, who was educated in the Soviet Union) have taken place.[2] Whatever substance there may be to these rumours, recent Soviet statements of policy have gone no further than to omit mention of Taiwan altogether,[3] thereby implying that they prefer not to be seen as supporting the Chinese People's Republic's claim that Taiwan is a part of its territory. It is on the whole unlikely that the Soviets would seriously contemplate making overtures to Taiwan as a partner in containment of China, for a number of reasons:

1.  There is no need. Taiwan's existence as an independent state was predicated on the doctrine that the mainland was the abode of rebels who would in due course be ousted. However unrealistic this belief might appear to most of the world, the United States has underwritten Taiwan's existence, maintained its territorial integrity by interposing a fleet between it and the mainland, and equipped armed forces which at present total some 522,000.[4] In response, the Mainland government has found it advisable to deploy the majority of its armed forces in

[1] Eg. in *Malaya Sovetskaya Entsiklopediya*, Vol. IX, Moscow, 1960, pp. 66-7.

[2] KMT tourism officials were permitted to visit Bulgaria in June 1969, the first visit by KMT representatives to any Communist country since 1949, but there were no apparent consequences; the grant of permission may have been designed to 'worry' the CPR. *New York Times*, 8 June 1969.

[3] Eg. Brezhnev, speeches of 7 June 1969 and 30 March 1971.

[4] *The Military Balance 1970-71*, Institute for Strategic Studies, London, p. 61.

positions from which they could readily move to repel an attempted invasion, thus limiting the force which it could bring to bear along the Sino-Soviet border, and improving the Soviet military position thereby.[5]

2. To enter into a relationship with Taiwan would be seen, and presented, by the Chinese, and many others in Communist parties throughout the world, as the most direct confirmation yet of Chinese charges that the Soviet Union and USA are acting in collusion against China, and is especially precluded by Taiwan's withdrawal from the United Nations.

3. Taiwan's future as an independent state depends to a large extent on the course of Sino-American relations. From 1949 to 1971 America has maintained the fiction that the government of Taiwan was the real government of China. It then attempted to substitute a 'two Chinas' policy of recognising both countries, while abandoning the fiction that Taiwan possessed even suspended authority over any part of the mainland. This was acceptable neither to the United Nations nor to the CPR, and the future of Taiwan will probably be decided in negotiation between a post-Mao and post-Chiang leadership. While Taiwan can rely on American support, it needs no Soviet buttressing; without American support, Taiwan's continued future is uncertain, and any militarily feasible Soviet support would be unlikely to make it viable again, even if it were not likely to be politically counterproductive. From Taiwan's point of view, Soviet support could be best expressed by drawing Chinese forces away to the Sino-Soviet border, an outcome which the Soviet Union has no interest in bringing about, especially on behalf of a state whose very future may be in doubt as a result of Sino-American rapprochement.

4. As Japan's strength increases, it is likely to assert a right to be consulted over the future of Taiwan, a territory which it ruled for fifty years prior to 1945, and with which it has strong economic links.[6] If there is a Soviet interest in containment of Chinese influence (military or political), Japan may well have a role in Soviet forward planning, not so much in the assumption of future alliance as in the assumption that a stronger Japan will be of concern to China. Both for this reason, and because of Japan's increasing importance as a trading partner

---

[5] This point is discussed in the chapter on 'Military Relations', q.v.

[6] For a summary of Japanese views on Formosan nationalism see Mendel, D., *The Politics of Formosan Nationalism,* University of California Press, 1970, pp. 196-224.

and co-developer of Siberia, Soviet leaders will wish to avoid actions in respect to Taiwan which might give China and Japan a common interest that they lack at present.

5.  Soviet statements have been careful to distinguish between the 'Mao Tse-Tung clique' on the one hand, and the mass of the Chinese Communist Party on the other,[7] reflecting a belief that with new Chinese leaders an amelioration if not a sinking of differences could take place. They would hardly expect the position of Chinese elements favouring such an outcome to be strengthened by a Soviet rapprochement with a government dedicated to the extirpation from China of any form of Communism.

6.  Rapprochement with Taiwan would require a degree of cynicism of which Soviet leaders have not showed themselves capable. It is one thing to woo non-Communist leaders against the wishes and interests of local Communist parties, or to intervene on an ally's territory to maintain the status quo. It is quite another to support a US-sponsored anti-Communist regime against a Communist one, however aberrant, and to justify it ideologically would require a surpassing mental agility.

7.  With erosion of the belief in the KMT's 'claim' to govern China, the Soviets may well expect that its claim to govern Taiwan will be openly questioned. Despite Taiwan's record of economic success, and its relative lack of rural unrest (the result, apparently, of land reforms sponsored during the period of Japanese rule rather than of specific actions by its present rulers), the rights of native-born Taiwanese have been subjected to considerable erosion by the post-1949 arrivals from mainland China.[8] It is possible that when Taiwan's future is considered, the Taiwanese themselves will press for independence or autonomy. To be associated with a KMT regime whose entire future would depend on denial of this option to self-determination could prove a further grave embarrassment for the Soviet government.

Though the idea that the Soviet Union would attempt to enlist Taiwan in its 'ring of containment' around China appears attractive on the surface, it seems likely that the most the Soviet

---

[7] Eg. in Sladkovskiy, M.I. (Ed.), *Leninskaya Politika SSSR V. otnoshenii Kitaya,* USSR Academy of Sciences, Institute of the Peoples of Asia, Moscow, 1969, pp. 159-256.

[8] Opposition by Taiwanese to mainland rule dates back to 1683; restoration of Chinese rule in 1945 was followed in 1947 by a Taiwanese uprising. See Kerr, G., *Formosa Betrayed,* Eyre & Spottiswoode, London, 1965.

leaders will feel required to do is to refrain from showing excess of zeal in support of the mainland government's claim to it. Recent speeches by Brezhnev indicate that this is precisely what they are doing; he did not even refer to the issue.[9]

### INDONESIA

The country in the Pacific area chosen for a major concentration of Soviet foreign policy effort was Indonesia. Prior to independence, the main Soviet link with it was through the Indonesian Communist Party (PKI), and it was untypical of the area in the strength of its early links with Moscow, through the Dutch Communist Party.

It was founded in 1920, and against the advice of the Comintern and most of its own small Moscow-trained cadre, attempted a revolt against the Dutch in 1926.[10] This failed, and the Party was outlawed, with most of its leaders interned or exiled. Until 1935, Stalin's rejection of alliances with the non-Communist nationalists, kept its influence low, and after 1935, its conformity to the Comintern policy of popular fronts against fascism led it to follow the Dutch Communist Party in deemphasising the issue of independence from Holland, and separated it from some non-Communist nationalists such as Soekarno. From 1942 to 1945 he collaborated with the Japanese in the belief that Indonesian independence would have to be secured within a Japanese-dominated Asia, but the abrupt collapse of Japan in August 1945 led to a confused situation, in which socialist and Islamic nationalists, the PKI and a Japanese-sponsored 'national-communist' movement (led by Tan Malaka, the former Comintern agent for South-East Asia) jockeyed for power, but without any indication of Soviet influence or control over the PKI's actions.[11] Indonesia's independence was proclaimed on 17th August 1945, but the Dutch determination to reestablish colonial rule led to a period of uneasy coexistence between Republican and Dutch forces which ended with the first major Dutch offensive in July 1947. During this period the exiled leaders returned, some reentering the PKI, but many others joining other parties, or working within the trade union, peasant or youth organisations to influence them in pro-Communist directions, and, later to take control of some of them. The PKI cooperated with the nationalists, held some governmental posts, and 35 out of 514

---

9   Eg. his 'Report of the Central Committee' at the 24th Party Congress, 30 March 1971.

10  Grant, B., *Indonesia*, Penguin Books, 1967, pp. 71-73.

11  Brackman, A. C., *Indonesian Communism*, Praeger, New York, 1963, pp. 33-43.

Parliamentary seats. It appeared set on a line of participation in the independence movement, cooperation, with non-Communist nationalists, especially the Socialists, and penetration of their organisations by 'undeclared' PKI members. However the fall of the Amir Sjarifuddin government in January 1948 eliminated the PKI from office, and a break-away of many socialists from the Socialist-Communist alliance in the same month tended to force the Party back to a more orthodox and differentiated position.[12]

The PKI's decision to operate through fronts and other political parties was later explained by Aidit as the result of 'failure to realise that the Dutch colonial era had ended and a new era opened'.[13] This is disingenuous; the PKI's leaders were not so blind to reality as that. It is more likely that the policy of concealment was adopted for reasons of international politics. In this period, which ended in Indonesia only in August 1948 with Musso's arrival from the Soviet Union, Stalin was attempting to avoid presenting an image of expansionism. In the Eastern European countries, for example, use of the title 'Communist Party' was being discouraged —Communists were enjoined to bring about mergers with left-wing socialists, and the offspring of these shotgun marriages to this day bear titles indicative of their mixed origin—the East German Socialist Unity Party, Polish United Workers' Party, and Hungarian Workers' Party.[14] While determined to exercise control over his new buffer zone, Stalin was anxious to avoid alarming the West by precipitate signs of Communist takeover, and for this reason all the states were described as 'People's Democracies', a title designed both to mark them off as lower on the Leninist ladder of social progression than the 'socialist' Soviet Union, and also to indicate that they were states of a new 'mixed type', allegedly retaining features of capitalism. With civil war in progress in China and the wartime alliance giving way to a cold war which must not become hot because the West held most of the cards (the Soviet economy having been devastated by war, that of the US stimulated by it, the Americans and British monopolising both sea and long-range air power, and the Americans also having the atomic bomb), Soviet policy, until enunciation of the 'two camps' theory at the end of 1947 aimed at not drawing attention to the extent of Soviet gains from the war. While the PKI remained in semi-concealment, Dutch attempts to blacken the image of the Indonesian indepen-

---

[12] *Ibid.*, pp. 64-79.
[13] *Ibid.*, interview with Aidit, 1960, p. 53.
[14] A cause of subsequent confusion, when pro-Chinese factions outside the countries concerned appropriated the titles of 'Polish Communist Party', etc. for the purposes of issuing anti-Soviet declarations.

dence movement could rely only on the fact that some of its leaders had collaborated with the Japanese, a fact hardly likely to impress the British, then negotiating with Aung San in Burma, or the Americans, who were swiftly adjusting themselves to the idea that the diligent and docile inhabitants of occupied Japan would make useful allies against the Soviets and Communist Chinese.

In 1948, this changed. By then Stalin had discarded the mask. Communist takeover was an established fact in all the countries of occupied Eastern Europe, and had been achieved without any military reaction from the West, beyond moves to form a defensive alliance. But during 1945-47 it was expedient to play down the importance of the PKI, and as circumstances made it possible for PKI members returning from exile, or emerging from the resistance, to conceal their affiliations, this was done. The ease with which the *revenant* from Moscow, Musso, was able to assume leadership of the PKI indicates that at that time it was extremely respectful to Moscow's wishes, even if its tactics were becoming tinged with a Maoist shade derived more from similarity of circumstances than conscious copying for its own sake. And during 1945-47, Moscow's wishes were that Communists should not draw attention to themselves if they could avoid doing so, especially in colonies of America's allies. That this diffidence was tactically sound was shown when Musso virtually forced the Party into the open in 1948; Dutch propaganda switched its emphasis from the pro-Japanese leanings of some nationalist leaders, to stressing the Communist involvement in the affairs of Indonesia.[15]

Musso, who returned in August 1948 was one of the founders of the Party, and had been in the Soviet Union since the end of the 1920s. As one of the PKI's delegates to the Sixth Comintern Congress in 1928 he had escaped the Dutch arrests and had remained outside Indonesia, apart from a visit during 1935 to re-organise the Party in accordance with the 'popular front' policy. He had been the PKI's titular leader ever since the Sixth Comintern Congress, and despite his remoteness from the local scene, was immediately accepted as leader and proceeded at once to implement a policy of organising all Communist elements into one avowedly Communist party. This involved dissolution of two other parties (the Socialist and Indonesian Labour Parties, whose leaders, including the ex-Premier, Sjarifuddin, announced that they

---

[15] On 20 September 1948 the Dutch offered to assist the Indonesian Republic in suppressing the Madiun rebellion. The Dutch Foreign Minister was in Washington at the time, and made the offer from there. The Republic rejected it.

had been Communists for many years),[16] the election of a new Politburo, and a lengthy process of reorganisation.

The 'new line' was to be based on a 'national front', for the purpose of 'completing the bourgeois-democratic revolution'; co-operation of non-Communists would be sought, but the nation must be led by the 'proletariat'.[17] So far Musso's policy was consistent with the idea of a 'two-stage' revolution, though the insistence on the need for 'the proletariat' to lead was unrealistic, given that the over-whelming majority of Indonesians were peasants. If, as so often in Communist statements, the 'proletariat' really meant 'the Party', there were overtones of the Maoist 'one-stage' revolution in Musso's draft resolution, but as a whole his statements, with their insistence on the abandonment of concealment in favour of overt PKI activity, and his attacks on the non-Communist leaders, especially Soekarno and Hatta for their willingness to negotiate with the Dutch, were typical manifestations of the 'two camps' doctrine.

However, before Musso could proceed far with his plans, the 'Madiun Incident' occurred. The genesis of this was to be sought in policies pursued by Sjarifuddin as Premier and Defence Minister in the latter half of 1947.[18] By then numbers of 'private armies' attached to political parties had come into being, and Sjarifuddin attempted to cut down the strength of those with right-wing affiliations, while fostering those of the left. This policy caused the Masjumi (Moslem) party considerable uneasiness, and it took the occasion of the unfavourable 'Renville' cease-fire agreement with the Dutch to withdraw its support and bring the government down. Sjarifuddin was replaced by a nationalist of the centre, Mohammed Hatta; the left demanded more portfolios than he was prepared to give, and he formed a government on 29th January 1948 which, for the first time since the declaration of independence, included none of the left-wing parties. It was this which led the non-Communist left to abandon its coalition with the PKI.

Hatta's 'rationalisation' of the armed forces, was to include demobilisation of many Communist-led units. Apart from its political implications, it accorded with the desires of the military leaders to produce a reformed army capable of better performance against the Dutch.[19]

Two concepts were discussed. Sjarifuddin, with Soekarno's

---

[16] Grant, *op. cit.*
[17] *Revolusioner*, 23 August 1948, quoted in Brackman, *op. cit.* p. 82.
[18] Hindley, D., *The Communist Party of Indonesia, 1951-63,* University of California Press, 1964, p. 20.
[19] Brackman, *op. cit.* pp. 74-5.

support, argued for a 'people's army' of irregulars recruited on a village basis, while Hatta, supported by the army leaders, favoured a smaller but more tightly disciplined and controlled guerilla-type regular force, on the grounds that a proliferation of irregulars was of doubtful military effectiveness and threatened to create problems of internal order. By September Hatta's view had prevailed, and it became clear that many Communist-led units would be disbanded or incorporated into the regular army.[20]

Musso, meanwhile, was engaged on a speaking tour attacking Hatta as 'leading the country back to colonialism', and claiming in the spirit of the 'two camps' theory that neutralism was wrong ('At present there are only two camps, the Soviet Union and those with colonies ... Can we maintain our neutrality in this controversy? Certainly not ...').[21] An attempt was made to persuade other parties to join Musso's proposed 'National Front', but these broke down. Skirmishing then broke out between Communist and government troops. On 16th September Hatta denounced the PKI for seeking 'to drag the Republic into a Soviet-American global conflict', and released the nationalist (and anti-PKI) Communist leader Tan Malaka.

From documents[22] subsequently produced by government forces, it appeared that the PKI was planning a military rising for November, with unrealistically high expectations of both military and popular support. For reasons still not fully explained, but probably connected with fear of the impending reorganisations, their armed units revolted instead on 18th September on a purely local basis at Madiun in East Java. They succeeded in capturing the city and some surrounding villages, but the revolt was quickly suppressed, and on 31st October Musso was killed. Several other Communist leaders, including Amir Sjarifuddin, were captured on 1st December, and three days later the government proclaimed the insurrection at an end. The Dutch attacked Indonesia again on the night of 18th-19th December 1948, and captured Soekarno with almost all his Cabinet. Before surrendering, it ordered the execution of all the prominent Communists, and a total of fifty-two were shot, leaving only six (three who had not been captured, and three who escaped). Tan Malaka escaped the Dutch encirclement and proclaimed himself leader of the resistance, denouncing all other leaders, including the PKI, but not Soekarno, as 'appeasers'. He was captured and executed by government forces in April 1949.

[20] *Ibid.*, p. 75.
[21] Speech at Madiun, 8 September 1949.
[22] Cited in Kahin, G. M., *Nationalism and Revolution in Indonesia,* Cornell University Press, 1952, pp. 270-1.

The PKI played very little part in the events following the second Dutch attack, because the executions in December had left it virtually leaderless. With the restoration of the Republic, its future was in doubt because of the Madiun revolt, and not until 7th September 1949 did the government decide against banning it.

As a decimated party, virtually bereft of leaders, and legally subsistent only by the grace and favour of the non-Communist government (whose charity was no doubt facilitated by the thought that it was advisable to allow it to operate in the open, where it would be easier to watch), the post-Madiun PKI was clearly in no fit state to pursue the tough line enjoined by the 'two camps' theory. The new titular leader, Alimin, was one of the few who had spent any time with the Chinese Communists, and he adapted Maoist theory to fit the reduced circumstances of the PKI. Indonesia's independence was imminent—it took effect on 27th December 1949, but the PKI was to regard it as unreal, because of the country's economic dependence on its former rulers.[23] On this basis, it was possible to argue that those members of the bourgeoisie who did not ally themselves with foreign financial interests constituted a 'progressive force', and to form an alliance with them, the petty bourgeoisie, workers and peasants for the purpose of fighting foreign capital and its allies, the 'comprador bourgeoisie'.[24] This was the policy which Alimin now began to advocate, and under Aidit, who succeeded him in January 1951, it was to be pursued to extravagant lengths.

As the negotiations with the Dutch moved towards independence, Soviet media continued their hostile blasts, *Red Star*[25] describing Hatta as a 'traitor' and a 'Quisling', and at the United Nations the Soviet bloc moved to overturn the Hague settlement, but without success.

Soviet hostility to the non-Communist leaders was as marked in Indonesia as elsewhere, reflecting Stalin's universal unwillingness to credit them with any aspiration to genuine independence. Soviet publications mentioned Indonesia hardly at all prior to enunciation of the 'two camps' doctrine, and after, it invariably presented the PKI as the 'real leader and organiser' of the Indonesian revolution, while the non-Communist nationalists were described in very hostile terms—as 'counter-revolutionary' (1948),[26] as a 'reactionary, bourgeois, feudal clique' responsible for 'division in the ranks

---

[23] Statement by PKI Politburo, 7 October 1948, and Aidit, 1955, cited in Hindley *op. cit.* p. 33.

[24] PKI programme, March 1954.

[25] *Krasnaya Zrezda*, Moscow 31 October 1949.

[26] Brackman, *op. cit.* p. 67.

of the national liberation movement', for which the people of Indonesia 'are now paying heavily' (1949).[27] It was claimed in 1950 that 'because of cynical betrayal by the Soekarno-Hatta clique', the struggle for independence had 'ended in abject defeat and the imposition of an American-Dutch imperialistic dual yoke disguised by the hypocritical sign of Republic'.[28] Until Stalin's death, therefore, Soviet relations with the actual wielders of State power were as negative in Indonesia as elsewhere in Asia.

The Soviet leadership showed as little interest in PKI matters from the Madiun incident to the death of Stalin, even though the speed with which the leadership of the PKI had been conferred on Musso indicates that he had returned with weighty credentials and an authority which only Moscow could then have conferred; this suggests that before Madiun Stalin considered the PKI's chances of gaining power to be better than the average for Communist parties in the emergent states.

But when the outcome of Madiun, and the death of most of the PKI's leaders, confirmed that leadership of the Indonesian revolution was firmly in the hands of the non-Communist nationalists, Stalin apparently lost interest. In any event, he had many other preoccupations between 1948 and 1953. The takeover of Czechoslovakia, the Berlin blockade, the Chinese Civil War and the Korean War all affected the Soviet Union far more closely than the fate of an unsuccessful Communist Party in a remote and unstable archipelago of South-East Asia.

The result was that, as had happened in China in the 1920s, a Party reduced to ruin by following Soviet guidelines was left to evolve policies of its own, based on close association with non-Communist elements which, in its weakened state, it could neither fight nor ignore. As the Chinese had concluded, so did the Indonesians, namely that they must prepare for a long power struggle rather than the quick *coup* which Musso apparently had in mind, and must wage it with the aid of a 'national front' comprising themselves, national bourgeoisie, petty bourgeoisie, workers, intellectuals and peasants.[29] This was a somewhat broader concept than that of Mao, or Alimin, but was essentially Maoist rather than Muscovite in inspiration, because of the similarities in the situations of the Indonesian and Chinese parties.

The main similarity in the situations was evident in that peasants formed the majority in society, while the 'workers' were few in

[27] *For a Lasting Peace, For a People's Democracy,* 15 February 1949.
[28] Potekhin, I. I., in *Sovetskaya Etnografiya,* No. 3/1950, p. 235.
[29] Hindley, *op. cit.* pp. 39-59.

number and found only in a small number of cities. A Bolshevik-style attempt at a *coup* had failed, and little further help could be expected from Moscow. Indonesia could be represented, as had China in the 1920s, as 'semi-colonial' because of its economic dependence, as its few industries and much of its exportable primary production were dominated by outside interests.

But there were also significant differences. Central government was weak in Indonesia, as it had been in China, but not so weak that generally acknowledged national leaders were lacking, and these leaders provided a focus for alternations to Communism with more attractive power than Chiang Kai-Shek had ever possessed. The strength of Islam represented another counter-force with no exact parallel in China; for though the PKI was able to make considerable headway among 'nominal' Moslems, a large Moslem hard-core remained impervious to it[30] and found political expression in a succession of right-wing parties. PKI strength, though at times high in parts of Sumatra and Kalimantan, was centred in East-Central Java, and remained regionalised, which made it easier to combat. And, perhaps more important, no outside enemy comparable to Japan emerged. It had been possible in China for the Communists to attract support for their national front from patriotic non-Communists who contrasted their vigorous opposition to the Japanese with Chiang's ineffectiveness.[31] No such possibility was open to the PKI, for two reasons. In the first place, the Madiun collapse showed the unlikelihood of success in any attempt at maintaining an armed force against the Indonesian Army; in the second, the Dutch in the late 1940s could not plausibly be represented as an equivalent to the Japanese of the 1930s.

This last factor proved crucial. The PKI's programme for a national front, leading in the long term to a socialist revolution, depended on the argument that Indonesia's semi-colonial status resulted primarily from a Dutch economic stranglehold into which she had been delivered by the non-Communist nationalist leaders headed by Soekarno. But as Soekarno reduced this 'stranglehold' by cancellation of Indonesia's debts to the Netherlands (1956), the expropriation of all Dutch-owned businesses (1957) and the takeover of Dutch New Guinea (1961-2), PKI arguments for the proposition became more and more difficult to sustain. There was little that the Soviets could or would do to bolster the PKI's case

---

[30] For a discussion of the division between Santri and Abangan Moslems, and its political implications, see Hindley, *op. cit.* pp. 11-12 and 223-225, 229.

[31] Fitzgerald, C. P., *The Birth of Communist China*, Penguin Books, 1964, pp. 88-89.

during the Soekarno years; after Stalin's death Soviet attention in Indonesia as elsewhere focused on the governing group rather than the local Communists, while PKI anti-imperialist agitation broadened to include the USA. Nor, in face of the signs of Soviet and Chinese favour for Soekarno, was it politically feasible for the PKI to continue to attack him as a tool of neocolonialism, and after 1952 such attacks ceased. The foremost non-Communist leader therefore became virtually immune to PKI attacks on 'neocolonialism', which had not been the case in China, and this circumstance lent the PKI's situation an additional particularity. The new policy of the PKI under Aidit was to cooperate with the 'middle forces', ie. those which were non-Communist (rather than specifically *anti-*Communist) and 'anti-imperialist'.[32]

Aidit spent several months in the Soviet bloc from November 1952, where he presumably gained Soviet support for his policies of cooperation, conversion of the PKI into a mass party, and the seeking of power by Parliamentary means.

To do this involved a delicate balancing of interests, and a programme which although inspired by the Chinese example, led to actions which could be defended only in terms of the internal situation, actions such as the advocacy of strong protectionist tariff policies designed to further the interests of local businessmen. Theoretically this could be justified as helping to complete the bourgeois revolution, a necessary prerequisite to a Socialist revolution, whether the two were seen in Leninist terms as consecutive or in the Roy-Mao conception as simultaneous, but in practice it was defended as furthering the cause of the 'united front' by defending the reasonable interests of the national bourgeoisie.[33] The policy of cooperation was shown mainly in the PKI's readiness to collaborate with other parties against the right-wing Masjumi (Moslem) party, in return for 'toleration'. Between 1951 and 1955 PKI membership increased from a few thousand to almost one million, with its associated trade union, peasant and youth movements showing similar increases, while the Party's support in Parliament occasionally proved crucial to incumbent governments. But the fragmenting of the non-Communist parties made coalition governments inevitable, while the ineffectiveness of these governments in solving economic problems and (especially after Masjumi's withdrawal in January 1957) their identification with Javanese interests, lowered their acceptability to the other islands. A decline in confidence in the Parliamentary system resulted, and

32 Hindley, *op. cit.* p. 57.
33 *Ibid.,* pp. 234 & 350.

the situation threatened to polarise between the Army on the one hand and Soekarno on the other.

This faced the PKI leaders with a problem of reevaluation. The elections of 1955, and still more those of 1957, vindicated their decision to rely on mass organisation and participation in Parliament, but the position of strength which they appeared to indicate was to a great extent illusory, because the collapse of Parliamentary institutions was imminent.

During May-August 1956 Soekarno visited a number of foreign countries including the United States, Soviet Union and China. On his return he expressed his 'amazement' at the enthusiasm with which workers in the Communist states laboured to create a new society, and both then and subsequently singled out the Chinese People's Republic as the most impressive example.[34] On 30th October 1956 he first used the term 'guided democracy' to describe his intentions, subsequently arguing that Western-style democracy required a degree of literacy and prosperity which Indonesia did not yet possess.

Considerable unrest resulted from his statements which appeared to portend the disappearance of political parties, and on 22nd February 1957 he elaborated the concept to provide for a continuation of parties, Parliament, and a free press, but to divorce them from executive power by constructing cabinets on an all party basis, and by forming a National Advisory Council made up of 'functional groups' (peasants, workers, intellectuals, etc.), chaired by himself. This plan was supported by the PKI in the expectation that it would receive a share in power. In fact, no PKI members were included in the Cabinet, and only 9 of the 45 National Council members had PKI affiliations.[35]

The Soviet Union welcomed 'guided democracy'.[36] It may have had reservations about Soekarno's attachment to the Chinese example, but since the Sino-Soviet dispute was not then at an acute stage it is unlikely that his references to it were taken as anti-Soviet in intent. In any case Soekarno threw in a number of complimentary references to the Soviet Union. In a gesture which was

---

[34] Eg. in speeches of 14 November 1956 and 27 August 1957.

[35] Hindley, *op. cit.* p. 263. Brackman (p. 237) considers that 12 of the 45 members were 'well-known Communists and fellow-travellers'.

[36] Apart from sending President Vorosholiv on a state visit coinciding with the inauguration of guided democracy, Soviet press and radio frequently referred to Soekarno in favourable terms and refrained from criticism of the restrictions placed on the PKI, as on other political parties. See also the very favourable review given by G. Kesselbrenner to Soekarno's book *Dibawah Pendera Revolusi* (Under the banner of Revolution) Vol. I, 1959, in *Narody Azii i Afriki* 4/1961, pp. 211-3.

presumably meant to have symbolic significance, though this was not specifically emphasised, the Soviet President, Voroshilov, arrived in Djakarta to commence a goodwill visit on 6th May 1957, the day 'Guided Democracy' was inaugurated. On the next day Voroshilov reiterated Soviet support for Indonesia's claim to Dutch New Guinea,[37] and the two leaders then embarked on a tour of the country.

Local elections were in progress at the time, and the results indicated large PKI gains. But most of these were at the expense of the Indonesian Nationalist Party (PNI), which Soekarno had founded, and only in Central Java were they sufficient to make the PKI the largest single party. Elsewhere the votes of the two Moslem-based parties, Masjumi and NU, remained large and stable; in Java, with an increase of over one-third in its vote compared with 1955, the PKI gathered 27.4% of votes, but nowhere else did it approach this level.[38] The success was in any case a relatively hollow one. On the one hand, Parliament had just been virtually stripped of its powers by 'Guided Democracy' so that electoral success would in future count for less. On the other, the increase in PKI electoral strength, dependent as it was on signs of Soekarno's favour and the presence of the Soviet head of state, served to alert the anti-Communist elements in Indonesian society and cause the PKI to turn more to Soekarno for protection, thus leading it to become closely identified with him and hence with his progressively greater leaning towards Peking, while not being sufficient to enable it to secure a real share in power.

With the discrediting of Parliamentary government, and the possibility that political interests would henceforth tend to polarise around Soekarno or the army, the PKI gravitated naturally towards support of Soekarno. It had long ceased its attacks on him, and welcomed as a sign of common interest his frequent declarations that the Indonesian revolution was not yet complete,[39] as well as his occasional public statements that it should be accorded a share in the government. In his search for allies against the army during 1955-6, he was attracted by the size and efficiency of the PKI and its associated organisations, while in its turn the PKI sought association with him in the belief that only he could prevent the establishment of an Army dictatorship or a right-wing civilian government, either of which would give power to the anti-Communist forces and bring an end to 'toleration'. Being still more

[37] Speech of 7 May 1957.
[38] Hindley, *op. cit.* p. 223.
[39] Eg. in speech of 17 August 1952.

amenable to Soviet thinking than most Asian Communist Parties, it was also, no doubt, influenced by the signs of Soviet favour to him. By 1957 Indonesia had received $US106.7 million worth of aid, and to help in coping with unrest in the outlying islands the Soviets varied the terms of their loan to permit the Indonesians to use some of it for the purchase of light military vehicles. Little use was made of this at the time, but in April 1958, after first approaching and being refused by the United States, the Indonesians announced receipt of a $400 million credit for arms purchases, nominally from Poland and Czechoslavakia.

During the period of guided democracy, the PKI became more and more unconditional in its support of Soekarno. In October 1959 it went so far as to endorse in toto his version of the five principles of Indonesian nationalism, enunciated by him on 1 June 1945 (and subsequently entitled 'Pantjasila' in confusing reference to the Panch Sheel, or five principles of *peaceful coexistence* listed by Nehru in 1955). As these included 'belief in Almighty God', it could well be argued that the Party leaders, at least, were straining their consciences in support of Soekarno. But the episode illustrated their dependence on him, as did the habit which arose of justifying Communist policies by quotations from his writings.

The Soviets, themselves committed to support Soekarno as a charismatic anti-Western nationalist leader, were as slow to detect the dangers in the PKI's position as the PKI leadership. In general they welcomed 'guided democracy' partly for the restrictions it placed on right-wing political parties, and partly for its talk of planning Indonesia's economy. One Soviet writer,[40] warned of the danger to the PKI, as the best-organised and most rapidly growing party, of the policy of restricting party political activity and of the growth in the Army's importance, but most Soviet comment emphasised the blows dealt to the Right-wing by, for example, the banning of the Masjumi and PSI in 1960.[41]

Having first placed its faith in parliamentary processes only to see the role of Parliament whittled down, the PKI began gradually to react to the restriction of the role of political parties. During 1959 it protested ineffectually as higher government officials were ordered to leave political parties, as the government announced its intention to extend the appointive system from parliament to local levels of government, and at the government's denial of parliamentary control over the Budget. In March 1960 Soekarno dissolved parliament, and Aidit requested either elections or appointment of

40 Lavrent'yev, A., in *Aziya i Afrika Segodnya* No. 3, 1961.
41 *Respublika Indoneziya,* Moscow 1960, foreword.

a new parliament to reflect the distribution of popular support. Soekarno gave way to the extent of appointing a new parliament in which 30 seats out of 261 were granted to the PKI. But in conformity with 'guided democracy', a bare majority of seats (131) were awarded not to political parties, but to functional groups, and 35 of these seats went to the Army.[42] Having enrolled the PKI's assistance to contain the Army, Soekarno was also using the Army to contain the political parties. Apart from distribution of seats in parliament, he used as a weapon the State of Emergency which had been proclaimed in March 1957 during the provincial unrest which followed the announcement of the guided democracy concept. Under this, Army commanders had wide powers to control political party and press activities, and frequently used them against the PKI. Not until May 1963 were these restrictions lifted.

The PKI's support for Soekarno, however much its leaders believed it to be rooted in their own internal circumstances, led it inexorably in his wake to policies amenable to Peking rather than to Moscow. While in receipt of vast amounts of Soviet military and economic aid, Soekarno took a pro-Chinese line in the Sino-Indian exchanges over Tibet in 1959, and the PKI followed suit, despite the acceptance of the Indian position implicit in the Soviet statement of 12 Sep. 59. What the PKI had conceived as an alliance was by no means an alliance of equals. The concessions to its viewpoint were few; it was unable to prevent erosion of representative institutions to any important extent, or to gain access to power. Its ability to act as a focus for discontent, social or economic, was gravely impaired by its unwillingness to attack Soekarno; instead it sought to show its militancy by attacks on his ministers, or demonstrations against economic conditions which frequently ended in repression by the Army, and were not effective in preventing deterioration in the standard of living. Even the admission of Aidit and Lukman into the government in March 1962 served only to increase their problems, because their admission (as Soekarno probably intended it should), served only to identify the PKI with government-imposed hardships, without giving them any power to alter conditions.[43] The PKI made half-hearted attempts to maintain an appearance of neutrality in the Sino-Soviet dispute, by refusing to take sides and by endorsing some of the propositions of each protagonist. Its attachment to the basic Khrushchevian position that Communist parties could achieve power by peaceful means was inherent in its post-Madiun policies, and therefore required no

[42] Hindley, *op. cit.* p. 274-6.
[43] *Ibid.*, pp. 294-7.

ideological adjustments on its part, while at the same time it derived more from Maoist than Soviet experience and was therefore unlikely to attract Chinese hostility. But its following of Soekarno into pro-Chinese positions, and persistence in supporting him over confrontation after the Soviets had begun to register disillusionment with him, in fact placed the PKI in the Chinese camp. Three statements must suffice to summarise trends in opinion within the PKI on the crucial question of 'peaceful transition to socialism' between the introduction of 'guided democracy' and the attempted *coup* of 1965.

1.  Aidit, 1957: 'If it depends on the Communists the best way, the ideal way, for transition to the system of people's democratic power . . . is the way of peace, the parliamentary way.'[44]
2.  Aidit, 1960: 'The prospects for a peaceful transition to socialism, as laid down by Khrushchev at the Soviet 20th Party Congress, are the brightest, and the opportunities most bountiful, in two countries; namely Cuba and Indonesia.'[45]
3.  Resolution of National Conference of PKI, 1964: 'The experience of the Indonesian people themselves has proved that only when they do not give up the weapons in their hands can they carry through the struggle against imperialism and old and new colonialism and win success.'[46]

Confrontation with Malaysia brought new strains in relations between the Army, Soekarno and the PKI. Briefly the Army leaders were wary at the prospect of having to send their best units to Borneo, leaving Java to an increasingly influential PKI. Nor were they happy at the increased role now given to the Air Force, which was a more left-wing body than the Army and more enthusiastic for confrontation.[47]

From the PKI point of view, undue emphasis on the military aspects of confrontation threatened to strengthen the armed forces at the expense of the political parties, and PKI statements on the subject showed some concern to stress other factors, such as pressure in the economic or political fields, for example nationalisation of British firms or recognition of an independent state of North Kalimantan.[48]

The circumstances surrounding the unsuccessful *coup d'état* of 30 Sep. 65 are still not entirely clear. Circumstances in the third quarter of 1965 would have pointed to the Army leaders rather

[44] *Bintang Merah,* Djakarta, October-November 1957.
[45] Interview 1960, cited in Brackman, *op. cit.* p. 302.
[46] *Peking Review,* 24 July 1964, p. 14.
[47] Weinstein, F., *Indonesia Abandons Confrontation,* Cornell, 1969.
[48] Eg. Aidit, *Harian Rakjat,* 14 October 1963.

than the PKI as the element in Indonesian government most likely to wish for a change of leadership. While Soekarno's leanings towards China as a 'distant friend' were clear, his treatment of the Chinese in Indonesia had shown him to have considerable reservations about nearby Chinese communities, and one factor in confrontation was a fear that the Chinese, who comprised 40% of Malaysia's population, would come to dominate the new Federation. But the expulsion of Singapore in August 1965 removed this possibility, and therefore took away one of the reasons for confrontation. Also in August 1965 occurred what amounted to the promulgation of an 'Asian Axis' with China, North Vietnam, Cambodia and North Korea, an event which seemed likely to estrange Indonesia from its two main suppliers of military and economic aid:—the United States, already gravely embarrassed by Indonesia's conflict with three of its allies, Britain, Australia and New Zealand; and the Soviet Union which was sufficiently disenchanted with both Soekarno's and the PKI's pro-Peking tendencies to have put out feelers for an exchange of diplomatic representatives with Malaysia (in July 1964, while Mikoyan was proclaiming Soviet support for confrontation in Djakarta).[49] It is possible that the PKI leaders contemplated a *coup* to replace the anti-Communist army heads, but it may be that they feared an army *coup* directed at ending confrontation, switching Indonesian foreign policy away from its pro-China path, and reducing the influence of the PKI, and were acting to forestall it. An additional incentive for them was the illness of Soekarno, and the fear that his removal from the scene would be followed by army action against them.[50]

Whatever the circumstances, the *coup* of 30 Sep. 65 was carried out mainly by Air Force officers. The PKI's newspaper welcomed it, but none of the Party's mass organisations took part or were even prepared to cope with the fierce anti-Communist reaction which took place after it had failed. If it was masterminded by the PKI's leaders, as the anti-Communists later alleged, it was done with extreme ineptitude.

Although Soviet dissatisfaction with Soekarno had been registered before the *coup* (Malaysia ceased to be denounced by the Soviet media as a neocolonialist artefact in 1964, when his policy of 'confrontation' was still in full swing), and after his fall in 1966 a Soviet article criticised him for sliding into the Chinese embrace, withdrawing from the United Nations and for pressing confronta-

[49] *Asian Almanac* 1963-64 (1), p. 405c.
[50] Soekarno fell ill at Bogor on 4 August 1965.

tion until Indonesia was on the verge of economic disaster, the circumstances of his fall gave them little cause to expect that his successors would be more amenable to Soviet interests. Nevertheless, for over eighteen months after the September *coup,* Soviet comment on Indonesia was optimistic. It was hoped that anti-PKI sentiment could be restrained from developing into a generalised anti-Communism, that the blame for the PKI's disaster could be attributed to the pro-Peking orientation of Aidit and other leaders, and that a weakening of the Chinese position vis-a-vis Indonesia could be turned to the advantage of the Soviet Union as Indonesia's largest creditor. But the scale, ferocity and duration of the anti-Communist pogroms, the return of Western assets to their owners, the efforts of the Indonesian government to attract Western capital, and its hedging over payment of its large debts to the Soviet Union, appear to have convinced the Soviet Union that its former restraint was no longer justified.[51] By April 1967 'downgrading' of Indonesia was apparent; the slogans for May Day included only *'friendly* greetings to the *workers* of Indonesia', as compared with those of October 1965, which had sent *'warm* greetings to the *great* Indonesian *people.'*[52]

The initial mildness of Soviet reactions to the destruction of the PKI after the attempted *coup* of 30th September 1965 was most likely motivated by the feeling that not much had been lost. The lavishness of Soviet economic and military aid to Indonesia had not prevented development by Soekarno of a strongly pro-Chinese line from 1963 onwards, nor had it averted a lean towards Peking on the part of the PKI. The new regime's abandonment of Soekarno's pro-Chinese line was welcome, while its easing of 'confrontation' meant that Soviet relations with Malaysia and Singapore could develop without the inhibitant imposed by fear of offending Indonesia. Soviet leaders may also have expected a political settlement, involving compromise between the army leaders and the more left-inclined navy and air force. At the very least, they may have also felt that a post-Soekarno leadership, having given up the adventuristic nationalism of his later years, could be a less embarrassing associate, and that consequently judgment on it should be reserved until its intentions had become clearer.

However, as it became clear that the new regime intended to make maximum use of foreign capital to rehabilitate the Indonesian economy, and was prepared to denationalise foreign firms in order

---

[51] For a discussion of the issues see Howard, P., 'The USSR and Indonesia', *Mizan* No. 3/1967, pp. 108-117.
[52] Moscow Radio, 17-18 April 1967.

to ensure a return of capitalist confidence (and funds), Soviet doubts began to surface. A number of articles and statements drew attention to the increase in right-wing influences and expressed regret at the continued persecution of PKI members,[53] but up to March 1968, at least, the Soviet media reprinted Indonesian claims to be adherents of non-alignment without comment, thus implying a willingness to believe them. At the same time the Soviet Union took a hard line over the accumulated Indonesian debts (which according to Adam Malik stood at $US931 million, of which $127 million was interest). Rescheduling was agreed in November 1966, but not ratified until May 1968. A number of projects were cancelled others postponed, and Indonesia was committed to pay off the accumulated debts by the middle of 1981. Only the oceanographic facility at Ambon and some road-building in Borneo were to continue.

During the summer of 1968 the worsening situation in Czechoslovakia, culminating in the Warsaw Pact invasion in August, caused complication in the Soviet international position which was soon to be reflected in its relations with Indonesia. While it may have suited Soviet policy that the pro-Peking orientation of the PKI be removed by Indonesian government action, the anti-Communist purges made no distinction between pro-Peking and pro-Moscow PKI members. In the summer of 1968 the Soviet Government was preparing to invade one of its allies for propagating a 'wrong kind' of Communism, and it knew from the support given to Dubcek by numerous Communist parties outside the Soviet bloc, that its action would be widely condemned by them as well as by non-Communists. Within the international Communist movement it was clear that many voices would be raised in support of charges, which the Chinese had been making publicly since 1963, that the Soviet leaders were concerned to exalt a narrowly-defined national interest above that of Communism as an internationally applicable political philosophy. The split in the movement exemplified by the Sino-Soviet dispute had brought an end to the ability of Soviet leaders to maintain with any chance of being universally believed the Leninist tenet that Soviet and Communist interests were globally synonymous. If the Soviet leaders were to be in a position to defend before a hostile Communist movement their actions over Czechoslovakia, it was expedient and necessary for them to prove themselves 'good Communists', at least in declaratory policy, by a more convincing display than hitherto of concern

---

[53] Eg. Moscow radio several times weekly in various services, from end of October 1965 to mid-1968. *Izvestiya,* 27 February 1968 etc.

for the fate of the PKI's three million members. It is therefore understandable that from the middle of 1968 onwards the tone of Soviet comment on Indonesian affairs became considerably more hostile, as uneasiness over trends in Indonesian foreign policy was reinforced by the imperatives of intra-Communist politics.[54]

Though deprived of its leaders for the third time, and with many of its most active members dead, the PKI still exists, and there is a struggle for influence over its remnants, in which the main issue is attribution of responsibility for its downfall, with the corollary of extracting the appropriate conclusions for its future policy. In September 1966 the PKI Politburo issued a 'self-criticism', which remains its most authoritative post-1965 statement. It contained little to encourage the Soviets, because it blamed the disaster on the willingness of the Aidit leadership to trust to legality and alliances with elites, its reluctance to organise peasant unrest, and its unpreparedness for counterrevolutionary violence. The only true road to power, the Politburo argued, was to establish a 'revolutionary united front aiming at an agrarian revolution and a people's democratic regime'. The components of the united front should be, as before, the 'national bourgeoisie', the urban petty bourgeoisie and the peasants, under the direction of the PKI, a clear sign that the rump PKI was as influenced by Maoist thinking as it had been before 1965.[55]

A pro-Soviet PKI group had been formed in Moscow after the 1965 *coup* from pro-Soekarno diplomats, students and Army officers who were training in the Soviet Union at the time. This group appears to have provided a leader and perhaps some members for a Communist guerilla group operating on the Kalimantan-Sarawak border in 1968 and subsequently. Although these were sufficient of a nuisance to necessitate a joint Malaysian-Indonesian operation in early 1971,[56] they hardly constituted evidence either that Muscovite influence in the PKI was strong, or that attempts to compete in militancy offered much hope of enhancing it. In any event, Soviet media have shown little enthusiasm for militancy. Attempts by the PKI to reorganise in Eastern Java during 1967, apparently with the intention of launching a guerilla campaign, were accompanied by encouragement from the Chinese press and radio which was not matched in their Soviet counterparts. Efforts to launch rural uprisings in mid-1968 eventually led to action by

---

54 For a fuller discussion see Howard, P., 'Moscow, Jakarta and the PKI' in *Mizan*, March-April 1969, pp. 105-118.
55 Summarised by McVey, R. T., in *Problems of Communism*, January-April 1971, pp. 25-36.
56 *Djakarta Times*, 7 January 1971.

the Indonesian Army, in which most of the new Politburo members were killed. The Chinese reaction was to argue that the campaign showed the 'revisionist road of peaceful transition . . . is the road to burying the revolution . . .', and that Suharto's successes would not have been possible but for Soviet-US 'collaboration' in supplying his army.[57] The Soviets riposted by accusing the Chinese of 'adventurism' in urging the PKI into becoming 'a weapon of its great-power policy in South-East Asia',[58] and arguing that the Indonesian Army's success in the operations of July-August 1968 proved the futility of Peking-inspired 'insurrectionism'.[59]

The Soviet ideological counter to the Politburo's views of the causes of the 1965 disaster was to blame it on the pro-Pekingism of Aidit and the other leaders. Thus a *World Marxist Review* article in 1969 argued that

> We should explain to the masses that the responsibility for past mistakes does not rest with the PKI and its three million members, or with any one person, but with a group of leaders who in point of fact had detached themselves from the Party, and, willingly or unwillingly, voiced interests alien to the Party . . .; that the group's political line did not accord with Party decisions, but was blindly conducted according to Peking's will and wishes; that the group's actions ran counter to the line of the international communist movement, and that its ideological slogans were not based on Marxism-Leninism . . .'[60]

but in the absence of similar statements from the PKI leadership itself, it must be assumed that this represents at the most the view of a small minority within the PKI, and there has been nothing since 1969 to suggest that this view is gaining ground.

By 1969 Soviet disenchantment with, and distrust of, Indonesia was manifest. Commentaries on Indonesian affairs emphasised the resurgence of Western influence, the repression of PKI members and the insincerity of Indonesian protestations of non-alignment.[61] At a further series of talks on rescheduling Indonesian debts the Soviet negotiators proved unforthcoming, reluctant to complete a number of unfinished aid projects, and unwilling to supply spare parts for the armed forces' Soviet-made equipment except for cash.

[57] Cited in *Far Eastern Economic Review,* 12 June 1969, p. 615.
[58] *Pravda,* 30 July 1968.
[59] *Pravda,* 10 September 1968. See also *Summary of World Broadcasts* SU/2871/A3/2 (10 September 1968), SU/2888/A3/3 (29 September 1968) and CPSU Central Committee statement of 10 October 1968 (SWB SU/2897/A3/1)
[60] *World Marxist Review* 9/1969, pp. 64-66.
[61] Eg. *Izvestiya,* 21 February 1969, and weekly Moscow Radio broadcasts.

Throughout 1970 the tone of pessimism about Indonesia's foreign policy course persisted and deepened; Indonesian cooperation in ASPAC, ASEAN and ASA was especially suspect, as the Soviet Union had since their inception regarded these organisations as US-sponsored attempts to 'substitute for SEATO'.[62] In January 1971 one Moscow Radio commentator said that 'the Djakarta authorities are gradually abandoning non-aligned policies, and now follow the generals who are ready to rearm the army and assist their Western allies . . .', while three weeks later another said that 'Indonesia has played an increasing role in turning ASEAN into a military bloc under the Pentagon's protection'. Although a 'presence' was being maintained through continued progress of fairly small Eastern-European (Polish and Czech) aid projects, some interest was being displayed in completing some Soviet projects left unfinished in 1966[63] and Soviet purchases of Indonesian rubber continued at a fairly high level, politically the Soviet interest amounted to no more than 'keeping a foot in the door'.

The basic problem for the Soviet leaders was that maintenance of a 'foot in the door' necessitated reconciling a number of conflicting requirements. Repayment of Indonesia's large debts had to be sought (the consequences within the international movement of financial leniency towards so determinedly anti-Communist a government could not be ignored, nor could a precedent be set which other non-aligned recipients of Soviet aid might follow), and one way to exert pressure was to insist on hard cash payment for spares with which to keep the Indonesian Navy and Air Force's equipment functioning.[64] But such a policy threatened to be self-defeating in two ways: in the first place, it could prompt the Indonesians to a more rigorous examination of their military needs, from which the dominant political force (the Army) might well conclude that the Navy and Air Force were far larger than Indonesia's defence needs required or her economy could sustain. (This seemed to have happened when in August 1970[65] many of the Navy's Soviet-built ships were put up for scrapping.) In this case, an opportunity for creating a continuing relationship was lost. And in the second place, subsequent replacements were hardly likely to

---

62 See eg., Pavlovskiy, V., 'Problems of Regionalism in Asia', in *International Affairs,* (Moscow), April 1969, pp. 46-51.

63 Moscow Radio, 5 December 1970.

64 Antara (Indonesian News Agency) reported on 16 May 1969 that the Soviet Union had stopped sending spares for the missile-firing fast patrol boats of the Indonesian Navy.

65 *The Australian,* 18 August 1970.

be sought from a supplier which had proved as uncooperative as the Soviet Union in keeping the equipment serviceable.

Rescheduling of Indonesia's economic and military debts, was also to be sought if any kind of influence was to be retained; but at the same time, the preservation of reasonable state-to-state relations with the Suharto government must take into account the possibility that the PKI would one day revive. In its previous incarnation it had leaned heavily towards Peking, but having been so thoroughly shattered, it was possible that the revived party would be more susceptible to influence from Moscow, and to be too solidly identified with the government responsible for the biggest slaughter of Communists since Stalin's purges could harm Soviet standing in the eyes of a resurgent PKI. At the same time, too distant an attitude to Indonesia's present rulers could merely deliver the country over to the Western countries with which they have considerable affinities, and tempt Indonesia to abandon what is left of its non-alignment. Soviet reluctance to foreclose possible policy options—or perhaps even simple inability to predict what those options might be—was shown in Brezhnev's speech to the 24th Party Congress,[66] where fifteen Asian countries were mentioned, but not a single word was said about Indonesia.

### LAOS AND CAMBODIA

Both these states had been the objects of a struggle between Thais and Vietnamese in the period before French colonisation during the 19th century, a struggle which was renewed in a 'globalised' form after 1954, with their territorial integrity frequently violated by North and South Vietnam and the USA. The course of internal political events in them after 1954 differed considerably, and so, in detail, did the Soviet espousal of the neutralist forces in both.

*Laos.* The origins of Laotian Communism date to the end of the Second World War, when members of the anti-French Lao Issara (Free Laos) movement came in contact with the Viet Minh operating along the border with Vietnam and among the Vietnamese minority in Laos. The head of the Laotian independence forces, Prince Souphanouvong, cooperated with the Viet Minh and because of this was relieved of command in 1949, whereupon he set up a movement known as Pathet Lao, operating mainly in the north-eastern provinces of Sam Neua and Phong Saly, which border

---

[66] 'Report of the Central Committee', 30 March 1971.

on China and North Vietnam and were effectively under the control of the Viet Minh. The Pathet Lao's role in the fighting was secondary to that of Viet Minh forces, which used Laotian territory to provide extra space for manoeuvre in the Vietnam war and in 1953 penetrated deeply into Laos in the course of operations against the French. By then the non-Communist nationalists had succeeded in negotiating Laotian independence within the French Union, and the Pathet Lao (most of whose support came from minority hill tribes)[67] was not able to establish a monopoly on the appeal to nationalism as the Viet Minh had succeeded in doing in Vietnam. At the 1954 Geneva Conference on Indo-China it attempted to secure international recognition as 'the' Laotian independence movement, but neither the Soviets nor the Chinese pressed its interests with diligence, and the most it was able to secure was the allocation of the Sam Neua and Phong Saly provinces as an area in which to regroup pending a political settlement to be supervised by the International Control Commission (India, Canada and Poland).[68]

The Pathet Lao set terms for political unity which went beyond what the neutralists and pro-Western elements were prepared to accept, and after almost a year of negotiation general elections were held in the provinces not under Pathet Lao control in December 1955. In March 1956 Souvanna Phouma became Prime Minister, and reopened negotiations, with the Pathet Lao and its political organisation Neo Lao Hak Xat leading to agreement (December 1956) which extended Royal Government control to the whole country. The Soviets viewed the moves to political integration benevolently, but the American reaction was hostile, especially when Souvanna Phouma included the NLHX leaders in his government in November 1957, and supplementary elections in the Pathet Lao provinces in May 1958 resulted in 13 out of the 21 seats being won by NLHX or left-wing neutralists. Souvanna Phouma was later to allege that American opposition was responsible for his (Souvanna's) dismissal from office and replacement by Phoui Sananikone. The Phoui government, formed in August 1958, excluded the NLHX, and with American encouragement took a hard line towards the Pathet Lao including the arrest of sixteen of its leaders in July 1959.[69] In January 1959 it took

---

[67] For a discussion of the ethnic and political divisions see Toye, H., *Laos: Buffer State or Battleground,* Oxford University Press, 1968.

[68] Simmonds, E. H. S., in *The Far East and Australasia 1969,* pp. 428-9, and Smith, R., 'Laos in Perspective', *Asian Survey,* December 1963, pp. 61-68.

[69] Girling, J. L. S., *People's War,* Allen & Unwin, London, 1969, pp. 183-90.

'special powers' alleging North Vietnamese violations of the Geneva Agreement which a United Nations investigation later that year did not confirm[70] and in February it declared that it would no longer be bound by the Geneva Agreement, thereby implying an intent to abandon neutrality. The UN Secretary-General Dag Hammarskjold visited Laos in November 1959, and thereafter Phoui attempted to reconstruct his government along broader lines. This led to his dismissal by army elements headed by Phoumi Nosavan, who organised elections in April 1960, which resulted in a right-wing government.

So far, Soviet interest was limited to denouncing the American manoeuvres,[71] and even after Souphanouvong and the other NLHX leaders escaped in May 1960, no concrete indications were forthcoming of Soviet willingness to become involved. The situation changed only when on 9th August 1960 a neutralist army officer, Captain Kong Le, staged a successful *coup d'état* in Vientiane and asked Souvanna Phouma to form a government. Nosavan, who was in South Laos, received support from the Americans and Thais (who closed their border, thereby effectively blockading the neutralist-held areas), and advanced on Vientiane. Souvanna sought Soviet assistance in breaking the blockade, and an airlift was instituted. However, the neutralist forces were inadequately equipped to halt Nosavan's forces; Vientiane fell, and Souvanna Phouma fled to Cambodia. Thailand, the United States, and a number of other Western governments hastened to recognise the right wing government, but the Soviet Union, its allies, and the non-aligned countries, maintained their recognition of the neutralist government[72] which returned to Laotian soil and established itself near the headquarters of the Pathet Lao with which it entered into a working agreement.

The Soviet airlift was expanded to include arms for the neutralist and Pathet Lao forces, which engaged those of the right during the early months of 1961 with considerable success. The US government, which had rejected a Soviet request for the immediate recall of the Geneva Conference in September 1959, proved more amenable in 1961 when the defeats suffered by the right-wing forces caused President Kennedy to declare that Laos was the 'most

---

[70] Simmonds, E. H. S., *loc. cit.*
[71] For Soviet accusations against US activities in Laos, see Pavlovskiy, V., *Laos v bor'be za Svobodu* (Laos in the struggle for freedom), Oriental Literature Publishing House, Moscow 1963, pp. 71-120. See also eg., *International Affairs,* Moscow, July 1959, pp. 63-66, and January 1961, pp. 121-2.
[72] Girling, J. L. S., *loc. cit.* pp. 183-90.

immediate problem' he encountered on becoming President.[73] At his June 1961 meeting with Khrushchev, he found the Soviets amenable to the concept of a neutral and independent Laos.[74] A conference convened in Geneva found that the major difficulties were not between the Americans (whose crudely-executed attempts to exclude the Pathet Lao from the political mainstream had had the opposite effect) and the Russians (whose airlift had underlined their support of Laotian neutrality at relatively small cost), but the reluctance of the three Laotian factions to come together. Although the agreement which was reached in July 1962 proved unworkable it has nevertheless succeeded in minimising the international implications of Laos' internal disorders.

For the Soviets the Laos situation appears to have little interest *per se*.[75] In view of Laos' precarious location between Thailand and Vietnam, both of which have in the past controlled most of it, its meagre resources and ethnic diversity (only about 60% of the population are Laotian; the rest are hill tribes, found also in Vietnam and Thailand, Vietnamese or Chinese) they probably consider that its future will only be solved as a byproduct of the war in Vietnam. In any event, their standard policy of courting the forces which hold power is virtually impossible to apply in a country which has been engaged in an almost continuous civil war since 1949, and in which no faction has gained ascendancy for long. *Cambodia.* Internal stability, which has eluded Laos, proved easier to achieve in Cambodia, and centred on the personality of Norodom Sihanouk. A resistance movement, the Khmer Issarak, formed in 1945 to gain independence from France, collaborated with the Viet Minh along the eastern borders of Cambodia but never became as dependent on them as did the Pathet Lao, nor as influential a force within the country. Sihanouk succeeded in securing independence in November 1953, and led the country as King, Prime Minister, or Head of State, until his overthrow in March 1970.

For most of that time his authority was not seriously challenged.

[73] Speech of 23 March 1961.

[74] Speech of 6 June 1961.

[75] The most authoritative Soviet foreign policy journal *Mezhdunarodnaya Zhizn,* (also published in English under the title *International Affairs*) carried only eight articles devoted solely to Laos during the period 1 January 1963—31 December 1969. None were more than one page long, all either linked US activities in Laos with events in the Vietnam war, or demanded adherence to the 1962 Geneva agreement, or did both. During the same seven-year period the most scholarly Soviet journal of contemporary Asian studies *(Narody Azii i Afriki)* carried *no* articles solely devoted to Laos.

His foreign policy was one of neutralism, but its particular features were dictated by its location between its longstanding enemies, the Thais and Vietnamese, and Sihanouk's personal assessments of the outcome of the Vietnam War.

The fact that Thailand and South Vietnam were firmly locked in American alliance, while North Vietnam was in effect at war with both, dictated a complicated pattern of relationships. Border disputes with Thailand and South Vietnam dictated friendship with larger Communist powers, to neutralise those countries' alliances with America. Violations of Cambodia's frontiers by both North and South Vietnamese forces were frequent, but those by the North were more regular and persistent, because of the utility of eastern Cambodia for infiltration from North Vietnam through Laos into the Saigon and Delta areas of South Vietnam. If the North's abuse of Cambodian territory was not to exacerbate relations with South Vietnam and the United States and threaten Sihanouk's internal standing, some means must be found of controlling it. This required cultivation of the nations best placed to put pressure on North Vietnam—China and the Soviet Union.

Sihanouk therefore pursued an intricate policy, whose details varied with his assessment of the situation in Vietnam. The outcome of the Laos conference in 1962 persuaded him that Communist victory in Laos and Vietnam was beyond American will or capacity to prevent, and he consolidated his relations with both China and the Soviet Union against a future in which Thailand would be Cambodia's only non-Communist neighbour, China would be the dominant power in South-East Asia, and Soviet friendship might be required as a counterweight to it.[76]

For the Soviets, relations with Cambodia presented few problems. Sihanouk's control of the country appeared unchallengeable; his neutralism was beyond question, and little was required of them except some aid and affirmations of support for Cambodia's territorial integrity, which they gave formally after his recognition of the South Vietnam National Liberation Front in June 1967. Some perturbation may have been caused by his reference to China as Cambodia's 'Number One Friend' after 1964. At this time, apparently in the belief that a Viet Cong victory was imminent, he refused all further American economic and military aid,[77] but the Soviets did not attempt to replace it, indicating that their interest in Cambodia was limited.

---

[76] For a discussion of Sihanouk's views on foreign policy, see Armstrong, J. P., *Sihanouk Speaks*, Walker & Co., New York, 1964, pp. 77-151.

[77] Leifer, M., in *The Far East and Australasia 1969*, p. 381.

Sihanouk's charisma waned within Cambodia during the latter half of the 1960s. Most of the reasons for this were internal, but one at least had considerable foreign policy implications—the continued presence of North Vietnamese and Viet Cong in northeast Cambodia. Still believing in the inevitability of a Viet Cong victory, Sihanouk was prepared to tolerate this presence within reason, but its proximity to Saigon made the NLF's presence permanent and growing, and the area was virtually sequestrated from Cambodia, whose army was in no fit state to restore it.[78] In an effort to bring external pressure to bear on Hanoi, Sihanouk left on a visit to Paris, Moscow and Peking early in 1970. He was deposed on 18th-19th March, and for the first time in their relations with Cambodia, the Soviets were forced to make a choice between him and another power-wielding group, a choice made the more significant in that he was actually in Moscow when his deposition was announced. His presence in their capital did not tempt the Soviet leaders to precipitate utterance on his behalf. On the contrary, for the first week after his overthrow, the Soviet media reported events in Cambodia on a facts-only basis, relying on Western sources. Only on 25th March, by which time Sihanouk had left for Peking, did they essay to comment on the Cambodian situation, and then an article in *Pravda*[79] repeated Soviet support for the neutrality, independence and territorial integrity of Cambodia within its existing borders, but said nothing in support of Sihanouk. The implications were that provided Cambodia remained neutral the Soviet Union was not concerned who governed it.

By mid-April South Vietnamese troops were operating in force in Cambodia, and Sihanouk was receiving strong verbal support from China. Soviet media now began to accuse the CIA of instigating the *coup,* and to describe the pro-Sihanouk forces in Cambodia in favourable terms, while a message of support sent to the 'Indochinese peoples' conference' held on 24th-25th April declared Soviet support for the 'Indochina peoples' anti-imperialist united front', without being specific about the extent or nature of the support to be given.[80]

When United States and South Vietnamese forces entered Cambodia in May 1970, Soviet comment became much more hostile in tone, but displayed some interesting reservations. The

78 Osborne, M., *Region of Revolt; focus on South East Asia,* Pergamon Press Australia, 1970, pp. 151-4.
79 Mayevskiy, V., in *Pravda,* 25 March 1970.
80 *Pravda,* 30 April 1970.

Lon Nol government protested at the 'invasion' and Soviet commentators, given the option of treating the protest as genuine or as a mere formality chose the former course, describing the American action as aggression against Cambodia, and avoiding thereby condemning the Lon Nol regime as a 'puppet'.[81] However, despite a wide-ranging attack on US policies delivered by Kosygin at a press conference on 4th May, no promises of definite action were given, a question on possible Soviet recognition of Sihanouk's 'government in exile' was side-stepped, no comment was offered on Chinese actions, and no suggestion of Soviet initiatives to resolve the situation was made. On the other hand, despite Soviet suspicions of the Lon Nol regime, its diplomats in Phnom Penh stayed at their posts and references to Sihanouk in the Soviet press, while cordial, were infrequent. Towards the end of 1970 the Soviet Ambassador was withdrawn, possibly because of pressure from Hanoi, but the Embassy continued to function under a *chargé d'affaires*; the ceremony marking the declaration of a republic was boycotted by Soviet Embassy staff, but beyond that aroused no Soviet comment or action.

On the effects of the Cambodian *coup* and subsequent events, Soviet public comment showed three main preoccupations. First was to play down the importance of North Vietnamese and Viet Cong presence in North-East Cambodia in weakening Sihanouk's standing with the governing elites. This was achieved by mentioning the North Vietnamese presence as little as possible and, when doing so, by arguing that since both sides violated Cambodian territory, toleration of both was an essential part of Cambodia's neutrality.[82] Second, was to arouse international opinion against further US widening of the war, as at Kosygin's press conference of 4th May 1970, when he interpreted the US invasion of Cambodia as part of a plot to 'eliminate progressive regimes' in South-East Asia, and suggested that it undermined the credibility of any possible US signature to any international agreement. While further progress on the Strategic Arms Limitation Talks and Middle East crisis was slow, continuation of talks at least showed the Soviet statement to be intended merely as a caution. No doubt it was also made with Hanoi's reactions in mind, because of the third Soviet preoccupation, namely their belief that Sihanouk's overthrow and the subsequent events tended to increase Chinese influence among the revolutionary movements of Indochina. Soviet media expressed concern at this on several occasions during May-July, and even

[81] Eg. Kudryavtsev, V., in *New Times,* 18-19/1970, p. 21.
[82] *Ibid.,* p. 22.

went so far as to say that Chinese interference in Cambodia was one of the factors which precipitated the *coup* against Sihanouk.[83] As his 'government in exile' in China became more and more pro-Chinese in its utterances, the Soviet press virtually ceased to mention it, or Cambodia, suggesting that the *coup* was regarded as irreversible, and there was no interest in becoming involved in a civil war. In his major review of policy at the 24th Party Congress, Brezhnev referred to both Laos and Cambodia only as countries whose peoples were being 'subjected to US aggression', and expressed no value judgments on the government of either country.[84]

THE PHILIPPINES

In 1924 a leading American Communist visited Manila, and arranged for some Filipino labour leaders to attend a Comintern-sponsored conference in China. Several of these later helped to found the Philippines Communist Party in 1930. In accordance with the then Comintern policy on Communist parties in colonies, it was for some years placed under the tutelage of the US Communist Party, which supervised and financed it. It was banned in 1932, but continued to exist illegally until in 1938 it merged with the Socialist Party. Like its tutelary Party it was active mainly in urban areas, among workers and nationalist intellectuals, but was brought into contact with the peasants by the merger, as the Socialists had a strong rural base, especially in Pampanga province of Central Luzon, long a centre of agrarian radicalism. Thus the Hukbalahap (Anti-Japanese People's Army), founded in 1942, consisted mainly of Pampangan peasants, but was under predominantly PKP control. Though not the only guerilla army in Luzon, it was the largest and most effective, but US Far East Headquarters regarded it with suspicion, and after liberation in 1945 ordered it to be disarmed and arrested many of its leaders. Some stood, successfully, for political office in 1946, but were unseated on grounds of electoral irregularities, and the Huk insurgency, which began as a result, went on intermittently until the late 1950s.[85]

In 1950 the PKP leadership concluded that the Philippines' economic crisis was irreversible, and that power could be seized within two years. On this assumption it planned a large-scale expansion of the Huk forces, and a major offensive, but on 18th October 1950 the entire leadership of the Party was captured in Manila and the Huks, deprived of their whole Manila organisation

---

83  Eg. Ukraintsev, M., in *New Times*, 23/1970, pp. 14-15.
84  'Report of the Central Committee', 30 March 1971.
85  Saulo, A. B., *Communism in the Philippines*, Ateneo, Manila, 1969, pp. 12-61.

were forced back into the rural areas where they were gradually reduced to a purely local threat. The coalition between urban Communists and rural socialists disintegrated, and the Huk forces degenerated into small bands, which by 1965 numbered only a few hundred men, and were confined almost entirely to Eastern Pampanga, where some of them engaged in protection rackets and banditry.[86]

Some of them, however, remained ideologically motivated, and the long years of guerilla warfare had increased the influence of Maoist doctrines among the few surviving PKP members. In December 1968 these founded a 'PKP (Re-established)' and a 'New People's Army', both avowedly 'under the supreme guidance of Mao Tse-Tung'. They denounced the 'old' PKP for its 'peaceful and parliamentary supine attitude',[87] but the New People's Army has proved neither popular nor effective. It has moved to the less accessible Tarlac province, but has not apparently proved attractive to other than Pampangos, and in 1970 was estimated to have less than 800 combatants.[88]

Thus the fortunes of the PKP proved to depend more on local conditions than international events, and the post-war insurrection was not motivated by the 'two camps' doctrine, which was not enunciated until over a year after it had begun. As to actual Soviet or Chinese influence or involvement (beyond general ideological influence exerted by writings), the Deputy Chief of the US mission stated in 1969:

> The various factions in the field and the dissident Communist groups in the cities have operated essentially on an independent, national basis. Ties with other Communist countries, including particularly the Soviet Union and China, have not been significant . . . we have no evidence that either Soviet or Chinese Communist agents have established or attempted to establish control, or to assist the various dissident groups in any significant manner.[89]

---

[86] Lachica, E., *Huk: Philippine Agrarian Society in Revolt*, Solidaridad, Manila, 1971, pp. 118-154.

[87] Captured PKP-NPA documents quoted in Lachica, *op. cit.* p. 162.

[88] General Headquarters, Armed Forces of the Philippines, estimate quoted in Lachica, *op. cit.* p. 14. A similar figure was given to a U.S. congressional inquiry in 1969 by the U.S. Chief of Mission—Subcommittee on United States Security Agreements and Commitments Abroad of the Committee on Foreign Relations, United States Senate: 'United States Security Agreements and Commitments Abroad: The Republic of the Philippines,' U.S. Government Printing Office, Washington, 1969, pp. 226-7.

[89] U.S. Senate, Foreign Relations Committee (as in note 88 above), p. 354.

This isolation is confirmed by a writer in the 'World Marxist Review' in 1965.[90] According to him, there were four main reasons for the failure of the Huk insurrection.

1. The incorrect belief that the government's situation was irrecoverable, ie., that promises of reform would not affect the people's attitude to it.
2. The neglect of legal (ie. parliamentary) forms of struggle, the failure to form a 'united front', and antagonising of the 'national bourgeoisie', which therefore allied itself with Magsaysay, first as Secretary of Defense and later as President.
3. Overconfidence, leading to bad security, enabling Magsaysay in October 1950 to seize the entire Party secretariat and many other 'top-ranking cadres', plus complete files of documents and correspondence. All nine members of the Politburo were eventually killed or captured, as was the whole of the Central Committee.
4. Physical isolation and lack of support from abroad.

A subsequent article, published five years later,[91] substantially repeated this assessment, but went on to criticise the PKP (Re-established) as discrediting the popular movement by 'its highly provocative behaviour in precipitating violence during demonstrations, thus alienating sections of the population otherwise prepared to support the popular cause, in projecting ultra-extremist phrases and slogans that distort and confuse issues, and in advocating and seeking to promote immediate armed struggle in wholly premature and unfavourable conditions'.

Moscow Radio announced on 12th April 1971, that the PKP (pro-Moscow) had sent a message to the 24th CPSU Congress, blaming the defeat of Huks in the 1950s as due to its '*self*-isolation from the international Communist movement' since the 1965 article had spoken only of 'physical isolation', this suggested an attempt to blame Maoism retrospectively for the failure of the 1946-53 insurrection. That this was the objective of the pro-Moscow faction's message is confirmed by its criticism of the PKP (Re-established) as 'guided by the counter-revolutionary concept serving the Maoist leaders' aspiration to dominate in South-East Asia'.

At present the effectiveness of the Philippines Communists would appear to be diminished by their division into two hostile groups. According to documents captured in 1963, the PKP receives no 'directives from outside', but presumably its leaders have access

---

[90] Maravilla, J., in *World Marxist Review*, 11/1965.
[91] *World Marxist Review*, 12/1970.

to published documents. From captured PKP documents it would appear that the pro-Moscow Party is prepared to follow a non-violent line and to cooperate with non-Marxist groups in a united front, while the PKP (Re-established) adheres to a more militant line.[92] Even granted that the preferred Soviet alternative, the establishing of a relationship with the power-holders has been denied them by the Philippine Government's reluctance to establish diplomatic relations with any Communist country, the possibilities of exerting influence through the local Communists would seem decidedly limited.

The decidedly pro-American and anti-Communist orientation of successive Philippines governments provided no scope for the establishment of any form of relationship, even on the most formalistic basis—no diplomatic relations exist between the Philippines and any Communist countries. However, the assertion of Philippine nationalism has given the Soviets expectations of change. Although the final document of the 1969 World Communist Conference condemned the repression of Communists in the Philippines, most Soviet comment in recent years has concentrated on the growth of nationalism, chiefly in terms of its anti-American manifestations, ignoring questions of insurgency and avoiding abuse of the Philippines authorities.

The victory of the Nationalist Party and President Marcos in the 1969 elections was greeted by the Soviet Union with pleasure,[93] with special emphasis given to his undertakings to consider establishing diplomatic relations with Communist countries[94] and to repeal the anti-subversion law. Since then Moscow radio commentaries for South Asia[95] have referred to Soviet offers to buy 'traditional export products' on the normal settlement terms of Soviet trade agreements with developing countries, to grant long-term low interest credits and to assist in development projects. This suggests a revival of interest in trade relations which were first broached in 1967-68 but broken off by the Philippines after the Soviet invasion of Czechoslovakia. The volume of trade contemplated seemed small (one million dollars or less), but on the experience of some past agreements, it is possible that growth could be rapid. However, of the Philippines' main exports, sugar and copra would be in competition with established trading partners

---

[92] *Asian Analyst,* February 1970, pp. 23-5. See also Guerrero, A., *Philippine Society and Revolution,* Ta Kung Pao, Hong Kong, 1971, pp. 110-112.

[93] Eg. by Barezhnikova, O., *Moscow Radio,* 17 November 1969.

[94] Moscow Radio, 3 December 1969.

[95] Eg. on 1 January 1969 and 27 January 1970.

(Cuba, for example), while the Soviet Union itself is a major exporter of timber. The prospects of Soviet-Philippine trade becoming large enough to provide substantial diplomatic leverage do not therefore seem high. At the same time, establishment of a trading and diplomatic relationship with a state which has hitherto been among the most violently anti-Communist in Asia would mark a minor breakthrough for Soviet diplomacy, and is likely to be pursued.

JAPAN

The Soviet Union has been unable to base its post-war relationship with Japan on either the facts of underdevelopment or the need to 'decolonise'. Its holding of former Japanese territory has proved a stumbling-block to political *détente,* while the Japanese Communist Party has proved more diligent than most in defence of its independence. However, scope for Soviet rapprochement with Japan is to be found in the joint development of Siberian raw materials, and it is in this area that the most important initiatives have been made.

Before the Second World War, Soviet-Japanese relations were consistently bad. Japanese troops invaded Siberia during the Russian Civil War,[96] and in the late 1930s clashed with Soviet forces in the Soviet Far East and Outer Mongolia. Possibly prompted by the severe beatings they received in these encounters,[97] they chose to attack the colonial dependencies of the Western powers in 1941 rather than to pin down the Soviet Far Eastern Army, whose divisions were removed to defend Moscow.[98] The Soviet Union therefore entered the war against Japan only after the war in Europe had ended, and the United States refused its request for an occupation zone.[99] It was not, therefore, in a position to foster its socio-economic system in Japan as it did in Germany, and what influence it had exerted itself in the first instance through the Japanese Communist Party (JCP).

The pre-war Japanese Communist Party, founded in 1922 was

---

[96] Silverlight, J., *The Victors' Dilemma: Allied intervention in the Russian Civil War,* Barrie & Jenkins, London, 1970, pp. 34, 79, 351.

[97] Zhukov, G. K., *Memoirs,* Jonathan Cape, London, 1971, pp. 147-171.

[98] Seaton, A., *The Russo-German War 1941-45,* Barker, London, 1971, p. 189.

[99] The Americans refused to divide the Japanese main islands into occupation zones, or to grant the Soviets any right over appointment of the Supreme Allied Commander. See statement by President Truman 16 August 1945, *Keesing's Contemporary Archives 1945,* p. 7373, and Craig, D., *The Fall of Japan,* The Dial Press, New York, 1967, pp. 126-7.

small, illegal, and predominantly consisted of intellectuals. It was almost totally unconnected with Japanese political life, had no mass basis, nor hope of attracting one, given the efficiency of the secret police and the fact that the 'enemy' was not a colonial power against which nationalist feeling could be invoked, but an indigenous nationalist regime, firmly in control and ruthless in defence of its prerogatives.[1]

The leaders of the Japanese Communist Party had drawn their inspiration both from Moscow, via the Comintern, and from the Chinese Communists, but until 1945 the Soviet example predominated.[2] However, when the Party's leaders emerged from prison or exile, their dominant personality was Sanzo Nosaka, who had spent the war years at Mao Tse-Tung's headquarters in Yenan. In formulating a strategy for the now legalised Party, he settled on a combination of doctrines adapted in accordance with his own views of Japanese society. The Party declared Japanese imperialism, not American, to be the principal enemy of progressive forces in Japan, but opted to assist in 'two-stage' revolution, and spoke of a 'peaceful path to power' achieved by Parliamentary processes. By 1949 the Party had over 100,000 members, and it gained 10% of the votes in the general election held in that year.[3] However, concentration on the specifically Japanese situation, which in effect divorced the JCP from the Cold War, proved unacceptable to Stalin, and in January 1950 the Cominform journal[4] denounced Nosaka for 'grave mistakes'. Soon afterwards the same journal was to denounce the Indian Communist Party for excessive attachment to violence,[5] but in the case of Japan, Nosaka's 'sin' was to have attached insufficient importance to the need for anti-US action, at a time when Soviet-American confrontation had already taken place in Germany, over Berlin, and was about to erupt in the Korean War, in which Japan would be an important US base.

Faced with the disapproval of its mentors, the JCP abandoned its 'Parliamentary' course. Most of its leaders sought refuge in Peking, much of the Party apparatus reverted to an 'underground' status, the 'peaceful path to power' ceased to be mentioned and the

1 For a detailed account of Japanese Communism before 1945 see Beckman, G. M. & Okubo, G., *The Japanese Communist Party, 1922-45,* Stanford University Press, 1969.
2 Langer, P., 'The New Posture of the CPJ' in *Problems of Communism,* January-April 1971, pp. 15-16.
3 *Ibid.* p. 16.
4 *For a Lasting Peace, For a People's Democracy,* 6 January 1950.
5 *For a Lasting Peace, For a People's Democracy,* 27 January 1950.

'1951 Thesis' defined US 'imperialism' as the main enemy, against which direct and militant action should be taken. However, the effects of the militancy which the Cominform urged in Japan were precisely the same as that which it had condemned in India, namely decisive counteraction by the government, isolation from the non-Communist Left, and a loss of membership and votes (from 10% in 1949 to 2% in 1955) as the Party shed its image of a genuinely 'Japanese' political organisation and exposed itself to charges that it was an instrument of foreign powers.

After the death of Stalin, the emergence of the doctrine of 'different roads to socialism' justified a return to policies tailored to Japanese conditions, but the Party was divided in its analysis of Japanese society, one faction seeing it as still substantially feudal and subservient to America, the other viewing it as an advanced capitalist society. The differences were not purely theoretical, because they determined the views on how the party should act. The first school saw American domination as evidence that Japan was of quasi-colonial status, and therefore required a 'bourgeois-democratic' revolution directed primarily against the US 'imperialists' and 'feudal remnants', with a strong possibility of violence. The second faction held that the revolution could be 'socialist' and achieved peacefully, by gradual transformation of society through Parliamentary means.[6]

The debate was soon overlaid by the growing Sino-Soviet dispute, and the two schools became associated with the protagonists in it. The pro-Chinese faction proved stronger for a number of reasons: Japan's historical and cultural debt to China was strong, to Communist and non-Communist alike; the JCP's leaders' personal ties with China were far stronger than with the Soviet Union as many of them had spent the war and post-1950 years in China, and even those who had spent much time in Moscow were not familiar with the new Soviet leaders; moreover, the Soviet search for *détente* was not only repugnant to many Communists because of its lack of revolutionary content, but some of its manifestations, such as the pressure for a test-ban treaty, appeared not only to be aimed against China but to pose long-term electoral difficulties for the JCP itself.

The outcome of the intra-Party debate was the programme adopted at the 8th Party Congress in 1961, which defined the primary enemy as US 'imperialism', describing Japan as 'semi-occupied' and 'virtually dependent'. The Party therefore opted for

[6] Langer, *loc. cit.* pp. 16-18.

a two-stage revolution, retaining the option of violence, but recommending that parliamentary opportunities be used to the full.

From 1961 to 1965 the JCP's posture was substantially pro-Chinese. The Soviet attempt to retain doctrinal hegemony was criticised, though at first without names being used ('. . . no Party can place itself above any other . . . Nor can any party force others to obey . . .'),[7] while relations with the Chinese and other Asian Communist Parties were described in altogether more glowing terms ('. . . fraternal solidarity binds the Communist Party and people of Japan inseparably with the Communist Parties and peoples of China, Korea, Vietnam, Indonesia and other countries in Asia . . .').[8] In 1964, the pro-Moscow faction was extruded from the JCP because of its open support for the Moscow-sponsored nuclear test-ban treaty, and formed itself into a separate 'Voice of Japan' party. In subsequent correspondence between the Soviet and Japanese parties, the JCP blamed strained relations on Soviet demands for uncritical support in the Sino-Soviet dispute, and on 'unjustifiable interference in our internal affairs and disruptive activities against our party . . .'[9]

The Soviet leaders continued to support the 'Voice of Japan' group, but it never became an important force in Japanese politics. For the JCP independence of Moscow was followed by a similar, though more dramatic, rupture with Peking in 1966, according to the Japanese because 'the Mao Tse-Tung clique of China started to engage openly in disruptive activities, interference and subversion, directed against our party . . . they tried to force through the proposition . . . that the so-called Mao Tse-Tung thought constitutes the highest principle of world revolution, that the Chinese revolutionary formula should be the revolutionary formula for all countries, and that those who do not accept this proposition are nothing but counter-revolutionary elements and traitors . . .'.[10] The secession of a second faction aligning itself with a foreign Communist power left a somewhat reduced Japanese Communist Party (JCP) which nevertheless has been able to increase its electoral popularity by persisting in its independent line, and continuing to seek its political future in terms of adapting Communist doctrine to Japanese conditions. Relations with the Soviets have remained cool even after a visit in 1968 by a Soviet delegation headed by Suslov, the Politburo member then in charge of relations with

[7] *Akahata* (Red Flag) 10 November 1963.
[8] Resolution of 5th plenum of Central Committee of JCP, 15 February 1963, in *Bulletin—Information for Abroad,* March 1963.
[9] Letter from Central Committee to CPSU, 18 August 1964.
[10] Central Committee Report to 11th Party Congress, 8 July 1970.

foreign Communist parties, for despite JCP demands that support
be withdrawn from the 'Voice of Japan' group, the Soviets did not
comply.

The current Soviet view of the JCP is contained in an article in
*Party Life*.[11] The JCP is criticised for its reluctance to support the
non-proliferation treaty, its unwillingness to accept the Soviet viewpoint over Soviet-held former Japanese islands, its condemnation
of the invasion of Czechoslovakia and of Soviet negotiation with
America, and for its refusal to attend the 1969 International
Conference of Communist Parties. The JCP for its part blames
Khrushchev for initiating the split in the international movement by
his attacks on Albania, and the Chinese for retaliating in kind,
while the Russians are additionally charged with having 'departed
very far from Marxist-Leninism'.[12] Both are accused of 'great-
power chauvinism', the Russians particularly over Czechoslovakia
and the Kurile Islands and their readiness to treat with US
'imperialism'. The Chinese are accused more generally for their
attempts to impose the thought of Mao Tse-Tung on all parties, and
for subversive activities against the JCP, with which they broke off
relations during the Cultural Revolution.[13] Resistance to Soviet or
Chinese pressure is basic to the JCP's position, and it has stood by
the line defined by Nosaka, as its Chairman, in July 1967: 'In
learning from the experiences and theories of foreign revolutionary
movements, we must stand on a basis of independence and critical
judgment. To apply foreign experience blindly and mechanically
. . . will result in endless evils.'[14] Hence, issues on which it has taken
an anti-Soviet stand place it well within the mainstream of Japanese
political thought, even though some of them involve the echoing of
Chinese criticisms. That the JCP's independent line is viewed by
the Chinese as nationalist rather than as pro-Peking is shown by a
number of Chinese attacks upon its leadership as the 'Miyamoto
revisionist clique'. One such attack, for example, criticised its
opposition to violent revolution and accused it of tolerating 'US
imperialism and Japanese militarist violence'.[15] However, the
policies pursued have been electorally popular, and JCP voting
strength has recovered from the 2% of 1955 to 5% in 1967.

The development of political relations with Japan has been
inhibited in general by its close relationship with America, and
in particular by the question of the former Japanese islands taken

---

[11] *Partiinaya Zhizn*, Moscow, 13/1970.
[12] *Akahata*, 5 August 1970.
[13] Central Committee report to 11th Party Congress, 6 July 1970.
[14] *Akahata*, 16 July 1967.
[15] New China News Agency, 17 March 1971.

by the Soviet Union in 1945. The issue is complicated by differences in interpretation of past treaties, and over the status of the Yalta agreement.

The islands concerned stretch between the Soviet Kamchatka peninsula and Hokkaido. They are known as the Kuriles, though the Japanese and Russians disagree whether they can all be so described. According to the Japanese, treaties of 1855 and 1874 defined the Kuriles as extending only as far south as Uruppu, leaving the southernmost islands (Etorofu and Kunashiri) as part of Japan, and excluding altogether the Habomai Islands and Shikotan, which were regarded as part of Hokkaido. A secret protocol to the Yalta Agreement of 11 February 1945 approved restoration of Soviet rights forfeited as a result of the Russo-Japanese War of 1904-5, in return for Soviet entry into the war against Japan, and it was understood that these 'rights' were to include the Kurile Islands. In the event Soviet forces occupied all the islands between Kamchatka and Hokkaido, and in the San Francisco Peace Treaty of 1951 Japan renounced all title to the Kuriles. The Soviet claim therefore rests on the Yalta Agreement which Japan, of course, was not a party to, and the San Francisco Treaty does not apply to them, the Habomais, or Shikotan.

The Soviet Pacific Fleet suffers strategically from the fact that its main base, Vladivostok, is located on the Sea of Japan, whose exits can be tightly controlled from bases in the Japanese main islands. For the purpose of easing Soviet naval access to the Pacific, the Kurile Islands are therefore of limited utility. But for defensive purposes, the position is somewhat different. As long as Japan is militarily linked to the United States, attacks on Soviet naval units, whether by sea or air, would most likely be mounted from bases in Japan. But should Japan adopt the neutralist policy urged on it by both Soviets and Chinese, its territory would no longer be available for attacks upon Soviet Far Eastern bases or ships. Attacking forces such as aircraft carrier groups or submarines would have to approach either via the Straits of Tsushima, or the Sea of Okhotsk. In the event of Japanese neutrality, therefore, listening posts, airfields, or small-force bases in the Kurile chain could be extremely important to the defence of the Soviet Far East. However, it would not be necessary to retain every one of them, as the seas around the Japanese-claimed islands could be surveyed by aircraft or ships from South Sakhalin or the Soviet Kuriles. This probably explains why in 1956 the Soviets agreed that *after* conclusion of a peace treaty with Japan (they declined to sign the 1951 Treaty because it did not explicitly accept their title to the islands), they would return the Habomais and Shikotan to Japan. Presumably at that time they felt it unnecessary to spell out their unwillingness to conclude a peace treaty except on condition of Japanese neutrality; the Austrian State Treaty of the previous year had been concluded on that basis, and they may well have felt the assumption went without saying. However, in January 1960 they made this explicit, by declaring that the Habomais and Shikotan would not be returned as long as foreign bases existed in Japan. As those bases (American ones) are still there, no Soviet-Japanese Peace Treaty has been signed, and there has been no progress on the islands mentioned. As to Etorofu and Kunashiri, the Soviets decline even to discuss them, as they reject the Japanese contention that they form a separate 'South Kuriles' group.[16] Both parties agreed in January 1972 to open negotiations on a peace treaty before the end of the year, but neither has as yet indicated what points will be raised or hinted at possible changes in substantive positions on the future of the islands or of the American bases in Japan.

Soviet expectations in relations with Japan centre on two focal points. The first is that of economic cooperation in exploiting the resources of the Soviet Far East, especially Siberian timber and Yakutian coal, oil and natural gas. So far modest progress has been made, though the Japanese have shown no inclination to be hurried into the Yakutian oil-natural gas project, and have turned down a Soviet proposal that they should help to finance extension of the Trans-Siberian pipeline (which connects East Siberia with the very large West Siberian and somewhat smaller Urals fields) from Irkutsk to Khabarovsk.[17] Apart from its mutual economic advantages, cooperation would presumably give Japan an interest in preserving Soviet territorial integrity against putative Chinese threats, give the Soviets some leverage against a possible recrudescence of Japanese expansionism, and in due course counterbalance, at least in part, the political leverage which the United States is felt to derive from Japan's dependence on American markets. The second hope is that the growth of Japanese neutralism can be fostered to the point that American bases are withdrawn, but contained short of assertion of Japanese power in military terms commensurate with its economic strength. It is possible that secretly the Soviet leaders would welcome an increase in Japanese military power for its containing effect upon China, but if this is so they have given no hint of it; all references to the possibility of increases in Japanese military appropriations have been hostile. Soviet fears,

16 *Asian Research Bulletin* Vol. I, no. 1, Singapore, June 1971, pp. 7-8.
17 Connolly, V., 'East Siberian Oil' in *Mizan,* August 1971, pp. 15-22.

conversely, centre on the possibility of a revival of militarism, either in association with the United States or in opposition to United States wishes.

THE FUTURE

The course of Soviet relations with the countries of Pacific Ocean Asia has been markedly more convoluted than that which they have followed in regard to the Indian Ocean countries. One reason for this is that the Asian peoples of the Soviet Union are predominantly part of the Central Asian civilisation. They are Turkic or Iranian in race and have much in common in the way of background and customs with Turks, Iranians or Afghans. This facilitates dealings with the Soviet Union, whose representatives, diplomatic or technical, include a percentage of the Asian peoples or at the least of Europeans who have substantial experience of Central Asia. Where the societies of Pacific Ocean Asia are concerned, the typical Soviet representative fits in less well; apart from the relatively small numbers who have served or lived abroad, he or she has had little contact with the customs and habits of the countries where Chinese cultural influence is strong, while the minorities of Siberia and the Soviet Far East are neither sufficiently numerous nor, in general, sufficiently 'advanced' to figure largely in Soviet diplomatic or technical missions. In most countries of Pacific Ocean Asia, therefore, the Soviet representative is more obviously alien than in the Indian Ocean countries, more difficult for the beholder to differentiate from former colonial masters, and less identified with the past and present of the area than has been the case in India Ocean Asia.

Identification with an area does not necessarily ensure a more amicable reception; in many of the countries the ubiquitous presence of Overseas Chinese has proved a cause for suspicion and hostility on the part of the indigenes. But given Soviet insistence that their presence as advisers and aid-givers must be regarded differently from that of the Western powers, inability to dissociate themselves from the complex of Asian attitudes towards 'Europeans' in general places them at a disadvantage, and it is harder for them to achieve this dissociation east of the Malacca Straits than west of them. A Turk can identify to some extent with an Uzbek engineer on grounds of race, language and religion—and then only provided the Uzbek has remained unresponsive to Soviet anti-religious propaganda; an Indonesian or Malay can do so only on ground of religion; a Cambodian cannot identify with him on any of the three grounds.

Apart from this general difficulty of 'presentation', Soviet foreign policy in Pacific Ocean Asia presents a diffuse picture because the non-aligned countries of the area present no pivotal point comparable to India in size and importance. In the 1950's it appeared that Soviet policy-makers had cast Indonesia for this pivotal role, but for a variety of reasons it turned out otherwise; the internal confrontation between the Army and the Indonesian Communist Party was managed by Soekarno in ways which gradually led both him and the PKI to move in a pro-Peking direction, and the tendency to grandiose foreign policy adventures ran in parallel with economic deterioration too great to be countered by aid on the scale which the Soviet Union could supply. Furthermore, Seokarno elected to 'confront' a country—Malaysia—which was of considerable importance to the Soviet Union as a supplier of rubber, and therefore created a conflict between Soviet economic and political objectives which eventually caused them to retrench. No such conflict existed in Soviet relations with the countries of the subcontinent, because Pakistan supplies nothing that India cannot. In addition, the progress of the Sino-Soviet dispute tended to move the Soviet Union closer to India but further from Indonesia, even before the coup of 1965 deprived both Moscow and Peking of their main supporters in Indonesian politics. So Indonesia failed to become the 'India of the Pacific' looked for by Soviet foreign policy makers, and no other country was large enough, underdeveloped *and* non-aligned. China was large and underdeveloped, but Communist and hostile; and increasingly a rival rather than a partner. Japan was large in population, but industrially highly developed and linked to the United States for defence purposes, although potentially useful as a partner in developing Siberia and as a military counterweight to China. Soviet policy in the Pacific region has therefore tended to diffuseness, explained by the continuing dispute with China, the acute situation in Indo-China, and the developing economic relationship with Japan, and has lacked the focus provided in the Indian Ocean by India and in the Middle East by Egypt. Its focal points have varied from year to year, and will probably continue to do so. However, the need to contain China's influence around Soviet borders is likely to remain a dominant theme, given additional urgency by signs of settlement of differences between China and the United States. In relation to the non-Communist countries of the area this theme is already being expressed in a number of ways. The search for a collective security system, based on economic betterment and bilateral or regional non-aggression pacts is one of them. The increasing interest in economic cooperation with Japan is another; on the one hand it is expected to increase the 'habitability' of Siberia, enable it to support a larger population and make it a more attractive place to live. On the other, it is calculated to increase Japan's vested interest in the political stability of an area from which it may draw an increasing proportion of its raw materials. In the short term, the theme of containment of China is expressed also in Indo-China. Here the Soviet interest is to ensure that North Vietnam emerges from the conflict as the dominant power of Indo-China, strong enough to pursue policies at least as independent of China as are those of North Korea. This is not possible except through Viet-namese reunification, so the Soviet Union cannot pursue a lesser solution except as a tactical device to facilitate American disengagement. In Indo-China, therefore, as elsewhere in the Pacific region, the presence and influence of China have a more immediate and pervasive effect upon Soviet policy than in the Indian Ocean area, where China's is relatively remote compared with the Soviet Union, and therefore bulks less large in the consciousness of most of the states.

# 6

# Relationships with the Asian Communist Countries

Although Soviet relationships with the other countries of Asia have been conducted mainly on a basis of dealing with the established non-Communist governments and nationalist leaders, Communist parties have come to power since 1945 in China, North Korea and North Vietnam, while Mongolia has been a Communist-government state since the 1920s. Of the four Asian Communist countries three have borders with the Soviet Union (all except North Vietnam), and all are divided. The Mongolian government rules only Outer Mongolia (Inner Mongolia is a province of China), while in the case of the other three, territory to which they lay claim (Taiwan in the case of China), or which are inhabited by their compatriots (South Korea and South Vietnam) and which they argue should be reunified, are ruled by American-backed governments.

## MONGOLIA

Of the four Communist countries, Mongolia has presented the Soviets with the fewest problems. Its independence is buttressed by economic aid from the Soviet Union which is substantial on the scale of Mongolia, but a small drain on the Soviet economy, and apart from the need to defend it against a Japanese incursion in 1939, its defence has not involved any serious burdens either. In fact, the existence of a defence agreement facilitated the Red Army's advance into China against the Japanese in 1945, and has since 1966 made it possible for the Soviet Army to maintain troops there, presumably as a deterrent to Chinese escalation of the Sino-

Soviet dispute. The Mongolian People's Republic is the only Asian Communist state admitted to membership of the Council for Mutual Economic Assistance (CMEA or 'Comecon'), along with the Soviet Union and its Warsaw Pact allies, and was the only governing party in Asia to send delegates to the Soviet-summoned Conference of Communist and Workers' Parties held in Moscow in 1969.[1] Also, unlike the North Koreans and North Vietnamese, it has been firm in its support of the Soviet viewpoint in the Sino-Soviet dispute, though it has avoided excesses of anti-Chinese diatribe.

More Mongolians live outside the Mongolian People's Republic than in it, most of them in Inner Mongolia but some also in the Buryat Mongol and Kalmyk Autonomous Soviet Socialist Republics in the Soviet Union. The modern history of Mongolia, since it became autonomous under Chinese suzerainty in 1915, has been one of jockeying for position between the Russians and the Chinese, with the Russians on the whole regarded as protectors, and changes in Soviet internal policy followed quickly by similar shifts in Mongolia. Thus Lenin's 'New Economic Policy' of 1921-28 was copied in Mongolia, and collectivisation of agriculture, instituted in the Soviet Union in 1928-29 was also copied, with short-term results fully as disastrous in Mongolia as they were in Russia. Religious persecution in 1928-32 also followed the Soviet pattern, and its combination with the unpopular collectivisation measures led to large-scale uprisings which were put down with Red Army assistance. Stalin's purges of the Bolshevik Old Guard and the Army also had their Mongolian counterparts, and the adoption of the Cyrillic alphabet in Soviet Central Asia in 1939 was followed by its introduction in Mongolia in 1946. In later years Khrushchev's campaign for opening up the 'Virgin Lands' of Kazakhstan in the second half of the 1950s was imitated in a Mongolian campaign which began in 1959.[2]

Between 1955 and 1960 China appeared to be competing with the Soviet Union for the role of great and powerful friend to Mongolia with large gifts of money and labour towards road and housing construction. But as the Sino-Soviet dispute intensified and Mongolia's attachment to its pro-Soviet line became apparent, Chinese labour began to be withdrawn, and by 1964 virtually all the Chinese had left. Since then Soviet influence has been practic-

---

[1] *Conference of Communist and Workers' Parties,* Novosti Press Agency Publishing House, Moscow, 1969, pp. 5-7.
[2] Bawden, C., 'Mongolia' in *The Far East and Australasia 1969,* Europa Publications Ltd. 1969, pp. 830-834.

ally unchallenged. From 1966 Soviet troops have been stationed in the country; their numbers are estimated at three divisions (about 30,000 men),[3] and their role has clearly nothing to do with Mongolia's internal security, though their engineer regiments spend much of their time in construction of roads or buildings for civilian use. The excess of Soviet exports to Mongolia over imports from it was 129.1 million roubles in 1969,[4] most of this representing Soviet project aid. 102.3 million roubles[5] worth of Soviet exports consisted of machinery of various kinds, in continuation of an export policy which has enabled Mongolia to make a modest beginning with industrialisation and to some extent reduce its dependence on Chinese-made consumer goods. In view of the Mongols' distrust of China, the country's economic reliance on the Soviet Union, and its leaders' political indebtedness to Russia, a relatively smooth relationship appears likely to continue at least through the 1970s.

NORTH KOREA

The division of Korea at the 38th Parallel of latitude was the result of a Second World War arrangement; it was the demarcation line between Red Army forces entering from the north and US forces coming from the south. As Korea had been ruled by Japan since 1910, after a period of Russo-Japanese struggle for control of it, there was no ready-made indigenous authority to which power could be transferred once the Japanese forces had surrendered and their administration had been removed. However, shortly before the US forces landed in the south (8 September 1945) a nationalist movement, with large left-wing and communist components formed a 'National Construction Preparatory Committee' and adopted a provisional constitution. The Americans, however, refused to recognise the Committee and instituted military government in their zone, pending the return of exiled Korean leaders, including Syngman Rhee, from the United States and elsewhere. The Soviets, for their part, recognised the Committee within their occupation zone, and allowed it to set up a provisional administration for North Korea, under a non-Communist chairman (Cho Man Sik), but insisted that half the members should be Communist, and placed controls on all movement across the demarcation line, thus in effect converting it into a political boundary.

---

3 *The Military Balance 1970-71,* Institute for Strategic Studies, London, 1970, p.67.

4 *Vneshnyaya Torgovlya SSSR ZA 1969 god* (Foreign Trade of the USSR for 1969), Moscow 1970, p. 13 (hereafter referred to as *V.T.*).

5 *V.T.,* 1969, pp. 239-241.

The Korean communists comprised three groups, those who had remained in the country clandestinely, those who had fought alongside the Chinese Communists, and those who came in with the Red Army in 1945. Among the last group was a guerilla leader who had fought the Japanese in the 1930s, and had taken refuge in the Soviet Union after a Japanese military expedition against him. This man, Kim Il Sung, was to become the key figure in the Communisation of North Korea.

In October 1945 a North Korean bureau of the Korean Communist Party was established with Kim Il Sung as its chairman, a counterpart to the organisation in the American occupation zone headed by Pak Hon Yong, one of the 'underground' Communists who had come into the open when the Americans permitted the resumption of political party activity. At that stage the division of Korea was still officially viewed as temporary (the Great Powers had agreed in December 1945 to establish an all-Korean provisional government, and had set up a US-USSR Joint Commission to arrange for its establishment), but even before the Commission met, a North Korean Provisional People's Committee (headed by Kim Il Sung, with the leader of the 'Chinese' group, Kim Tu Bong as his deputy) began functioning in the North in February 1946. It immediately directed a land reform, splitting up large estates and giving ownership of the land to the peasants, following these measures with a nationalisation of industry, banks and communications. These steps aroused no particular opposition in North Korea, as most of the facilities concerned had been Japanese-owned.[6] However, the conversion of the military demarcation line into a political one, the placing of Communists in the leading positions in government, the land reform and nationalisation all pointed to the intention to consolidate Communist rule and establish the infrastructure of a socialist state in the North, whatever happened in the South, where the Communist party continued to function but administration was in US hands with Korean advisors chosen from the non-Communist political leaders. Many members of the non-Communist parties in the North fled to the South, and many South Korean Communists to the North, thus increasing the polarisation of Korean political life.

Some slight indications of friction between the Korean Communists who had returned from China and those who had come from the Soviet Union were evident when the 'Chinese' Koreans in

[6] 96% of industrial capital was Japanese owned according to Paige, Glenn, D., *The Korean People's Democratic Republic,* Hoover Institution Studies, 11., Stanford, 1966, p. 57.

March 1946 renamed their Independence League the 'New People's Party', thus in effect setting up a competing Communist Party. Three months of negotiation were needed to bring about a merger, and in the new body (the North Korean Workers' Party) Kim Il Sung held only the Vice-Chairmanship with Kim Tu Bong, his deputy, on the Provisional People's Committee as Chairman.[7]

The Joint Commission met in early 1946 and again in May-June 1947 without reaching agreement on an all-Korean government, and in September 1947 the United States referred the matter to the United Nations. This body established a Temporary Commission and proposed UN-supervised elections in both halves of Korea for an all-Korea House of Assembly. The Soviet Union, however, refused to admit the Commission to North Korea—partly because it feared that all-Korean elections would result in the extinction of the Communist regime in the North (whose population, about 10 million, was less than half that of the South), and partly because it distrusted the built-in pro-United States majorities inherent in the structure of the United Nations as it was then. The Americans thereupon arranged for general elections to be held in South Korea in May 1948 for a House of Assembly which was to draw up a constitution and elect a government. This government was inaugurated on 15 August 1948, and in October a Communist-led revolt broke out in the south-west. This was suppressed, and the remaining Communist leaders escaped to the North after the Party was banned in the South. Several months of mutual exchanges of threats to invade followed, and the Americans took the South's threat against the North sufficiently seriously to keep Syngman Rhee's forces short of supplies and ammunition.[8] This proved unfortunate, because in June 1950 North Korea launched an invasion, routing the South Koreans and initiating the three-year Korean War.

Soviet complicity in this undertaking was clearly shown in that the North Korean Army was entirely supplied with Soviet arms, but what is not clear is whether they agreed on the timing of it. The arms supplied included large quantities of armour, which suggests far more than an intention to provide North Korea with the wherewithal to defend itself, but Soviet diplomatic support in the United Nations proved ineffective and badly coordinated. On 12 January 1950 the US Secretary of State, Dean Acheson, had made a speech

---

[7] Yang, K. P., 'Korea', in *The Far East and Australasia 1969*, pp. 785-6 and 788.

[8] 'The Military Situation in the Far East', Joint Senate Committees on Armed Services and Foreign Relations, Hearings, Washington 1951, pp. 2010-12.

in which he had outlined the US defensive perimeter in the Far East as including Taiwan and Japan, but not South Korea. That this was followed within six months by a North Korean invasion suggests that Stalin took the Acheson speech (preceded during 1949 by the withdrawal of all US forces) as indicating a lack of interest in Korea's future. He had withdrawn the Red Army by the end of 1948, but had built up the North Korean forces in response to Syngman Rhee's verbal bellicosity, and intensified the supply of weaponry to them in the first half of 1950, thus giving them the capacity to invade without requiring the involvement of Soviet forces. But the Soviet UN delegation had withdrawn in protest at the American-organised refusal of the United Nations to expel the Chinese delegation and give its place (including its permanent membership of the Security Council) to the newly-victorious Chinese Communists, and was still boycotting the UN's proceedings when news of the Korean invasion arrived.[9] It was therefore unable to use its veto to prevent the United States' enlistment of UN support for aid to South Korea, and did not choose to involve its own forces in support of its protege against the United States. With the possibility of escalation to world war in mind, Stalin ordered the terms of conscript service in all the Soviet armed forces to be increased by one year, thus doubling them in size (from 2,874,000 in 1948 to 5,763,000[10] by the time the war ended). However, for fear that the Americans would conclude from it that he intended aggression and would therefore strike first with their nuclear weapons, of which they possessed a near monopoly, he did not announce the fact (it was officially admitted only in October 1967)[11] or authorise Soviet intervention. Instead it was the Chinese who were to intervene in the war, and later to allege that the Soviets had made them pay for the weapons provided to the Chinese 'volunteers'. Furthermore, liquidation of the venture was undertaken at Soviet initiative, as part of the post-Stalin search for *détente* with the West, not in pursuit of any specifically Korean interests.

While North Korea's dependence on the Communist countries increased in the post-war period because of its need for their assistance in rebuilding the war-shattered economy, the exclusive relationship with the Soviet Union was considerably weakened. At the time of need, when North Korea was on the verge of political

[9] Lockie, R., *The Korean War*, Putnam, New York, 1962, pp. 48-55.

[10] Khrushchev, N.S. speech of 14 January 1960.

[11] Grechko, Marshal A., speech to the Supreme Soviet, *Pravda*, 13 October, 1967, pp. 5-6.

extinction, it had been saved not by Soviet but by Chinese intervention. Chinese troops remained in the country until 1958, while Chinese aid (estimated at $1.8 billion up to 1961)[12] was almost as large as Soviet ($2 billion)[13] with the Eastern European Communist countries contributing a further $620 million.[14]

Politically, the years 1953-55 saw the elimination of the 'Southerners' as a potential 'national Communist' faction, with the execution of their leader Pak Hong Yong, and 1956-58 the removal from power of both pro-Soviet and pro-Chinese factions. As Soviet influence had been paramount during 1945-50, the diversification of North Korea's trade and political relationships after 1955 tended to reduce it more than it reduced the much lower Chinese influence. The failure of an attempt by a faction within the party to follow the Soviet example of destalinisation in 1956 (in the form of an attack on the 'cult of personality of Kim Il Sung') left Kim in an unchallenged position, which he has retained as a 'Korean Stalin'.

It appears that the Soviet party attempted some form of interference at the time of the 1956 attack on Kim Il Sung and subsequently.[15] At the 4th Congress of the Korean Workers' Party in September 1961, Kim Il Sung claimed that all factionalism had been eradicated,[16] but in 1964 he attacked the leadership of the Soviet Communist Party for attempting to exercise a hegemonial relationship. Korean opposition to this was put in the form of a total rejection of any patterns of hierarchical authority within the international Communist movement: 'All fraternal parties are equal and independent . . . there may be a big party and a small party, but not a higher party and a lower party, nor a guided party and a guiding party' . . . 'no majority principle or centralised discipline is applicable to the relations between fraternal parties.'[17]

This expressed a fusion of Communism and nationalism which remains dominant. At times North Korea has appeared to lean towards China, the more especially in that Kim Il Sung's personality cult is very much modelled on that of Mao Tse-tung.

[12] Far Eastern Economic Review Year Book for 1962, p. 149.

[13] *Ibid.*

[14] Asahi Shimbun, Tokyo 14 July 1961, p. 3 quoted in Paige, *op. cit.*, p. 43.

[15] Eg. in the attack on the Kim Il Sung personality cult, and the dispute over the priority given to heavy industry, Yang, *loc. cit.* p. 789.

[16] For a discussion of the issues see Scalapino, R. A. 'The Foreign Policy of North Korea' in *China Quarterly* April-June 1963, pp. 30-50, and Bradbury, J., 'Sino-Soviet Competition in North Korea', *China Quarterly*, April-June, 1961.

[17] Pyongyang Radio, 31 August 1964.

Thus the virtue of 'self-reliance' has been lauded above all others (to the dismay of the Soviets, who noted that among the fruits of self-reliance displayed to foreign visitors are industrial plants built by the Soviet Union or Eastern European countries), and the history of Korean liberation from Japanese rule has been rewritten to eliminate almost completely all elements except the guerilla activities of Kim Il Sung. The Korean War has been rewritten to describe it as a victory of North Korea over American imperialism and its lackeys, in which the Soviet Union and China played minor supporting parts.[18] Although the Soviet Union remains North Korea's largest trading partner, Japan, China and a number of other countries have become of growing importance in North Korea's foreign trade.

The current Soviet attitude to North Korea is correct but cool. In the major review of policy given by Brezhnev at the 24th Party Congress,[19] North Korea was one of the four Communist-ruled states whose relations with the Soviet Union were not described as including 'friendship'—the other three were Yugoslavia, China and Albania. He voiced approval in respect of only two foreign policy objectives—reunification and withdrawal of US troops from South Korea—and abstained from comment on North Korea's internal situation. Otherwise he described the growth of ties only as 'meeting the interests of the peoples of both countries', a formula frequently applied to relations with non-Communist countries, and indicating a lack of political closeness with the North Korean regime.

NORTH VIETNAM

The circumstances in which the Vietnamese Communists came to power owed more to the cross-purposes of American, French, Nationalist Chinese and British policy than to Communist doctrine. President Roosevelt was particularly concerned to avoid recreating the French colonial empire in Indochina, and it was therefore decided at the Potsdam Conference that after surrender of the Japanese there, British forces from India should occupy the south and Nationalist Chinese from South China the north, the 16th Parallel serving as the demarcation line between them. The French had banned the Indochina Communist Party in 1939, and a number of its members led by a certain Nguyen Ai-Quoc took refuge in Southern China, where they joined with non-Communist nationalist Vietnamese in forming in May 1941 the Revolutionary League for

18 Eg. in Baik Bong, *Kim Il Sung, Biography,* Vol. I, Miraisha, Tokyo, 1969, pp. 529-32.
19 *Report of the Central Committee of the CPSU,* 30 March 1971, Novosti Press Agency Publishing House, 1971, p. 15.

Vietnamese Independence, Viet Minh for short. Nguyen Ai-Quoc was reluctant to cooperate with the Chinese, but after some pressure (notably a long term of imprisonment) he agreed, and in March 1944 a Vietnamese Provisional Government was proclaimed in China. Viet Minh forces returned to Indochina, to operate as guerillas against the Japanese, supply intelligence to the allies, and spread its own propaganda in favour of independence among the population. Nguyen Ai-Quoc had by now changed his name to Ho Chi Minh ('He who Enlightens') for security reasons, and was unchallenged leader of the Viet Minh. On VJ-day, 13 August 1945, the Indochinese Communist Party decided to disarm the Japanese before the allied occupation forces arrived, and thus greet them as the effective authority in Hanoi and Saigon, hoping in this way to forestall any idea of restoring French control.

The British forces in the south arrived promptly, but with too few men to do more than occupy Saigon and its immediate environs. The Chinese forces were much larger but moved very slowly and long before they arrived in Hanoi, Viet Minh troops had occupied it, on 2 September proclaiming the 'Democratic Republic of Vietnam' there. Arms secured by disarming the Japanese were supplemented by weapons which the Japanese had taken from the French forces, and further arms of American origin were acquired by various means from the Chinese Nationalist occupying forces.[20] In this way arms for the nucleus of a 'People's Army' were secured, and these were the resources with which the war against the French was mainly fought.

In 1945 the French Communist Party was in a very strong position, so much so that continuation of the wartime alliance with the Soviet Union seemed likely, and the accession of the French Communists to power only slightly less so. A Communist uprising in a French colony, even if the Soviet Union had no hand in it, could well hamper the process by its adverse effects on French non-Communist voters. Therefore, French Communists in Saigon warned the Viet Minh in 1945 not to seek independence 'prematurely', and so strongly did domestic considerations continue to pre-occupy them that in 1947 the Communist members of the French Cabinet voted in favour of the fight against the Viet Minh, believing that they were thereby serving their own and Soviet interests.[21]

[20] For an account of this period see Isaacs, H. R., *No Peace for Asia* 1947 pp. 145-175, or extracts in Gettleman, M. E., (Ed.), *Vietnam,* Penguin Books, 1966, pp. 42-61.
[21] Girling, J. L. S. *People's War,* George Allen & Unwin, London, 1969, p. 18.

At the outset, Chinese influence was pronounced, whereas Soviet influence was negligible. Most of the original Viet Minh commanders had learnt the art of 'protracted war' in China, and their numbers were supplemented by newly-trained officers and troops when China became a 'sanctuary' and training ground, after Chinese Communist forces occupied the areas bordering on Tonkin in the latter part of 1949. But at the same time, anti-Chinese reservations were widespread in Vietnam; and the Viet Minh sought to stress its continuity with past Vietnamese liberation movements by naming its offensives after historic figures in the fight for Vietnamese independence, most of whom had in fact fought against Chinese armies coming down from the North.[22]

After the Communist victory in the Chinese Civil War, China provided much aid and the Soviet Union provided a little, but the Viet Minh's effort was not dominated by the need for outside supplies. Soviet aid was especially tardy; the first French observations of Soviet-built trucks occurred as late as November 1952, when some were captured at Phu-Doan,[23] while the increased strength of the Viet Minh after mid-1953 was the result not of increased Soviet aid, but of an inflow of Chinese instructors and equipment of Chinese, Soviet and American origin from Korea, after the armistice came into force in July.[24]

In 1954 the Viet Minh successes raised the question of abandonment of Indo-China by France, and a possible Communist takeover of the whole of Vietnam. A fourteen-power conference was convened at Geneva to deal with both Korea and Indochina, and its opening coincided with a major Viet Minh victory at Dien Bien Phu. But any hopes the Viet Minh might have had of acquiring all of Vietnam were to be subordinated by the Soviet leaders to their policy aims in Europe.

The Geneva Conference coincided in time with a crisis in European politics over the question of the European Defence Community. This proposal—for integrating the armed forces of several European members of NATO—was meeting fierce opposition in France from the Gaullists, who disliked the diminution of sovereignty involved, and from many of the centre and left, who believed it harmful to the possibilities of *détente* with the Soviet Union apparent in the post-Stalin period. The Soviets allowed their hostility to EDC to be known, and some observers have argued,

22 Fall, B. B., *The Two Vietnams,* second revised edition, Pall Mall Press, London, 1967, p. 108.
23 Fall, *op. cit.,* p. 120.
24 Eisenhower, Dwight, D., *Mandate for Change,* Doubleday, New York, 1963, p. 338.

though the evidence is not conclusive, that Soviet willingness to urge a cease-fire upon the Viet Minh was conditional upon French refusal to ratify EDC.[25] If this was so, then the Soviet Union, conversely, was under an obligation to moderate its support for the Viet Minh in order to ensure that a cease-fire eventuated; otherwise the French might well revive the EDC proposal. Whatever the reasons, the Soviet delegation at Geneva proved cooperative both in reaching an agreement which left the Vietnamese Communists in control of only half the country, and in persuading them and the Chinese to accept American and South Vietnamese refusal to sign the agreement.[26]

Up to 1954 the success of the Vietnamese Communists owed far more to China than to the Soviet Union, and their willingness to accept less than their military successes had entitled them to expect, was probably due less to fear of American entry into the war than to Soviet pressure to moderate their demands, coupled with a belief that South Vietnam would become theirs either as a result of the promised elections to take place in 1956 (which South Vietnam refused to hold, on the grounds that it had not signed the Geneva agreement and was not bound by it) or as a consequence of South Vietnam's disintegration under the weight of internal dissensions.[27]

In fact, events disappointed North Vietnamese expectations, as large-scale American aid enabled the South Vietnamese regime to overcome most of its difficulties and achieve some marked economic progress. Conversely, in the North, departure of the French and many French-trained Vietnamese technicians left its industries seriously short of skilled manpower and management, while a dogmatically-based and ruthlessly executed attempt at agrarian reform along Chinese lines caused agricultural unrest quelled only by mass executions and a reversal of policy.

The North Vietnamese government's economic policy required an expansion of agricultural production, but it was not likely that the country would become self-sufficient, as traditionally it had depended heavily on rice from the South, a source no longer available. If it were not to remain dependent on hand-outs of food from China or the Soviet Union (neither of which possessed large surpluses or, in some years, any surpluses at all), an attempt must

---

25 The French Government denied it at the time—*Times,* London, 7 June 1954. But see Mayne, R., *The Recovery of Europe,* Weidenfeld & Nicolson, London, 1970, p. 213 and Fall, *op. cit.* p. 124.

26 For an account of the Soviet role at Geneva see Lancaster, D., *The Emancipation of French Indo-China,* O.U.P. 1961, pp. 314-336.

27 Honey, P. J., *Communism in North Vietnam,* M.I.T. Press, 1963, p. 6.

be made to develop industry, based on raw materials known or believed to exist within the country, so that manufactures could be sold abroad to purchase food. In the summer of 1955, Ho Chi Minh visited China and the Soviet Union and signed aid agreements with both. But restoration of existing mines and factories, exploration for new sources of minerals, and building and equipping of new factories, were tasks in which China could offer little assistance. Within the bloc only the Soviet Union and its Eastern European allies could provide expertise and equipment of the requisite kinds and on the necessary scale. The pursuit of Chinese advice proved near-disastrous in the agricultural field, and a counterpart to the Chinese 'Hundred Flowers' campaign in 1957 proved so productive of criticism of Party and government that it was abandoned even more hastily than its model, so Chinese influence sank as Soviet influence rose during 1957-58.[28]

In May 1957 the Soviet President, Voroshilov, visited North Vietnam, and on 6 July Ho Chi Minh left for a tour of all Communist countries, probably in search of further aid. It is possible that there was a serious dispute within the Party, in which Ho's leadership came into question; he remained out of the country until December, but there is almost no evidence as to what was happening, or whether it involved relations with the Soviet Union and China—Ho stayed for a time in both countries during his absence.

Whatever had been happening, his return was followed by a 'Three Year Plan' in which quietist policies were pursued at home in the interests of industrialisation and of making the agricultural reform work. During most of this period North Vietnam's 'middle course' bore a slightly pro-Soviet tinge. For example, there was no suggestion that the Chinese 'Great Leap Forward' should be imitated even in token fashion, while at the time of the North Vietnamese Communist Party's 3rd Congress in September 1960 more prominence was given in the press to Soviet attacks on the Chinese, which were fully reported, than to Chinese attacks on the Soviets, which were toned down or edited out. Pronouncements made by the North Vietnamese themselves, however, were pro-Soviet, but only very cautiously so, and contained no attacks on China. At the November 1960 meeting of 81 Communist Parties in Moscow, the North Vietnamese were more concerned to avoid a split between their 'great and powerful friends' than to take sides, and their official pronouncement on the Conference statement was careful to pay tribute to both; 'The Soviet Union is the mightiest country in

[28] *Ibid.*, pp. 10, 16-17, 48.

the socialist camp . . . at the same time, the Soviet Union and China are the two largest countries in the socialist bloc, and the CPSU and CCP are the two largest and most responsible parties in the international Communist movement . . .'[29] Both at this meeting, and in the communique issued after a visit by Pham Van Dong, Prime Minister of North Vietnam, to Moscow in July 1961, the North Vietnamese confined themselves to pronouncements on matters which were not the subject of controversy within the international Communist movement.

However, during 1958-61 the pressures for renewal of the Vietnam war were building up, and in December 1960 the National Front for the Liberation of South Vietnam was set up. Commitment to the cause of forcible unification increased the importance of Chinese support, as the Soviet government was heavily engaged in the pursuit of *détente* and disarmament. At the same time, North Vietnam's dependence on the Soviet Union both for aid in industrialisation and for assistance in deterring greater American involvement in the Vietnam war, precluded over-enthusiastic endorsement of Chinese positions.

An example of the delicacy with which Ho Chi Minh balanced between his benefactors at this time is given by Bernard Fall. Ho was an honoured guest at the Soviet 22nd Party Congress in October-November 1961. In the course of it the Chinese delegation walked out and returned home. He also left the meeting, but before returning home went on a tour of European Russia, and wrote a brief article in which he thanked the USSR and its Eastern European allies for their economic aid, making no mention of China's contributions in the field, which at that time were probably larger than any other especially in the supply of food and consumer goods. But on arrival in Hanoi he arranged a special exhibition to mark the seventeenth anniversary of China's sole European ally, the Albanian People's Republic.[30]

During 1960-61 the rate of infiltration from North to South Vietnam increased sharply, and in January 1962 Hanoi Radio announced the formation of the 'Marxist-Leninist Vietnamese People's Revolutionary Party', a device for absolving the North Vietnamese Communist Party from direct linkage to the war in the South, while at the same time giving a public indication of close Communist involvement in it.[31] During 1961-63 Chinese leaders

[29] Nhan Dan, Hanoi, 7 December 1960.
[30] Fall, *op. cit.*, p. 102.
[31] Glaubit, J., 'Relations between Communist China and Vietnam' in Rupen, R. A., and Farrell, R., (Ed.), *Vietnam and the Sino-Soviet Dispute*, Praeger, New York 1967, p. 62.

paid a number of visits to Hanoi, but North Vietnam continued to pursue a middle line on the Sino-Soviet dispute; even when in May 1963 Liu Shao-chi, in a speech in Hanoi declared that 'in such an important battle for principles we cannot be spectators or follow a halfway line',[32] the North Vietnamese refused to take a position on the Sino-Soviet dispute as a whole. Only in one major respect did they 'lean' towards China; while war in the South was intensified during 1962-63 the Soviets were involved in negotiating the partial test ban treaty, and did not welcome developments which threatened to exacerbate their relations with the United States. The North Vietnamese echoed Chinese opposition to the Test Ban Treaty and refusal to sign it. At the same time, they avoided giving excessive offence to the Soviet Union by playing down the importance of the test ban issue, as opposed to the line taken by the Chinese, who described it as yet another instance of Soviet-US collusion in pursuit of 'joint world domination'.[33] There are some indications, nevertheless, that even the limited support given to China aroused fears among pro-Soviet elements in the Central Committee of the North Vietnamese party that public estrangement from the Soviet Union would follow, and America would consequently be emboldened to attack North Vietnam.[34] That the Soviet Union chose to deliver no assurance on the issue is indicated by the fact that in February 1964 the North Vietnamese Party's theoretical journal *Hoc Tap* discussed the possibility of such attacks, said that if they occurred the Americans would face resistance not only from North Vietnam but also from China, and made no mention of possible Soviet support. A further possible indicator of strains in Soviet-Vietnamese relations is the sharp reduction in Soviet deliveries to North Vietnam, from 51 million roubles worth in 1963 to 42.5 million roubles in 1964, most of the reduction being in deliveries of machinery and equipment (from 30.6 to 22.3 million).[35] However, the Tonkin Gulf incident of August 1964, and subsequent escalation of the war to include regular bombing of North Vietnam posed new requirements, especially in anti-aircraft defence, which China was in no position to satisfy. A new trade agreement was concluded in December 1964 and Kosygin visited Hanoi in February 1965. Soviet economic aid resumed the upward trend which had been interrupted in 1964 and military aid was stepped up both in quantity and, especially, in scope, to include

[32] *People's Daily,* Peking, 16 May 1963.
[33] The role of the Test Ban Treaty is discussed in the section on Sino-Soviet relations later in this chapter.
[34] Glaubitz, *loc. cit.* p. 63.
[35] *V.T.*, periodical issue, 2 November 1965, p. 4.

surface-to-air missiles as well as large numbers of anti-aircraft guns with the necessary ancillary equipment.

On his departure from Hanoi (10 February 1965), Kosygin issued a communique stating:

> ... the only correct way to settle the South Vietnam question is for the United States to fulfil the Geneva agreements; to stop the war of aggression at once; to withdraw its forces, military personnel and weapons from South Vietnam; to cease interference in the affairs of South Vietnam, and give the South Vietnamese people the right to decide their internal affairs for themselves.

Despite minor tactical shifts of emphasis, this has remained the Soviet position. The Conference of Communist and Workers' Parties held in Moscow in June 1969 used virtually the same words in its main document:

> ... The Conference calls on all who cherish peace and national independence to intensify the struggle in order to compel US imperialism to withdraw its interventionist troops from Vietnam, cease interfering in the internal affairs of that country and respect the right of the Vietnamese people to solve their problems by themselves.[36]

In similar fashion, Brezhnev endorsed the North Vietnamese position in his speech at the 24th Party Congress in March 1971: 'There is only one way of solving the Vietnamese problem. It is clearly indicated in the proposals of the DRV government, and the Provisional Revolutionary Government of South Vietnam, proposals which we firmly back'.[37]

No details of military aid provided by either the Soviet Union or China are available, nor are there any of Chinese economic aid and trade. The Soviet Union, however, publishes full details of its trade with North Vietnam annually, and the imbalance between exports to it and imports from it gives some indication of the scope of Soviet loans or grants. Since trade began in 1955, Soviet exports have always exceeded imports from North Vietnam, but the major increases from the Soviet side were in 1959 to 1966 (reflecting assistance for the 1960 industrialisation plan), and again in 1967 to 1970, indicating a stepping-up of aid to offset the effects of American bombing (1965 to 1968) and continuing attempts to restore and expand the economy after bombing ended. The peak years for North Vietnamese exports to the Soviet Union were 1963

---

36 *Documents adopted by the International Conference of Communist and Workers' Parties*, Novosti Press Agency Publishing House, 1969, p. 51.
37 *Report of the Central Committee*, Novosti, 1971, p. 29.

and 1964 (just over 31 million roubles' worth in each year), and by 1968 they had declined to just over half that level. The four-yearly averages show the stepping up of the Soviet effort; the figures give the *annual* average of Soviet exports to and imports from North Vietnam in millions of roubles.[38]

Table 15

|         | 1955-58 | 1959-62 | 1963-66 | 1967-70 |
|---------|---------|---------|---------|---------|
| Exports | 6.2     | 31.8    | 55.7    | 153.3   |
| Imports | 3.3     | 21.3    | 28.3    | 16.7    |

The major items exported by the Soviet Union have been equipment for complete factories, lorries and spare parts, oil and oil products, ferrous metal components and food (mostly wheat)—in 1968 these accounted for 58% of the traffic by value. Principal items in the much smaller return flow from North Vietnam in 1968 were clothing, vodka and liqueurs, which totalled 57% by value.[39] The very high ratio of exports to imports indicates heavy commitment to support of North Vietnam (though modest compared to American expenditure on and in South Vietnam), a commitment which is unlikely to be reduced for some years in view of the role played by the DRV in Sino-Soviet, Soviet-American and Sino-American relations.

While the support of North Vietnam involves drain on Soviet economic resources, this has not been large in terms of the Soviet economy. It has, though, been vital to North Vietnam, but despite this has done no more than ensure that the North Vietnamese pursue a middle of the road policy in the Sino-Soviet dispute. While the North Vietnamese leaders frequently pay tribute to the aid received from both major Communist nations, they avoid commenting on Soviet charges that the Chinese interfere with their aid shipments on their way by rail through China, certainly giving no support to their allegations that the Chinese reluctance to intervene in Vietnam results from a tacit understanding with the United States, rather than from fear of a US retaliation against China.

Soviet freedom of manoeuvre in the Vietnam situation is extremely limited by the dispute within the international Communist movement. To urge an accommodation on Hanoi in the interests of Soviet objectives in other parts of the world, as was done in 1954, is no longer possible. To do so would inevitably lead to further charges of betrayal from the Chinese, and probably from

[38] *V.T.* 1918-66, pp. 202-5, 1968, pp. 214-8, April 1971, p. 57.
[39] *V.T.* 1968, pp. 214-8.

the Vietnamese as well. At the same time, the development among Soviet leaders of a less holistic view of the international scene has enabled them to continue negotiation with the USA and other Western powers on matters such as strategic arms limitation or European security, and though existence of the Vietnam problem may well have slowed down progress towards agreement on these other issues, it has not rendered it impossible to discuss them. There is no reason to expect that the Soviet Union will exercise pressure on Hanoi or on the National Liberation Front to extract the United States from its dilemma in Vietnam. Some observers claim to detect stronger pro-Peking tendencies among the NLF leaders than are to be seen in the North Vietnamese government itself. Without attempting to push these potential differences too far or to minimise the extent to which the government of North Vietnam controls the NLF, it is not difficult to conceive how, in terms of Soviet experience and policies in Asia, Soviet leaders should be easier and more confident in their relations with an established government than with a revolutionary movement. But even if they wish the war ended, both they and the Chinese are sensitive to charges of collusion with the United States. In this regard the US blockade and resumption of bombing constitute a challenge to both which neither can ignore in the short term, whatever either's final objectives. Nor can they be certain that public withdrawal of North Vietnamese support for the NLF would in fact be synonymous with actual withdrawal or even that, if genuine, it would end the campaign by the South Vietnamese Communists. (It would undoubtedly much reduce their effectiveness, but that is not the same thing; the Viet Minh's ability to survive and operate without a secure rear area was shown by its campaigns of 1946-49, before the Chinese Communist successes provided sanctuaries for it.) All they can be certain of is that pressure to end the war would cause further internal rifts in the international Communist movement; and although this movement is no longer the reliable foreign policy tool that it was, it still provides the Soviet Union with a powerful international forum and body of support. At its present level of strong verbal, economic and military support short of actual involvement, Soviet foreign policy towards North Vietnam balances between the extremes of pusillanimity on the one hand and dangerous bellicosity on the other. That there is little room for manoeuvre is the result more of the strains within international Communism than of tensions in relations with the non-Communist world. To the extent that this is so, the Vietnam situation has been 'sealed off' by Soviet policy, which has not, for example, made progress in the Strategic

Arms Limitation Talks contingent on US withdrawal from Vietnam, but has used the Vietnam situation as a stick with which to beat the Chinese, by alleging that US 'aggression' is facilitated by Chinese-induced splits in the 'socialist camp'.

## CHINA

As has been indicated in the foregoing sections, Soviet dealings with the lesser Communist-ruled countries of Asia have in large measure been determined by its relationship, and theirs, with China. It is therefore apposite at this stage to examine in some detail the relations between the Soviet Union and China, and in particular the differences on a range of issues comprised within the general title of the Sino-Soviet dispute.

When the Chinese Communists proclaimed the People's Republic in Peking on 1 October 1949, there was a tendency among Western leaders to assume that a mere extension of Soviet power had occurred; this was exemplified in Dean Rusk's description of Communist China as unfit for recognition on the grounds that 'It does not meet the first test . . . it is not Chinese'. Although for some years Chinese behaviour was in fact that of an ally, if not a satellite, there were in fact a number of reasons why the Chinese leaders should view Soviet hegemony within the Bloc with less than rapture. Not least of these was the highly ambiguous nature of Stalin's attitude towards them ever since the 1920s. The results of following Soviet advice to 'base themselves on the urban proletariat' and operate in the open (making common cause with the KMT with a view to capturing it from within) had been near-disastrous. It meant that the Party had been led to neglect the largest source of recruits—the peasantry—in favour of a small segment of the population, easily controlled by KMT security forces because it was concentrated in a small number of cities, and easily eliminated when its members abandoned their semi-clandestine existence to stand up and be counted.[40] For Stalin, as for European Communists in general, the peasants were a reactionary force which could be recruited into the service of revolution by promises of land, but were by themselves not capable of forming a Communist nucleus, while the essence of Leninism, Lenin's major contribution to Communist organisational practice, was the concept of the small centralised party. This remedy was natural enough for the circumstances of the European Left, constantly reft by factional struggles, but not particularly adapted to the different circumstances of China

[40] Eudin, X. J., and North, R. C., *Soviet Russia and the East, 1920-27*, Stanford University Press, 1957, pp. 288-310.

where left factionalism was in no way comparable in scale. The obedient application of unimaginative Soviet advice in 1926-27 brought the Chinese Communist Party to the verge of extinction, and it had to extract itself by its own efforts.[41]

During the protracted Civil War in China, Stalinist policy continued to display features explicable on grounds of *raison d'état,* but hardly consonant with proletarian internationalism. Aid was given to the KMT, which from 1937 onwards was fighting both the Communists and the Japanese. It included military advisers, aircraft and pilots who remained in China until 1942;[42] as far as can be ascertained they were employed only against the Japanese, but their availability naturally enabled some KMT resources to be diverted into anti-Communist operations; nor is there any record of similar Soviet assistance being given to Mao Tse-Tung's forces at any time.

In August 1945, in a campaign which was a logistic tour de force, but involved relatively little heavy fighting, the Red Army swept into Manchuria to demolish Japan's last remaining major ground force—the Kwantung Army. When the Soviet forces withdrew, no clear picture of cooperation with the Chinese Communist armies emerged—in some cases Soviet withdrawal permitted Communist troops to occupy the abandoned territory and occasionally to take over arms dumps which the Japanese had surrendered to the Soviets, but in most cases KMT takeover of the cities was facilitated. Certainly local Soviet commanders made no extraordinary efforts to ensure that their withdrawal was arranged to strengthen the Chinese position, and almost everywhere they used the argument that Manchuria's industries, having been built up by Japan, were war booty, to justify removing most of the equipment of China's only major industrial area to the Soviet Union.[43] This behaviour contrasted vividly with their conduct in respect to Silesia earlier in the same year—there the commander of the Soviet troops in the area received and executed specific instructions from Stalin that the Silesian industries should, if possible, be captured intact, as they were to be ceded to Poland in part compensation for Soviet acquisitions of territory in Eastern Poland. He therefore phased his operations in such a way as to invite a speedy German withdrawal, thus avoiding damage to the area from demolition or fighting at the

41 Fitzgerald, C. P., *The Birth of Communist China,* Pelican Books, 1964, pp. 58-68 and 72-85.
42 Chuikov, Marshal A. I., *The Beginning of the Road,* McGibbon and Kee, London, 1963, p. 13.
43 Fitzgerald, *op. cit.,* pp. 97-100.

expense of allowing the German forces to escape.[44] If provision of a heavy industrial base for Poland was an act of policy, then the removal of China's heavy industrial base a few months later, an act which required elaborate organisation, is hardly likely to have been viewed by the Chinese Communist leaders as a fit of absent-mindedness. In addition, as he subsequently disclosed to a Yugoslav delegation, Stalin in 1946 advised the Chinese Communists to seek a *modus vivendi* with the KMT and dissolve their army.[45] His reasons for doing so are a matter for speculation—no doubt he did not wish to antagonise his allies of the late war, at a time of great Soviet weakness, by catering to their fears of militant Communism—certainly in Eastern Europe at the same time he was discouraging militant local Communists from overt seizures of power. But in view of his past record of ambiguity towards the Chinese revolutionaries, it is at least possible that he did not relish the prospect of their coming to power. One of the features of his rule was the subservience of other Communist parties to Soviet policy, and he may have foreseen that a Communist China, with over three times the Soviet Union's population and an experience in making revolution extending over 20 years, would be a fruitful source of pluralist tendencies in a hitherto monolithic bloc. If he foresaw the possibility he might well have believed that a weak KMT-dominated government, harassed by centrifugal tendencies within its own ranks, as well as by a Communist movement strong enough to disrupt but too weak to seize power, offered the best prospects for Soviet aggrandisement, including annexation of peripheral areas such as Sinkiang, where Soviet influence was high in the 1930s and 40s, and was being exerted in the direction of separation from China.[46] In view of the lack of reliable evidence about his motives, the precise degree of hypocrisy behind official Soviet welcomes to the new Chinese government cannot be ascertained. The Soviet Ambassador remained accredited to the KMT until the very end, accompanying it as it moved from one temporary capital to another, until its departure for Taiwan, when he returned to Peking to become accredited to the new regime.

That Mao Tse-Tung had not only adapted Marxism to Chinese conditions, but that the Chinese Party leadership was fully aware of his importance as an innovator, emerged even before the end of

[44] Konev, Marshal, I. S., *Sorok Pyaty* (Forty-five), Moscow 1968, pp. 3-4.
[45] Dedijer, V., *Tito,* Simon & Schuster, New York, 1953, p. 322 and Djilas, M., *Conversations with Stalin,* Penguin Books, London, 1962, pp. 164.
[46] See Fleming, P., *News from Tartary,* Jonathan Cape, London, 1936 pp. 245-270, 345-351. See also Whiting, A. S., and Sheng Shih-ts'ai *Sinkiang; Pawn or Pivot?* Lansing, Michigan, 1958, pp. 21-267.

the war. The 'Resolution concerning Several Questions of the History of Our Party' of 20 April 1945 stated specifically 'Comrade Mao Tse-Tung has splendidly *developed* the Leninist doctrine on the Revolutionary movement *in colonial and semi-colonial countries* (my italics) . . .', and after the Communist victory in the Chinese Civil War the claims made for Mao as an innovator became bolder, and in 1951 it was officially claimed that 'Mao not only adapted Marxism to new circumstances, he advanced its development. He created a Chinese, or Asiatic, form of Marxism'.[47] For all the other Communist Parties, only the Stalinist model was valid, until Tito challenged his authority in 1948, and for most, for long thereafter. But the statements made on behalf of Mao indicated no willingness to accord doctrinal hegemony to Stalin; on the contrary, the claim that Mao had created a new form of Marxism was more ambitious than anything ever claimed on Stalin's behalf. In 1956 the Peking *People's Daily* staked an even bolder claim for Chinese doctrinal hegemony among Asian revolutionary movements by declaring 'The classic type of revolution in imperialist countries is the October Revolution, the classic type of revolution in colonial and semi-colonial countries is the Chinese Revolution . . .'.[48] Chinese ideological claims were muted between 1951 and 1956, but probably more because of China's need for Soviet economic and military support in the reconstruction and Korean War period, than because her leaders had ceased to believe them. And the Soviet press, though for a time appearing to concede the special relevance of the Chinese revolutionary experience for insurrectionist movements in Asia, fell far short of endorsing the claim that Mao had created a specifically Asian form of Marxism.

A Treaty of Alliance and two Aid Agreements were signed in February-April 1950, on terms not particularly favourable to China. The Alliance covered only attack by Japan, or states allied to it, thereby not automatically covering general war, ie., not guaranteeing Chinese assistance to the Soviet Union in the event of war in Europe, nor Soviet assistance to China in the event of war in the Far East in which Japan provided bases but did not itself participate. This turned out to be more than a mere legal quibble, as the outbreak of the Korean War was only four months away; in it, despite Chinese participation, the Treaty was not invoked. The Aid Agreements provided for a Soviet loan of $US300 million, and

[47] Statement at meeting to celebrate 30th Anniversary of founding of the Chinese Communist Party, quoted in Mehnert, K., *Peking and Moscow,* Mentor Books, 1964, p. 430.
[48] *People's Daily,* 8 November 1956.

for exploitation of oil and mineral resources (including uranium in Sinkiang) by joint stock companies, similar to those formed in Eastern Europe (and already under strong public attack by the Yugoslavs as instruments of Soviet economic exploitation).[49] Rights of control over the North Manchurian Railway (which provides a more direct route between Eastern Siberia and Vladivostok than the Trans-Siberian Railway proper), traditional since Tsarist times, were restored to the USSR, as was the use of the naval base at Port Arthur on the Liaotung Peninsula (valued by the Tsars and their successors because it is ice-free and has relatively easy access to the open sea, unlike their main fleet base at Vladivostok), though this latter right was to lapse in 1952 (or on conclusion of a Japanese Peace Treaty if that occurred before 1952). When the Sino-Soviet dispute became public, the Chinese were to charge that most of the loan was in fact used up in military purchases, necessitated by the Chinese involvement in the Korean War, and that Soviet insistence on payment for military equipment (needed, as the Chinese saw it, for use in a war instigated without consultation by the Russians, but which exposed China to danger from the United States because of Soviet miscalculations) had rendered the loan virtually useless for the economic purposes which it was meant to serve.[50]

The Port Arthur base was retained beyond 1952 because of the Korean War, but Stalin's successors agreed in October 1954 to evacuate it, liquidate the joint stock companies, and hand over control of the North Manchurian Railway to China. All this was achieved during 1955, in which year a new agreement was signed, under which, among other things, The Soviet Union agreed to provide China with a non-military nuclear reactor and to build a railway from Alma Ata into Sinkiang, to improve the links between Soviet and Chinese Central Asia.[51]

During 1955 several events occurred which in retrospect appear to have indicated both a Chinese desire to assume a role of regional leadership of Asian Communism, and a Soviet attempt to reassert its hegemony and the indivisibility of Communism as a world movement. The Soviet Union was excluded from the Bandoeng Conference of Asian states, even though it is the largest Asian state by area, and one of the largest by population, and Khrushchev and

---

[49] For a discussion of Sino-Soviet economic relations prior to 1963 see Griffith, W. E., *The Sino-Soviet Rift*, George Allen & Unwin, 1964, pp. 231-8.

[50] Whiting, A. S., 'Contradictions in the Moscow-Peking Axis', *Journal of Politics*, February 1958 quoted in Mehnert, *op. cit.*, p. 325.

[51] Mehnert, *op. cit.*, p. 298.

Bulganin visited Afghanistan, Burma and India. The visit was marked by a number of anti-colonial speeches, but also served as a demonstration of Soviet interest in Asia, despite exclusion from Bandoeng, and as a sign that the Soviet Union did not intend to 'sub-contract' leadership of Asian Communism by according regional overlordship to the Chinese, despite the Chinese claims that their revolutionary experience was more relevant to Asian conditions than the Soviet.

The first overt sign of disagreement occurred when Khrushchev in February 1956 introduced the de-Stalinisation campaign and the doctrine of 'different roads to socialism'.[52] This last, which declared the Soviet model to be no longer obligatory, was to lead to mild rebuke of the Soviets by the Chinese, for failure to consult them before beginning de-Stalinisation.[53] However, public relations remained cordial, and even the emerging differences were not seen as irreconcilable. China supported Soviet handling of the Polish and Hungarian crises of 1956,[54] though its offering of advice indicated its insistence on its right to consultation over events in Europe. Soviet trade with China went on increasing (in 1955, Soviet-Chinese trade turnover, imports and exports combined, was 21.4% of all Soviet foreign trade),[55] the numbers of Soviet experts working in China was stepped up (211 factories were being built with Soviet assistance during 1956),[56] as were the numbers of students from China in the Soviet Union. However, by comparison with Western aid programmes to non-Communist Asian countries, and with China's needs, the Soviet programmes were exceedingly modest in scale. (Only 11,000 Chinese students were received in the Soviet Union during 1951-62, an annual average of less than 1,000,[57] and the total value of Soviet equipment for the 211 factories was 2.5 billion pre-1961 roubles,[58] ie., about $US275 million, hardly an

[52] Speech at 20th Party Congress, 14 February 1956.
[53] Chinese letter to Soviet Party, 10 September 1960, quoted in Zagoria, D. S., *The Sino-Soviet Conflict*, Princeton University Press, 1962, pp. 42-3.
[54] Eg. in *People's Daily*, 10 November 1956.
[55] *V.T.*, 1918-66 (Summary Volume) Table V.
[56] For a Soviet account of aid to China see Sladkovskiy, M. I., (Ed.) *Leninskaya Politika S.S.S.R. v otnoshenii Kitaya* (The Leninist policy of the USSR towards China) Moscow, 1968, pp. 201-203.
[57] *Ibid.*, p. 204.
[58] Attempts to price the Soviet pre-1961 rouble are fraught with uncertainty. The equivalent in dollars given here is based on the 1961 rouble, which equalled ten old ones. Prior to 1961 it was customary to take 4 roubles as = $US1. On this basis, the aid would have been worth $625 million, still very modest. See Chu-yuan Cheng, *Economic Relations between Peking & Moscow 1949-63*. Praeger, New York, 1964, pp. 27-47.

impressive total for an aid programme which had been under way for almost six years.) Nor did they even compare well with aid programmes being offered by the Soviet Union to non-Communist Asian countries, so it would not appear that the Soviet Union was prepared to make extraordinary efforts to develop the Chinese economy. However, the emphasis in Sino-Soviet relations was about to shift into the military field.

During 1955-56 an intensive debate took place in China's Defence Ministry about the alternative courses open to China in acquiring modern weapons.[59] One school advocated a long-term programme related to development of China's own industrial capacities, with reliance in the meantime on the Soviet 'nuclear umbrella'; others (mainly on the General Staff) argued for extensive purchase from the Soviet Union of modern equipment, to provide China with up-to-date defence as quickly as possible, at the expense of longer-term dependence on the Soviet Union for spares. It was eventually decided to follow the first course.[60]

The Soviet Union in August 1957 became the first nation to make a successful test of an intercontinental ballistic missile (ICBM) to full range, and followed this feat on 5 October by the first launching of an artificial earth satellite. Ten days later a Sino-Soviet treaty covering 'new technology for national defence' was signed. It was a secret treaty, whose existence was disclosed by the Chinese only in 1963,[61] and very little is known of its provisions. However, Soviet indignation and embarrassment at the Chinese disclosure tends to suggest that it contemplated the provision to China of know-how related to weapons not provided to their Warsaw Pact allies, ie., long-range missiles (though not necessarily ICBM's), and perhaps of military nuclear technology including a 'sample' atomic bomb.[62]

The episode is hardly consistent with Soviet policy of non-dissemination of advanced military weapons information to allies, or of subsequent arms control and disarmament policy, nor does it fit well into the general picture of a gradually deteriorating relationship. What it does suggest, however, is that the Chinese were anxious to possess advanced weapons, as was implied in the outcome of the military debate, and that their requirement from the

[59] Hsieh, A. L., *Communist China's Strategy in the Nuclear Era*, Prentice-Hall, New Jersey, 1962, Chapter II.

[60] *Ibid.*, and Clemens, W. C., *The Arms Race and Sino-Soviet Relations*, Stanford University Press, 1968, pp. 16-19.

[61] 'Statement by the Spokesman of the Chinese Government 15 August 1963'. *Peking Review*, 16 August 1963, pp. 7-15.

[62] For a discussion of the 'secret treaty' see Clemens *op. cit.*, pp. 13-57.

Soviet Union was more for knowledge on how to manufacture advanced weapons, than for weapons in quantities suitable for deployment. Soviet motivation for the secret treaty is less clear, but Khrushchev may have expected to retain a lever on Chinese defence policy by some limited dissemination and hoped by this gesture to salvage a relationship which though deteriorating was still far from the point of no return.

With his internal position secured through defeat of the 'anti-Party Group', and his external position enhanced by the ICBM and Sputnik successes, Khrushchev convened an international Communist meeting in Moscow for November 1957, the fortieth anniversary of the Bolshevik seizure of power. A Declaration, issued on 14 November, reaffirmed the 20th Congress theses of non-inevitability of war, possibility of peaceful revolution, and of different roads to socialism, but qualified them by reference to the continued danger from 'imperialism', by implying that peaceful Communist takeover was only possible in advanced countries and therefore not applicable to most of Asia, and by stressing the perils of 'revisionism' and 'dogmatism' when attempting to pursue roads to socialism other than the Soviet model. While stigmatising both these deviations, the Declaration branded 'revisionism' (a term used in particular to describe the Yugoslav brand of Communism, with its rejection of Soviet claims to doctrinal hegemony and its extensive experimentation) as the greater danger.

The main Soviet concern in sponsoring the Declaration was the reassertion of a doctrinal hegemony which had been threatened by the upheavals of 1956 and the dissensions within its Presidium in 1957. For the Chinese, their co-sponsorship of the Declaration had a different meaning; it signified equality of status with the Soviets and, as Mao's speech at the meeting showed,[63] a belief that Soviet power should be used in the interests of the international revolution.

Fortified by the secret defence agreement, Mao stated that the 'East Wind prevails over the West Wind'. This has sometimes been taken to mean simply that he believed the Soviet success with Sputnik I and its achievements in development of thermo-nuclear warheads, had placed the Communist bloc in a position to intensify pressure on the 'capitalists' even at the risk of world war, but in fact this interpretation is over-simplified. Mao's stigmatising of the atomic bomb as a 'paper tiger' had made no exception for Soviet bombs, and the 'East Wind' comprised not merely the Soviet ICBM

[63] Chinese Government Statement of 1 September 1963, *Peking Review*, 6 September 1963, pp. 7-16.

but the totality of 'anti-imperialist' forces—the proletariat, the peoples of the Communist countries, the national-liberation movements, newly independent countries, plus the Soviet technological achievements.[64] Whatever may have been said afterwards, the Soviets are unlikely at the time to have encouraged Mao in any simplistic belief that a handful of successful tests constituted a major change in the strategic balance. The Soviet ICBM of 1957 (SS-6) was to prove a very reliable vehicle for the space programme, but as a military weapon it had a number of quite important defects. It was very large and therefore quite uneconomic to 'harden' by placement in a reinforced concrete underground silo; it used volatile liquid fuels and therefore could only be kept ready for launch for limited periods; and it was radio-guided and therefore vulnerable to a jamming signal which could send it off course.[65] Only small numbers of it were ever deployed, and it is very likely that the Soviet Union intended it mainly for use in its space programme, as two other types, much more suitable for military use, were well on in development by the time it first flew. Moreover, despite the amount of propaganda use the Soviets made of it, it is highly improbable that in private meetings they would have allowed Mao to propound a belief that it made World War III 'feasible'— if that was what he believed.

What both Mao and Khrushchev did believe was that the Soviet technological 'firsts' increased the strategic power of the Soviet bloc —as indeed they did, though the advantage was to prove neither decisive nor long-lived. Where they differed was in the uses to which they wished to put their enhanced bargaining power. China wished to put pressure on Taiwan, and in September 1958 was to cause the Quemoy crisis, in which the Soviet Union eventually warned the United States that it would retaliate with nuclear weapons if US nuclear weapons were used against China. The Chinese later charged the Soviets with having made this declaration only after the crisis was over,[66] implying that they had expected the Soviets to make it earlier, and that invocation of the Soviet 'nuclear umbrella' formed part of their strategy for managing it.

The Soviet Union had entirely different preoccupations. Though Khrushchev had come to power with the support of the 'heavy industry' lobby, including the military, his policy was geared to

---

[64] Simmonds, J. D., *China's World: The Foreign Policy of a Developing State*, Australian National University Press, Canberra, 1970, pp. 56-58.

[65] For a discussion of the 1957-60 Soviet ICBM deployment see Horelick, A. L., and Rush, M., *Strategic Power and Soviet Foreign Policy*, Chicago University Press, 1966, pp. 35-70 and 105-116.

[66] Chinese Government Statement of 1 September 1963.

improvements in living standards, especially through housing and light industry, and he was engaged in reducing where possible the demands of defence on scarce resources. As part of that policy he had already begun reductions in the armed forces which were to reduce their numbers from 5.75 million in 1955 to 3.6 million in 1959,[67] and was pursuing the aim of a total test ban. This had several objectives—to regulate the speed of the arms race, to complicate NATO arrangements (where multilateral control of nuclear weapons was widespread, whereas in the then recently formed Warsaw Pact all nuclear weapons were under exclusive Soviet control), and to reduce the risks of proliferation—which posed more hazards to the Soviet bloc, as most potential nuclear powers were countries such as France, Germany and Japan, members of US-sponsored alliances.

From an internal point of view, resistance to Khrushchev's arms control policy could be disarmed if a test ban could be negotiated while the Soviets were 'ahead'; and in the sense that the Soviet ICBM 'worked' while the US counterpart (Atlas) did not, the Soviet Union was 'ahead' in late 1957. A total ban on nuclear testing, if negotiated then, would have impeded American development of miniaturised warheads for its missiles which were needed to bring their payloads up to those of their Soviet counterparts. There were therefore several reasons why the shift from war-fighting capabilities (conventional forces) to deterrence (nuclear weapons carried by long-range bombers and later by missiles) should have appealed to Khrushchev as a means of cutting defence expenditures and releasing manpower for the labour force—needed for the building industry, the 'Virgin Lands' policy and the attempt to increase the population east of the Urals—and several reasons why he should have used the technological 'firsts' of 1957 as the basis not for increased militancy, but for the pursuit of *détente* and disarmament. But as pursuit of *détente* with a suspicious West was hardly possible without deemphasis of the theme of 'world revolution' in Communist dogma, the difference between his military aims and those of the Chinese inevitably spilled over into the ideological field.

It is possible, though the evidence is fragmentary, that the secret treaty's provisions on nuclear weapons were conditional on China's agreement to subscribe to a nuclear test ban treaty if it proved possible to conclude one. Certainly during 1958 the Chinese publicly supported a ban, and assailed US and British counter-arguments. But at the end of 1958 there was a change in the Soviet position on the proposed treaty.

Until December 1958 the Soviet delegation maintained that the treaty should cover only the then three existing nuclear powers, and opposed British and American insistence that it should contain provision for accession by other states, arguing that such provision could be misused to put off the time at which a treaty would come into effect. At the beginning of January 1959 the Soviets abandoned this position, provided that operation of the treaty by existing nuclear powers should not be made contingent on accession of non-nuclear states.[68] It is not clear why they abandoned their earlier view that the moral force of the treaty would be sufficient to prevent its violation by non-signatories, but only two countries announced during 1958 their intention to proceed with nuclear weapons programmes—France and China.

1959 was the climactic year of the dispute. The Soviet Union, having already gone far under the secret agreement (and the earlier agreement on non-military nuclear technology) to provide China with the prerequisites of a nuclear weapons programme, unilaterally abrogated it on 20 June, and withdrew its defence scientists and technologists.[69] Shortly afterwards it ceased to deliver even advanced aircraft, including Tu-16 bombers, which were supplied to non-Communist countries (Egypt and Indonesia) but not to China.[70] In September it declared its neutrality in the Sino-Indian border dispute,[71] thereby indicating to the Chinese not merely a support for the status quo which ill became an avowedly revolutionary party, but implicit support for a government of India which had only recently removed from office the Communist state government of Kerala. In September-October Khrushchev visited the United States, unveiled a Utopian plan for general disarmament, and was coldly received in Peking on his way back.

But the explanation for the deterioration in Sino-Soviet relations during 1958-59 is not to be sought solely in differences in foreign policy attitudes or in views of the strategic balance. More important was the challenge to Soviet primacy in the building of a truly Communist society implicit in the Chinese announcement in May 1958 of the 'Great Leap Forward'.[72] In the then accepted Commu-

---

[68] Clemens, *op. cit.*, pp. 27-28.
[69] 'Statement by the Spokesman of the Chinese Government 15 August, 1963', *Peking Review*, 16 August 1963 pp. 7-15.
[70] *The Military Balance 1969-70*, pp. 37, 40, 44.
[71] TASS statement, 12 September 1959.
[72] Liu Shao-chi, 'Report on the Work of the Central Committee', at Eighth Party Congress, Second Session, 5 May, 1958.

nist hierarchy of social structures, all the Communist-ruled states except the Soviet Union were in the stage of 'People's Democracy', with the 'progressive forces' engaged in building the prerequisites of socialism under Communist guidance. Only in the Soviet Union had the 'remnants of capitalism' been liquidated and the state become socialist on the principle of 'from each according to his ability, to each according to his work'. It was assumed that the Soviet Union would be the first to enter on the building of a true Communist society, on the principle 'from each according to his abilities, to each according to his needs', but there had been no attempt to lay down a blueprint of such a society on an authoritative basis. Party theorists assumed that it would involve the abolition of financial relationships, and therefore could not come until 'abundance' had been created. Lenin had made no such assumption; instead he had emphasised the restructuring of human nature which would produce voluntary self-rationing; the Soviet action in making abundance a precondition for full Communism was further evidence to the Chinese of the embourgeoisement of the CPSU.[73]

The second session of the Chinese 8th Party Congress took place from 5 to 23 May. Liu Shao-chi spoke of the next three years as the 'actual beginning of Communism', in which private property and want would be done away with through a proliferation of 'People's Communes'. The lower levels of society would create their own wealth, complete with the later notorious backyard furnaces and coal mines. The communes would also serve as the basis for a national militia, so that participation, whether in agriculture, industry or defence, would be near-total.

The 'Great Leap' programme was more than a Utopian attempt to short-circuit the processes of industrial development as hitherto conceived. By the constant reiteration of its role in 'beginning Communism', it constituted an ideological challenge to the Soviet Union, which after forty years of Communist rule had not yet set out the criteria for completing the building of socialism and the subsequent transition to Communism. The resolution on the communes spoke of the possibility that the building of socialism would be completed in three years in some places, longer in others, but implied that it would be completed everywhere by the late 60s or early 70s and the transition to Communism would follow at once.[74] Not until the 22nd Party Congress in late 1961 did the Soviet Party leaders begin to talk of the 'building of Communism',

---

[73] 'Open Letter from the CPSU Central Committee to Party organisations and all Communists of the Soviet Union', *Pravda*, 14 July 1963.
[74] 'Resolution on People's Communes', *Peking Review*, 16 September 1958.

and then only in terms of a modest beginning by 1980.[75] In short, by launching the 'Great Leap Forward' China's leaders served notice that despite its continued acknowledgement of the Soviet Union as the leader of the 'socialist camp', and the CPSU as the leader of the world-wide Marxist-Leninist movement, it expected to lead the camp into Communism.

Soviet comment on the 'Great Leap' was to ignore it; for months after the resolution which initiated it, the Soviet press was silent about its consequences, confining itself to oblique warnings of the impossibility of short cuts to Communism. Later, as the economic and social chaos caused by over-enthusiastic introduction of communes and fragmenting of industry became apparent, the Chinese Communist Party, in the Wuhan Resolution of 10 December 1958 reintroduced the concept of 'gradualness' in the achievement of Communism, and, by admitting the prior necessities of a heavy industrial base, of payment according to work and retention of private property, conceded implicitly that Soviet scepticism had been justified.[76]

The Wuhan resolution marked a retreat in the ideological challenge for leadership, and was followed by a period of relative quiescence on the doctrinal front. At the Soviet Twenty-First Party Congress in February 1959 Chou En-Lai withdrew any claim of priority in the march to the Communist society, when he made it clear that under the Wuhan resolution the process of 'building *socialism*'—was expected to take 15-20 years or more, in contrast to statements made at the start of the Great Leap, which had talked of building *Communism* in 10-15 years. He also emphasised that the communes were a product of Chinese conditions, and not necessarily meant either to be compared with the collective farms of other Communist countries, or to be used as a model for the future.[77] On the Soviet side, Khrushchev conceded the possibility that the advanced Communist countries would develop so fast that they would be in a position to aid the less developed members of the camp on such a scale that all would 'attain Communism' virtually at the same time. But any hopes the Chinese may have had that this concession would bear fruit in increased aid soon were crushed by further arguments that abundance on the scale necessary would not be attained in the near future, and by evidence of

[75] Khrushchev, N. S., Report of the Central Committee to the 22nd Party Congress, 18 October 1961.

[76] 'Resolution on some Questions concerning the Peoples' Communes', *Peking Review*, No. 43, 1958, pp. 10-19.

[77] *Pravda*, 29 January 1959.

Soviet reorientation of their trade away from China towards India, Japan and the United Arab republic, as the table shows.

Table 16: Soviet Trade with selected countries (imports and exports combined), as a percentage of total foreign trade[78]

|        | 1955 | 1960 | 1966 |
|--------|------|------|------|
| China  | 21.4 | 14.9 | 1.9  |
| India  | 9.2  | 1.0  | 2.3  |
| Japan  | 0.1  | 1.2  | 2.8  |
| U.A.R. | 0.4  | 1.7  | 2.1  |

The apparent ideological lull proved no more than an isolated phenomenon. The unilateral Soviet denunciation of the secret defence treaty was to take place only four months after Chou En-Lai's speech, and the latter half of 1959 saw a determined Soviet ideological offensive on the theme of the 'transition to Communism', clearly intended in the main as a response to the abortive Chinese challenge, and pursued in the belief that the Chinese retreat signalled in the Wuhan Resolution would prove to be temporary only. In contrast to the almost total lack of discussion of the subject before the 'Great Leap', over 100 books and pamphlets on the features of a true Communist society appeared during 1959-60.[79] In part these were a response to the numerous Western writings on Communism, but these have appeared for a great many years and there was no particular reason why Soviet theorists and publicists should become sensitive to them at that particular time rather than any other. Within Soviet society, 'comrades courts' and 'druzhiny' (a type of unofficial police) began to assume some of the functions of the law courts and police—a modest and token beginning to the 'withering away of the State', a process which is held by Marxists to be possible only when the achievement of Communist society has abolished exploitative class relationships, and the restructuring of human nature has produced a society in which the coercive apparatus of a state is no longer needed.

The dispute was still not officially acknowledged to exist—neither the existence of the secret defence treaty nor the Soviet abrogation of it were to be revealed until 1963,[80] and in public attacks the Russians used 'Albania' as a surrogate for China, while

[78] *V.T.*, 1918-66 pp. 70-1.
[79] Mehnert, *op. cit.*, p. 410.
[80] New China News Agency, 16 August 1963.

the Chinese made similar use of 'Yugoslavia', or, when not prepared to be even that specific, the Russians attacked 'dogmatism'
and the Chinese 'revisionism'. However, the Chinese chose to make
the dispute public in three articles under the general title of 'Long
Live Leninism', published in the Peking *People's Daily* beginning
on 16 April 1960. These constituted an attack on the guiding
principles enunciated by Khrushchev at the 20th Party Congress
in February 1956, and used as the rationale for Soviet policy since
then. These 'Theses' contained three main new propositions, which
the Chinese now set out explicitly to demolish, as they had been
doing implicitly hitherto.

First, Khrushchev had argued that war was no longer inevitable
because the Soviet Union had 'liquidated the capitalist encirclement'. His prime justification for this in 1956 would have been
the arrival in service of the first intercontinental bombers, capable
of conveying thermonuclear weapons to American targets, just as
American bombers had been capable of reaching Soviet territory
since 1945 from bases in Europe and elsewhere; by 1960 they had
been supplemented (though not yet supplanted) by the first intercontinental ballistic missiles. Second, he had argued that Soviet
attainment of strategic parity made peaceful coexistence possible
on a stable and long-term basis, rather than as the 'breathing space'
which Lenin had conceived it to be in the early 1920s.[81] No longer
was America invulnerable; no longer, therefore, could it contemplate nuclear aggression against the Soviet Union. The struggle for
influence would shift more and more into 'peaceful economic
competition'. Third, the likelihood of 'peaceful transition' to
socialism in a number of states was increased because fear of Soviet
retaliatory capability would erode American willingness to oppose
'progressive' movements in other countries by violent means.

Up to 1960, little had happened to controvert the Khrushchev
theses. The debate in NATO on nuclear strategy, British persistence with maintenance of an independent nuclear force, and the
French decision to develop and deploy nuclear weapons, had taken
place against a backdrop of concern, often openly expressed, that
the United States' commitments to use nuclear weapons in defence
of its allies could no longer be taken seriously. Concern over the
prospects of 'peaceful economic competition' against centrally-
directed Soviet economic offensives had been widely voiced in the
West, suggesting that the Soviet forecast of a long period of
'competitive' peaceful coexistence was both shared and feared by

---

[81] Eg. in 'The Home and Foreign Policy of the Republic', 25 December
1921, *Collected Works*, Vol. 33, pp. 117-52.

Western leaders, while the leftward inclination of countries such as Ghana, Guinea, Mali and Indonesia also tended to confirm that the Khrushchevian vision had substance. Later events were to show that Soviet optimism was excessive, but when the Chinese chose to attack it in 'Long Live Leninism' this had not yet become apparent. They dismissed the idea of concentrating on economic competition as a fallacy, with scornful references to Titoism. They emphasised the importance of violence in the 'anti-imperialist' fight; while imperialism existed, local wars were inevitable and more likely to be contained by resoluteness than by irresolution, which would merely tempt the imperialists to repeat their aggressions. Without naming the Soviets, they dismissed the entire attempt of its leaders to adjust to a world of nuclear parity with the patronising statement, 'There are some people, not revisionists, but well-intentioned persons, who want to be Marxists, but are confused in the face of certain new historical phenomena and thus have some incorrect ideas'.

The reference to Titoism was particularly wounding, as Yugoslav-Soviet relations were at a low ebb, but even more so was the description of 'some people' (who could be nobody but the Soviet leaders) as 'wanting to be Marxists, but confused'. 'Long Live Leninism' was more than an attack on specific policies, it was yet another challenge to the idea that the Soviet Union had any special status among the Communist parties of the world.

The ostensible occasion for the publication of 'Long Live Leninism' was the 90th anniversary of Lenin's birth on 22 April, but with Khrushchev due to attend a Summit meeting in Paris with Eisenhower, MacMillan and De Gaulle in the following month the contents of the articles were of more than ritual significance, because what they chose to do was to foredoom, by selective quotation from Lenin, the entire Soviet policy of *détente*. The fortuitous shooting down on 1 May 1960 of an American U-2 photographic reconnaissance aircraft near Sverdlovsk—1200 miles inside Soviet territory—provided the Chinese with ammunition against the Soviet policy, and against Khrushchev's oft-stated belief that Eisenhower was a 'man of peace'. Khrushchev abandoned the Summit meeting, refused to negotiate further with Eisenhower, but divorced the man from the office by declaring his willingness to resume discussion with the next American President, due to be elected in November. Any idea that the setback to his policy would lead to a composition of ideological differences with China was dispelled by events of the summer. In June 1960, *Pravda* chose to riposte to 'Long Live Leninism' by celebrating a Lenin anniversary of its own choosing

—the 40th anniversary of the publication of his 'Left Wing Communism—an infantile Disorder', an attack on the 'Left Deviationists' who had assailed his policies of compromise with capitalism. The editorial[82] hit out impartially at the Yugoslavs ('building socialism on imperialist handouts'), and at the Chinese ('skipping entire historical stages'), and reasserted Soviet primacy in the bloc. A few days later the first explicit criticisms of the Chinese by a Soviet ally appeared in East Germany, the newspaper *Neues Deutschland* rejecting the Chinese communes as a model for collectivisation of East German agriculture and the Prime Minister, Walter Ulbricht, declaring 'dogmatism' (ie., the Chinese view of the world scene) to be as dangerous as 'revisionism' (the Yugoslav view). The two shorthand terms were to be of increasing importance in the months ahead. In the same months, two other events of more immediate significance than the bandying of quotations took place—violent verbal clashes between the Soviet delegation (led by Khrushchev), and the Chinese (led by P'eng Chen, Mayor of Peking) occurred at the Roumanian Communist Party Congress, in the presence not only of the Roumanians but of the largest gathering of 'fraternal' Communist Party delegates since the 1957 meeting; and on 16 July the Soviet government notified the Chinese that experts working in China were to be withdrawn immediately. In many cases they took their blueprints and working drawings with them leaving the Chinese with numbers of half-completed projects that they lacked even the basic data to complete.[83]

At a Moscow Party meeting on 26 July, Suslov (the Presidium member responsible for relations with foreign Communist Parties) said that difficulties with China were 'as bad as those with Yugoslavia' and that the best that could be done was to preserve 'State relations' (ie., that relations between the two Communist Parties were already minimal). He told his audience that economical and technical assistance was no longer justified, but not that it had already been decided to terminate it.

In August the Chinese press began to extol self-reliance and several Soviet newspapers published an article warning China of the dangers of isolation from the socialist camp. The Chinese in the following month made their first approaches to non-bloc oil companies, indicating readiness to increase their dependence on the non-Communist world, rather than knuckle down to their opponents within the bloc. To make their position even clearer, the *People's Daily* on 6 and 7 October reviewed the fourth volume of

[82] *Pravda*, 12 June 1960.
[83] *Peking Review*, No. 9, March 1963, pp. 10-11.

Mao Tse-Tung's collected works in terms which disclosed both uncompromising revolutionary ardour ('we can only eliminate wars through wars', 'we are advocates of thoroughgoing revolution') and contempt for Soviet pretensions to doctrinal hegemony ('Mao Tse-Tung is the greatest Marxist-Leninist of our time').

With the withdrawal of Soviet technical aid, the split had clearly become very deep; while Soviet experts in India, Egypt and elsewhere helped to develop the economies of 'bourgeois-nationalist' states, China was deemed unworthy of such assistance. From now on, the trend of the dispute, despite periodic attempts at alleviation, would be for each to depict the other as not merely an erring Communist, but no Communist at all.

But this point had not yet been reached in 1960. For the moment an attempt was to be made not so much to compose the differences as to conceal them if possible, or clarify them if not, so as to draw the lines between the disputants clearly and attempt to range as many supporters as possible behind the banner of each.

To this end a conference (subsequently known as 'The Conference of Eighty-One Communist and Workers' Parties) was held in November 1960. It had a number of unusual features for an international Communist meeting on such a scale; invitations were issued privately; all meetings were held in camera; even the fact that it was taking place was kept secret; and it went on much longer than intended (10 November-1 December, whereas it was intended to finish on 15 November).

For the other Parties apart from the protagonists, the meeting presented a number of delicate problems, reflecting the diversity of the movement and the increasing realisation among its members of the prevalence of local factors over universalist dogmas. For the European parties, both the ruling ones and the large French and Italian parties, there could be little problem of choice. Operating in countries which were all numbered among the 'advanced', they could have little sympathy for the Chinese exaltation of will over material resources, nor, living in the area of direct confrontation between the major military forces of the two alliance systems, could they view with approbation the Chinese hard line on local war or their almost insouciant dismissal of nuclear weapons as a 'paper tiger'. For the Western European parties, in particular those of France and Italy, commitment to success in free elections was reflected in the Soviet doctrine of 'peaceful transition to socialism'; to revert to the idea that the transition would almost inevitably have to be by violent revolution was counter to a generation of party tradition, and tantamount to electoral suicide. Whatever might be the case in the Third World, the Chinese position did not correspond to European realities, and they could not endorse it. But at the same time, to expel China, or force it to walk out, would restore Soviet doctrinal hegemony in a rump bloc, and put a brake on the polycentric tendencies within the movement, which most of them had found working to their advantage. Their impulse, therefore, was towards compromise to keep the Chinese and their allies in the bloc, as was that of many who supported the Chinese viewpoint but realised that in the current balance of forces within the movement it could not prevail. The outcome was a 'Declaration' and an 'Appeal to the Peoples', which all could subscribe to, and which either side could use, by selective quotation, to establish that its viewpoint had prevailed.

The 'Declaration' made some verbal concessions to the Chinese with regard to militancy towards the West, and stigmatised 'revionism' as the main danger to ideological purity of the movement. But on the main essentials it satisfied the Soviets and reflected their majority support in the world Communist movement. It accepted and proclaimed peaceful coexistence as the general line of Communist world strategy, and affirmed that Communism could defeat capitalism in peaceful economic competition. While not denying the need for violence in certain circumstances, it recommended Communists to seek power where possible by gradualist methods, and endorsed the policy of making common cause with bourgeois elements, some of whom it described as 'viewing the world situation sensibly'. In addition, it qualified its references to revisionism as the main danger, by strongly emphasising the perils of dogmatism as well.

Since the Declaration was meant to be all things to all men, it was only to be expected that the disputants would use it as such. Thus on 18 January 1961 a Soviet Party Plenum acknowledged revisionism as the chief current danger, but said 'sectarianism and dogmatism' could also *become* 'maximum dangers' if not combatted constantly, and Suslov reemphasised the importance of *détente* as part of Soviet policy by expressing the government's determination 'to strengthen in every way personal contacts with heads of state and government of capitalist countries'. Since President Kennedy was to be inaugurated two days later, and Khrushchev had signified his intention to seek a summit meeting with Eisenhower's successor, Suslov's statement was no mere verbal flourish. The Chinese press, on the other hand, edited the Soviet Plenum resolution, removing the references to 'sectarianism and dogmatism', and the party passed a hostile resolution of its own. This, in turn, was edited before publication in the Soviet press, to remove some violently anti-American remarks and a reference to the adaptation of Communist doctrine to Chinese conditions.

Certain decencies were still observed in the polemical exchanges which continued throughout 1961-62. In public, at least, the Russians referred to 'dogmatists' or 'Albanians' when they meant 'Chinese', and the Chinese talked of 'revisionists' or 'Yugoslavs' when they meant 'Russians'. But during 1960-61 Chinese attention focussed on Soviet activity in the field of arms control and disarmament, and demonstrated great hostility to it.

Prior to Soviet abrogation of the secret defence agreement in 1959, there had been no distinctive Chinese position on arms control. In 1946 Mao had reiterated his belief in the supremacy of man over weaponry when he said '. . . in the end, the (atomic) bomb will not annihilate the people. The people will annihilate the bomb', a line not greatly different from the Soviet attitude of the time, when the atomic bomb was still an American monopoly, and into the 1950s Chinese arguments had echoed Soviet ones, with particular emphasis on the fact that as a predominantly agricultural country with large terrain, scattered population, and few concentrated industrial targets, China was less vulnerable than other countries to nuclear attack. A typical example of Chinese public denigration of the atomic bomb stated 'Those who think the atomic weapon is omnipotent should consider which country is most scared of the atom bomb. Is it the Soviet Union, whose territory extends from Europe to Asia; is it China, which has such a vast expanse of territory and whose population is so dispersed; or is it New York, Washington or London, whose population is highly congested?'[84]

This line of argument was, of course, spurious. In 1950 the Soviet Union had very few atomic weapons and no means of conveying them to the United States, while China had neither weapons nor delivery systems. But it closely followed the line taken by Soviet leaders at the time, and used by Khrushchev, after Soviet attainment of delivery capability, to show that America was more vulnerable than the Soviet Union. It continued to be used by the Chinese and Soviets for six years, but Chinese arguments about readiness to ignore the casualties which even the 'paper tiger' atom bomb could cause were more strongly worded than Soviet ones. Leaders in both countries frequently stated up to 1957 that nuclear war would lead only to the collapse of capitalism, but Soviet leaders never hinted at the price they would be prepared to pay for such

[84] *People's Daily,* 12 November 1950.

a result. On two occasions, however, Chinese statesmen were explicit. Marshal Peng Te Huai said on 22 August 1956:

> . . . we are not afraid of atomic warfare. Why? Because China has 600 million people. Even if 200 million were killed by atomic weapons, 400 million would still survive. Even if 400 million people were killed, 200 million would still survive. Even if 200 million survived, China would still constitute a big country in the world. Furthermore, these 200 million people will absolutely not surrender. Therefore, at the end, America will lose the war.

In November 1957, Mao himself adverted to the question, in words which were not made public for another six years.

> I debated this question with a foreign statesman. He believed that if an atomic war was fought, the whole of mankind would be annihilated. I said that if the worst came to the worst, and half of mankind die, the other half would remain, while imperialism would be razed to the ground and the whole world would become socialist. In a number of years there would be again 2700 million people and definitely more.[85]

By this time Soviet spokesmen, while still maintaining that world war would put an end only to capitalism, were more and more emphasising the destruction that such a war would cause to mankind as a whole, and the importance of avoiding or quelching local conflicts to prevent their escalation into the world war which was, in Soviet doctrine, to be opposed to the utmost. Mao's statements were therefore to serve as grist to the Soviet propaganda mill in later years, because they apparently showed a readiness to disregard the consequences of reckless action. In fact, Mao went on to say:

> . . . if imperialism insists on fighting a war, we will have no alternative but to make up our minds and fight to the finish before going ahead with our construction. If every day you are afraid of war, and war eventually comes, what will you do then? First, I have said that the East wind prevails over the West wind, and that war will not break out, and now I have added these explanations about the situation in case war should break out. In this way, both possibilities have been taken into account.

At this stage, therefore, the differences between Chinese and Soviet thinking were not as absolute as both sides later claimed them to be. Both maintained that world war could be prevented; both

[85] Chinese Government Statement of 1 September, 1963, and Soviet Government Statement of 21 September 1963, according to which the 'foreign statesman' was Nehru.

insisted that if deterrence failed, the socialist states would win; both disclaimed any desire to start it, and both emphasised its destructiveness—though the Chinese, verbally at any rate, dismissed this destructiveness as transitory.

A few months later the first references were made to the possibility of Chinese nuclear weapons. On 12 May 1958, Chen Yi said 'At the moment China does not have atomic weapons, but we shall have them in the future', and eleven days later a senior Air Force general, Liu Ya Lou, amplified Chen Yi's remarks:

China's working class and scientists will certainly be able to make the most up-to-date aircraft and atomic bombs in the not too distant future. By that time in addition to the political factor, in which we always occupy an absolutely predominant position, we can use atomic weapons and rockets, made by the workers, engineers, scientists of our country, in coping with the enemies who dare to invade our country and undermine world peace . . . The revolutionary movement in the world in general, and Asia in particular, will advance with more vigorous steps.

When these statements were made, the secret agreement on new defence equipment had been in force for about seven months, and Liu Ya Lou's vision of the future must have been in part derived from it. His view of a world-wide revolutionary movement 'and Asia in particular', invigorated by China's possession of new weapons derived from Soviet technological expertise, was to prove over-optimistic; more to the point, and very likely a contributory factor in Soviet cancellation of the agreement just over a year later, it was much at variance with Soviet practices in the Third World, where aid was being given to non-Communist movements and governments—thereby incidentally strengthening their ability to resist their indigenous Communist movements—and with the Soviet moves to use their improved strategic position not as the basis for pressure on 'imperialism', but as grounds for pursuit of a *détente*. The differences between the Soviets and Chinese in their interpretation of the socio-political implications of the new weaponry were far more radical than those in their respective assessments of the strategic consequences.

On the arms control front, 1959 saw little in the way of publicly expressed polemic. But in other respects it saw many important developments in Sino-Soviet relations, with the outbreak of the Tibetan revolt in March causing Sino-Indian tensions, abrogation of the secret defence treaty in June, the Soviet declaration of neutrality in the Sino-Indian dispute in September, and Khrushchev's visit to the United States in October during which he unveiled his proposals for general and complete disarmament. On 14 January 1960, however, Khrushchev delivered a major policy speech, in the course of which he announced that Soviet armed forces manpower would be reduced from 3.6 to 2.4 million by the end of 1961. To his posing of a future dominated by a choice between nuclear holocaust or coexistence and disarmament, 'Long Live Leninism' defiantly retorted

> We are opposed from start to finish to criminal wars launched by imperialism, because an imperialist war would mean enormous sacrifices for all people, including the people of American and other imperialist countries. But if the imperialists impose these sacrifices upon the heads of everyone, we believe that just as was experienced in the Russian and Chinese revolutions, these sacrifices would be worthwhile. On the debris of a dead imperialism, the victorious people would create very swiftly a civilisation thousands of times higher than the capitalist system, and a beautiful future for themselves.

On 7 June *People's Daily,* without identifying him as their source, picked up some phrases used by Khrushchev in order to refute them.

> The post-war history of the struggle for disarmament shows most clearly that the aggressive nature of imperialism will never change . . . the possibility of preventing a global war does exist at present, as a result of the change in the balance of world forces, and the unprecedented might of the forces of peace, but we cannot say that 'war can be eliminated for ever' at present, or that 'there exists at present the practical possibility of fundamentally eliminating war from the life of modern society, still less that mankind has entered the epoch of lasting peace'.

In August 1961 the Soviet Union denounced the moratorium on nuclear testing which had been observed by all nuclear powers except France since 1958, and conducted a series of tests, including one of 58 Megatons. China supported the Soviet action as necessitated by American failure to agree to a ban on nuclear weapons, and on 5 September Chen Yi responded belligerently to US criticism: 'We wish to challenge the USA; dare you or dare you not destroy all nuclear weapons? Dare you or dare you not agree to carry out general disarmament . . . Your hullabaloo . . . reveals only your hypocrisy and cowardice . . .' However, Chinese support indicated not a lessening in the dispute but a desire to protect its own position as a potential tester of nuclear weapons. In October 1961 Chen Yi granted an interview, in which he explained that China favoured a ban on the manufacture and testing of nuclear weapons, but felt that if agreement to this effect proved impossible, 'when more countries possessed atomic weapons, the chances of war would be lessened'.[86] In other words, proliferation was preferable to continuation of the existing monopoly by a handful of powers. With this statement, Chen Yi placed China in opposition to both Soviet and American policy, which at that stage was beginning to focus on the idea of a ban on nuclear testing, in part as a means of reducing the speed of the superpower arms race, but more importantly, as a way to slow down the rate at which the 'nuclear club' would expand. Existence of a formal treaty would make it easier to bring pressure on potential 'Nth Powers' not to conduct nuclear tests, and be more effective as an anti-proliferation measure than an informal moratorium, which had not prevented France's beginning tests in 1960.

The main problems of a nuclear test ban lay in verification of compliance; in particular, distinguishing between underground tests of low-yield devices and minor earth tremors presented acute problems. Technical studies (in which Soviet collaboration began in 1958) suggested a reasonable probability that one or more of a series of tests in areas of low seismic activity would be detected, but that tests conducted in 'earthquake zones' could go undetected because they would tend to be 'masked' by the natural seismic activity. In the Soviet Union, Central Asia and the Kamchatka-Kuriles area would, it was felt, prove difficult to police by inspection of seismographic records. There was a good deal of shadow-boxing in the positions of both sides—Soviet refusal to accept Western doubts on the policing of low yield tests was motivated by a desire to restrain outside access to a minimum, while Western proposals tended to overstate the amount of inspection needed, as well as to overlook the inherently low probability that a would-be violator would risk conducting a series of tests deep underground in areas prone to earthquakes. But for the Chinese, the technical details of the test ban discussions were less menacing than the fact that by engaging in them at all, the Soviet Union confirmed itself as interested in confining membership of the nuclear club to itself and three of its enemies, (America, Britain and France), while denying entry to China in two ways—first by denying it the nuclear technology promised in 1957, and second by helping to create an international atmosphere inimical to Chinese attempts to develop nuclear weapons themselves.

On 3 April 1962, therefore, the *People's Daily* indicated its displeasure at progress of the test ban negotiations by emphasising

[86] Interview with Walter Cole of Reuter's Newsagency, 11 October 1961.

that while it favoured general disarmament 'as the Chinese government has time and again emphatically stated, it will not undertake
any obligation regarding any disarmament agreement or other international agreement in the discussion of which no Chinese representative has taken part, and which no Chinese representative has
signed'. The reference to 'other international agreement' was never
explained, but in the arms control context would cover a test ban
agreement which involves no disarmament as such—the Chinese
were later to make this very point, when they accused Khrushchev
of having 'separated nuclear testing from disarmament' in 1956,
by proposing to discuss it as a separate measure, without making
its conclusion contingent on some measures of arms reduction.[87]

The test ban negotiations proceeded nevertheless. It proved
impossible to reach agreement to ban underground tests, ostensibly
because of the verification problem. In view of the large number
of US and Soviet tests conducted underground in the late 1960s, it
is more likely that both sides wished to continue testing, and were
satisfied with a partial agreement, committing future aspirants to
the more expensive method of underground testing; an agreement
banning all testing in the atmosphere, on the earth's surface, or
under water therefore became the object of negotiation.

As the negotiations proceeded, the Chinese generalised their
support for the Soviet tests to cover themselves against possible
criticism of future tests conducted by themselves, and on 9 August
1962 the New China News Agency argued that nuclear testing by
Socialist countries was 'entirely different in nature from nuclear
weapons in the hands of the imperialist bloc and nuclear tests conducted by that bloc. For the socialist countries to hold nuclear
weapons and carry out nuclear tests can only be a telling blow to
the imperialist policy of nuclear buildup and nuclear blackmail, and
is therefore beneficial to the prevention of nuclear war; will help
force imperialism to accept some kind of agreement on discon-
tinuance of nuclear testing and the prohibition of nuclear weapons,
and so will help the cause of world peace.' This tortuous reasoning
had no discernible effect on the Soviets; on 29 August the Russians
abandoned their tactical negotiating position, which linked a test
ban to progress on a disarmament agreement, thus removing the
last barrier to a partial test ban. On 12 September the Chinese at
last exposed their concern that such a ban was aimed at them,
when *People's Daily* linked the test ban issue to that of nuclear
proliferation: 'the treaty will make it easier to prevent the spread
of nuclear weapons to countries not possessing them . . . Washing-

[87] Eg. in Chinese Government Statement of 31 July 1963.

ton is anxious to tie China's hands . . . only a complete ban on nuclear weapons, and the unconditional destruction of all existing nuclear weapons can prevent a nuclear war . . .' Only the hope that Moscow could be persuaded to change its mind prevented *People's Daily* linking it to 'Washington'. The Chinese government later stated that on 3 September and 20 October it sent two memoranda to the Soviet government, warning that it would oppose any Soviet-American treaty aimed at depriving China of the right to acquire nuclear weapons, and would make its opposition public.[88] This it proceeded to do, first within the international Communist movement, at various Party Congresses between October 1962 and April 1963, accompanying its private onslaughts with public criticism aimed at Party leaders by name, such as the Italian, Togliatti[89] who supported Khrushchev. A third government-to-government memorandum of 6 June 1963 was followed by a Soviet refusal to withdraw from the negotiations, and public defence of positions— the Chinese on 14 June, the Russians a month later which, for the first time identified the dispute as between Soviets and Chinese, rather than between 'Albanians' or 'dogmatists' and 'Italians', 'Yugoslavs', or 'revisionists'. The Partial Test Ban Treaty was signed on 25 July, and on 31 July the Chinese government issued a statement which finally made public the depth of the dispute:

> . . . This is a Treaty signed by three nuclear powers. By this treaty they attempt to consolidate their nuclear monopoly and bind the hands of all the peace-loving countries subjected to the nuclear threat. This treaty signed in Moscow is a big fraud . . . (it) actually strengthens the hands of the nuclear powers for nuclear blackmail . . . The interests of the Soviet people have been sold out, the interests of the people of all countries of the socialist camp, including the people of China, have been sold out, and the interests of all the peace-loving people of the world have been sold out.

The Statement went on to propose total destruction of all nuclear weapons and means of delivery, beginning with the removal of all foreign military bases, a ban on all testing, and on the export or import of nuclear weapons or information on their manufacture, and the establishment of nuclear free zones in (1) Asia and the Pacific including the USA, Soviet Union, China and Japan; (2) Central Europe; (3) Africa; (4) Latin America. It called for a meeting of all heads of government to discuss its proposals. There

---

[88] *Ibid.*
[89] 'The Differences Between Comrade Togliatti and US', *People's Daily*, 31 December 1962.

can have been no expectation on the part of the Chinese that the proposals would be taken seriously, as all the measures had been under discussion for a number of years without result; their objective was to embarrass the perpetrators of the 'Big Fraud' and make a counterbid to the Soviet 'General and Complete Disarmament' proposals of 1959 and 1960. From 31 July 1963 onwards, China's distinctions between the Soviet and American governments became less and less meaningful. A Chinese delegate to the Hiroshima Conference against nuclear weapons on 6 August put the question bluntly to the Soviet delegation: 'You said that by possessing nuclear weapons, the Soviet Union has protected the socialist camp. But how can we have any trust in you? . . . we can list a hundred cases of your capitulation to imperialism . . .'

Publication of the Chinese attacks on the Test Ban Treaty brought further polemical exchanges, in which, for the first time, the Soviet side charged China with 'non-Socialist' ambitions. A government statement of 21 September charged China with repeated border violations ('over 5,000 times during 1962'), of attempts to annex Soviet territory, of having attacked India in 1962 'at the same time as the Soviet Union was attempting to achieve relaxation of international tensions' (ie. when it was attempting to negotiate an end to the Cuba crisis), and, most serious of all, of 'Great-Power' ambitions: 'From our point of view, the very idea that there is a need for them to acquire their own nuclear weapons could occur to the leaders of a country whose security is guaranteed by the armed might of the camp of socialism, only in the event of their developing some sort of private aims and interests which cannot be supported by the military forces of the socialist camp.' The importance of this statement was that for the first time in the dispute the Soviet leaders indicated doubt of China's credentials as a member of the 'socialist camp'; this point was made even more forcefully on 3 October by an editorial in the Soviet Party journal *Kommunist,* which declared that the Chinese leaders' views had 'nothing in common with Marxism-Leninism', and were 'hostile to the general line of the international Communist movement'. Although in his interview with the General Manager of Reuter's a few days later, Chou En-Lai maintained that the dispute was one between Parties, not states and that 'those who think they may use differences between the Chinese and Soviet Communist Parties to deal with China and the Soviet Union separately are certain to be disappointed',[90] he had in fact been pre-empted by the two preceding declarations from the Soviet government and Party, which made

[90] *The Times,* London, 14 October 1963.

it clear that the differences were not mere disagreements between Party theorists. A number of personal attacks on Khrushchev had appeared in the Chinese press, but so far there had been no Soviet retaliation. This self-denying ordinance was breached on 23 October in *Kommunist,* which accused Mao of 'replacing Leninism with Mao Tse-tungism', said further 'we are witnessing a campaign against the very fundamentals of Marxism-Leninism such as has not occurred since the days of Trotsky', and 'to judge by their actions the Chinese leaders have decided to demolish the international Communist movement and create some sort of new movement under their own aegis'. Abuse now began to escalate. Khrushchev said the Chinese would have to go without trousers to meet the cost of nuclear weapons,[91] the Chinese accused the Russians of racist arguments ('raising a hue and cry against the yellow peril and the imminent menace of Genghis Khan'),[92] and said that Khrushchev was as good a servant of neocolonialism as 'the old revisionists' had been of colonialism.[93] But while these exchanges made a refreshing change from the unrelieved turgidity of most Communist prose, and showed the depths of personal animosity involved, the doctrinal differences were of longer-term importance. The Russians accused the Chinese of having invented a theory of 'some sort of special common interest of the peoples of Asia, Africa and Latin America' which 'fully contradicted Marxism-Leninism' and served 'as an instrument for isolating the peoples of these continents from the socialist states'.[94] The Chinese replied that 'the attitude of the Soviet leaders towards the liberation struggle of the oppressed nations of Asia, Africa and Latin America is passive, or scornful, or negative', and that they had 'worked out a set of nostrums' for the ills of the oppressed peoples—peaceful coexistence, peaceful competition, aid to backward countries, disarmament, and elimination of colonialism through the United Nations'.[95]

Dissension was now spreading through the international movement, and the Australian Communist Party provided the occasion for the next Chinese blast. In late March 1964 its pro-Peking faction seceded from the Party, and announced that it had set up the 'Communist Party of Australia (Marxist-Leninist)', and a week

[91] For some pointed observations on Soviet vulgarity see Crankshaw, E., *The New Cold War, Moscow v Peking,* Pelican Books, 1965, p. 142.

[92] *Peking Review,* 25 October 1963.

[93] *Ibid.*

[94] *Kommunist,* 18 October 1963.

[95] 'The leaders of the CPSU are the greatest splitters of our times', *Peking Review,* 6 February 1964, pp. 5-21.

later, on 29 March, the Chinese Communist Party invited others
to follow suit when it issued a statement calling on all Communist
parties to abandon the 'revisionist quagmire', repudiate and liquidate the revisionism of Khrushchev ('the most pernicious of
revisionists and the greatest capitulationist in history', who was
'leading the Soviet Union along the road back to capitalism'), and
follow the 'Marxist-Leninist line' of the Chinese Communist Party.
It repudiated outright Khrushchev's argument of 1956 that there
could be a peaceful transition from capitalism to socialism,
admitted that it had endorsed this line at the 1957 and 1960
meetings, but said it had done so only for the sake of unity, and
accepted that it deserved to be criticised for doing so.[96]

This time the Russian riposte was to hand in the shape of a
speech made by Suslov on 14 February 1964, but not previously
published. In it he reviewed the dispute at length, claimed that
nationalism was becoming the mainspring of Chinese actions, and
called for a meeting of world Communist parties. He did not
suggest that the meeting expel China from the movement, but since
the Soviets already knew that a majority of parties supported them,
and each side had denounced the other's policies root and branch
and invited the other to remove its leaders, it is difficult to see what
other outcome was envisaged.[97]

Relations had now reached so low an ebb that very little else
could happen to make them worse. After Khrushchev's removal in
October 1964, the new Soviet leaders attempted to lower the
temperature by abstaining from polemic for several months, but as
the Chinese did not follow suit, denigration of China was resumed.
The oddities of the cultural revolution added new fuel to the flames,
with Soviet diplomats in Peking harassed, and violent demonstrations against the respective embassies. Trade sank to infinitesimal
levels (Sino-Soviet trade, which in 1955 had been 21.4% of all
Soviet trade, was down to 0.5% by 1965)[98] trade with the Eastern
European countries also sank, and China's commercial contacts
with the West increased rapidly.

The Soviet campaign for an international meeting met with very
limited success, as a number of influential parties had no desire
either to split the movement irrevocably by formally excommunica-
ting the Chinese and their allies, or to restore Soviet doctrinal

---

[96] NCNA 29 March 1964.
[97] Speech of 14 February 1964, 'On the Struggle of the CPSU for the
Solidarity of the International Communist Movement', *Pravda*, 3 April,
1964.
[98] *V.T.*, 1965, Table V.

overlordship and reverse the polycentric tendencies which suited their local circumstances. Not until June 1969 did it take place, and the Chinese did not attend. On 2nd, 4th and 15th March major incidents took place on the border in the Far East, on an island in the Ussuri River known as Damanski Island by the Russians and Chenpao by the Chinese. What happened is not clear; each side blamed the other but as 31 Soviet border guards were killed, as well as an undisclosed number of Chinese, there was obviously a major affray. From the Soviet point of view, the incidents were a useful prelude to the international meeting which took place in Moscow on 5-17 June 1969. At this meeting, Brezhnev devoted almost one-eighth of his main speech[99] to discussion of Sino-Soviet differences; by virtue of the occasion, the speech constituted a definitive indictment of Chinese foreign policy at the highest possible level, and the main charges are therefore summarised as follows:

1. Since 1960 Mao and his supporters have been attacking the principles of scientific Communism, and the Communist movement.

2. The scale of this offensive has grown steadily, and since the 9th Party Congress (early 1969) has amounted to a definition of all Communist Parties not sharing China's view as 'revisionists'.

3. Peking aspires to hegemony in the Communist movement because it has great power aspirations, including territorial claims against the Soviet Union.

4. The Chinese are being conditioned to the idea of nuclear and conventional war against the Soviet Union.

5. Peking's 'splitting' activities, and its hostility to the world Communist movement aid imperialism by dividing the anti-imperialist forces. Its reduction in trade with the 'socialist' countries, and its 'flirting' with big capitalist powers, including West Germany, indicate a foreign policy which is not socialist or internationalist (and therefore, by implication, China is no longer a 'socialist state').

If the Soviets had hoped to range the international movement behind them against China, they were to be disappointed. The documents adopted by the conference[100] made no specific charges against China, and, more fundamental still, most Asian communist

---

[99] 'For Greater Unity of Communists, for a fresh Upsurge of the Anti-Imperialist Struggle', 7 June, 1969.

[100] *Documents adopted by the International Conference of Communist and Workers' Parties, Moscow June 5-17, 1969*, Novosti Press Agency Publishing House, n.d., 96 pp.

parties did not even accept invitations to attend. Those present from Asia and Australasia (excluding Asian Arab countries) comprised only the Communist Parties of Australia, Ceylon, East Pakistan, India, Iran, Mongolia and Turkey. Absent were Afghanistan, Burma, Malaysia, Singapore, Thailand, Cambodia, Laos, North Vietnam, South Vietnam, North Korea, China, the Philippines, Indonesia, Japan and New Zealand. Thus of the four Asian Communist governments, only Mongolia was represented, and of the large non-governing Communist parties in Asia, all except that of India (whose pro-Chinese faction formed itself into a separate Party) absented themselves.[101] This did not mean even to participate in the conference at all was regarded as a sign of commitment in the dispute which most of the Asian parties were not prepared to make.

In his speech at the conference, Brezhnev said, 'We are of the opinion that the course of events is also putting on the agenda the task of creating a system of collective security in Asia.' He did not specify the country or countries against which the Asian collective security system should provide protection, but it was widely assumed both in the West and among the Asian governments that it was China which he had in mind. The response in Asia was unenthusiastic, and Soviet advocacy of it is sporadic. In its original form, put forward in *Pravda* on 29 May 1969, Afghanistan, Burma, Cambodia, India, Pakistan and Singapore were mentioned as possible members, and it was implied that the superpowers should not belong to it, but a much later reference (Radio Moscow to South East Asia, 11 September 1970), suggested an 'anti-imperialist' emphasis as well as participation by both the Soviet Union and China. This may have been a response to the Malaysian proposals for a neutralised South East Asia, guaranteed by the USA, USSR and China, adjusted by the Soviets in an attempt to exclude the USA as 'non-Asian', as well as an effort to reduce the apparent anti-Chinese bias of the 1969 proposals, which has contributed to their unacceptability in Asia.

Since emergence of the dispute into the open, Chinese charges have centred on allegations that the Soviet Union has abandoned the revolutionary cause and opted instead for 'joint world domination' with the United States, including the possibility of a joint war of aggression against China. The Soviets, for their part, describe China as a 'military-bureaucratic state', ie., implicitly no longer a member of the 'socialist camp' and therefore a potential enemy like any other powerful non-socialist state. They have also from time

101 *Ibid.,* Communique, pp. 5-7.

to time referred to alleged Chinese 'collusion' with the United States.

The likelihood of major war between them has been discussed elsewhere, and assessed as not high. Of more immediate relevance to consideration of Soviet policy in Asia are questions of 'containment' of China, of attempts to influence Asian governments and revolutionary movements, and the effects on these policies of changes in the Soviet or Chinese leadership.

As has been suggested, the elements of the Sino-Soviet dispute are many. They include not merely ideological factors, but state interests which do not depend on ideology, though it is sometimes used to justify them, and historical memories (on the one side, Soviet representation of the Chinese as the 'new Mongols'; on the other, Chinese mistrust of European influence, Communist or otherwise, resulting from China's humiliation in the 19th Century, the unfortunate results for the Chinese Communist Party of following Soviet advice in the 1920s and later, and the brusque removal of Soviet experts in 1959 and 1960). Although the characterisation of each side by the other is exaggerated, it is true that Soviet influence is directed predominantly towards existing governments, that their attention towards revolutionary movements has been generally dilatory and perfunctory, except perhaps where they can be represented as extensions of existing governments (such as in the relationship between the Government of North Vietnam and the National Liberation Front), and that they normally give their relationship with an existing government (irrespective, within wide limits, of its political tinge), priority over the fortunes of the local Communist Party.

The Chinese, on the other hand, still place more emphasis on relations with Asian Communist Parties, irrespective of their short-term prospects of winning power, and reject the Soviet support of 'national democracy' on the grounds that cooperation with the non-Communist Left in order to seize power should be undertaken only where the Communists control the alliance, so that the bourgeois revolution is automatically and rapidly succeeded by the Socialist one. This distinction is not rigorous; the Chinese do in fact give aid to several non-Communist states of Africa and the Middle East, as well as to the erstwhile military dictatorship in Pakistan, but do not give it preference over aid to Communist governments or movements. These differing practices correspond to the national assets of each; the Soviet Union is much more able than China to use economic instruments such as trade and aid which are eminently applicable to existing governments, while China's experience of seizure of power in a predominantly peasant society is more obviously relevant to conditions in a number of Asian countries than the Soviet experience (*coup d'état* in a rapidly industrialising society by a small body of intellectuals controlling a disciplined group of workers and soldiers to exploit a temporary breakdown of authority). The distinction in approach is of relatively long-term validity, since the nature of the instruments available to each will not change quickly; further economic development will enhance the absolute amounts of aid each can make available and will increase the opportunities for trade, but it does not appear that in the short term China's capabilities in this regard will increase relatively to those of the Soviet Union. Equally, while the post-Mao leaders in China may be less dominated by their revolutionary experience, and more akin to the post-Stalin Soviet leadership, 'convergence' towards the Maoist model through the accession to power in the Soviet Union of a generation of peasant revolutionaries is, to put it mildly, not very likely. Nor is it probable that new Soviet leaders will be prepared in the interests of doctrinal purity to forego influence in the present for the possibility of influence in the future. It seems probable, therefore, that through the seventies at least, the established modes of acquiring influence will continue to be employed by each.

One characteristic shared by Communist-controlled governments where transfers of power from one leader to another have taken place (ie., in all except Yugoslavia, East Germany and North Korea) has been the unpredictable nature of the process, both in timing and consequences. About all that can be said with confidence about the post-Mao leadership of China is that it will lack his charisma and unique authority in the eyes of the people and the outside world. Few regimes are less based on charisma than the Brezhnev-Kosygin-Podgorny triumvirate and, though the possibility of a return to one-man rule in the Soviet Union can never be ruled out, a new collective leadership appears more likely as the increasing complication of Soviet society makes the governing of it more and more a matter of reconciling the interests and claims of different elite groups. While the unity of the international Communist movement has traditionally been high on the list of Soviet objectives, polycentrism has made it a less reliable instrument of Soviet foreign policy than in Stalin's time and has correspondingly reduced its value. The history of the Sino-Soviet dispute showed that the Soviets were not prepared to abandon important points of principle in order to maintain unity, in particular on foreign policy matters involving risks of war (even though it can be argued that their emplacement of missiles in Cuba in 1962 was far more adventuristic than anything China has done), or internal policy concerned with the pace and nature of the transition to Communism. It is not likely, therefore, that they will make even the limited efforts of the 1957-60 period to restore Bloc unity. The Yugoslav, and later, Chinese example of disruption of it, in conjunction with the doctrine of 'different roads to socialism' has engendered centrifugal tendencies which will not easily be suppressed. The Soviet invasion of Hungary in 1956 was followed by large numbers of individual resignations of members of Communist Parties outside the Bloc; that of Czechoslovakia in 1968 had no comparable effect; instead it was denounced by the *leaderships* of a large number of parties, because by 1968 it was no longer necessary to prove one's credentials as a Communist by unconditional support of the Soviet Union, and to do so was recognised in many countries as detrimental to electoral prospects. Therefore, unity of the international movement has already ceased to be of high priority, and restoration of it will not play an important part in motivating attempts to solve Sino-Soviet differences, though each will freely use allegations of disruptive activity to discredit the other.

More important is the border question. While the Chinese have shown no sign of demanding back the Soviet territories acquired under the 'Unequal Treaties', both they and the Soviets have regulated traffic across their frontiers as strictly as on their borders with the non-Communist world, and disputes over sections of the borders where there is no agreed demarcation have prompted the despatch by each country of sizable military reinforcements. With extensive commitments elsewhere, and the difficulties of campaigning over remote terrain, a new generation of leaders is likely to accord high priority to border demarcation, with adjustments on a limited scale to facilitate policing.

Development of relations between the two countries is subject to a number of factors outside their control. While Chinese characterisation of the Soviet Union as its prime enemy owes something to ideological fervour (the Soviet Union, as a socialist country which has 'gone rotten' being more villainous than the United States, which in their view has never been anything else), the long-term problems of Sino-American relations are largely soluble in terms of postural readjustments on both sides. With a reduction in American commitment to the Asian mainland (as is currently in progress), and defusing of the Taiwan problem, plus US recognition and Chinese admission to the UN, a partial American-Chinese 'disengagement' will be effected; whereas the Soviet Union cannot disengage from its Central Asian and Far Eastern proximity to China. The extent to which China seeks rapprochement with the Soviet Union will depend on the progress of thaw in Sino-American relations, and that the Soviet Union is concerned about the possibility of a Sino-American thaw is shown by its accusations that Chinese tolerance of US activities in Vietnam indicates covert co-operation with the USA, as well as by its hostile comments on President Nixon's visit to China.

A major consequence of the Sino-Soviet rift has been the almost total cessation of trade between them. Although it is not known to what extent this fall-off is attributable to Soviet action on the one hand, or Chinese on the other, the main result has been the finding by each of other trading partners; in China's case these have been Western European countries, Canada and Australia, and whatever ideology may dictate, the Chinese will have noticed that trade with these is less affected by changes in political relationships than are transactions with the Soviet Union. In 1971 Brezhnev indicated that a new trade agreement with China had been signed, providing for some increase in trade, but it is not likely that it will come again to occupy anything like the importance it possessed for both countries during the 1950s.

Both sides have left open possibilities for rapprochement following a change of leadership, by describing the other's leaders in terms which suggest they are a small and unrepresentative clique. But it is not likely that even in the improbable event of full composition of the present issues between them, either would wish to restore the pre-1955 relationship.

At the 24th Party Congress, Brezhnev referred to 'signs of some normalisation' in Sino-Soviet relations, following the meeting between Kosygin and Chou En-Lai in September 1969—negotiations on the border issues, an exchange of ambassadors, and a slight increase in trade. At the same time he charged the Chinese with the spreading of slanderous anti-Soviet inventions and, while expressing willingness 'to help not only to normalise relations but also to restore neighbourliness and friendship between the Soviet Union and China', gave no indication of Soviet readiness to yield on any major points at issue.[102] As they stand now, these points may be briefly summarised as follows:

*On war,* the Soviets advocate and practice avoidance of direct involvement, and justify this in terms of the danger of escalation and the importance of mobilising peace-loving forces' against the

[102] *Report of the Central Committee,* 30 March 1971.

use of war as a policy instrument. The Chinese argue that this position permits the 'imperialists' to practice nuclear blackmail, and that Communists should neither seek war nor admit to being afraid of it. In practice, they have shown no desire to involve themselves in wars outside their borders since Korea.

*On arms control,* the Soviets argue for large-scale reductions in both conventional and nuclear forces, advocate the abolition of military alliances and foreign bases, and urge the nuclear non-proliferation treaty. The Chinese do not deny the advantages of disarmament, but claim it is not feasible until imperialism has disappeared, and oppose the non-proliferation treaty as a Soviet-US device to perpetuate 'joint world domination'. But the Soviet Union's interest in arms reduction has not led it to make any large unilateral cuts since 1961, while it maintains 33 or 34 divisions outside Soviet borders; China maintains no forces outside its borders apart from some construction troops in North Vietnam, and has shown no inclination as yet to proliferate nuclear expertise or weapons to any other country.

*On foreign aid,* the Soviet Union continues to channel its assistance mostly to non-Communist nationalist governments, in opposition to the Chinese argument that preference should be given to the poorer Communist countries. In practice, China also aids non-Communist regimes, but would argue that it does not give them preference over Asian communist countries such as North Vietnam, or its one European ally, Albania.

*On trade,* the Soviets allege that China has deliberately cut its trade with the 'socialist countries' and increased that with capitalist countries. That Chinese trade had been reoriented towards Western markets is true, but without knowing to what extent the reduction in Soviet-Chinese trade was at the initiative of either, it is difficult to judge how much substance there is to this allegation. The Chinese may well have felt it desirable to reduce their dependence on uncertain allies for essential products during a violent ideological dispute. Soviet attempts to buttress the argument statistically confirm that a fall has taken place (eg., trade with the Soviet Union was 50% of all Chinese foreign trade in 1959, but only 15% in 1965), but do not justify their allegations of Chinese 'malice aforethought', as Soviet trade with a number of capitalist countries also increased during the same period.

*On 'national liberation movements',* the Chinese make more violent verbal declarations of support, but the Soviet Union grants greater actual aid in the form of hardware both to governments 'struggling to protect their independence', and to insurrectionists, such as the NLF, who may be viewed as extensions of those governments. On the other hand, the Soviet policy of supporting non-Communist governments with economic and military aid strengthens them against such movements, whether or not Communist-led, while Chinese methods and doctrines have probably proved more useful to the leaders of insurrections in Asia than the hardware provided by either China or the Soviet Union has to governments.

The Vietnam situation has shown divergencies between Soviet and Chinese policies, with the Russians contributing military hardware, such as guided missiles and interceptors, which China is not capable of supplying. If there were no Sino-Soviet dispute, such action would appear no more than a natural division of labour between allies, but during 1966 and early 1967 the Russians accused the Chinese of delaying, or in some cases, confiscating, Soviet supplies on their way by rail through China to Hanoi, and for future deliveries adopted the practice of handing them over to North Vietnamese representatives before they left Soviet territory. The respective roles of the Soviet Union and China in the Vietnam situation have already been discussed; it is sufficient here to note that generally the Soviet Union has been, at least in public, more favourable to a negotiated settlement than has China, and less willing to make verbal declarations of willingness to assist with troops, but in practice China has not done more than provide non-combatant engineer troops for rail and road-building and repair (in part because communications between Yunnan and the rest of China depend on the rail links through Hanoi), while the Soviet Union has not noticeably urged a modification of North Vietnam's will to pursue military victory, and has provided over 400 million dollars' worth of economic support since 1954, in addition to its military assistance. Before and during President Nixon's visit to China in February 1972, Soviet comment on the Indo-China situation assured North Vietnam of continued Soviet support, indicating both a fear that Sino-American discussions would lead to a settlement in Indo-China in which Soviet interests would be ignored, and a readiness to support North Vietnam not merely against American but also against Chinese pressure. To that extent the partial thaw in Sino-American relations forced the Soviet Union into public commitment on North Vietnam's behalf beyond that undertaken in 1954.

The relationship with China would inevitably have dominated Soviet dealings with Asian Communism even had there been no Sino-Soviet dispute, because China is so much larger and more influential, culturally politically and economically, than the other Asian Communist countries. It is beyond the scope of this review to argue whether China's size and potential for influence made the dispute inevitable, or whether it resulted from a combination of historical and psychological factors. But whether inevitable or not, it occurred, and has dominated not merely Soviet relations with Asian Communism, but relationships within the international Communist movement. Unconditional support for the Soviet Union, was considered so basic a duty of foreign Communists that it was laid down as one of the "21 Conditions" for admission to the Comintern.[103] The Sino-Soviet dispute has eroded this obligation to vanishing point; the Soviets have moved from implicit to explicit statements that the Chinese Communist Party no longer exists[104] but the majority of the international movement declines to follow the Soviet lead.

Inherent in the Soviet attitude to the U.S. feelers for rapprochement with China is the fear that the "capitalist encirclement" of the Soviet Union, which Khrushchev proclaimed had been "liquidated" in his speech at the 20th Party Congress in 1956, is being resurrected. It has been the habit of maritime powers to consider that "the first line of defence is the enemy's ports", and, in the spirit of the maxim, to attempt to extend their perimeters of defence to the opposite shores of the seas which protect them. American efforts to project conventional power to the Arctic Ocean, Eastern Mediterranean and Western Pacific, and, on a smaller scale, Australian adherence to concepts of "forward defence", show this thinking to have survived the advent of the thermonuclear warhead and intercontinental ballistic missile. For the Asian territories of the Soviet Union the "first line of defence" against China cannot be drawn at such a comforting distance—it lies, at the furthest, on the other side of a river, and in Central Asia at the other side of a frontier marker post. In view of the omnipotent malevolence ascribed to China in the past by the United States and Australia,

---

[103] "Every party which wishes to join the Communist International is obliged to give unconditional support to any Soviet republic in its struggle against counter-revolutionary forces . . ." From Condition 14 of "Conditions of Admission to the Communist International Approved by the Second Comintern Congress, August 1920". De Gras, J.; (Ed.), *The Communist International 1919-43, Documents*, Vol. I, R.I.I.A./ Oxford University Press, 1956, pp. 168-172.

[104] E.g., "In the course of the 'cultural revolution' in China the system of revolutionary-democratic dictatorship of the people and, above all, its nucleus, the Communist Party, was destroyed. . . . The IX Congress of the CCP in fact laid the foundation of a new Maoist governing party . . ." *Kommunist Vouruzhennykh Sil* (Armed Forces Communist) No. 5, March 1972, p. 19.

neither of which was within physical reach of China's armed forces, it would be unwise to dismiss Soviet apprehensions as fabricated, solely because the Soviet Union is a much stronger military power than China. It always has been stronger than China, and, prior to 1964 was relatively much stronger than it is now, because it had nuclear weapons and China did not. This did not prevent the Chinese attempt to seize doctrinal hegemony of the Communist movement in 1958, nor inhibit their denunciations of Soviet policy, which began in veiled form in 1960, and became open in 1963, fifteen months before the first nuclear explosion. As the Soviet leaders see it, a lone China, without nuclear weapons, did not hesitate to pose a major challenge to the Soviet Union; its differences with America once composed, what may a nuclear-armed China not dare? This apprehension is behind much of Soviet policy in Asia, and is likely to be of growing importance as American presence on the Asian mainland is reduced or withdrawn. Because unlike America or Australia, the Soviet Union cannot "pack up and go", any more than China can.

# 7

# Economic Relationships

There is no private foreign trade in the USSR, and almost all importing and exporting activities are covered by trade agreements, while all trade is conducted by state-owned trading corporations.[1]

Care must be taken to distinguish between *trade* agreements and *aid* agreements as such. Western commercial trade is mostly private, and normally only in the event of a loan or grant being made by a government or international agency is an agreement required at government-to-government level. The signing of a trade agreement by the Soviet Union is entirely concerned with establishing or renewing a trading relationship, and where loans or grants are concerned, these will be the subject of a separate payments agreement.

Soviet import statistics sometimes appear to violate this rule by recording imports from countries with which no trade agreement existed at the time they were made.[2] In some cases (such as imports of Australian wool prior to 1965), trade was conducted without an agreement, but in most the violation is more apparent than real, since the Soviet practice is, where possible, to record imports by their country of origin even if the actual purchase has been made via an intermediary.[3] This practice also helps to account

---

1 Details of trade agreements are published in monthly issues of the Soviet publication *Vneshnyaya Torgovlya* (Foreign Trade), usually soon after signing, and have not therefore been separately referenced in this chapter.

2 Summary volume *Foreign Trade of the USSR, 1918-66* (in Russian), Moscow, Ministry of Foreign Trade, Economic Planning Directorate, 1967. Volumes have subsequently been published annually, and are hereafter referred to as *V.T.* for the relevant year. Summary tables for, eg., Argentina, Turkey and Indonesia record trade in years before signing of trade agreements.

3 *V.T.,* 1968, p.6.

for discrepancies between Soviet figures of imports from particular countries, and the exports to the Soviet Union recorded by the countries concerned. An example of this may be found in the case of Malaysian rubber, where the Soviet figures of imports are frequently substantially higher than the Malaysian figure of exports. The reason is that the Soviet Union purchases much of its rubber in the United Kingdom or Singapore, but records it as of Malaysian origin, while Malaysia recorded it as exported to the United Kingdom or Singapore.[4] Apart from minor discrepancies common to all foreign trade figures, caused by differences in calculating exchange rates or wastage of goods in transit, a further cause of discrepancies between Soviet figures and those of their trading partners is that some of the recipients of Soviet aid do not include goods received under aid agreements in their import figures, whereas Soviet export statistics make no distinction between goods exported on normal commercial terms and those covered by an aid agreement. In addition, the Soviet Union records not only exports but also imports at F.O.B. ('free on board' at foreign port) prices, whereas the practice of most countries is to record exports f.o.b. and imports c.i.f. ('cost, insurance, freight'). This means that Soviet figures for their import prices do not include the cost of transport, so that the cost to the Soviet Union of its imports is understated.[5] But provided these factors are borne in mind, Soviet foreign trade statistics are reliable and, as they are very much more complete and detailed than those of most of the developing countries with which the Soviet Union trades, must inevitably form the major statistical source when considering its economic relations with the Third World.

Prior to 1955 trade agreements existed with only four non-Communist countries in Asia (Afghanistan, Iran, India and Turkey) and only four with the rest of the Third World (Egypt, Lebanon, Argentina and Uruguay). As part of the general post-Stalin drive to increase relations with the developing countries (and perhaps spurred by exclusion from the 1955 Bandung Conference as 'not an Asian state'), trade agreements have since then been concluded with Burma (1955), Japan and Indonesia (1956), Cambodia (1957), Ceylon (1958), Laos (1962), Pakistan (1965), Singapore (1966), and Thailand (1970).[6] These formed

---

[4] *Ibid.*, pp.5 and 6.
[5] *United Nations Statistical Yearbook*, 1969, table 142, p. 370, note 10 and *V.T.*, 1968, p. 5.
[6] *V.T.* monthly issues, *passim*, and Müller, K. *The Foreign Aid Programmes of the Soviet Bloc and Communist China; an Analysis*, Walker & Co., New York, 1967, pp. 138-9. (hereafter cited as 'Müller').

part of a general expansion of relations with the states of Africa, Asia and Latin America, under which agreements were signed with 30 countries between 1955 and 1965 alone.[7]

In the initial stages, there were close linkages between military and economic aid, and between aid and trade, but these later diminished, and in any event approximately five-sixths (84%) of Soviet trade with non-Communist Asian developing countries has been on a purely commercial basis involving no loans, while a percentage of Soviet loans (which cannot be determined with any precision) would rank as a commercial credit rather than as aid. Before discussing trade, however, it is advisable to consider the role which aid, military and economic, has played in the development of Soviet economic relations with Asia.

Compared with the West, the Soviet Union's aid-giving potential was, and has remained, relatively small, and the enhancement of the Soviet image to be expected from it was modest unless special steps were taken to ensure publicity. This publicity has been achieved in the main by the use of three techniques —

1. To emphasise the difference in character which the Soviets claim exists between their 'aid' and Western 'exploitation'.[8]
2. To concentrate relatively large amounts of aid on a limited number of countries and, within those countries, on a relatively small number of large projects, eg., the Aswan Dam in Egypt, or the Bhilai and Bokaro steelworks in India.[9]

This concentration has been very marked. At least 29 Third World countries were known to have received Soviet loans between 1954 and 1966, but four of them (India, Egypt, Afghanistan and Indonesia) accounted for 61% of the amounts negotiated.

Table 17: Soviet Loans negotiated to 'Third World' Countries—1953-66.[10]

| | Total $US 4,302 million | |
|---|---|---|
| *of which* | | |
| | | %age of total: |
| India | 1,018.5 million | 22.8 |
| Egypt | 824.5 million | 18.6 |
| Afghanistan | 488.2 million | 11.1 |
| Indonesia | 374.2 million | 8.5 |

[7] *V.T.*, 11/61, p. 4, 11/62, p. 25, 11/65, p. 9.

[8] For exposition of Soviet declared policy on aid and trade with Third World countries, see eg., *The National Liberation Movement* (in Russian), Moscow, 1967, pp. 195-301.

[9] Arnold, H. J. P., *Aid for Developing Countries*, 2nd ed., The Bodley Head, London, 1963, p. 103.

[10] Derived with minor amendments from Müller, *op. cit.*, p. 219, and *Voprosy Ekonomiki* (Problems of Economics), Moscow, 2/65, p. 72.

3. To ensure maximum publicity by concluding both aid and trade agreements in 'skeleton' form, followed by agreement on prices, subject to annual review. As each stage is reported in the mass media, it is easy for the public to be left with the impression that a *series* of *aid* agreements is being concluded, rather than the reality, that *one credit* is being negotiated through several stages.

The Soviets argue that their economic aid programmes differ in principle from those of Western powers, which they claim are exploitative in character, designed to perpetuate colonial rule in a new (economic) form, by keeping the newly independent countries in their 'traditional' role of suppliers of raw materials and food. They claim that the purpose of Soviet aid, on the contrary, is 'to help the formerly enslaved peoples put an end as soon as possible to their dependence on imperialism, and create an economy based on modern industry, without which the well-being of the people cannot be assured'. There is no reason to doubt the sincerity of the principle involved here, as it fits their own experience of rapid industrialisation in the 1920s and 30s, and the aspirations of the newly independent countries themselves. However, Soviet sincerity of belief is tempered in practice. The volume of aid is low, maximum publicity is gained for it by the methods of negotiation, or refusal to channel it through multilateral agencies, and it is tied to Soviet-supplied equipment. This does not mean that Soviet aid is cynically motivated, but does tend to show a more lively awareness of possible political benefit than they will normally acknowledge. Between 1955 and 1962, aid agreements were concluded with over 20 countries for the construction of about 500 industrial facilities. They claim that their rate of interest, almost always 2.5% per annum, is much lower than that charged by Western countries (which was true up to 1961, though offset by the fact that a much higher proportion of Western aid is in the form of direct grants), and that by accepting payment in local currency they ease the burden on foreign exchange reserves of the developing countries. With this last claim, they are on much less sure ground. It is true that Soviet loans are usually repayable in local currency or products, but some agreements (such as that with Ceylon of February 1958, and the 1962 Payments Agreement with Egypt),[11] contained options for payment in convertible currencies. In any event, acceptance of payment in local products economises foreign exchange

---

[11] *Vedomosty Verkhovnogo Soveta SSSR* (Proceedings of the Supreme Soviet of the USSR), 11/58, pp. 564-5, and text of Soviet-Egyptian Payments Agreement of 23 June 1962.

only if the products cannot be disposed of for convertible currency, or if the Soviet lender is prepared to purchase at above free market prices. This has happened occasionally (particularly with regard to Cuban sugar or the Egyptian cotton crop), but in general Soviet purchasing organisations work on a basis of world prices, and have a reputation for businesslike bargaining.

In professing that their aid programmes are based on unalloyed altruism, the Soviets are not unique. In fact, an aid programme can become self-financing in time, with repayments of principal and interest under previous loans providing the basis for new ones. Soviet loans are almost invariably tied (as is 75% of the Soviet contribution to various UN funds for technical training)[12] so that the equipment to be provided under them is of Soviet origin, which has not always proved suitable for operation in warm climates, or as technically satisfactory as similar equipment of Western origin (often because of higher running costs and lower engine life-between-overhauls). Spare parts have often been priced highly and are not readily available (a shortcoming frequently apparent in the Soviet Union itself), leading to long periods out of service after only minor malfunctions. While these shortcomings should not be exaggerated, they have carried sufficient weight with some recipients of Soviet aid to make them unwilling to purchase further equipment on commercial terms. Since one of the longer-term purposes of tied aid is to create a continuing market for the donor country's products, shortcomings of this nature cause results to fall short of expectations. The most spectacular instance of this has occurred in the military aid field. Indonesia in the post-1965 period has found it increasingly difficult to keep its Soviet-supplied warships in service, and in January 1971 invited tenders for the scrapping of about 100 of them—almost half of its navy. Success in the vending of military aircraft has not been parallelled in the civil airliner field; and though the technical characteristics of air-craft such as the IL-62 are comparable to Western counterparts (Boeing 707, DC-8, VC-10), operating costs per seat mile and availability of spares to ensure maximum use have proved sufficiently unfavourable to render them unattractive in many cases. Outdatedness of products and high production costs have caused a number of complaints in India (especially in regard to plants for producing antibiotics and surgical instruments),[13] and dissatisfaction has been expressed there at the high costs of maintaining Soviet technicians (which have to be met out of the loans). Here the main

---

[12] Müller, *op. cit.*, p. 274.
[13] *Far Eastern Economic Review*, 22 January 1970.

problem appeared to be not the excessively high living standards
of individuals, but the excessive numbers employed compared with
similar Western projects (during the simultaneous construction of
steelworks by German, British and Soviet interests in India, Soviet
technicians numbered between 600 and 1,000, while the British
project required only 200).[14] This probably reflects Soviet practice
at home, rather than 'overloading' with spies or commissars—
contrary to some popular conceptions there have been almost no
recorded instances of subversive activity by Soviet engineers
working abroad. It is also fair to add, in the case of the Bhilai
project, that although begun at approximately the same time as the
British-built works at Durgapur and the West German plant at
Rourkela, it was completed some two years ahead of either.
Contrary, also, to some fears expressed when Soviet aid programmes began, behaviour of Soviet technicians has not been
particularly 'democratic'—they do not in general mix with the
'natives', live at the local standard, or act as ambassadors—it is
only the Chinese who write into their agreements that the living
standards of their technicians shall not exceed those of their local
counterparts. The impression which they leave on their hosts is not,
in fact, strikingly different from that left by their Western equiva-
lents.

In the early days of Soviet aid programmes it was alleged by
some of their competitors that their criteria for examining the
necessity or feasibility of the large projects which they agreed to
finance were deficient; in other words, that they were ready to
pander to the whims of inexperienced leaders who hankered for the
status symbols of a modern industrial state. In fact, greater
experience of Soviet behaviour in aid programmes has tended to
dispel this view, which was based largely on the single instance of
their readiness to finance the Aswan Dam after the Americans withdrew their offer in 1956. The Soviet engineers who were brought
in made a number of modifications to the plan, but in any event,
the allegations against their espousal of the project would be more
convincing, were there reliable evidence that they were based on
considerations other than political pique. There have been some
excesses in pursuit of industrialisation (India's current efforts to
secure markets for railway wagons in the Soviet bloc suggest she
may have been provided with iron and steel capacity beyond her
home market's ability to utilise to the full at present, for example),
but the most Soviet engineers can be accused of at Aswan is a

[14] Müller, *op. cit.,* p. 211.

neglect for the ecological consequences, a fault hardly unknown among engineers of other nations.

The charge could be levelled with greater accuracy at the military aid programmes; it seems clear that Egypt Afghanistan and Indonesia were provided with weapons in quantity and sophistication beyond their capabilities to operate or maintain.[15] In the non-military programmes, however, although there is evidence of mistakes arising from lack of foresight, ignorance of local conditions, technological shortcomings, or excessive attachment to the belief in primacy of heavy industry, there is little, if anything, beyond that.

Another allegation occasionally made is that the Soviet Union engages in profitable re-export of primary products and minerals purchased from Asian countries, thereby not merely gaining convertible currency which the original supplier could have obtained by making the sales itself, but damaging its long-term interests in the market concerned. A few cases of re-export are known to have occurred, but the frequency and value of such occurrences does not appear to have been significant, except within the Communist bloc itself, where it is covered by existing agreements, and does not deprive the supplying country of convertible currency, since no Communist bloc currency is convertible. Re-export within the Bloc appears to be used as a device for disposing of occasional surpluses which occur because of the bilateral nature of most Soviet or East European trade agreements.[16]

In terms of per capita aid, Afghanistan has been the largest recipient, with about $US32.50 per head over the period 1954-66, but in absolute terms, loans to India obviously bulked largest; for comparative purposes, India's foreign aid position in respect to some major creditors is given as at September 1967:[17]

Table 18

| Lending country | Total authorised (million $US) | Total utilised (million $US) |
|---|---|---|
| USA | 7648.9 | 6652.9 |
| German Fed. Rep. | 989.1 | 822.7 |
| UK & Colombo Plan | 1431.7 | 1272.2 |
| USSR | 1362.0 | 666.0 |

[15] Arnold, *op. cit.,* p. 113.

[16] Fluctuations in Soviet sugar exports to Eastern Europe may reflect re-export of Cuban sugar, but the Soviet Union is itself the world's largest sugar producer and it is not possible always to trace flows back to their origin.

[17] *The Far East and Australasia 1969,* Europa Publications Ltd., London, 1970, p. 202.

In round terms, therefore, US aid *actually utilised* was ten times the Soviet figure, that from the Colombo plan countries (UK, Canada, Australia, New Zealand) twice the Soviet aid actually drawn, while although Federal Germany had *granted* less aid than the Soviet Union, it had actually supplied more. The Western aid also included grants ($US822.9 million), whereas all Soviet aid was in the form of loans. To avoid overestimating the scope of Soviet aid and the influence which it is presumed to confer, it comprised only 5½% of all foreign aid extended to India up to 1967. The USSR ranked 4th as a provider of aid in all forms (after the USA, World Bank, UK and Colombo Plan partners), but 6th (after the foregoing plus the IDA and the German Federal Republic) in amounts actually utilised up to September 1967.

In trade, the USSR was 6th among exporters to India (after the USA, UK, German Federal Republic, Japan and Canada), and 4th among importers from it (after UK, USA and Japan). Economically, therefore, its position, while important, was hardly dominant.[18]

The impact of Soviet aid (like Soviet-bloc aid in general) is limited by its relatively small scale comparative to that made available by Western countries. In the first ten years (1954-63) of their aid to the 'Third World' Soviet credits totalled $US3,921.5 million, of which only one-third had actually been drawn by 1963.[19] Strict comparisons between Soviet and Western 'aid' are difficult to make; some of what is called 'aid' is no more than normal commercial credit, most of which in the West is made by private institutions and distinguished from government-to-government loans. In the case of Soviet credits, however, this private component has no counterpart; all loans can be called 'aid' even where they are comparable to a Western commercial credit. By the early 1960s credit from Western advanced countries (by all sources) was running at a rate of over $US7,000 million *per annum,* excluding grants.[20] Soviet loans, therefore, at an annual average of less than $US400 million were only 5.7% of the credits provided by the industrial West, and the position did not alter substantially after 1963. Soviet loans in 1967 were only 5½% of all government-to-government loans or grants utilised by India.

[18] *Ibid,* p. 203.
[19] The slowness with which Soviet aid is drawn is characteristic of their aid programmes, reflecting slowness in bureaucratic procedures and also production lags—see Indian complaints of delay in deliveries to Bhilai steel works in *The Current* (Bombay), 25 October 1969.
[20] *UN Statistical Yearbook,* 1969, Tables 192 and 193, pp. 667-669, and equivalent tables in earlier years ('Net movements of long-term capital and official donations from developed market economies to developing countries and multilateral institutions').

## MILITARY AID

In view of Stalin's professed belief that the former colonies were in no way truly independent, and the almost complete absence of trade relations with most of them, it is not surprising that no monies were allocated for either economic or military aid to them.

After Stalin's death, however, the adoption of more outward-looking policies, coincident with US efforts to expand the ring of 'containment' around the Soviet Union's periphery, focused attention on ways in which Western, especially US, influence in the states between Turkey and China might be countered. One of these ways was military aid, and in this field American attempts to extend the ring of containment eastwards from Turkey created possibilities for a Soviet military aid counter-programme, at a time (1954-60) when the Soviet armed forces were being substantially reequipped and very considerably reduced in size, thus rendering large stocks of equipment available for disposal.[21]

The first opportunity for exertion of influence in Asia through closely limited military and economic aid policies arose not in a former colony, but in Afghanistan. As the buffer zone between the Russian Empire in Central Asia and the British Empire in the Indian sub-continent, Afghanistan had been the subject of jockeying for influence from the 1830s until 1907, when concern over the growing menace from Germany prompted the British and Russians to resolve their differences in Central Asia, by a Convention which virtually neutralised Afghanistan, while leaving its external relations under British control. Creation of the independent states of India and Pakistan bequeathed Pakistan the North-West frontier problem over the Afghan population (the so-called 'Pushtunistan' issue). The accession of Pakistan to the South-east Asia Treaty Organisation (September 1954) and the Baghdad Pact had already been preceded by a US grant of military aid to Pakistan in February, and more was to come. The Afghan government, which was receiving Soviet economic assistance on a small scale (a loan of 3.5 million dollars for construction of grain mills and silos)[22] requested US military aid to counterbalance that given to Pakistan, but was refused. It then turned to Moscow, but not until after Khrushchev and Bulganin had visited Kabul (December 1955) was its request granted. Formal agreements were signed with

---

21 On force reductions, see Khrushchev's speech to the Supreme Soviet, 14 January 1960. On restructuring and re-equipment, see Wolfe, T. W., *Soviet Power and Europe, 1945-70,* Johns Hopkins Press, 1970, pp. 160-194.

22 Müller, *op. cit.,* p. 220.

the Soviet Union and Czechoslovakia, under which deliveries of small arms, radios, helicopters and aircraft began almost at once. No ground attack aircraft or bombers were included, but total deliveries were estimated at over $US100 million by 1960.[23] The agreement was justified by the Soviet Union in terms of concern for its own safety through strengthening the defences of a neighbour whose security was threatened by Pakistan's US-supplied weapons, and military assistance was accompanied by economic aid projects designed to reduce Afghanistan's dependence on outlets which lay under Pakistan's control. Most Afghan trade with the outside world had passed by road from Kabul to Karachi, until Pakistan closed the road in late 1955, so the military aid agreement was accompanied by economic agreements under which the Soviet Union built roads from its railhead at Kushka to Herat and Kandahar, and from Kabul through the Hindu Kush to the Soviet river port and railhead at Termez. When completed, these links would free Afghan trade from dependence on Pakistan for transit, and provide all-year-round alternatives via the Soviet rail network. A further source of revenue for Afghanistan, and a means of repaying Soviet aid, is the supply of natural gas to the Soviet Union from a gas field discovered by Soviet exploration teams and a pipeline supplied under Soviet aid.

Soviet action in respect to Afghanistan was explained in terms of its proximity to Soviet borders and the need to balance US military aid to Pakistan. No such explanation is tenable in the case of Indonesia, the next Asian recipient of Soviet arms aid. In the late 1950s the endemic discontent against Java felt in the outlying islands came to a head in a number of armed rebellions, motivated by discontent at the priority felt to be given to Java and, in some cases, at the influence of the Indonesian Communist Party upon government policy. In 1957 the Soviet Union, which had already granted Indonesia $US106.7 million in economic aid varied the terms of its loan to allow part of it to be taken in light military vehicles,[24] but no weapons were supplied, and when the Indonesian government felt that arms were required to crush the revolt in Sumatra it first approached the United States. Whether this approach was genuine may be doubted, as insofar as the Indonesian government did not believe America to be implicated in the revolts, it believed the Netherlands, the USA's ally in NATO, to have

---

[23] US Congress, House of Representatives, Hearings for Fiscal Year 1962, Committee on Appropriations, Subcommittee on Foreign Operations, Washington 1961, p. 703.

[24] Antara (Indonesian News Agency), 17 July 1957.

instigated them, and expected the request to prove embarrassing to Dutch-US relations, in view of the campaign it was then conducting for the surrender of Dutch New Guinea. Whatever the Indonesian motives for making the request, it was refused and Indonesia then approached the Soviet Union. The outcome was a grant of about 400 million dollars for arms, announced on 19 April 1958, the nominal suppliers being Poland and Czechoslovakia. However, a US-Indonesian rapprochement followed suppression of the Sumatra revolt, and the Soviet military loan was taken up only in part.

India was to be the next recipient of Soviet military assistance. Until 1960 most of its defence needs were met by the purchase of British weapons, or their manufacture in India under licence. This dependence on a major member of the Western alliance systems was tolerable on grounds of compatibility with those systems to which the Indian armed forces were already accustomed before independence, but imposed some strains on the policy of non-alignment. These became more acute after the Tibetan revolt of 1959, and the open rift with China over border questions led China to cast public doubts upon the sincerity with which India pursued non-alignment. On the one hand, India wished to diversify its sources of supply as an earnest of its non-alignment. On the other, while the rift with China might have been seen as posing a long-term danger of border conflict, a far more pressing problem for the Indian military was that of Pakistan, where the Kashmir issue was a perpetual source of a future war. India fully shared Afghanistan's concern at the US supply of arms to Pakistan, as it rejected American apprehensions about a Communist military threat either from the Soviet Union or from China, and therefore regarded US military aid supplies to Pakistan as far more likely to be used against itself. With a particular requirement for transport aircraft and heavy lift helicopters for its forces in Kashmir it approached both the United States and the Soviet Union.

From the Soviet angle, the Indian approach was welcome on a number of counts. It provided an opportunity to riposte to American arms aid policy in Asia; it clearly provided a propaganda advantage in the eyes of the Third World, by being seen to assist a country whose non-alignment credentials were impeccable, against one widely regarded at the time as a Western puppet. By reducing India's reliance on Western suppliers, it increased India's ability to respond to Soviet urging on future occasions to act against Western interests, whether in the UN or elsewhere; and to supply arms to India would reduce the fears of other non-aligned countries that to accept Soviet arms was to forfeit non-alignment, thus improving long-term prospects for Soviet arms aid as a diplomatic weapon. Against that, to be seen supplying a country with which another Communist bloc member (China) was in dispute, and whose government was taking stern action against its domestic Communists, was difficult to explain within the international Communist movement. However, by the end of 1960 the lines in the Sino-Soviet dispute were already clearly drawn, and the Soviet Union had breached Communist unity by declaring itself neutral in the Sino-Indian border question a year earlier.[25] On balance, therefore, the advantages of acceding to the Indian request outweighed the snags, and the Soviet Union outbid the United States by offering the required equipment at a lower price[26] and agreeing to accept payment in Indian currency or goods, a most important inducement to India in view of its shortage of convertible currencies. The Soviet offer was accepted, and it thereby gained an important footing in the Indian arms market. A further agreement was concluded in July 1962, covering purchase of additional transports and helicopters, MIG-21 interceptors (to offset Pakistan's acquisition of American aircraft), and containing an unusual (by Soviet standards) provision—assistance in constructing factories so that MIG-21s and jet engines could be produced in India. This provision proved unsatisfactory in practice; the MIG-21 factory had still not produced its first aircraft by the end of the decade, by which time the aircraft was becoming obsolete as an interceptor, and after testing samples of Soviet jet engines the Indians decided to use a British engine in the Hindustan HF-24 'Marut' supersonic fighter of Indian design.

These earlier agreements—with Afghanistan in 1954-6, Indonesia in 1957-8 and India in 1960—were motivated by a general desire to counter Western (particularly American) arms diplomacy and sponsorship of manifestly anti-Communist treaties (viewing the Indonesian case as a 'counteroffensive'), as well as by a desire to court influence with the countries concerned, by gaining their good-will, enhancing their freedom of anti-Western action and, perhaps, limiting their freedom of anti-Soviet action by control over their supplies of spare parts.

The pattern of military aid provision after 1960 indicated that the struggle to contain Chinese influence was having its effects in the military aid field as in other areas of Soviet policy towards Asian countries. Only in late 1962, when China invaded the Indian

---

[25] TASS (Soviet News Agency) statement, 12 September 1959.
[26] *The Hindu* (Delhi), 10 April 1961. See also Stein, A., *India and the Soviet Union,* University of Chicago Press 1969, pp. 203-8.

North-East Frontier Agency, did the Soviets show signs of faltering. The Cuban missile crisis was still in progress when the Chinese attacked on 20 November 1962, and Soviet uncertainty as to its outcome led to short-lived attempts to play down their role in arming India[27] whose support was clearly less important to the Soviet Union than would be China's if the Cuban crisis could not be resolved quickly. However, by December 1962 the Soviets had withdrawn their hints of possible cancellation of the MIG-21 licensing agreement and, spurred by the dangers that India might abandon non-alignment (having noted that America had been quick to reply to its call for assistance), the first MIG-21 deliveries were made early in 1963. Further deliveries of MIG-21s, transports and helicopters followed during 1963-64, and agreement was reached to install an air defence system. By mid-1964 Soviet arms supplies to India, all on a basis of payment in local currency or commodities, were estimated to have totalled $US140 million[28] India, however, faced with the twin defence preoccupations of China and Pakistan, needed to re-equip its forces on a more comprehensive scale, and in September 1964 the Soviet Union granted a credit for the purchase of approximately $US300 million worth of arms, including 44 more MIG-21s, helicopters and, for the first time, combat equipment for the Indian Army (70 PT-76 amphibious tanks).

One of Pakistan's objectives in joining CENTO and SEATO had been the hope of receiving Western support in its dispute with India over Kashmir, and it began seriously to doubt the wisdom of this policy on noting the Kennedy Administration's concern to bolster India as a counterweight to China. When the Indo-Pakistan war over Kashmir broke out in September 1965, China gave verbal support to Pakistan, while the Soviet Union, like the United States, brought pressure to bear for a cessation of hostilities. Unlike the United States, however, it did not terminate arms deliveries. In fact, it profited from the Western embargo to conclude a deal for the one armed service so far not in receipt of Soviet equipment—the Indian Navy—undertaking to supply frigates, patrol boats and four modern 'F' class submarines. Having acquired the position of arbiter in the sub-continent through its role in bringing about the Tashkent agreement, it found its arms traffic something of an embarrassment. The opportunity to extend its influence by taking advantage of the Western embargo was too good to resist, but to broaden it by supplying Pakistan threatened its position with the

[27] Discussed further in the section on Sino-Soviet relations, q.v.
[28] 'Soviet Military Aid to India', *New York Times,* 13 May 1964.

Indians; on the other hand, to deny Pakistan risked providing China with an opportunity by default.

In June 1966 precisely that happened. The Pakistan government made a formal request for military assistance, Moscow temporised, and the Chinese provided Pakistan with an unknown number of interceptors, light bombers and medium tanks of Soviet design but Chinese manufacture.[29] To counteract this, the Soviet Union in late 1967 began to supply Pakistan with helicopters and lorries, attempting to blunt Indian protests by an almost simultaneous agreement to deliver 140 SU-7 ground attack aircraft to the Indian Air Force. Private assurances were given to the Indians that no offensive weapons systems would be supplied to Pakistan and that in any event the aid was given only so that the Soviet Union would have a 'lever' over Pakistani behaviour. By 1969, with the delivery of 60 Soviet tanks to Pakistan announced, the value of the first assurance was being widely doubted in Indian governing circles, while with the MIG-21 factory still not in production, seven years after the original agreement, it was becoming apparent in New Delhi that the Soviet argument about 'levers' was even more applicable to India, with its much greater stocks of Soviet-made weapons.[30] By 1970, with 120 MIG-21s in service, and 140 SU-7B in course of delivery, over one-third of the air force's combat strength was Soviet-built. So too were 450 of India's 1150 tanks, about one-sixth of its artillery (490 out of 3,000 guns), and half of its helicopters (109 out of about 200), while its navy, though still overwhelmingly British built or designed, had no submarines other than Soviet-built.[31] Among non-Communist countries in Asia, only Afghanistan (whose small armed forces are almost totally Soviet-supplied and trained) and Indonesia had a higher proportion of Soviet equipment. For both India and the Soviet Union the Indonesian experience contained a lesson—for the Soviets, on the very limited utility of arms aid in ensuring long-term influence (a lesson to offset the success of the same policy in regard to Egypt), and for India on the possible consequences for defence capability of governmental action hostile to Soviet interests.

The initial modest provision of light military vehicles for the Indonesian Army in 1957 proved the precursor to the largest Soviet arms aid operation in Asia. Whereas the estimated value of Soviet

---

[29] *Strategic Survey 1967,* Institute for Strategic Studies, London, 1968, p. 33.
[30] Verbal information to author, New Delhi 1969.
[31] *The Military Balance 1969-70,* Institute for Strategic Studies, London 1970, pp. 62-63.

equipment provided to India up to 1967 was between $US600 and 750 million, that supplied to Indonesia totalled about $US1,100 million;[32] furthermore, while India paid for most of what it received and has maintained its payments on the credits which covered the rest, most of the Indonesian arms were never paid for despite several reschedulings of debts.

The Soviet opportunity in Indonesia arose in part out of Soekarno's policy of forcing the Dutch out of West New Guinea. This inhibited US willingness to supply arms for use against a NATO member, partly out of the obvious implications for the then British colonies if the 'West Irian confrontation' succeeded (which ruled out the British as suppliers of arms), partly from geography (which created a demand for naval weapons and sophisticated air-craft, such as China was not in a position to supply, even if it had wanted to—which was unlikely, given the vigorous discrimination then being pursued by the Soekarno government against the Chinese of Indonesia). With large numbers of warships available for disposal (1950-60 had been a period of great expansion of the Soviet Navy, and the 1960s were showing that many of the ships built were surplus to requirement—or obsolete for the type of naval warfare to be expected if a general war broke out in Europe), and with no competitor in sight, the Soviet Union appeared uniquely placed to isolate the Indonesian armed forces from their former suppliers. During 1960-63 Soviet low-interest credits ($2-2\frac{1}{2}\%$ interest) totalling almost $US1 billion were granted, most of them under an arms agreement concluded in January 1961, and to make it clear that the Soviet Union did not interfere with Indonesian policy, it made no attempt to ensure that Indonesia's orders corres-ponded to its capabilities or its requirements. As a result, not merely did Indonesia order far more ships than it could man effectively (including a 19,000 ton cruiser, 14 submarines and 14 destroyer escorts),[33] and far more aircraft than it could properly maintain or operate[34] (including 25 strategic bombers), a major opportunity to influence the main anti-Communist force in the country—the Army—was missed.

Indonesian politics at the time were somewhat convoluted. President Soekarno was balancing to the left, under increasing influence from the Indonesian Communist Party, and his success in acquiring Dutch New Guinea prompted the launching in 1963

---

[32] Author's estimates based on quantities supplied, and prices of com-parable Western equipments; believed subject to error of ± 20%.
[33] *The Military Balance 1970-71*, pp. 63-4.
[34] Verbal information, Djakarta 1969.

of 'confrontation' with the British-sponsored Federation of Malaysia. The PKI, which had moved towards the Chinese position in the Sino-Soviet dispute, was already doctrinally committed to a 'one-stage' revolution (ie. an eventual seizure of power). The enthusiasm of the army leaders for confrontation waned rapidly as they realised that it would entail long periods of acute discomfort on outlying islands, while the PKI enhanced its position in Java.[35] That China enthusiastically advocated confrontation[36] merely made the PKI more arrogant and more suspect to the army leaders, whose ill-equipped forces received little from the massive Soviet military aid programmes, while distrust of the more Left-inclined airforce increased with each new delivery of Soviet aircraft. Eventually the airforce-PKI *coup* of 30 September 1965 roused the army to take over power itself, and led to an orgy of slaughter in which both pro-Peking and pro-Moscow PKI members perished equally. The Soviets cut off the supply of spare parts, and Indonesia was forced to deactivate, and later to scrap, almost all its Soviet-built warships. A major Soviet exercise in military aid had brought no tangible benefit.

No other Asian non-Communist countries have received substantial Soviet military aid, and the armed forces of these countries still to an overwhelming extent receive their weapons from the United States, the United Kingdom or France, reflecting the fact that the countries apart from India and Indonesia, on which Soviet military aid has been concentrated (Egypt from 1955, Syria from 1958, Iraq from 1958 to 1963, and Algeria since 1963), lie outside Asia as defined for the purposes of this study. There is obviously scope for further grants of Soviet military assistance but it will be limited somewhat by problems of compatibility with existing equipment. However, in the naval field, it has available large numbers of a class of warship hitherto somewhat neglected by western navies. This is the fast patrol boat, with a displacement between 25 and 200 tons, and a speed of 35-50 knots.[37] Several classes of this generic type are in service with the Soviet Navy (it is estimated to have about 500 of them),[38] in configurations which include patrol boat, anti-submarine vessel, motor torpedo boat, or missile firer, capable of attacking the largest types of surface warship at ranges of 20 miles or more. They are essentially inshore boats,

---

[35] See Weinstein, F. B., *Indonesia Abandons Confrontation,* Cornell University Press, 1969.

[36] A policy described as 'Let's you and him fight', W. A. C. Adie, Canberra, 1971.

[37] *Jane's Fighting Ships, 1969-70,* pp. 555-7.

[38] *Ibid.,* pp. 578-9.

but in the islands and enclosed seas of South-East Asia, can perform a number of duties as efficiently as larger conventional types of warship, at modest expense and with small crews. Similar boats ordered new from British suppliers are in service with the Malaysian Navy, but only the Soviet Navy possesses the type in numbers sufficient to dispose of secondhand models. Only in this category of weapon does the Soviet Union appear to have a supply advantage; it supplied 30 to Indonesia between 1961 and 1965, and India received five in 1967.[39]

SOVIET AID TO ASIAN COMMUNIST COUNTRIES

Compared with Western (especially US) aid to its Asian allies, Soviet aid to China was very modest—according to Chou En-Lai (in a speech on 21 December 1964), it totalled 1,406 million roubles ($US1,562 million)—though it may well have been of critical importance in beginning China's programme of industralisation. The last Soviet credit to China was extended in 1957, and deliveries under it ended in 1960. It is not known whether the termination of the Soviet aid programme was by mutual consent, Soviet abrogation, or Chinese refusal to accept further Soviet aid. But 1957 was the year of the secret Sino-Soviet defence agreement,[40] and Chinese anger at the abrupt withdrawal of Soviet experts in 1960 argues that they still felt themselves in need of assistance. So on balance it seems that the cessation of aid was by Soviet decision; the defence agreement (unilaterally denounced by the Soviets in 1959) may have been a means of softening the blow. It is not clear why the Soviet Union should have terminated its aid programme, but there is evidence which suggests (1) that the Soviet leaders decided to give priority to aiding non-Communist Asian and African countries (loans extended to Third World countries 1954-57 totalled $US632 million, 1958-61 $2,421.5 million, ie. they almost quadrupled);[41] (2) that the unrest in Poland and Hungary in late 1956 necessitated the making of loans and an increase in exports to improve consumer wellbeing in the Eastern European countries;[42] and (3) the requirements of the Soviet Seven Year Plan (1959-65), which envisaged large increases in housing and consumer goods, created resource alloca-

---

[39] See sections on Indonesian and Indian Navies, issues of *The Military Balance* for 1961-62, 1965-66, 1966-67.

[40] Discussed in chapter on Sino-Soviet relations, q.v.

[41] Müller, *op. cit.* p. 219.

[42] Speech by N. S. Khrushchev at Csepel Iron and Steel works, Budapest, 9 April 1958.

tion problems.[43] But from the Chinese point of view, these factors, singly or in combination, could hardly be convincing. They regarded it as the 'revolutionary duty' of the more advanced countries of the Soviet bloc to assist the less developed, and could hardly be convinced that they should take second place either to non-Communists such as Nehru or Nasser, or to raising the living standards of Poles, Hungarians and Russians who were already affluent by Chinese standards. Soviet aid policy towards China was an important factor in the decline of Sino-Soviet relations, and is therefore discussed in more detail in the chapter on those relations.

Mongolia publishes few statistics, but most of its trade is with the Soviet Union. Soviet figures of trade with the Asian Communist countries for 1967 to 1969 showed that North Korea and China fell into the 'balance' category (though the Soviet Union had a large favourable balance with North Korea in 1968 which may indicate implementation of a Soviet loan), while the favourable balance with North Vietnam and Mongolia undoubtedly reflected Soviet loans or grants, and gave a rough indication of the cost of non-military aid to the North Vietnamese economy, surprisingly cheap at 114-155 million roubles per annum.

Table 19: Soviet trade with Asian Communist countries 1967-69 (million roubles).[44]

|  | 1967 | | 1968 | | 1969 | |
|---|---|---|---|---|---|---|
|  | Exports | Imports | Exports | Imports | Exports | Imports |
| North Korea | 99.3 | 97.2 | 155.0 | 108.8 | 181.4 | 113.9 |
| North Vietnam | 132.9 | 18.8 | 143.3 | 16.1 | 170.4 | 15.2 |
| Mongolia | 167.8 | 55.9 | 174.5 | 47.8 | 176.6 | 47.5 |
| China | 45.3 | 51.0 | 53.4 | 33.0 | 25.0 | 26.1 |

MILITARY AID TO ASIAN COMMUNIST COUNTRIES

Mongolia's armed forces are so small[45] that military aid would not be significant; the true Soviet military support for Mongolia comes from its defence pact with the Soviet Union and its remote-

[43] Speech by Khrushchev, 14 January 1960. The resource allocation problem during the Khrushchev period is discussed, eg. in Bloomfield, L., Clemens, W., and Griffiths, F., *Khrushchev and the Arms Race: Soviet interests in Arms Control and Disarmament, 1954-64*, M.I.T. Press, 1966, pp. 229-287.
[44] *V.T.*, 1967, 1968, 1969, data on the countries listed, Tables IV & XIX.
[45] 24,700 men, according to *The Military Balance, 1970-71*, p. 67.

ness from likely attackers. Soviet military aid to North Vietnam has comprised surface to air missiles, anti-aircraft guns and radars, interceptor aircraft, some light bombers (which as far as is known have never been used in actual combat since their arrival there in 1965-6), and 16 patrol boats (four of 250 tons and 12 of 50 tons) transferred between 1961 and 1964.[46] North Korea possesses about 1100 tanks and self-propelled guns, 8,000 artillery weapons, about 900 armoured personnel carriers and other military vehicles, about 300 air defence missiles, all of Soviet design and about 90 ships, most of them small patrol types, but including four submarines.[47] The terms on which military equipment was furnished to North Vietnam and North Korea are not known; it cannot therefore be said whether they constitute trade or aid, but it is probable that most if not all of North Vietnam's supplies are grant aid, and most or all of North Korea's have been paid for or are supplied against credits.

THE GROWTH OF SOVIET FOREIGN TRADE

The expansion of Soviet foreign trade in general, and its distribution by groups of countries, is illustrated in the following table.[48] Figures given are in millions of roubles (at official exchange rate 1 rouble = $A1 or $US1.11).

Table 20

|  | *1950* | *1960* | *1969* |
|---|---|---|---|
| *Total:* | 2925.5 | 10072.9 | 19784.0 |
| Of which CMEA members (Warsaw Pact members plus Mongolia): | 1678.6 | 5343.3 | 11213.0 |
| Advanced non-Communist countries: | 440.2 | 1917.3 | 4331.4 |
| Developing Communist Countries: | 694.2 | 2026.3 | 1727.4 |
| Developing non-Communist countries: | 112.5 | 784.8 | 2512.2 |

Where individual Asian countries are concerned, their 'specific weight' (ie. the percentage of all Soviet foreign trade for which they account) was as follows:[49]

46 *Ibid.*, pp. 69-70.
47 *Ibid.*, pp. 64-5.
48 *V.T.* 1918-66, pp. 62-3, 1969, Table III, p. 10.
49 *V.T.* 1918-66, pp. 14, 70-1, 1969, Table V, p. 16.

Table 21

|  | 1950 | 1960 | 1969 |
|---|---|---|---|
| Afghanistan | 0.1 | 0.4 | 0.3 |
| India | 0.2 | 1.0 | 1.8 |
| Indonesia | 0.0 | 0.4 | 0.1 |
| Turkey | — | — | 0.4 |
| Malaysia | — | 1.0 | 0.6 |
| China | 17.7 | 14.9 | 0.3 |
| North Korea | 3.5 | 1.0 | 1.5 |
| North Vietnam | — | 0.4 | 0.9 |
| Mongolia | 2.5 | 1.3 | 1.1 |
| Japan | 0.1 | 1.2 | 2.8 |

By the end of the 1960s Japan was vying with the United Kingdom as the Soviet Union's most important non-Communist trading partner, but to keep the matter in perspective, the German Democratic Republic (East Germany) with a population of 17 million accounted in 1968 for 15.5% of all Soviet external trade, and Poland for 10.4%, compared with the 10.3% of all the countries listed in the table above.[50] The decline in trade with China reflected the course of the Sino-Soviet dispute—its peak was in 1955 (21.4%).[51]

LIMITING FACTORS

For many years Stalin pursued policies aimed at making the Soviet economy as autarkic as possible; the trend to reduce or inhibit the growth of foreign trade which this implied, was accelerated after the war by the American-sponsored policy of embargoing goods and raw materials of possible strategic value from export to Communist-controlled countries. This policy played a part in forcing the Soviet Union to broaden its industrial range, and exploit its ample raw material resources—a process which would have occurred anyway, but probably at a slower pace. The cumulative effect of the search for autarky, the possibilities for it offered by the extent, climatic diversity and mineral resources of the country, and the policy of strategic embargo, was to limit the Soviet Union's potential for, and need of, foreign trade. Despite the abandonment of autarky after Stalin's death, and the 'trade and aid offensive' into the Third World from 1954 onwards, the Soviet share of world trade grew only slowly to 1960, and has since then shown a slight tendency to grow at a slower rate than world trade as a whole. Its combination of *absolute* growth with *relative* decline

[50] *V.T.* 1968, p. 16.
[51] *V.T.* 1918-66, China section of summary tables, 'Specific weight of individual countries in Soviet foreign trade'.

may be seen by comparing the two following sets of percentages; in each case the figures from which the percentages have been derived are for turnover (imports and exports added together).

Table 22

1. *Percentage growth of Soviet foreign trade, 1955-68.*[52]

| | |
|---|---|
| 1955 | 100 |
| 1960 | 181 |
| 1968 | 314 |

2. *Soviet trade turnover as a percentage of world trade 1953-68.*

| | |
|---|---|
| 1953 | 3.42 |
| 1960 | 4.24 |
| 1968 | 4.08 |

Thus despite its growth the Soviet contribution to world trade is a modest one, and as only a little over one-tenth of it (11.3% in 1968, 12.7% in 1969) is with the developing countries of Asia, Africa and Latin America, it can be seen that even if the Soviet Union should seek to dominate the Third World economically, it would be in no position to do so without expanding its trade by an entire order of magnitude.

It has already been noted that the Soviet Union compensates to some extent for the modesty of its aid programmes by concentrating a major proportion of them upon a small number of countries. A similar concentration is to be seen in its foreign trade (naturally, in view of the predominance of tied loans in Soviet aid), and is illustrated in the following table, in which foreign trade turnover figures of a number of Asian countries for the latest available year have been examined to determine (1) the percentage of each country's trade which is with the Soviet Union and (2) the position occupied by it among the country's trading partners.[53]

Table 23

| Country | Year | Percentage of foreign trade with USSR | USSR's ranking among trading partners |
|---|---|---|---|
| Afghanistan | 1968 | 20.98 | 1st |
| Burma | 1966 | 1.80 | 9th |
| Cambodia | 1967 | 0.83 | 18th |
| India | 1967-68 | 10.24 | 3rd |
| Malaysia | 1967 | 2.77 | 6th |

[52] Part 1 derived from *V.T.* 1968, Tables VI and VII, p. 17. Part 2 derived from *UN Statistical Yearbook,* 1969, p. 370.
[53] Derived from relevant country sections of *Asia and the Far East, 1969.*

A much heavier Soviet predominance in trade is seen in the case of the Asian communist countries. Unfortunately available figures for North Korea and North Vietnam are incomplete since neither issues figures of its imports and exports, and they have therefore been compiled from the estimates of the countries which trade with them, among which China, a large trading partner of both, also issues no figures. The figures which follow are therefore those of Soviet percentage share of foreign trade of North Vietnam and North Korea (imports and exports combined) other than trade between the two countries, or between them and China.[54]

Table 24

|               |      |       |     |
| ------------- | ---- | ----- | --- |
| North Korea   | 1966 | 64.62 | 1st |
| North Vietnam | 1966 | 46.26 | 1st |
| Mongolia      | 1960 | 64.28 | 1st |

Although trade with China had slumped to 0.3% by 1969 and therefore become economically of very low significance to the Soviet Union, figures published by China's trading partners indicate that the Soviet trade was still of some importance to China; in 1966 the Soviet Union was China's third largest trading partner, after Hong Kong and Japan. However, between 1966 and 1969 Soviet imports from China were substantially reduced, while Chinese purchases from non-Communist countries increased. Even in 1966, Chinese trade with Western Europe (UK, France, West Germany, Italy) had outstripped that with European Communist countries (USSR, East Germany, Poland)—673 million dollars versus 439 million—and the statistical yearbooks of China's trading partners indicate that the gap has continued to increase.

Since the USSR proclaims itself to be in competition not merely with particular capitalist countries, but with capitalism as a system, a comparison may legitimately be made between its trade with the non-Communist developing countries of Asia as a whole, and those countries' trade with the 'developed market economies', ie. the advanced industrial countries of North American and Western Europe, plus Japan, Australia, New Zealand and South Africa. This, too, indicates that the absolute increase, though large, has been insufficient to prevent a decline in the Soviet share of this trade over the past decade, relative to the countries with which it claims to 'compete'.

[54] *Ibid.*

Table 25: Trade between Asian developing countries and other parts of the world (Figures are in millions of $US)[55]

|  | 1958 | 1968 |
|---|---|---|
| 1. Total | 14830 | 26740 |
| 2. 'Western' share | 8960 | 18030 |
| As % of (1) | 55.5 | 67.4 |
| 3. Soviet Union | 315 | 680 |
| As % of (1) | 2.1 | 2.6 |

Thus while the Soviet share of trade with the non-Communist developing countries of Asia increased only from 2.1 to 2.6 per cent, the 'Western' share went up from just over half to just over two-thirds. The USA, Western Germany, the United Kingdom, Japan and France all outranked the Soviet Union in trade with Asia, while the combined total of Australia and New Zealand in 1968 also outweighed the Soviet share of trade with the Asian developing countries (exports, $US320 million versus 295 million Soviet; imports, 405 million, versus 385 million Soviet), though as the Soviet import figures did not include the cost of transport, the difference is somewhat smaller than the figures indicate. It should be noted, however, that the other Eastern European countries are also involved in trade with Asia, and that in most years their combined trade with it has slightly exceeded that of the USSR.[56] Since this book is concerned with Soviet, not CMEA relations with Asia, their contribution is not analysed here, but even if it were added, the European Communist countries' share of trade with non-Communist Asia would be increased only to between 5 and 6 per cent, still exceedingly modest compared with the 67.4% share of the advanced non-Communist states.

Because of its unconvertible currency, the tying of almost all its loans to purchases in the Soviet Union alone, and, perhaps, a preference of its planners for the ease of management which it affords, Soviet foreign trade is conducted on a more strictly bilateral basis than is that of countries whose currencies are freely convertible, and with considerable regard for the achievement of as perfect a balance of trade as possible within reason. This is particularly marked within its own bloc in Europe, as the 1967 to 1969 export-import figures illustrate.

[55] Derived from *UN Statistical Yearbook* 1969, Table 143, pp. 376-383.
[56] See annual volumes of Soviet publication *Vneshnyaya Torgovlya Sotsialisticheskikh Stran* (Foreign Trade of the Socialist Countries), and tables 'World Exports by provenance and destination' of *UN Statistical Yearbook*.

Table 26: Soviet exports to and imports from East European Communist countries 1967-69 (million roubles)[57]

|  | Soviet Exports | Soviet Imports | Imbalance |
|---|---|---|---|
| Bulgaria | 2417.8 | 2375.8 | +42 |
| Czechoslovakia | 2803.7 | 2778.2 | +25.5 |
| East Germany | 4195.5 | 4182.6 | +12.9 |
| Hungary | 1764.9 | 1786.7 | −21.8 |
| Poland | 2845.2 | 2752.4 | +92.8 |
| Roumania | 1158.9 | 1197.2 | −38.3 |
| Total | 15186.0 | 15072.9 | +113.1 |

The inbalance represents 0.38% of the turnover on total Soviet-East European trade over the three years.

Trade with the Third World as a whole is an exception to the general rule of 'balance where possible'—in 1969 Soviet exports to it were 1,520.1 million roubles, imports from it 992.1 million.[58] Some of the difference is accounted for by Soviet loans, but the overall balance shows that the 1955-60 willingness to accept an unfavourable balance of trade while establishing a foothold in new markets has been reversed. With the Soviets' largest Asian trading partner, India, trade was in almost perfect balance in 1968, exports totalling 165.0 million roubles, imports 164.7 million, but in 1969 exports declined to 154.2 million, while imports rose to 199.3 million.

Of the 21 non-Communist Asian developing countries with which the Soviet Union trades, 13 showed a balance of trade favourable to the Soviet Union (that is, it exported more to them than it imported from them) in all three of the years 1967-69, exports totalling 1004.8 million roubles, imports 422.1 million. Seven of these countries were in the Arab world, but the other six (Afghanistan, Iran, Pakistan, Singapore, Thailand and Turkey) took 673.1 million roubles' worth of Soviet exports, while the Soviet Union received only 328 million worth of imports from them, the imbalance in Soviet favour equalling 34.5% of the turnover. Two countries only—Malaysia and Indonesia—showed an unfavourable balance of trade in all three years, reflecting Soviet requirements for natural rubber which could not be met from elsewhere, and which had to be met irrespective of the reluctance of these countries to accept Soviet-made goods in part-payment.

[57] Compiled by addition of relevant country entries in *V.T.* 1967, 1968, and 1969, Table IV 'Scope of foreign trade of the USSR'.
[58] *V.T.* 1969, Table III, p. 10.

Table 27: Value of Soviet exports from and imports to Malaysia and Indonesia, 1967-9 (million roubles)[59]

|  | Malaysia | | Indonesia | |
|---|---|---|---|---|
|  | Soviet Exports | Soviet Imports | Soviet Exports | Soviet Imports |
| 1967 | 0.1 | 86.9 | 4.7 | 21.9 |
| 1968 | 0.1 | 90.4 | 4.7 | 17.2 |
| 1969 | 1.5 | 109.6 | 3.2 | 21.4 |
| Total | 1.7 | 286.9 | 12.6 | 60.5 |

While the modesty of Soviet foreign trade should be evident from the foregoing discussion, two things remain to be considered —the extent to which their trading record justifies the claims they have made for the character of their trade, and its prospects for future growth.

Despite denigration of Western trade with the Third World as designed to keep the new states in their colonial position as mere suppliers of raw materials and food, the Soviet Union has not so far offered them any convincing alternative. The table which follows illustrates the typical items of Soviet trade with the Asian countries. In each case, the products listed comprised at least half the exports or imports by value during 1969.[60]

The overall pattern is clear. Naturally the ability of the Asian countries (except Japan) to export industrial products is limited, but even the industries which have been begun with Soviet bloc help receive no special favour in the Soviet market. For example, efforts made between 1968 and 1970 to conclude an agreement for supply of railway wagons by India to the Soviet Union fell through, the Soviet offer being assessed by the Indians as below the cost of manufacture.

Soviet economists argue that their practice of granting loans on easy terms and at a low rate of interest has benefited the Third World countries by forcing the West to revise its usurious practices. Soviet loans are normally repayable over 12 years at an interest rate of 2.5% per annum, and while interest is payable from granting of the loan, repayments of the principal do not normally begin until the facility built with the credit has begun to produce, or until one year after the Soviet Union has made the last deliveries under the credit. Certainly Western loans during the 1950s and early 1960s usually carried much higher rates of interest, and it

[59] *V.T.* 1968 and 1969, Table IV.
[60] *V.T.* 1969, extracted from Table XIX.

Table 28

| Country | Principal exports to USSR | Principal imports from USSR |
|---|---|---|
| Afghanistan | Cotton, wool, fruit | Machinery |
| Burma | Rubber | Ferrous metals |
| Cambodia | Rice | Metal products, machinery |
| India | Tea, coffee, skins, jute, cashew nuts textiles, footwear | Machinery |
| Indonesia | Rubber | Textiles, machinery |
| Iran | Cotton, skins, wool textiles, ores, dried fruit | Machinery |
| Malaysia | Rubber | Plant seeds, cotton cloth |
| Mongolia | Wool, cattle | Machinery |
| Nepal | Jute | Machinery |
| Pakistan | Jute, cotton, textiles | Machinery |
| Singapore | Coconut Oil | Textiles |
| Thailand | Rubber | Textiles |
| Turkey | Fruit, nuts | Machinery, metal products |
| Ceylon | Coconut oil | Oil products, plywood, cement |
| Japan | Machinery, textiles | Timber, cotton, metals |
| North Korea | Metal products construction materials | Machinery, oil products, metal products |
| China | Textiles, ores, foodstuffs | Explosives, metal products, machinery, cable, spare parts |

could well be that organisations such as the US Agency for International Development and the International Development Association, which offer loans on much easier terms than the Soviet Union (interest rates in some cases as low as 0.75%, and repayment terms up to 50 years) were called into being by Soviet competition.

A further argument put forward by Communist publicists on their 'superiority' as trading partners is that their planned economies offer a stable and long-term market, free from the fluctuations of markets not subject to central control. On the whole, the record of Communist trading with the Asian countries does not sustain this claim. While there have been occasions when Soviet purchasing has provided a market for goods which a particular primary producing country was having difficulty in selling, there have been wide fluctuations both in quantities purchased, and in the prices which the Soviet purchasing commissions are prepared to pay—their practice of annual renegotiation of prices has been noted. The following example indicates the fluctuations in prices paid for jute in 1967, 1968 and 1969.

Table 29.[61]

| Country | Price per ton 1967 | (roubles) 1968 | 1969 |
|---------|------|------|------|
| India | 286.27 | 262.08 | 340.29 |
| Nepal | 297.50 | 260.00 | 291.43 |
| Pakistan | 314.74 | 268.50 | 308.25 |

Even allowing for differences in supply and quality, the varia-tions between prices paid in the three countries in the same year, and those in prices paid in each country in the three successive years, indicate bargaining situations rather than stable long-term deals. Those for other primary products showed similar or greater fluctuations, and market studies performed in 1963 and since confirm that the variability in quantities taken and prices paid, visible in the Soviet foreign trade statistics, is of a similar order to that found in Western markets.

It can, of course, be argued with some justice that the Soviet purchasing commissions have no obligation to pay excessive prices, and that they are in any event competing with Western traders whose generally much larger orders determine the market prices. This is a valid point, though it does not alter the fact that for the developing countries the Soviet market is as variable as any other. But even if this be conceded, the main basis of the Soviet claim is not this point, but an assumption of greater predictability based on the fact of a centrally-planned economy which determines its future demand by acts of volition rather than the blind interplay of market forces. The validity of this claim, insofar as it affects tropical food producers, can be examined by reference to the Soviet Union's own assessment of its growth prospects to 1970 and 1980 as an importer of tropical food products, contained in its submissions to the United Nations Conference on Trade and Development (UNCTAD), in the early 60s. The figures for actual purchases in 1970 are not yet available, but those for 1967 and 1969 have been included to

[61] Derived from relevant country entries, Table XIX, *V.T.* 1967-9, entry 51010.

indicate the extent of the progress towards the level which they then expected to reach by 1970 (all figures are in thousand metric tons).[62]

Table 30

|  | 1967 (actual) | 1969 (actual) | 1970 (forecast) | 1980 (forecast) |
|---|---|---|---|---|
| Cocoa beans | 81.7 | 98.6 | 120 | 350 |
| Coffee | 24.7 | 48.0 | 60 | 120 |
| Citrus fruits | 252.5 | 299.2 | 180 | 750 |
| Vegetable fats (coconut & palm oil, etc.) | 90.7 | 119.2* | 300 | 1000 |

*1968

From the figures it would appear that while imports of citrus fruits have grown much faster than expected, the estimates for coffee and cocoa beans have proved too optimistic, while those for vegetable fats were extremely unrealistic—even the low figures given above have been obtained only by including imports of olive oil, not all of which comes from tropical areas or developing countries. In the same document the Soviet Union indicated that it intended to increase its imports of tea, bananas, pineapples, spices, cotton fibre, wool, minerals, raw materials for the chemical industry, manufactures and semi-manufactures, but made no attempt at a quantitative forecast. In view of the discrepancies between expected and actual rates of growth of imports in those commodities where it felt able to give figures for the others, it would not appear that the Soviet market is any more stable or predictable in the medium and long term than any other.

Although the purpose of some Communist, as of Western, trade and aid is political, it undoubtedly serves a number of economic purposes as well and the examples given of hard bargaining behaviour indicate that most is undertaken for strictly economic reasons. Until recently the European Communist countries (especially the USSR, Poland, Hungary, Bulgaria and Roumania) were themselves large-scale exporters of primary products and raw materials, and their reliance to an increasing extent on imports of these from developing countries has reflected not merely agricultural inefficiency (of which there has been plenty), but the progress

[62] Cols. 1 & 2 *V.T.* 1967-8-9, Table XVIII; Cols. 3 & 4 *Economic Survey of Europe*, UN, 1961, Chapter V, p. 17.

of industrialisation carried out with a labour force drawn largely from agriculture. The backwardness of the agricultural sector in the Soviet Union is a byword, but the purpose of collectivisation was not so much to increase production as to provide surplus labour for the new industries, and this it has achieved. That it should seek to exchange industrial for agricultural products is therefore not surprising, though to do so damages the claims of its leaders that they are assisting the developing countries to free themselves from dependence on primary production. But Soviet purchases of rubber in South-East Asia, especially Malaysia, came at a time when traditional customers for rubber were turning increasingly to synthetics. By opening up a new market, they have helped to avert what could have become a serious economic crisis in rubber producing countries (which would inevitably have had serious repercussions upon their internal stability), while easing their own transition into the age of synthetics. However, Soviet production of synthetics is increasing at a rate which suggests an intention to reduce their dependence on natural rubber. In 1969 the Soviet Union purchased 295,000 tons of natural rubber (235,300 tons of it from Malaysia and 44,000 tons from Indonesia); but it also imported 33,400 tons of synthetic rubber, and exported 58,300 tons of it.[63] The likelihood that Soviet purchases of rubber will provide a fast growing long-term market for Malaysia and Indonesia is not high. However, the Soviet Union is beginning to expand its production of motor vehicles dramatically, and natural rubber still offers some advantages over synthetics for motor and truck tyres, which should maintain Soviet demand for natural rubber at or above its present level for the foreseeable future. Development of synthetic production in the Soviet Union and Eastern Europe is likely also in the long term to affect the demand for cotton, jute, wool, hides, skins, and some mineral ores, though it is not possible to estimate the extent of the effects.

The idea that the Soviet Union and its allies should increase their imports of manufactures and semi-manufactures from Asian countries, has so far not led to any governmental action, but it is an obvious step for improving the economic viability of the industries established in the new countries with Soviet assistance. Some Soviet and Eastern European economists have recently extended its scope by suggesting that regional cooperation be increased, and that industrial plants in the new countries manufacture goods for delivery to other countries in the area as part of Soviet aid programmes. This too, may have some possibilities, but

[63] *V.T.* 1969, Tables XVII and XVIII, entries 35001 and 35002.

there are some fairly serious obstacles in the way of increased Asian exports of manufactures.

The Soviet bloc countries are themselves large-scale producers of manufactures, and their interest in shopping for industrial products in the West has been in advanced technology—computers, scientific machinery, complete factories for such things as cars, petrochemicals and so on. Many of the products of nascent Asian industries may be susceptible to the same criticisms of out-of-dateness, lack of sophistication, poor finish or performance, as have beset Soviet industrial products in Western markets. The Soviets may, as their own modernisation advances, find it advantageous to procure the simpler types of manufacture from an Asian country, especially in view of the continuing latent demand for consumer goods in the USSR. But this will not meet their stated aim, or the aspiration of many Asian leaders, to eliminate backwardness and reliance on 'traditional' exports; it will merely shift it one rung higher up the industrial ladder. Another disadvantage is the relative smallness of the 'socialist countries' as a market—the Soviet Union's foreign trade was only 4.08% of world trade in 1968, and that of the 'advanced' socialist countries combined (the USSR, Poland, Hungary, East Germany, Czechoslovakia, Bulgaria and Roumania) only 10.2%. Furthermore, most of their trade is with each other or with advanced non-Communist countries, and this proportion is not merely expected but planned to grow. In 1967-69 Soviet foreign trade was divided as follows:[64]

Table 31

| Group of countries | Percentage of Soviet foreign trade, (imports and exports combined) | | |
|---|---|---|---|
| | 1967 | 1968 | 1969 |
| CMEA members (Warsaw Pact countries plus Mongolia) | 57.1 | 57.5 | 56.7 |
| Other Communist countries (Yugoslavia, Cuba, China N. Vietnam, N. Korea) | 10.7 | 9.9 | 8.7 |
| Advanced capitalist countries | 20.6 | 21.3 | 21.9 |
| 'Third World' | 11.6 | 11.3 | 12.7 |

Since then the new Soviet Five Year Plan has stated that the increase in foreign trade under it will mostly take the form of increased exchanges between the European Communist countries

[64] *V.T.*, 1969, p. 16.

themselves. Only limited provision appears to be made for the developing countries to share in these exchanges.

Despite its limited scope and failure in some ways to live up to expectations, the expansion of Soviet foreign trade has conferred benefits on both sides. The rapid growth of the Soviet industrial sector has generated demands for raw materials which have in large measure been satisfied by imports from the developing countries, especially of rubber, jute, cotton and mineral ores. Equally, the comparative neglect of Soviet agriculture, resulting from the priority given to industrial growth has in part been possible because of the availability of primary products from the Asian developing countries—tea, coffee, fruit and rice in particular. While Soviet interests might have been better served by devoting more resources to agriculture, at the expense of slowing industrial expansion, the ability to pursue industrialisation, and pay for food imports in industrial products, has enabled the Soviet leaders to follow their inclinations and to that extent has increased their freedom of action. Furthermore, they have been able to export industrial goods difficult to market in the West, because of poor finish or bad styling rather than engineering faults, but which are acceptable in developing countries where, for shortage of foreign exchange or marketable products, such considerations are relatively unimportant. In return, their presence in the market has conferred economic benefit upon the primary producing countries by absorbing surpluses which could otherwise be sold only at a reduced price, if at all, and has, particularly in the countries where they have concentrated aid and trade, made a visible contribution to their economic advancement. However, the non-convertibility of the rouble, as well as the predilections of Soviet planners for bilateral arrangements, have created difficulties where individual countries have accumulated rouble surpluses which they cannot convert for purchases elsewhere, and which they do not wish to use for further purchases in the Soviet Union. Soviet claims that their trading practices offer a more stable market than the West does, have not been borne out by their trading record, but in most cases (the abrupt drop in trade with China being the outstanding exception) they have not been found to exploit their position as trading partners in political ways.

In summary, therefore, it can be said that the pattern of Soviet trade with Asia, as it has unfolded over the period since 1954, and the current plans for industrial and agricultural development, hold out no promise to the developing countries of dramatic new trade prospects, but the growing affluence of the Soviet consumer will increase markets, in particular for semi-luxury food items where there is considerable latent demand, and the continued expansion of Soviet industry will provide outlets for raw materials, though prospects for non-edible primary products may diminish.

While official pronouncements about prospects of growth in trade between the Soviet bloc and the developing countries are invariably optimistic, academic assessments by Soviet economists have during the late 60s pointed to problems as well as opportunities. Articles by academic economists do not, of course, constitute statements of policy, but do occasionally bear on it. As early as 1966, one such article, referring to 'non-traditional' exports (manufactures and semi-manufactures) argued that low productivity, lack of modern equipment, inadequate quality control, and operation of plants below capacity, rendered many 'non-traditional' products of Asian countries uncompetitive on European markets, and suggested that the countries concerned cooperate to market them regionally, advocating, as Soviet economists normally do, that this be done under state control. This was justified by the argument that only under state control could resources be concentrated on the most important objectives, and maximum economies of scale achieved.[65]

A writer on 'Problems of improving economic cooperation between socialist and developing countries' in 1968, went into considerable detail about the prospects and difficulties of increased trade. He pointed out that the concentration of Soviet bloc trade on a relatively small number of countries caused 'instability' because of dependence of both sides on a small number of markets. Apart from specific difficulties such as the UAR's import licensing system, and India's high tariff barriers, he cited a list of general obstacles to growth of trade. The main one, in his view, was the political and economic instability of some developing countries, but 'differences in socio-economic systems', difficulties of industrialisation in new states, the depredations of neocolonialism and imperialism, the lack of official trade relations (ie. of trade agreements, without which the Soviet 'investment' is felt to be inadequately protected), and inadequate realisation of export potential, whether due to failure to produce suitable goods, or to mutual ignorance of export requirements. Rather than 'tinker' with the existing trade pattern, he advocated a change in its structure to take account both of the increased industrial capacity of the socialist countries and changes in the nature of demand from their trading partners in the Third World. In sum, he suggested that the socialist countries should import more manufactures, thus enabling

[65] Pavlov, V. G., 'Non-traditional exports of developing countries' in *Narody Azii i Afriki,* (Peoples of Asia & Africa) 3/1966.

developing countries which had already made some progress with industrialisation (such as India, UAR, Brazil) to construct larger plants and achieve a better 'spread' of orders, thus reducing unit costs of production and increasing their interest in establishing permanent trading relationships with the socialist countries. However, as this could not be achieved overnight, the Soviet bloc should increase its imports of 'traditional' products; as they were short of raw materials, while the capitalist world had a surplus of many, an increase in Soviet bloc imports would assist the developing countries to resist a fall in prices, so the interests of both parties would be served.

He also argued for an increase in export of equipment which would enhance the capacity of Third World countries to produce 'non-traditional' goods needed by the socialist countries, noting that the basis for such a policy existed already in trade agreements which provided for payment in products from facilities built with Soviet bloc aid. Co-production agreements should replace credits as far as possible, provided that (a) government-to-government trade agreements could be negotiated to protect the capital invested and (b) that the proposals for co-production were carefully costed against alternatives, including production entirely within the Soviet bloc. Co-production could be especially useful to countries which were encountering difficulties in exploiting facilities built for them by socialist countries 'because of lack of capital or expertise' (he could have added 'or because the size of the market had been over-estimated by them or their Soviet bloc advisers', as seems to be the case with some plants in India).[66]

The future of military aid is not a subject which Soviet academic writers are encouraged to discuss, so even less can be said about its future prospects. On the one hand, it is relatively free of economic considerations, as the weapons supplied are for the most part obsolescent or obsolete in the Soviet armed forces, and would be stockpiled or scrapped if not disposed of to Third World countries. Their true cost to the Soviet Union is therefore scrap value of obsolete items or the cost of producing extra units for the stockpile of reserve weapons. On the other hand, at least one very large venture into military aid (Indonesia) has proved politically unfruitful, though others (Afghanistan, India and Egypt) have probably proved beneficial to the furthering of Soviet interests, at least for the time being. The acceptance by Ceylon of Soviet military aid, and Malaysia's declaration of intent to send some

---

[66] Yu. F. Shamray, 'Problems of improving economic cooperation between socialist and developing countries' in *Narody Azii i Afriki* No. 4/1968.

officers for training in Communist countries, as well as its denial of any opposition in principle to the purchase of arms from them, may indicate some further scope for the gaining of political influence by military aid or trade.

# 8

# In Place of Conclusions

A general study such as this cannot pretend to exhaustiveness; the most it can do is to aspire to illustrate the observable trends in Soviet policies in and towards Asia since 1917 and especially since the death of Stalin in 1953. In brief, the policy towards the Asian parts of the Soviet Union has been to develop them by policies aimed at diminishing or eliminating economic and social shortcomings compared with the European USSR. In respect to the Transcaucasians and Central Asian nationalities in particular, this process, while not yet bringing conditions up to those of the European USSR has significantly narrowed the gap and provided standards of living, education, and social welfare considerably above those of their neighbours. In return the Central Asians have found it necessary to tolerate a large immigration of Russians and other Europeans, who in some Republics play a disproportionately large role in political and economic management, but whose role tends to diminish as development proceeds. Repression of religion has been practised in Central Asia, as elsewhere in the Soviet Union, but the Central Asians have not been uniquely discriminated against in this respect, as the same policies have been applied to religious believers in the European USSR.

The Soviet leaders avoid describing their achievements in terms which would suggest merely that they are more successful empire-builders than other nations; their ideology requires that the relationships between the disparate elements of their multiracial society be described in terms which assign to the Great-Russians an 'elder brother' rather than an imperial role. Nevertheless, their own experiences in providing social and economic advancement to particularly backward areas of a state which was in most respects underdeveloped gave them useful expertise with which to approach the developing countries of Asia. That they have not chosen to emphasise this aspect of their approach is no reason for us to ignore it.

In the immediate post-Stalin years their interest in the countries along the southern borders was stimulated by American attempts to draw those countries into alliances hostile to the Soviet Union and its allies. Their policy towards them originally contained strong elements of universalist dogma, but was from the beginning based on dealings with the effective governments rather than revolutionary movements, and has become more specific to each country as their familiarity with local conditions has improved and with their realisation that the Third World countries lack easily-defined common interests beyond the improvement of their material conditions. Though as consumers of Third World traditional exports and as providers of aid, they are of far less importance than the Western countries, and have not always lived up to their own claims to provide long-term and stable markets, their presence in the trade and aid field has been welcomed by many of the Third World countries for its favourable effects both upon prices of their own exports and on the terms of Western loans to them.

Politically, their decision to concentrate their efforts upon dealings with incumbent nationalist governments, virtually without reference to the ways in which those governments treat native communists, has exposed them to attacks from the Chinese and pro-Chinese parties for 'betraying the revolution', but has enabled them on the whole to avoid charges of interference in the internal affairs of the Third World, at any rate from the non-aligned. Despite occasional incidents, their actual conduct towards non-aligned governments has not been in conflict with their professed aim of enabling non-aligned countries to reduce their dependence on the West without interfering in their internal affairs. As a matter of self-interest, this policy is probably dictated by the realisation that Western economic assistance is still needed, as is Soviet capacity to replace it limited, and that it would be unrealistic to urge abandonment of it upon governing elites whose class backgrounds in Marxist terms bind them to some extent to the former colonial powers, as well as by a belief that to foster revolution would be to expose their supporters to failure, as happened in a number of countries after the war, or to deliver them into the hands of pro-Chinese Communist movements. Whatever the mixture of ideological and self-interested motives behind Soviet policy in the Third World, the result has been to lend their conduct a sophistication and understanding not always seen by the neutrals to be present in American conduct. To many of them, the list of virtues of some American-supported regimes (eg., those of Phoumi Nosavan in Laos or Diem in South Vietnam) has appeared to begin and end with anti-Communism, and inevitably Soviet willingness to assist anti-Communist governments provided they maintain non-aligned foreign policies has been contrasted favourably.

Economically, the Soviet capability is limited in both the trade and aid fields, with the one exception of military aid (where Soviet surplus stocks have been adequate to meet the usually modest requirements of new states without difficulty). However, this handicap has largely been overcome by concentrating both trade and non-military aid upon a relatively small number of countries, by concentrating within countries on large projects designed in the main to build up the state-owned industrial sector, and by the astute use of publicity-gaining devices, such as refusal to sink aid within the relative anonymity of multilateral organisations, and the practice of negotiating agreements in several stages. In Asia at any rate (the same may be less true of some African countries), Soviet aid projects have been justifiable on strictly economic grounds of 'mutual benefit', and, though there have been errors of judgment it is generally true that both aid and trade patterns are rational. They have given few grants, and have been businesslike both in trade negotiations and in relation to defaulting debtors. It would be hard to sustain the charges made in the early days of their aid and trade programmes, that they were prepared to pander to the whims of inexperienced heads of new states, by providing them with 'status symbol' projects of doubtful economic relevance. There have been no recorded instances of major subversive activity by Soviet personnel working on aid programmes in Asia, nor have their been any major recorded scandals of corruption in connection with them, a circumstance which contrasts with some Western-sponsored programmes.

Militarily, their major preoccupation in the area has been with China, but their deployments, even allowing for reinforcement of their Eastern frontiers between 1969 and 1971, still indicate that they regard NATO as their major antagonist. Despite the publicity it has received, and the apprehensions it has aroused, their presence in the Indian Ocean has been small, occasional, and more readily explainable in terms of desires to (a) 'show the flag' and (b) produce pressure for agreement to limit naval activity by non-local powers, than as part of a plan for interference with trade routes of which they are themselves major users. Their preference for sponsorship of neutralism over local Communist parties, their manifest unwillingness to sponsor military alliances apart from those conceived in the most general terms (such as the Asian regional security pact suggested by Brezhnev in 1969), and the smallness of their military presence away from their own borders, contrasts with their activity in the trade and aid field to suggest that strategic considerations are not high on their list of priorities. The picture of an 'optimal Asia' which they paint in their theoretical journals and attempt to further by their actions since 1953 is one of gradual development under predominantly non-Communist but nationalist and socialistic governments of states with mixed economies, but with a large and growing state-owned industrial sector whose existence justifies description of them as 'taking the non-capitalist road'. Ideologically such development, leading to the formation and growth of an industrial working class, is seen as leading to improved prospects for an eventual socialist revolution, but it is not suggested that this process will be anything but protracted, or that it can be forced.

Essentially the Soviet view of the world is dynamic and based on a conflict model; moves must therefore be ideologically justified in terms of a 'world conflict between two opposing social systems', and while the 'peaceful coexistence' of states, especially great military powers, is an objective necessity, 'there can be no peaceful coexistence of ideologies'. Consequently, Soviet policy towards the Third World, as Soviet policy in general, is habitually described in quasi-military terms, and for that reason often sounds more militant than it is. Khrushchev, for example, justified more flexible and pragmatic policies by transferring the Third World Countries in ideological terms to a 'zone of peace', that is, by representing them as allies, actual or potential, of the Soviet bloc. Failure of the Third World to conform either to Soviet hopes or to Western fears resulted mainly from a nationalism which both sets of outsiders had tended to underrate, but which could be more readily accommodated within a Western frame of reference than within the Soviet concept of an international class struggle in which developments had to be presented in terms of success. The Soviet ideologists have found it necessary to modify a number of assumptions, notably those which in the field of political philosophy presented the domination of the Third World by 'bourgeois nationalists' as a short-term phenomenon, denied to the Third World any specific interests of its own distinct from those of the Soviet bloc, and presented their continued relations with the West as a colonial legacy of which they would be anxious to rid themselves. Some Soviet publicists still argue that their relations with Third World countries are based on a 'community of interests in the struggle against imperialism', and rationalise those countries' acceptance of Western aid as 'co-operation in form, but struggle in substance' (in that the ultimate goal which it serves is to end dependence and enable the 'non-capitalist road' to be taken), but others accept their links with the West as a fact of life, and the general thrust of Soviet foreign policy since 1953, with its emphasis on incumbent governments, has been to enhance area stability rather than to subvert it.

If these conclusions are justified, what are their implications for Australia? As this book, which is about Asia, has said almost nothing about Australia and New Zealand, and is not, in any event, a policy-oriented study, it would be rash to attempt to enjoin specific reactions. In any case, there is nothing to suggest that during the reformulation of policy which took place after Stalin's death (and may even have been initiated before it), the Soviets had any reason to take account of either country. Relations with both were glacial, both were bound closely into Western alliances, neither was underdeveloped in the Asian-African sense, neither was capable of posing military threats on its own, and neither was even particularly interested in Asia at that stage. On the general scale of this book neither would rate more than a few paragraphs, and they have been denied even that. If broadcasting time in the Soviet overseas services may be taken as an indicator of level of interest, it is worth noting that broadcasts beamed to Australia and New Zealand total 4 hours daily (2 hours in English, 2 in Russian), compared with 17 hours for Latin America, 64 hours for Africa and 127 hours 20 minutes for Asian audiences, suggesting that Australasia still ranks low in Soviet interest.

However, the low level of Soviet interest in Australia and New Zealand does not mean that Soviet actions in Asia are of no interest to those countries. Without presuming to suggest policy guidelines, it is perhaps apposite to suggest that when considering reactions towards Soviet involvement in Asia a few simple precepts should be borne in mind.

1. Soviet involvement in Asia is not new; Russia has been the largest Asian state in terms of area since the mid-19th Century, and has become one of the largest in terms of population and industrial capacity during the last fifty years.

2. The Soviet Union has a large Asian population; its third most numerous nationality (after the Russians and Ukrainians) is the Uzbeks, who are Asians, and its Asian component is growing somewhat faster than its European.

3. Well over half its land borders are with Asian countries.

4. Its Asian areas have been developed to an extent equalled only by Japan over the last fifty years; they have to a certain extent provided other Asian countries with a model, and Soviet managers with expertise which may be particularly relevant to the needs of Third World countries.

This list could be extended further, but even at the above length it is sufficient to illustrate that Soviet involvement in Asia is natural and inevitable, considerably more so than the Asian engagement of America, to which none of the above points applies. To view as desirable and natural, or, worse still, to attempt to base policies upon, an American presence on the mainland of Asia, while at the same time raising cries of alarm at the presence of the Soviet Union is unrealistic. Nor are Third World leaders likely to be impressed by suggestions from afar that the Soviet Union is out to dominate them. Apart from the fact that it does not square with their own experience, it suggests that a distant white race is more capable of detecting Soviet ulterior motives than yellow, brown, or black races which live much closer to the Soviet Union and have relations with it far more widely ramified than ours. It would be difficult to find a government which has conducted its international relations with more sophistication than that of India and to suggest that the Soviet Union will become the 'dominant power' in the sub-continent (as opposed to becoming more influential than, say, Britain) is to assume that India is unable to look after itself. So far twenty-three years of Indian independence do not warrant such assumptions, because whatever its economic and military shortcomings, it has been exceedingly successful in recruiting international support without greatly reducing its freedom of action. Few leaders in the Asian Third World regard Soviet involvement in their affairs as showing either the advent of the millennium or the elevation of the Antichrist; they do not regard with favour attempts to persuade them that either happening is imminent, and the abandonment of overtones of the Apocalypse is a prerequisite for Western dialogue with them.

Obviously not every Soviet initiative will be consonant with the interests of either Australia or New Zealand, however defined, but the automatic assumption that all Soviet moves must be to our detriment is as unwise as assumptions about the inherent identity of British or American interests with our own have proved to be in the past. Every Soviet move must be looked at in its direct and immediate context, without undue attempts to make it consistent with putative global plans. Most governments are more concerned with getting through the next six months than with devising plans for twenty or fifty years ahead, and despite its high-sounding claims to be guided by an all-foreseeing ideology, the Soviet government's crystal balls are no more effective than anyone else's. Its leaders are as concerned to maximise Soviet influence in the international environment as is every other government of a large and powerful state, but this is very different from concern to overturn the system and replace it with another. Soviet leaders still from time to time voice sentiments indicating that that is what they would like to do, but in Asia, at any rate, their actions over the last eighteen years have suggested that they are more concerned with evolution than revolution, and their forecasts indicate that they intend to continue in this vein.

# Select Bibliography

1. OF GENERAL RELEVANCE TO ONE OR MORE ASPECTS OF THE SUBJECT

Arnold, H J P: *Aid for Developing Countries,* 2nd ed, The Bodley Head, London 1963
    *Aid for Development: A Political & Economic Study,* The Bodley Head, London 1966

Avtorkhanov, A: *The Communist Party Apparatus,* Regnery, Chicago 1966

Barnett, D (Ed): *Communist Strategies in Asia,* Praeger, New York, 1963

Beckman, G M & Okubo, G: *The Japanese Communist Party 1922-45,* Stanford University Press, 1969

Bloomfield, L Clemens, W & Griffiths, F: *Khrushchev and the Arms Race,* Massachusetts Institute of Technology Press 1966

Brackman, A: *Indonesian Communism,* Praeger, New York 1963

Brezhnev, L I: *Report of the Central Committee of the CPSU to the 24th Party Congress, 30 March 71,* Novosti, Moscow 1971

Brimmell, J H: *Communism in South-East Asia: A Political Analysis,* Oxford University Press 1959

Carr, E H: *The Bolshevik Revolution 1917-23,* Macmillan, 1953

Chu-Yuan Cheng: *Economic Relations between Peking and Moscow 1949-63,* Praeger, New York 1964

Clemens, W C: *The Arms Race and Sino-Soviet Relations,* Stanford University Press, 1968

Crankshaw, E: *The New Cold War, Moscow v Peking,* Pelican Books, London 1965

Degras, J: *Comintern Documents 1919-43,* Oxford University Press 1956-65 (3 volumes)

Deutscher, I: *Russia, China and the West,* Oxford University Press 1970

Djilas, M: *The New Class: an Analysis of the Communist System,* Thames & Hudson, London 1957

Druhe, D N: *Soviet Russia & Indian Communism 1917-47,* Bookman Associates, New York 1959

Eudin, X J and North, R C: *Soviet Russia and the East, 1902-27,* Stanford 1957

Fall, B B: *Street without Joy: Indochina at War 1946-54,* Stackpole 1961
    *The Two Vietnams,* 2nd Revised ed, Pall Mall Press, London 1967

Fischer, L: *The Soviets in World Affairs*, Princeton University Press, 1951

Fitzgerald, C P: *The Birth of Communist China*, Pelican Books, London 1964

Gankovskiy, Yu V: *Natsional 'nyy Vopros i Natsional 'nyye Dvizheniya v Pakistane*, USSR Academy of Sciences—Institute of the Peoples of Asia, Moscow 1967

Girling, J L S: *People's War*, George Allen & Unwin, London 1969

Grant, B: *Indonesia*, Penguin Books 1967

Griffith, W E: *The Sino-Soviet Rift*, George Allen & Unwin, London 1964

Herrick, Cdr R W USN (Ret'd): *Soviet Naval Strategy* US Naval Institute, Annapolis 1968

Hindley, D: *The Communist Party of Indonesia 1951-63*, University of California Press 1964

Honey, P J: *Communism in North Vietnam*, Massachusetts Institute of Technology Press 1963

Hsieh, A L: *Communist China's Strategy in the Nuclear Era*, Prentice-Hall, New Jersey 1962

Kahin, G M: *Nationalism and Revolution in Indonesia*, Cornell University Press 1952

Kazemzadeh, F: *The Struggle for Transcaucasia 1917-21*, George Ronald, Oxford 1951

Khrushchev, N S: *For Victory in Peaceful Competition with Capitalism*, Hutchinson, London 1960

Kotovskiy, G G & Popov, V A (Ed): *Krestyanskoye Dvizhenie v Stranakh Vostoka*, USSR Academy of Sciences, Institute of the Peoples of Asia, Moscow 1967

Kautsky, J: *Moscow & the Communist Party of India*, Wiley, New York 1956

*Communism & the Politics of Development*, Wiley, New York 1968

Lancaster, D: *The Emancipation of French Indo-China*, Oxford University Press, 1961

Lavrishchev, A A (Ed): *Razvivayushchiyesya Strany v Mirovoy Politike*, Moscow 1968

Leifer, M: *Cambodia: the Search for Security*, Praeger, New York 1967

(Ed): *Nationalism, Revolution & Evolution in South-East Asia*, University of Hull 1970

Lenin, V I: *Collected Works*, Lawrence & Wishart, London 1960

Lockie, R: *The Korean War*, Putnam, New York 1962

Mackintosh, J M: *The Strategy & Tactics of Soviet Foreign Policy*, Oxford University Press 1962

Mao Tse Tung: *Selected Works*, Foreign Languages Press, Peking 1965

Mehnert, K: *Peking and Moscow*, Mentor Books, New York 1964

Menon, K P S: *The Flying Troika*, Oxford University Press, 1963

Moraes, F: *India Today*, Macmillan, New York 1960

Müller, K: *The Foreign Aid Programmes of the Soviet Bloc and Communist China: An Analysis,* Walker & Cox, New York 1967

Naik, J A: *Soviet Policy Towards India,* Vikas, Delhi 1970

Nove, A & Newth, J A: *The Soviet Middle East: A Communist Model for Development,* George Allen & Unwin, London 1967

Novosti Press Agency, Moscow: *Documents on International Communist Meeting, 1969, and 24th Party Congress, 1971*

Osborne, M: *Region of Revolt: Focus on South East Asia,* Pergamon Press, Australia 1970

Overstreet, G & Windmiller, M: *Communism in India,* University of California Press 1959

Paige, Glenn D: *The Korean People's Democratic Republic,* Stanford University Press, 1966

Park, A G: *Bolshevism in Turkestan 1917-27,* Columbia University Press, New York 1957

Pipes, R: *The Formation of the Soviet Union,* Harvard University Press 1954

Rakowska-Harmstone, T: *Russia & Nationalism in Central Asia,* John Hopkins Press 1970

Rothermund, I: *Die Spaltung der Kommunistischen Partei Indiens,* Harrassowitz, Wiesbaden 1969

Samra, C S: *India and Anglo-Soviet Relations 1917-47,* Asia Publishing House, Bombay 1959

Schapiro, L: *The Communist Party of the Soviet Union,* Methuen 1963

Simmonds, J D: *China's World: The Foreign Policy of a Developing State,* Australian National University Press, Canberra 1970

Smirnova, A A (Ed): *Strany Yuzhnoy Azii (Politiko-Ekonomicheskiy Spravochnik),* Moscow 1968

Sokolovsky, Marshal V D (Ed): *Voyennaya Strategiya,* Ministry of Defence Publishing House, Moscow 1st ed 1962, 2nd ed 1963, 3rd ed 1969

Stein, A: *India & the Soviet Union: The Nehru Era,* University of Chicago Press 1969

Tinker, H: *The Union of Burma,* Oxford University Press 1957
*India and Pakistan,* Pall Mall Press, London 1962

Tyurin, V A: *Problemy Sovremennoy Indonezii,* USSR Academy of Sciences, Institute of the Peoples of Asia, Moscow 1968

USSR Academy of Sciences: *Dalniy Vostok* (The Far East), Moscow 1966

United States Congress, House of Representatives: *Hearings for Fiscal Year 1962,* Committee on Appropriations Sub-committee on Foreign Operations, Washington 1961

United States Senate: Committees on Armed Services & Foreign Relations: *The Military Situation in the Far East, Joint Hearings,* Washington 1951

Wilber, C K: *The Soviet Model & Underdeveloped Countries,* University of North Carolina Press 1969

Wolfe, T W: *The Soviet Union and the Sino-Soviet Dispute,* Rand Corporation 1965
Yegorov, Yu (Ed): *Natsionalno—Osvoboditelnoye Dvizhenie Politizdat,* Moscow 1967
Zagoria, D S: *The Sino-Soviet Conflict,* Princeton University Press 1962

2. OF UTILITY IN ESTABLISHING PARTICULAR POINTS

Armstrong, J P: *Sihanouk Speaks,* Walker & Co., New York 1964
Baik Bong: *Kim Il Sung, Biography,* Miraisha, Tokyo 1969
Balabushevich, V V and Prasad, B (Ed): *India & The Soviet Union —A Symposium,* People's Publishing House, New Delhi 1969
Broido, E: *Memoirs of a Revolutionary,* Oxford University Press 1967
Burchett, W G: *Mekong Upstream: A Visit to Laos & Cambodia,* Seven Seas Books, East Berlin 1959
Chuikov, Marshal A I: *The Beginning of the Road,* McGibbon & Kee, London 1963
Clark, A: *Barbarossa,* Hutchinson, London 1963
Conquest, R: *The Great Terror,* Macmillan 1968
Craig, D: *The Fall of Japan,* The Dial Press, New York 1967
Dedijer, V: *Tito,* Simon & Schuster, New York 1953
Dinkevich, A I (Ed): *Kredit i Kreditnyye Systemy Stran Azii,* USSR Academy of Sciences, Moscow 1968
Djilas, M: *Conversations with Stalin,* Penguin Books, London 1962
Eisenhower, Dwight D: *Mandate for Change,* Doubleday, New York 1963
Fleming, P: *News for Tartary,* Jonathan Cape, London 1936
Gettleman, M E (Ed): *Vietnam,* Penguin Books 1966
Greiner, H & Schramm, P: *Kriegstagebuch Des Oberkommandos Der Wehrmacht,* Vol I Bernard und Graefe, Frankfurt-am-Main 1965
Gupta, S: *India and Regional Integration in Asia,* Asia Publishing House, Bombay 1964
Horelick, A L & Rush, M: *Strategic Power and Soviet Foreign Policy,* Chicago 1966
Hough, R: *The Fleet That Had to Die,* Hamish Hamilton, London 1958
Indian Council on Current Affairs: Research Committee on Foreign Aid, Indian Economic Council. *Foreign Aid: A Symposium, A Survey, and A Reappraisal,* Calcutta 1968
Israelyan (Ed): *Soviet Foreign Policy: A Brief Review 1955-65,* Progress Publishers, Moscow 1967
Karanjia, R K: *The Philosophy of Mr. Nehru,* George Allen & Unwin, London 1966
Kerr, G: *Formosa Betrayed,* Eyre & Spottiswoode, London 1965
Khan, Ayub: *Friends, Not Masters,* Oxford University Press 1967
Konev, Marshal I S: *Sorok Pyaty,* Moscow 1968
Laird, R D & B A: *Soviet Communism & Agrarian Revolution,* Penguin Books 1970

Lane, D: *Politics and Society in the USSR,* Weidenfeld & Nicolson, London 1970

Lipper, E: *Eleven Years in Soviet Prison Camps,* London 1951

Luke, Sir H: *The Old Turkey and the New Bles,* London 1955

Marx, K: *Collected Works*

Mayne, R: *The Recovery of Europe,* Weidenfeld & Nicolson, London 1970

Mendel, D: *The Politics of Formosan Nationalism,* University of California Press 1970

Pavlovskiy, V: *Laos v Bor'be za Svobodu,* Oriental Literature Publishing House, Moscow 1963

Roy, A: *Planning in India—Achievements and Problems,* Calcutta 1965

Roy, M N: *Our Differences,* Saraswati, Calcutta 1938

Rudnev, V S: *Malayziya 1963-68,* Nauka, Moscow 1969

Rupen, R A & Farrell, R (Ed): *Vietnam and the Sino-Soviet Dispute,* Praeger, New York 1967

Salisbury, H: *The Coming War Between Russia & China,* Norton, New York 1969

Seaton, A: *The Russo-German War 1941-45,* Barker, London 1971

Silverlight, J: *The Victors' Dilemma: Allied Intervention in the Russian Civil War,* Barrie & Jenkins, London 1970

Sladkovskiy, M I (Ed): *Leninskaya Politika SSSR v Otnoshenii Kitaya,* Moscow, 1968

Toye, H: *Laos: Buffer State or Battleground,* Oxford University Press 1968

Trotsky, L: *Between Red and White: A Study of some fundamental questions of revolution, with particular reference to Gargia,* Communist Party of Great Britain, London 1922

Trotsky, L: *The Revolution Betrayed,* Faber & Faber, London 1937

USSR Ministry of Defence: *Istoriya Velikoy Otechestvennoy Voyny Sovetskogo Soyuza*—6 volumes, Moscow 1961-5

Watt, Sir A: *Vietnam: An Australian Analysis,* Cheshire, Melbourne 1968

Weinstein, F: *Indonesia Abandons Confrontation,* Cornell University Press 1969

Whiting, A S & Sheng Shih-Ts'ai: *Sinkiang—Pawn or Pivot?* Lansing 1958

Wolfe, T W: *Soviet Power and Europe 1945-70,* Johns Hopkins Press 1970

Zhukov, G K: *Vospominaniya i Razmyshleniya,* Moscow 1969
    English E. *The Memoirs of Marshal Zhukov,* Jonathan Cape, London 1970

Zorin, V A (Ed): *Vneshnyaya Politika SSSR na novom etape Politizdat,* Moscow 1964

*The Gulf: Implications of British Withdrawal,* Georgetown University Centre for Strategic & International Studies, Washington 1969

3. YEARBOOKS

Europa Publications—*The Far East & Australasia, 1969*
*Far East Economic Review*—Yearbook
Institute for Strategic Studies, London—*The Military Balance: Strategic Survey*
*Jane's Fighting Ships 1969-70*
*Lloyd's Register of Shipping—Statistical Tables*
Soviet Central Asian Republics, Archive Directorates—*Statistical Yearbooks*, esp. 1962
USSR Central Statistical Directorate—Annual Yearbooks: *The National Economy of the USSR* and *Foreign Trade of the USSR*
USSR Ministery of Foreign Trade—*Vneshnyaya Torgovlya Sotsialisticheskikh Stran* (Foreign Trade of the Socialist Countries)
United Kingdom—Ministry of Defence—*Defence White Paper 1968*
United Nations—*Economic Survey of Europe*
—*Yearbook of Statistics* (esp. 1969)

4. PERIODICALS OF MAJOR UTILITY

*Asian Recorder*
*Asian Research Bulletin*
*Aziya i Afrika Segodnya*
British Broadcasting Corporation—*Summary of World Broadcasts*
*China Quarterly*
*Asian Analyst*
*Asian Recorder*
*Asian Almanac*
*Far Eastern Economic Review*
*For a Lasting Peace, For a People's Democracy*
*Kommunist*
*Keesing's Contemporary Archives*
*Mezhdunarodnaya Zhizn* (English Ed: *International Affairs—Moscow*)
*Mizan*
*Narody Azii i Afriki* (Peoples of Asia and Africa)
*Novoye Vremya* (English Ed: *New Times*)
*Pravda*
*Peking Review*
*Problems of Communism*
*Times of India*
*World Marxist Review*
*Survey of the China Mainland Press*
*USSR and Third World*

5. USEFUL ON SPECIFIC POINTS

*Akahata*
*Annals of the American Academy of Political and Social Science*
*Asahi Shimbun*
*Asian Almanac*

*Asian Survey*
*Australian, The*
*Bangkok World*
*Bintang Merah*
*Bulletin of the Institute for Study of the USSR*
*Canberra Times*
*Current*
*Current Affairs Bulletin*
*Daily Telegraph, The*
*Dawn*
*Djakarta Times*
*Guardian, The*
*International Affairs (London)*
*Izvestiya*
*Journal of Politics*
*Kommunist Vooruzhennykh Sil*
*Krasnaya Zvezda*
*Nation*
*New Middle East, The*
*New York Times*
*Nhan Dan*
*Orbis*
*Partiinaya Zhizn People's Daily*
*South African Digest*
*Sovetskaya Etnografiya*
*Sovetskoya Vostokovedeniye*
*Statesman*
*Survey*
*Survival*
*The World Today*
*Times, The*
*Vedomosty Verkhovnogo Soveta SSSR*
*Vneshnyaya Torgovlya*
*Voprosy Ekonomiki*
*Voyenno—Istoricheskiy Zhurnal*
*Washington Post*
*World Politics*
*World Review (Queensland)*
*Yale Review*

# Index

## DATE DUE

| | |
|---|---|
| | |
| | |
| | |
| | |
| | |
| | |
| | |
| | |
| | |
| | |
| | |
| | |
| | |
| | |
| | |
| | |
| | |
| | |